W9-AUO-598

IN THE NAME OF HUMANITY

ALSO BY MAX WALLACE

The American Axis
Muhammad Ali's Greatest Fight
Love & Death (co-author)

IN THE NAME OF
HUMANITY
The Secret Deal to End the Holocaust

MAX WALLACE

ALLEN
LANE

ALLEN LANE

an imprint of Penguin Canada, a division of Penguin Random House Canada Limited

Canada • USA • UK • Ireland • Australia • New Zealand • India • South Africa • China

First published 2017

www.penguinrandomhouse.ca

LIBRARY AND ARCHIVES CANADA CATALOGUING IN PUBLICATION

Wallace, Max, author
In the name of humanity / Max Wallace.

Includes bibliographical references and index.
ISBN 978-0-670-06959-0 (hardcover)
ISBN 978-0-14-319493-4 (electronic)

1. Auschwitz (Concentration camp). 2. Holocaust, Jewish
(1939–1945)—Poland—Oświęcim. 3. World War, 1939–1945—
Concentration camps—Poland—Oświęcim. I. Title.

D805.5.A96W34 2017   940.53'1853862   C2016-907462-5

Cover and interior design by Jennifer Lum
Cover image by Alexander Vorontsov / Galeric Bilderwelt / Getty Images

Printed and bound in the United States of America

10 9 8 7 6 5 4 3 2 1

 Penguin
Random
House
ALLEN
LANE

To my late mother, Phyllis Bailey,
who taught me to never forget

CONTENTS

IN THE
NAME OF
HUMANITY

AUTHOR'S NOTE

When *Schindler's List* was released in 1993, Steven Spielberg's epic film served as a powerful antidote to decades of stories focusing only on the darkest elements of the Holocaust. Oskar Schindler, the German industrialist who saved more than 1000 Jews, served as an inspirational figure who came to epitomize the little-known area of Holocaust rescue and reminded the world that not all Germans had acquiesced in their country's crimes.

Five years later, I was working in Montreal as an interviewer for the Shoah Visual History Foundation—the institute Spielberg established with the proceeds of the film to document the video testimonies of Holocaust survivors and to ensure the world would never forget. Each week, I encountered men and women—Jews and non-Jews—who had endured and somehow survived the nightmare. Many of the stories I documented continue to haunt me to this day, each marked with common themes of death and despair, hardly redeemed by the fact that the subjects happened to survive while most of their loved ones ended up in Hitler's ovens.

After spending two years recording many such grim testimonies, however, I learned of a man living in another Canadian city who had a very different story to tell. In the summer of 2000, I traveled to Toronto to meet Hermann Landau—the last living eyewitness to an incredible chapter of history. As the secretary of a Swiss-based rescue organization, Landau had spent more than three years documenting the activities of an extraordinary band of Orthodox Jews who spent every waking moment on a mission that may have dwarfed the significant accomplishments of Schindler and others more familiar to history.

As he shared his remarkable story and generously opened his meticulous archives, I was astonished that the staggering achievements of this group were so little known. It led me to follow an historical trail that, more than fifteen years later, may very well rewrite the history of the Holocaust.

ONE

THE LIFEBOAT IS FULL

Early in the morning of November 25, 1944, prisoners at Auschwitz-Birkenau heard a deafening explosion. Emerging from their barracks, they witnessed the gas chambers and crematoria—part of the largest killing machine in human history—reduced to rubble. Most assumed they had fallen victim to inmate sabotage and thousands silently cheered. However, the Final Solution's most efficient murder apparatus had not been felled by Jews, but rather by the ruthless architect of mass genocide, SS chief Heinrich Himmler.

On his first morning in Germany—April 20, 1945—Norbert Masur woke up in a cold sweat. From all corners of the Fatherland, leading Nazis were already converging on Berlin for a celebration of Adolf Hitler's fifty-sixth birthday, set to take place that evening in the Führerbunker where Hitler had retreated while his Thousand Year Reich crumbled around him. Among the invited guests, in fact, was the man whom Masur had secretly flown to meet.

As he anxiously waited for the meeting to take place, Masur couldn't help but wonder why he had agreed to make the trip, which had been undertaken the night before in the strictest of secrecy. It was a journey fraught with danger and not just from the nearly constant strafing of Allied aircraft while he was driven from Berlin's Tempelhof Airport to the lavish estate of the host who had arranged the historic meeting.

Norbert Masur had traveled from Sweden as a representative of the World Jewish Congress to meet the man who had almost single-handedly been responsible for the decimation of his people. If the Führer, holed up in his bunker, were to discover that a member of the hated race was waiting nearby to meet with his most powerful lieutenant, the consequences would almost certainly be catastrophic.

As Masur waited, he had no idea of the events that had led to this improbable journey, nor the role played by an ultra-Orthodox woman he had never heard of in bringing about his fateful mission.

For Hitler, only one task remained before he and his mistress took the cyanide capsules that had been stashed in the bunker ahead of the approaching forces—a Red Army intent on capturing the man responsible for unleashing years of unimaginable suffering. But if the Reich was doomed, the Führer was determined as his last act to take every last Jew with him and complete the Final Solution, which had not yet achieved its ultimate aim.

The systematic extermination of European Jewry had come to a halt five months earlier with the destruction of the Auschwitz gas chambers on November 25. Since that time, tens of thousands more Jews had succumbed during brutal death marches, or from the disease and hunger that ravaged the remaining concentration camps. Now, those left alive faced the same fate as the nearly six million who had already fallen victim to the Nazis' monstrous genocide, unless something was done to countermand Hitler's orders.

Masur's mission, then, was no less than preventing the imminent extinction of European Jewry. The burden weighed heavily on him as he spent the day awaiting an unlikely encounter that few could have imagined possible. When he was still waiting at midnight, however, it appeared that his trip had been undertaken in vain. Finally, at precisely 2:30 a.m., he heard a car pull up. As the front door opened, Norbert Masur came face-to-face with the Devil.

The fact that there were any Jews left at all to save at this stage of the war could be explained by an extraordinary confluence of events and a disparate cast of characters. Heroes and villains alike came together at history's darkest hour for a variety of motives that historians still struggle to explain.

Today, visitors who flock to St. Gallen, Switzerland, can't help but feel that they've been transported into a picture postcard. Nestled in a valley between Lake Constance and the spectacular snowcapped mountains of the Appenzell Alps, the small city is surrounded by quaint timbered cottages, verdant rolling fields and medieval architecture that harkens back to the village's seventh-century founding by an Irish monk. An eighth-century abbey still towers over the city, its library designated a UNESCO heritage site. In the tenth century, the abbey housed a Benedectine nun named Wiborada, who warned locals of an imminent Hungarian invasion and lost her life saving the abbey. For her heroic efforts, Saint Wiborada was the first woman ever canonized by the Roman Catholic Church. Nine centuries later, an equally brave woman would make her mark on the city.

When Recha Sternbuch arrived in St. Gallen in 1928 to settle with her new husband, the city hardly looked different than it does today. She had imagined the town as a safe and prosperous place to raise a family. But as in Wiborada's day, there were dark clouds looming over the border.

Recha was born in Kraków, Poland, in 1905, the daughter of Rabbi Markus (Mordechai) Rottenberg, a respected Chassidic scholar whose Talmudic interpretations were known throughout Europe. At the beginning of the twentieth century, many Orthodox communities, especially in Western Europe, were succumbing to pressures from the younger generation toward a more liberal or modernized approach. This worried the elders, concerned about the encroaching influence of the Conservative and Reform movements sweeping Jewish communities throughout the world. The Belgian city of Antwerp, in fact, was one of the few Western communities where the ultra-Orthodox—or *Haredim*—still dominated Jewish life. During the Middle Ages, virtually all Jews had been expelled from the city as "usurers" or had been massacred during the 1309 Crusade of Pope Clement V.[1] When Austria took over the country in 1713, Jews were allowed to return in small numbers, though it took the French Revolution at the end of the eighteenth century to restore nominal rights. Full religious freedom only came in 1830 when the country achieved independence.

Antwerp had been known as one of the world's great diamond centers since the fifteenth century, when Lodewijk van Bercken pioneered a revolutionary diamond-cutting technique. By the time the first diamond bourse was established in 1893, the industry had been mostly taken over by Orthodox Jews—traders, cutters and polishers—many of whom had fled pogroms in Eastern Europe.[2] By the eve of the First World War, the Jewish population of Antwerp had mushroomed to approximately thirty-five thousand, most of whom had some connection to the diamond trade. And while the community was thriving financially, the elders worried that its spiritual needs were not being met. Jewish religious life had to be preserved and nurtured, lest the community suffer the same fate as Brussels, a metropolis whose Jewish community was dominated by largely assimilated French émigrés.

To that end, they issued a plea eastward to Poland, where word of a rabbi from Galicia known for his strict orthodoxy and compassionate wisdom had reached all the way to Belgium. In 1912, Markus Rottenberg arrived in Antwerp with his wife, Dvora, six sons and three daughters—including seven-year-old Rachel (Recha)—to take up the post as chief rabbi of the city's *Haredi* community.[3] Only weeks earlier, Rabbi Rottenberg had attended the founding conference of Agudath Israel in Katowice as a representative of the Council of Torah Sages. The goal of this historic gathering had been to strengthen Orthodox institutions throughout the world in the face of perceived threats from the growing liberal and Zionist movements. Recha's father's role in the founding of the Agudah would later provide her with crucially important credentials.[4]

Growing up in a religious community with rigidly defined gender roles, Recha had few opportunities for furthering her formal religious education. But the young girl had an unquenchable thirst for knowledge and would quiz her brothers when they returned home from yeshiva each day. As there were no Jewish schools in Belgium open to girls at the time, Recha attended a public school, where she learned French and a little Flemish. The Rottenberg household had become known as a gathering place for lively religious discourse. And when the learned scholars came to discuss the sacred books, young Recha took it all in—often lying in her bed listening to her father passionately interpret the *midrash* for the visitors who came from far and wide seeking his spiritual guidance. By the time she was a teenager, those same visitors were often surprised to find a girl participating fully and knowledgeably in their discussions.

In 1905, the same year that Recha Rottenberg was born in Poland, Naftali Sternbuch arrived in Basel, Switzerland, with his wife and seven children, including his ten-year-old son Yitzchok

(Isaac). He came not from the old country but from the United States, to which his family had fled after a pogrom in Moldova eight months earlier.[5] New York at the time was not a welcoming environment for an Orthodox Jewish immigrant. Sternbuch decided to book passage to Switzerland to start a new life in a quaint medieval metropolis on the Rhine known as Basel. The city's tiny Jewish community traced its roots to the French Revolution, when the town granted a request by France to allow the temporary settlement of a handful of Jewish families fleeing anti-Semitic violence in Alsace. By 1805, Basel's Jewish community numbered some 128 people.[6] The relative peace lasted a short thirty years before the Jews were expelled en masse when the separatist canton of Basel Land was established. It wasn't until 1866 that Jews were allowed to settle in the area for good. Two years later, the region saw the establishment of its first synagogue.

Only eight years before Sternbuch's arrival, Basel had played host in 1897 to the first ever Zionist Congress, chaired by the founder of modern Zionism, Theodor Herzl. In the decades before the Second World War, most *Haredim*—including Recha's father, Markus Rottenberg—were rigidly anti-Zionist. Many believed that Jews were forbidden to establish a Jewish state in Palestine before the coming of the *moshiach* (messiah).

It is possible, in fact, that it was the location of this historic Zionist conference that inspired Naftali to settle in Basel as his own one-man religious mission—determined that his piety would act as a counterpoint against the secular Zionist threat. Indeed, his arrival in 1905—sporting the long beard and black garments favored by the Chassidim—must have been quite a sight to the largely assimilated Jewish community who preferred not to call too much attention to themselves for fear of provoking anti-Semitism. Sternbuch soon founded Switzerland's first *shtiebel* (prayer house), which would serve the growing community of ultra-Orthodox who followed him to Basel in the years to come. His presence was initially met with suspicion and animosity, but he quickly succeeded in winning over his neighbors with his tremendous community spirit, generosity, devotion and warmth.[7] Many a neighbor—Jew and gentile—took note of the sheer joy that exuded from the Sternbuch household. Exuberant Eastern European dances, music, drinking and merriment were part of the Chassidic tradition, but few Jews had experienced these living among the staid Swiss community.[8]

As with the Rottenberg house in Antwerp, distinguished Orthodox scholars came from all over Europe to confer with Sternbuch and to assist him in his mission. He had gradually softened his stance against a Jewish state in Palestine in favor of a new movement known as religious Zionism, which sought to bring religion to the mostly secular settlers who had traveled to the Holy Land to establish a Jewish state. One of the movement's founders was the future chief rabbi of Palestine, Abraham Isaac Kook, who happened to be staying with the Sternbuchs when war broke out in Europe in 1914. He ended up residing with the family for nearly two years, though by this time they had already moved from Basel to St. Gallen.[9] Despite his embrace of Zionism, Kook continued to have strong reservations about its secular direction. When Theodor Herzl died in 1904, Rabbi Kook delivered a eulogy that pointed out what he called the fundamental failure of the Zionist enterprise, the fact "that they do not place at the top of their list of priorities the sanctity of God and His great name, which is the power that enables Israel to survive."[10] Kook's long stay with the Sternbuchs likely had a strong influence on the family's unusually flexible attitudes toward Palestine and would play a significant role in their later rescue efforts.

In 1928, tragedy struck the Rottenberg family when Recha's aunt died suddenly, leaving a four-year-old daughter, Ruth. Recha couldn't bear to see the young girl brought up without a mother. Still single, she startled her family by announcing her intention to adopt Ruth if she could find a man who was willing to marry her and raise the girl together. Word soon spread through *Haredi* circles. The daughter of the great Rabbi Rottenberg was available, but there was an unusual catch. Intrigued, Isaac Sternbuch—having failed to find a wife in the largely assimilated Swiss Jewish community—embarked on the journey to Belgium to meet the rabbi and his daughter. Such an expedition was perfectly in keeping with the Orthodox tradition of *shidduch*—a form of matchmaking from the Middle Ages—which had long been used to bring Jewish couples together. Still, most men would have been taken aback by the unusual condition that Recha had imposed for her hand. Charmed by the worldly young woman, however, Isaac had no hesitation. They were married within weeks. By the time the couple returned to Switzerland, they were accompanied by a young girl whom they would raise as if she were their own.[11]

Switzerland came as something of a culture shock to Recha at first. Having grown up surrounded by *Haredi* Jews in Antwerp as the daughter of a celebrated rabbi, she was surprised to arrive in St. Gallen and find only a tiny Jewish community, numbering around 650.[12] Most of them didn't share her Orthodox ways, despite Naftali Sternbuch's best efforts. The first Orthodox Jews had only settled in the canton in 1919 and, although there were two synagogues, both were too liberal for the Sternbuchs to attend. Instead, they worshipped at the makeshift *schul* that Naftali had set up in his home for the tiny Orthodox population. Fortunately, the Rottenbergs had spoken German at home and Recha attended a French school as a child, so when she arrived in Switzerland, she already spoke two of the country's three main languages without a trace of an accent.

St. Gallen was the capital of the Swiss textile trade at the time. Its close proximity to both the German and Austrian borders helped facilitate trade with its European neighbors that was critical to Switzerland's economic prosperity. Sternbuch had originally traveled there from Basel to open an embroidery factory. His sons, Isaac and Elias (Eli), ran the successful business with their father and each was prosperous. The success of the business had allowed Isaac to purchase a spacious and comfortable modern apartment, suitable for raising the large families that the *Haredim*, then as now, considered their obligation in order to ensure the future of the Jewish people. As a married woman, Recha was expected to keep her head covered for religious reasons. In later years, many ultra-Orthodox women would shave their heads and wear a wig to comply. But in that era women were more likely to wear headscarves or hats. Shortly after her wedding, Recha crafted a fashionable head covering that she described as a turban—and which would not have been out of place on the streets of Paris. It would become her trademark. Unlike the Orthodox men whose long beards and black garments made them immediately stand out as religious Jews, her appearance often proved useful in her skillful dealings with both gentiles and secular Jews, for which she would soon become known. As a result of her insular upbringing, Recha had never before experienced genuine anti-Semitism. It is not that Belgians were necessarily more welcoming of Jews than the Swiss. But in Antwerp, Recha had had little contact with the *goyim* (gentiles) except in school. To preserve their culture, the *Haredi* preferred to keep to their tight-knit religious community, except in matters of commerce.

———

It was not until 1874 that the Swiss constitution finally granted the nation's Jewish citizens full civil and religious rights, making it one of the last European countries to formalize Jewish emancipation. Nevertheless, the old prejudices flourished and Jews were still widely seen as alien to the Swiss way of life.

Swiss historian Simon Erlanger traces Swiss animus toward the Jews to a number of unique factors stemming from the country's fragmented political and socio-linguistic structures. When the Swiss state was formally established in 1848, there were twenty-five cantons[13]—administrative sub-divisions each with its own constitution, government and courts. While most of the cantons are predominantly German speaking, a good portion of the country is also French or Italian, which created further chasms along linguistic and cultural lines. It also created deep religious divisions between Catholics and Protestants. The largely pastoral nation landlocked in the middle of Europe consisted of skilled craftsmen, dairy farmers, tradesmen and merchants. The First World War caused massive upheaval that threatened to destroy the stability that had been carefully nurtured since the Congress of Vienna established Swiss independence in 1815. The Congress also formalized the single greatest factor that has ensured the country's survival for two centuries: its neutrality. And while this meant Switzerland didn't officially take sides during the Great War, the conflict saw much of the German majority siding with the Kaiser while the French- and Italian-speaking cantons tended to side with the Allied countries.

When peace came in 1918, the deep divisions had to be repaired. "Finding a common denominator became crucial," observes Erlanger. "And when a society has trouble defining a positive common identity, it can use a negative one instead; if you cannot say who you are, you can at least say who you are not. Thus, the nation united around the principle of not being Jews: being Jewish became the opposite of being Swiss. Jews were the essential 'Other' against which the collective was defined."[14]

Following the war, a new word began to slowly creep into the Swiss vocabulary—*Überfremdung* (over-foreignization). Increasingly, a xenophobia took hold that would have a far-reaching impact on governmental policy in the turbulent years ahead. As early as 1917, the Swiss state established a "federal police for foreigners"—known as the Alien Police—designed to combat foreign influence that was being blamed for threatening the national identity.[15] Interestingly, the number of foreigners living in Switzerland had actually decreased significantly since the war, suggesting that this threat was largely contrived. In 1910, the total percentage of foreigners living in Switzerland was 14.7. By 1920, that figure had dropped to 10.4 percent, and those numbers would continue to decline until 1941, when the total stood at only 5.2 percent of the Swiss population.[16] But it was becoming increasingly evident from the rhetoric around over-foreignization that the word was in fact synonymous with "Jewification" (*Verjudung*). (This was the conclusion of a 2002 national commission studying Swiss refugee policy during the Nazi era, which found that measures targeted at foreigners were mostly designed to restrict Jewish immigration.[17]) During the Great War, handwritten comments in the applications of Jewish immigrants were implicitly aimed at preventing them from obtaining Swiss citizenship. In 1919, the applications of Jews were even stamped with a Star of David, but by the 1930s the practice had been discontinued.

The Bolshevik revolution also likely played a part in exacerbating suspicion of foreigners among the Swiss. Vladimir Lenin had actually lived in Swiss exile during the First World War before returning to Russia in 1917 and leading the revolution there. And while Lenin wasn't Jewish, anti-Semitic leaflets distributed in Switzerland and elsewhere frequently linked the Bolsheviks to the Jews, thus inflaming suspicions. Ironically, the revolution had resulted in an influx of Russians fleeing to Switzerland to *escape* the Bolsheviks.

Even the most ardent anti-Semites, however, qualified their attitudes for Jews who were willing to assimilate into the Swiss way of life. Heinrich Rothmund had headed the federal Alien Police since its creation in 1919 and would become the embodiment of anti-Jewish Swiss policy in the years before the Second World War. But even Rothmund was quick to point out that his attitudes toward the Jews didn't apply to those who were willing to assimilate. His hostility, he emphasized, was aimed at the so-called Eastern Jews (*Ostjuden)* with their funny customs and clothing. Addressing Parliament about measures designed to normalize policies for Swiss Jews, Rothmund once declared, "As you will see, we are not such horrible monsters after all. But that we do not let anyone walk all over us, and especially not Eastern Jews, who, as is well known, try and try again to do just that, because they think a straight line is crooked, here our position is probably in complete agreement with our Swiss people."[18]

Although she had attained Swiss citizenship upon marrying Isaac, Recha Sternbuch and all *Haredim* would have most certainly fallen into Rothmund's idea of "Eastern Jews" alien to the Swiss way of life. Indeed, Recha felt much like an alien when she first arrived in St. Gallen to start a family. But she was determined to instill the same spirit and hospitality into her new household as she remembered from her Rottenberg home in Antwerp. It didn't take long. Most of the houses in the immediate vicinity of the Sternbuch residence didn't have running hot water. Instead, the water was heated with gas, which was rationed and to be used sparsely. Recha let it be known to her elderly and poorer neighbors that they were most welcome to use her house for laundry or bathing purposes.[19] When a baby was born, Recha was always the first to arrive at the new mother's house with offers of help, even after she gave birth to her first child, Avrohom, in 1929. She also poured herself into charitable causes, and word of her work quickly spread beyond St. Gallen.

In 1933, five weeks and 4000 miles apart, two men assumed the leadership of their respective countries. Adolf Hitler was appointed chancellor of Germany on January 30 and Franklin Delano Roosevelt was inaugurated president of the United States on March 4. The elevation to power of these towering figures would soon have profound effects on the world. But in Switzerland, the Nazis' ascent at first registered barely a ripple, least of all in the Sternbuch household.

In the immediate aftermath of Hitler's rise to power next door in Germany, two categories of refugees had begun to stream into Switzerland: political activists opposed to the regime—Communists and Social Democrats—who were already subject to persecution and physical violence at the hands of the Brownshirts even before the Nazis took power; and a small but steady number of Jews who had seen the writing on the wall early on.[20] In response to the influx, the Swiss federal government passed a law in 1933 distinguishing between political refugees and others. Only a select few fell into the former category, such as leaders of left-wing political parties, high state officials and well-known authors. Communists were the most unwelcome, and Swiss authorities let it be known that they would not be granted political refugee status under any circumstances. In all, fewer than four hundred applicants would be granted this status before the start of the Second World War.[21] All other refugees were simply designated as foreigners, and as such they fell under the Federal Law on Residence and Settlement of Foreigners. Many of the early refugees intended simply to pass through on their way to England and France, but the possibility of large numbers of Jews pouring into the country prompted Swiss authorities to impose a series of measures to ensure that Switzerland remained a *Transitland* (transit country), where foreigners were to be prevented from taking up permanent residence. Among the new rules was a ban imposed on any "professional activities."[22] Most refugees during this period, if they were lucky, would be issued "tolerance permits" by the cantonal government, permitting them to stay a few months at most.[23]

The various Jewish relief organizations active throughout the country had pledged to shoulder the costs for the care and accommodations of this first wave of refugees, thus relieving any burden on the state. Between 1933 and 1937, fewer than six thousand Jews were granted refuge in Switzerland. Of these, a significant number had made their way to St. Gallen. Word had spread of a woman living there who personified the Torah principle of *hachnasas orchim*—the welcoming of guests. During these years, the Sternbuch house was teeming with refugees. "The house was so crowded," observes Joseph Friedenson, who later tracked down a number of the guests, "that it was not uncommon for refugees to believe at first that the Sternbuch home simply *had* to be a small hotel—for no family home could be that open, crowded, or busy. Some neighbors complained and said, 'What's going on?' It was a quiet family and all of a sudden there were tens upon tens of people coming in and going out."[24] Recha worked tirelessly to locate temporary homes for the travelers, often finding safe houses in Zürich, home to nearly half the country's Jewish population at the time. It was here that Isaac maintained his factory, and his business contacts proved useful in helping Recha establish her underground network along with her own extensive Agudah contacts and close ties to the city's religious community.

When those accommodations filled up, the refugees simply stayed with the Sternbuchs, many for months at a time. One of those guests, Zecharia Reinhold, who had entered the country illegally, later recalled his arrival: "When I came in, there were tables surrounded with people as if at *simcha* [a festive occasion] where they ate and drank. . . . It was an open house . . . people coming and going all day. . . . The floors of the house were covered with mattresses for the people. . . . There were all kinds, not all *frum* [devout] . . . she helped everyone. A Yid is a Yid."[25] At one point, recalled Reinhold, the Orthodox refugees attempted to set up a temporary synagogue in a back room but were prevented from doing so by the less religious guests worried about disturbing the neighbors and provoking a potential anti-Semitic backlash. Recha settled the controversy by establishing a daily *minyan* (a quorum for prayer). Reinhold recalled the gentile neighbors coming by during Yom Kippur and staring wide-eyed at the refugees clad in *tallit* (Jewish prayer shawls). "They had never seen anything like it," he remembered. Although it took a while for the neighbors to warm to the Sternbuchs and their strange religious ways, stories would eventually circulate of gentiles climbing trees to cut down branches to help cover the traditional Jewish *sukkah* during the harvest festival of Sukkot.

During the first five years following the Nazis' ascension to power, many refugees managed to find their way to the Sternbuchs. The accumulating dark clouds of 1938, however, soon meant that henceforth Recha would have to go to them.

When Austrians woke up on March 12, 1938, they discovered German troops marching through their streets in what became known as the Anschluss. Instead of offering resistance, large crowds greeted the Nazi invaders with raucous cheers and Nazi salutes, leaving little doubt that most were eager to join the Reich. Carl Mogenroth, a German who had moved to Vienna in 1933 to escape the Nazis, later recalled watching the scene. "The Germans marched in to the jubilation of most of the Viennese," he recalled. "They went wild with joy."[26] Three days later, Hitler himself rode triumphantly through the streets of Vienna in an open-air convertible, acknowledging the cheers of the thousands of overjoyed Austrians. "It was like everyone all of a sudden became Nazi," recalled a Jewish Viennese resident, Herbert Jellinek.[27]

As they had watched the persecution of their brethren next door, most Austrian Jews had believed they were safe from a similar fate. The events of March 12, however, caused an overnight upheaval. William Shirer notes that the treatment of Jews in Vienna following the Anschluss was far worse than anything he had seen during his years as a Berlin-based foreign correspondent covering the Reich during its formative years. He describes the behavior of the Nazis in Vienna following the Anschluss as "an orgy of Sadism." In the immediate aftermath, Jews were forced to scrub election signs from the former regime off the walls and sidewalks. "While they worked on their hands and knees with jeering storm troopers standing over them, crowds gathered to taunt them," he observed. "Hundreds of Jews, men and women, were picked off the streets and put to work cleaning public latrines and the toilets of the barracks where the SA and the SS were quartered. Tens of thousands more were jailed. Their worldly possessions were confiscated or stolen."[28] The terror accomplished what may have been its goal. Between the Anschluss and the start of the war, almost 100,000 Jews fled Austria. Of this total, between 5500 and 6500 made their way to Switzerland.[29]

The prospect of thousands of Jews pouring across Swiss borders and swelling the ranks of Jews in the country set off immediate alarm bells, not least in the offices of Alien Police Chief Heinrich Rothmund.

In September 1938, Rothmund was invited by the German government to tour the Sachsenhausen concentration camp outside Berlin,
along with two prominent Swiss pro-Nazi figures: Robert Tobler, a
member of the Swiss parliament, and Benno Scaepi, a propagandist
for the pro-fascist National Front party. Upon his return from
inspecting the camp, Rothmund wrote the Swiss minister of justice
and police a telling memo, reporting on conversations he had just
had with Nazi officials: "I attempted to make it clear to the gentlemen that the people and government of Switzerland had long since
become fully cognizant of the danger of Judaization and have consistently defended themselves against it. . . . The peril can only be met
if a people constantly protects itself from the very outset against
Jewish exclusiveness and renders that quite impossible."[30]

Soon afterwards, the Swiss would implement an infamous policy
that would come to be known by its French name, *réfoulement*—the
practice of turning away Jewish refugees at the border and returning
them to the Nazis. Exploring the consequences of this policy in 2002,
the Swiss commission investigating the country's wartime refugee
policy observed, "The measures agreed in August 1938 to turn back
unwanted immigrants were implemented ruthlessly; despite their
awareness of the risk refugees ran, the authorities often turned them
over directly to the German police. It even happened that border
guards struck refugees with the butts of their rifles to bar them from
crossing the border."[31] There were exceptions enshrined for children
under sixteen, the elderly and the sick, but most others were to be
turned away.

If there was any doubt about which refugees Switzerland considered undesirable, it was dispelled when the Swiss legation in Berlin—
on Rothmund's recommendation—entered into negotiations with
Germany to stamp the passports of German Jews with a *J* to make it

easier for Swiss border officials to turn away "non-Aryans." It was long believed in Switzerland that the *J* stamp had been instituted by the Nazis as just another of their notorious anti-Semitic measures. But when the documents finally surfaced in the 1950s, it emerged that it was not the Germans who initiated the policy but the Swiss authorities themselves. On September 7, 1938, a directive was circulated to Swiss border officials instructing them to refuse entry to any refugees who attempted to cross without a visa, "Especially those who are Jewish or probably Jewish." Their passports were to be marked "Turned Back."[32] As part of a reciprocal arrangement, each country agreed that it would turn away Jews without the necessary "authorization" to cross each other's borders. The Swiss Federal Council adopted the new protocol on October 4, 1938. As the Swiss justice minister would later declare in response to the influx of refugees, "The lifeboat is full."[33]

TWO

THE SWISS SCHINDLER

S hortly after the first immigration restrictions were put in place in August 1938, the Sternbuchs received word from contacts in Austria that Jews were being turned away at the border in large numbers. Not for the last time, Recha's long-standing connections with the Agudah served as an informal network whereby Orthodox Jews throughout Europe functioned as a trusted clandestine intelligence and transportation network to facilitate an underground railroad devoted to rescue operations. A key element of the network—one that would later become an essential element of their rescue efforts during the Holocaust—was identifying and organizing sympathetic gentiles. Although many *Haredim* led insular lives, others such as Isaac Sternbuch and his brother Eli, were businessmen who interacted with gentile clients on a daily basis. Through these business connections, the family would cultivate an increasingly valuable list of contacts. Soon, a network of helpers—including farmers, truckers, taxi drivers and police officers[1]—was mobilized. Recha and others also used their own money to pay professional smugglers (*passeurs*) when necessary, though their services were expensive, some charging as much as 3000 francs per person. Willi Hutter preferred to call himself a "guide." His daughter later recalled his arrangement with the Sternbuchs, who would present him with 20 francs for every refugee he brought to them.[2] In 1938 currency values, it took just under 4.5 Swiss francs to buy a U.S. dollar, so this was not a great deal of money.[3]

Jewish refugees fleeing Austria were given instructions about the routes and rendezvous points that would provide a safe haven in Switzerland. Once over the border, they would be brought to St. Gallen, less than twenty miles away. One of the most popular crossing points was located at Diepoldsau in the Rhine Valley. Here, a bend in the river had been removed at the beginning of the twentieth century to prevent flooding. After the Rhine was redirected, it left an area of swampland covered by bush and shrubs. That made it easy to wade across from Austria without detection by border authorities.[4]

Back on land, the hapless refugees were often surprised to encounter a cheerful Orthodox woman waiting for them with coffee and a smile. They were then spirited away in a vehicle, often under a hay bale or a pile of produce. More often than not, Recha would be accompanied by a helper to drive, but on many occasions, she traveled alone. "When I arrived over the border, I was driven to St. Gallen by a woman dressed in black," recalled one Austrian refugee.[5] Recha's sister-in-law Gutta Sternbuch would later recall these early rescue missions. "She got word every night that there are Jews trying to get across the border, there are Jews that can't come over, the Swiss don't let, they throw them back. They throw them back to the Germans."[6]

Recha was hardly the only Swiss rescuer working to smuggle Jews into the country during this period. Throughout Switzerland, scores of political groups and religious organizations took advantage of contacts in Germany and Austria to smuggle thousands of Jews and political activists across the border. These rescuers included countless gentiles who defied their country's policies to save refugees fleeing from the Reich. Among these was a nineteen-year-old Swiss factory worker named Jakob Spirig-Riesbacher, who is estimated to have saved between 100 and 150 Jews by leading them across the Rhine from Germany or through Austrian forests.[7]

By the end of 1938, hundreds of refugees—mostly Jewish—had made their way to St. Gallen.[8] Having reached the safety of a neutral country, however, they still had one significant obstacle to overcome. Most of the new arrivals—especially the Orthodox—were conspicuous by their appearance. In a city as small as St. Gallen, newcomers stood out immediately. The Swiss authorities had already made it clear that they had no compunction about sending back Jews who had entered the country illegally. Among the many sympathetic gentile contacts that Recha had cultivated over the years, the most important proved to be the St. Gallen police commander, Captain Paul Grüninger, a much beloved local figure and former soccer star who had once played for the national team that won the Swiss Cup. Grüninger had been brought up as a Protestant, though his father was a Catholic. His parents ran a local cigar shop and were fixtures in the town. Following his discharge from the Swiss army after the First World War, Grüninger obtained a teaching diploma and worked for a time as a teacher at a primary school outside Zürich, where he would meet his future wife, Alice. During this period, he joined the country's powerful center-right Liberal Party, where political connections landed him a job back home as a lieutenant at the St. Gallen police department. The couple's only child, Ruth, was born in 1921. Four years later, he was promoted to captain and handed command of the cantonal police. The captain was widely known in St. Gallen for his compassion, especially among the less fortunate, to whom he and Alice would often bring food or clothing for the children. Grüninger had been horrified when he first received orders from his superiors in the spring of 1938 to be on the lookout for fugitive Jewish refugees. When Recha approached him with her plan, he didn't even hesitate. "I could do nothing else," he later recalled.

"As soon as she had one person or two or three persons or a whole family," recalled Gutta Sternbuch, "she went to Grüninger and Paul Grüninger wrote in a sort of a passport that they came legally. It was unbelievable for a Swiss to do this."[9] Despite this account, versions of which have been repeated for decades, Grüninger rarely put his own signature on the falsified documents. Instead, it was Jewish relief officials who issued the documents when Recha or even Grüninger himself brought them to the local refugee processing camp at Diepoldsau—set up on the site of an old embroidery factory—where they awaited permits authorizing a temporary stay.[10] After the war, many of the refugees who had been saved by Grüninger's actions described their interactions with the police captain.

Hilde Weinreb, born in Austria's second largest city, Graz, fled her homeland as a child in 1938. She remembers holing up for an entire day with her parents near the Swiss border, waiting for night to fall. "We were all wet from the rain when it finally grew dark. We sneaked out of our hiding place and warily approached the border. The closer we got, the muddier the terrain became and we could not see the path any longer. There was deathly silence, except for the noise our feet made in the mud and the beating of our hearts. Suddenly a man in uniform appeared out of nowhere. He held a [flashlight] in his hand, shining the light into our faces. We must have looked ashen and were convinced that this was the end. But the man greeted us with a kind smile on his face. I looked at him as if hypnotized. He told us not to be afraid but to come with him to Switzerland, and everything would be okay. It was as he said. Later on, I learned the name of the man. It was Paul Grüninger, the police commander from St. Gallen himself."[11]

There are no accurate records to assess how many of the refugees saved by Grüninger were brought to him by Recha Sternbuch, but the number was significant. Among these was Moritz Weisz, a Viennese merchant who later remembered crossing the Rhine near Hohenems in September 1938, along with his wife and seven other members of his extended family. Before setting out, they had been instructed to find the home of Recha Sternbuch in St. Gallen. Upon their arrival, Recha let them hide out in her apartment because they were in the country illegally and were afraid to emerge. Weisz recalls Recha heading out one day to arrange for Grüninger's assistance. "Soon afterwards, we got documents allowing all of us to stay in Switzerland," he recalled.[12]

Recha's daughter Netty, seven years old at the time of the Anschluss, remembers frequently giving up her bed and sleeping on the floor in favor of the refugees who passed in and out of the apartment.[13] All the while, Isaac remained supportive of his wife's activities, even as she went out until all hours of the night, frequently exposing herself to grave danger. "Isaac not only supported what Recha was doing, he worked harder at his factory to finance her operations which had a lot of expenses," recalls their niece Ruth Mandel.[14]

Grüninger's operation took care of the refugees whom Recha had personally smuggled in. But she was well aware that there were hundreds, perhaps thousands, of others scattered throughout the country, terrified that they would be rounded up and sent back to face the growing horrors of the Third Reich. Again, she activated her intelligence network to spread the word that she had discovered a way to normalize the status of Jews whose illegal entry put them in danger of imminent deportation. By day, she would race from town to town to gather the names of refugees, often driving as far as Zürich—a little over an hour's drive—where she had established dozens of safe houses and where Jews could more easily hide than in the tiny community of St. Gallen. By night, she continued her incursions to the border to retrieve the ever-growing numbers of refugees. When she wasn't on one of her missions, she worked the phones, calling her extensive network all over the country. Her phone bill during these years often exceeded 1000 francs a month, an enormous sum.[15]

Even for those who had entered the country legally, the restrictions were severe. Under Swiss regulations, refugees were forbidden to work during their stay. The rules were meant to encourage the visitors to be on their way as quickly as possible. Under no circumstances would they be making Switzerland their home. For Recha, this meant two separate phases to her operation. The first goal was to help Jews flee the Reich over the Swiss border. Next, she was determined to find safe passage for them to another destination where they would find a more permanent welcome. To this end, she utilized contacts in the Chinese and Cuban embassies who were willing to sell visas that could be used to expedite the transport of Jews to those countries. Eventually, a middleman in Zürich would supply a substantial number of visas for passage to Italy or China for the rate of 400 lira—about 20 U.S. dollars—apiece, though these countries were not their intended destination. Although she did not consider herself a Zionist, Recha used the clandestine underground network the Aliyah Bet, to facilitate the passage of countless refugees to Palestine in defiance of the British blockade and the strict quotas that were imposed after Arab uprisings in 1936.[16]

While Recha devoted herself full-time to this rescue work, other members of the family were no less devoted to the cause. Zecharia Reinhold, who had been captured by Swiss authorities shortly after entering the country from Austria, recalls what happened while he was awaiting deportation. "In the beginning Mrs. Sternbuch tried very hard to have us legalized. It was not easy, but she finally succeeded. They wanted to send us back. . . . We had been locked up as criminals—we were about twenty or thirty people. It was night and we were sitting in despair. We heard someone climbing up near the window and we were frightened. A voice at the window said, 'Don't be afraid.' This was Eli Sternbuch [Isaac's brother] bringing us the good tidings. In the morning we were taken to the police station, where they took our names and divided us among several villages."[17]

By the end of 1938, Recha's network was so widespread that a number of advocates were sending refugees from long distances to seek her services. An eighteen-year-old German refugee named Daniel Gromb, who had illegally entered the country on his own, recalls crossing Lake Constance from Austria and making his way to Zürich. There, a refugee lawyer referred him to a woman in St. Gallen who could arrange to legalize his status. When he reached the Sternbuch house, Paul Grüninger happened to be there meeting with Recha. "It was thanks to him that I could stay," Gromb later recalled.[18]

In addition to securing their papers, refugees remember Grüninger—sporting distinctive pince-nez glasses and an impeccable uniform—arriving at the refugee internment camp at Diepoldsau to enquire about their welfare. Stories abound of the captain using his own money to purchase shoes or winter clothing. He even took a young girl suffering from a toothache to the dentist and personally paid the bill.[19] By November 1938, hundreds of illegal refugees had already been "regularized" by the efforts of Paul Grüninger, the Sternbuchs and countless others. But if they already had their hands full keeping up with the steady demand, the events of November 9 and 10 would signal a desperate new phase.

On the morning of November 7, 1938, a seventeen-year-old religious Jew named Herschel Grynszpan walked into the German embassy in

Paris and shot a junior diplomatic official named Ernst vom Rath to avenge his family's recent expulsion from Germany to Poland.

Josef Goebbels immediately blamed the assassination on "world Jewry." The Führer, he announced, had decided that "demonstrations should not be prepared or organized by the Party, but insofar as they erupt spontaneously, they are not to be hampered."[20] This appeared to be a signal to launch the pogroms that the Nazis had seemingly been planning for some time but for which they had been awaiting an excuse. Those assembled for Goebbels's speech immediately took to the phones to give instructions to regional offices throughout the Reich.[21] Before long, "spontaneously" organized mobs of Germans went on a violent rampage through the streets of Germany and Austria, vandalizing and torching more than 7500 Jewish businesses, destroying more than 250 synagogues, and desecrating cemeteries and other Jewish institutions. Brownshirts also targeted the homes of Jews in Berlin and Vienna, looting valuables and assaulting residents. Rape was also widespread and a significant number of suicides were reported. The pogroms continued for two consecutive nights, leaving at least ninety-one Jews dead and massive destruction in their wake.

The shards of shattered glass left on the street from the vandalism would give the pogroms of November 9 and 10, 1938, the infamous name that some historians consider the true beginning of the Holocaust—Kristallnacht (the Night of Crystal, or Broken, Glass). As the violence was winding down on November 10, state security chief Reinhard Heydrich sent a telegram to all police headquarters marked "Measures Against the Jews Tonight." Among its directives, he ordered, "As soon as the course of events during the night permits the release of the officials required, as many Jews in all districts—especially the rich—as can be accommodated in existing prisons are to be arrested. For the time being only healthy male Jews, who are not too old, are to be detained. After the detentions have been carried out, the appropriate concentration camps are to be contacted immediately for the prompt accommodation of the Jews in the camps."[22]

Acting on these instructions, police arrested more than thirty thousand Jewish men and incarcerated them in three concentration camps—Dachau, Buchenwald and Sachsenhausen—that had previously been reserved for political prisoners. There, they were kept for weeks under brutal conditions. Many were only released after they promised to leave the Reich immediately. Among these was an Austrian named Brucharz who later recalled conditions inside the camps: "The bloodhounds arrested men, cripples and even children of 11 and 12 years and brought them to the camp. How they attacked them is unbelievable. There was not one of the more than 10,000 in the camp who did not have at least a hole in his scalp. . . . Hundreds became insane and we had later to carry corpses from the washrooms where we had put them."[23]

The events of November 9 and 10 served as a wake-up call for the tens of thousands of Austrian Jews who had failed to emigrate following the Anschluss. For those who had once believed the Nazis were a mere nuisance, the events of Kristallnacht signaled that they were no longer safe in the country of their birth. In the days and weeks that followed, Recha Sternbuch would be confronted with a massive increase in the number of Austrians seeking illegal refuge. Her underground network was stretched almost to the breaking point.

THREE

BETRAYED

As fast as the Sternbuchs and their network could smuggle refugees into the country, Paul Grüninger arranged to legalize them. By the time the Swiss Federal Council convened to discuss the "problem" in January 1939, there were nearly twelve thousand refugees in Switzerland, most of them Jewish. And then catastrophe struck. The first indication of trouble had come the previous November 23, when the Swiss Alien Police chief, Heinrich Rothmund, discovered that an unusually large number of visas—more than 2900—had been granted to Jewish refugees in just three Swiss consular offices near the Swiss–Austrian border—in close proximity to St. Gallen. It's likely that Jewish relief groups had chosen those offices to file the papers because they were known to be more sympathetic to the plight of refugees or because they had been working with inside contacts, drawn to the cause for mercenary or humanitarian reasons. Ernst Prodolliet fell into the latter category. While stationed at the Bregenz consulate, the former businessman turned diplomat— responsible for processing passports and visas—was caught in October 1938 issuing falsified transit visas for refugees to continue their onward journey through Italy to Palestine and other destinations. At the disciplinary hearing against him, Prodolliet was told by his Swiss Foreign Office superiors, "Our consulate's job is not to ensure the well-being of Jews."[1] Still others let it be known that their services were for sale. The large numbers of Jews arriving in the St. Gallen canton didn't seem unusual at first, given its proximity to both the Austrian and German borders. But when Rothmund analyzed the data, indicating almost three thousand arrivals in a period of just a few months, he was immediately suspicious. The Alien Police chief issued a formal directive requesting an investigation by local authorities and demanding that appropriate "sanctions" be applied against those responsible.

The Sternbuchs always believed that Rothmund had been alerted by "informants," though no evidence has ever emerged to point the finger at any specific culprit. Although St. Gallen was one of the more liberal Swiss cantons, the town also boasted a sizable contingent of the far-right National Front as well as a chapter of the NSDAP, the Nazi Party.[2] After the war, an anonymous tract was found in the police archives dating from the summer of 1938, entitled "The Jews of St. Gallen." It listed a number of prominent Jews residing in the canton, including "The German Jew Kleinberger, the dirty Polish Jew Teitelberg, the very dangerous Jew Sternbuch, and the dirty Jew-in-chief Wyler." These and other "foreign racial elements" had earned a place on the "Blacklist" because they "exploit the Swiss people, abuse our daughters, poison, rape, and contaminate our brave trusting Christians."[3] There is evidence that two prominent local textile barons, Arnold Mettle-Spaeckler and Max Stoffel, had been financing propaganda pamphlets against what they described as the "monopoly of Jews and Free-Masons"—material apparently designed to discredit business rivals such as Isaac Sternbuch and others whose names appeared on the list.[4] The presence in St. Gallen of larger numbers of Jews than usual had in fact inflamed the far right and prompted many such anti-Semitic outbursts.[5]

The turning point came near the end of 1938. On December 21, a communiqué was received at Heinrich Himmler's SS headquarters in Berlin from a police outpost in Bregenz, Austria. It alerted the German authorities that a suspicious truck registered in St. Gallen had been spotted outside a Bregenz café the night before. At approximately 8 p.m., the truck had been stopped and searched as it approached the Swiss border. Inside, Reich police found two Jewish women hiding under a blanket. The smuggler was a St. Gallen police officer, Karl Zweifel, under the command of Paul Grüninger. Upon Zweifel's return to Switzerland, Grüninger was left with little choice but to arrest him and a fellow police officer accomplice who had traveled to Germany to retrieve his comrade.

The arrests of two St. Gallen officers for smuggling refugees now placed the canton firmly in Rothmund's crosshairs. Grüninger was ordered to assemble a report detailing precise immigration figures to account for the "surprising proportions" of refugees in the region.[6] On January 26, the captain issued his report. There were currently 859 Jewish refugees present in St. Gallen. Of these, 262 had arrived *after* the immigration restrictions were imposed in August 1938.[7] Appearing to anticipate that the elevated numbers would give away his activities, he provided an addendum to accompany the report. "We have been active mainly for humanitarian reasons," he explained. "We could not force ourselves—we were not hard-hearted enough— to send back any of the stream of refugees after [Kristallnacht]. It would have been shameful behavior on our part because these people had escaped an ill fate only under great hardship. We were led by the public opinion of the majority of the Swiss people, the media and political parties. Whenever we did attempt to refuse someone entry to the country, there were heartrending scenes. The police staff and border guards declared that they would not go on doing service in such inhumane circumstances."[8]

Perhaps hoping to reassure authorities that the illegal refugees had no intention of staying in Switzerland, Grüninger wrote, "Together with the Swiss Association of Jewish Refugees, we are looking for possibilities of an onward journey for the refugees, and it appears that several hundred of them could soon leave Switzerland for Palestine. For this reason, we have not seen any problem in granting them a limited residence permit."[9] He had hoped that this explanation would relieve the pressure and enable him to resume his important rescue work. He assumed he would be backed up by his supervisor, Valentin Keel—a Social Democratic politician who had aided the refugee smuggling operation for months. Unbeknownst to the captain, however, Keel was in the process of betraying him. On January 28, Keel submitted his own report to Rothmund, alerting the Alien Police chief that his office had "discovered that some officials of the cantonal police have not complied with the instructions to refuse illegal immigrants, mainly in cases where their health and life were in danger." Here, he attempted to save his own skin and set the stage for the events to follow. "We have, however, given strict orders that absolutely no illegal crossings of the border must be allowed any longer. Nevertheless, Police Captain Grüninger has continued to allow people to get in. According to our information, there are 859 immigrants in the canton of St. Gallen at the present time."[10]

Two weeks later, on February 11, Rothmund delivered his response. He noted that he had personally given Grüninger "clear instructions" in the past not to allow refugees over the border. "Nevertheless," he wrote, "it appears that this civil servant and officer sanctioned or even provoked illegal immigrations off his own bat." The captain's fate was sealed.

A month later, a St. Gallen police officer reported that a Jewish refugee had confessed that he had entered Switzerland after August 1938, contradicting the papers filed by the Swiss Association of Jewish Refugees, which had been backdated as usual. For the first time, a Jewish organization had been linked to the illegal smuggling of refugees.[11]

On April 3, 1939, Grüninger made his way from the upper flat he shared with his wife and daughter to police headquarters in the Klosterplatz, where the cantonal government offices were located. On his way in, he was stopped by an officer who informed him that he had been suspended from duty pending an investigation into the "human smuggling" of refugees.[12] He would never again set foot in his old office. Two weeks later, an official from the canton arrived at his apartment to demand he hand over his uniform.[13]

At first, Grüninger denied all knowledge of illegal smuggling. To avoid a paper trail linking him to these operations, he had for the most part refrained from putting his name on the falsified papers issued to refugees after August 1938. Instead, the papers were usually signed by the scion of one of Switzerland's oldest Jewish families, Sidney Dreifuss, who headed the local Jewish relief organization, the Israelitische Fluechtlingshilfe. The two had worked closely for months. In October 1938, Dreifuss had sent Grüninger a birthday note expressing the best wishes of his organization: "It is our ardent desire to thank you, honored Captain, and to wish you well in the name of all the members of our organization. We would like to express our deep gratitude for your humanitarian activities for all of us and especially for the pitiful refugees. Please do not regard it as a hackneyed phrase but be assured that these thanks come from the bottom of our hearts."[14]

But now, confronted with more than 130 backdated visas that bore his signature, Dreifuss was forced to come clean. He had falsified the documents at the request of Captain Grüninger, he admitted. Recalling that Grüninger would often appear at his office twice a day, he declared that he was grateful to the Swiss police official for helping Jews "escape the utter hell of the German Reich" but that it was in fact Grüninger who ordered him to falsify the documents and that he was left with little choice but to comply.[15]

Six months earlier, the ten most affluent Jews in St. Gallen had been summoned to the office of Saly Mayer, a retired knitwear and lace manufacturer who had headed the Union of Swiss Jewish Communities (SIG) since 1936. Mayer explained that the Jewish community was expected to finance the care and feeding of the refugees who were pouring over the border to escape the Reich. The group contributed the not inconsiderable sum of 400,000 marks to finance ongoing refugee relief. At this meeting, one of the assembled industrialists, Ernst Kleinberg, cautioned the group that the Jews of St. Gallen needed to be careful about taking on too high a profile. "Hitler's going from success to success," he noted, "and we're sitting on a powder keg because we don't know when it will be our turn."[16] Undoubtedly, the prospect of a prominent Jewish leader linked to an illegal smuggling operation could have had far-reaching implications. "Dreifuss was in a very dangerous place both for himself and his people," notes St. Gallen historian Stefan Keller. "He had been caught [red handed]. If he took responsibility, he would have likely been arrested and there would have been serious repercussions for the Jewish community and for future refugees. I think he thought he was left with little choice but to name Grüninger."[17]

Recha herself had worked closely with Dreifuss, though she had kept her distance for some time from his boss, Saly Mayer, as a result of an altercation between her and the Jewish leader a year earlier. At that time, Recha had received word that two brothers named Blum had been caught entering the country illegally and that Swiss border guards were preparing to deport them back to the Reich in accordance with the *réfoulement* policy. Recha decided to pay a visit to Mayer, who was said to enjoy cordial relations with Heinrich Rothmund himself. At the SIG offices in St. Gallen, she implored Mayer to use his influence to save the brothers from a tragic fate. To her dismay, the Jewish leader refused to intervene. Instead, he chose to admonish her. "Frau Sternbuch, if you were a good Swiss citizen you would consider it your duty to take the two men who had crossed illegally by the collar and hand them over to the police. You know the Jewish rule of *dina demalchusa dina*—the rule of the land has the [validity of religious law]."[18] Recha would not be lectured to by this officious bureaucrat, especially on matters of religion. "Herr Mayer, you obviously don't know me. I am a Jewish mother and I don't know what the law says. I only know that we have to save these people. If you refuse to be of any help, I will have nothing further to do with you." In years to come, in fact, members of Recha's rescue network would accuse Mayer himself of informing on Paul Grüninger, though no evidence has ever emerged to support this accusation.[19]

Dreifuss's confession had dealt the final blow. On May 12, 1939, Grüninger was formally dismissed from his post and had criminal charges brought against him. A year later, in the fall of 1940, a panel of judges declared him guilty of "violating his oath" and falsifying the papers of twenty-one illegal refugees. "Such underhanded practices threaten the necessary trust and the respectability of authorities and the reliability of subordinates," the court declared.[20] He was also cited for arranging for at least 118 questionnaires to be doctored at the

Jewish relief camp. The tribunal stripped him of his pension and left him virtually unemployable.

Left penniless after his dismissal, the forty-nine-year-old struggled to make a living with a series of odd jobs. When Recha heard of the financial plight of the man who had been so instrumental in her own rescue operations, she and her husband provided the funds for Grüninger to open up his own store in Basel, selling raincoats manufactured by Isaac's brother, Eli. They also arranged a job for Ruth in the family textile business.[21] For decades, Switzerland resisted calls to pardon the man who is today often referred to as the "Swiss Schindler." In December 1970, after a series of media reports about his efforts, the Swiss government finally sent a letter of apology, but still refused to reinstate his pension. A year later, Yad Vashem bestowed on Grüninger the title of "Righteous Gentile Among the Nations," just a few months before he died. His conviction was finally overturned by Switzerland in 1995.

If the suspension of her powerful police ally had dealt a severe setback to Recha Sternbuch's efforts, what happened next proved fatal to the operation. On the very same day that Paul Grüninger was officially dismissed—May 12, 1939—Recha was ordered to report to St. Gallen police headquarters. Upon arrival, she was presented with a long litany of criminal charges against her, likely gleaned from the investigation into Grüninger.

Among the most serious of these charges was "collusion"—the accusation that she had worked with a vast underground network to illegally smuggle refugees into the country. She was also charged with bribing a consul to obtain Cuban visas. It didn't take long to discover what the authorities were after. It was made clear that if she was willing to supply a list of her accomplices, she could escape harsh punishment. When she refused to do so, she was arrested and placed in custody. In a letter she sent to the prosecuting attorney from the detention center in May, Recha politely explained her reluctance to share the names of her collaborators. In this document can be found telling clues as to her motivations. It is especially important because Recha rarely spoke of her extraordinary actions, even to family and friends: "I always believed that when innocent persecuted people ask me for help and nobody suffers a loss through my help, that only I will be punished. I will gladly choose to be punished because if one has seen the mental and physical exhaustion of these people when they come from the border, one would prefer, with satisfaction, to endure punishment rather than to send them back."[22]

Although the Sternbuch family business was thriving and she could likely have afforded to hire the best criminal attorney in northern Switzerland, she at first chose to defend herself against the charges. Her statement makes it clear that she considered herself a Swiss patriot: "I was so agitated yesterday when they sent me a lawyer. I don't want anybody to cover up my actions or try to cast them in such a light that I would escape punishment. . . . Your demand however . . . that I should denounce human beings that haven't harmed anyone, and for the most part are poor, decent workers who could not bear to suffer punishment, be it financial or a loss of their employment for a few months, bringing extreme hardship to their wives and children, this I cannot do. Do you really expect me to denounce the fathers of these families and bring them misfortune?"[23]

By the time her case came to trial, Recha had reluctantly agreed to retain a lawyer to fight the charges. She could not save Jews, she reasoned, sitting behind bars. On the stand, she once again reiterated her unequivocal objection to naming names, though she had no hesitation admitting to her own role in smuggling refugees. Asked to swear an oath, she declared, "My willingness to give truthful information as far as the investigation concerns me. However, I refuse to provide any information about third parties who in any way or manner were helping me with the illegal entry of immigrants into Switzerland." She proceeded to explain how she cared for approximately fifteen or twenty immigrants in her own home in August 1938 but a month later furnished a larger home where many of them were moved. "I have financed these immigration transports out of my own means; when these refugees didn't have the money, I paid their debts to chauffeurs and others . . . because I didn't want these people to suffer damage."

She was ordered to name these chauffeurs who had participated in the clandestine operations. "It is quite impossible for me to permit myself to be used as an informer, and I think it grossly unfair to expect such a thing of me," she responded. The prosecutor had in his possession a thick dossier of individual cases where Recha was alleged to have participated in illegal smuggling, but his line of questioning made it clear that the authorities were not terribly interested in the cases where she had assisted refugees after they made their way over the border. Instead, he was intent on identifying upper-level officials and police accomplices who might have aided her operations—activities that would "naturally discredit the Swiss in the eyes of the Germans." He pressed her about one case dating to New Year's Eve 1938, in which she had a taxi driver take her to the St. Margarethen border station to pick up a family. "It has been reported to us that prior to the arrival of this family, you contacted the police there. . . . We wish to learn from you the names of all your middlemen of whose services you have availed in order to bring immigrants illegally and unobserved over the Swiss border. We have some definite evidence in this respect."[24]

Recha was unbending. "I will not answer that," she replied. The trial eventually turned to the more serious charge. Confronted with evidence that she had obtained visas from a gentile named Menzel in exchange for a fee, Recha did not deny that she had on occasion resorted to bribery: "Conditions today are unfortunately such that many times it appears impossible, or is in fact impossible, to obtain a visa in a legal manner and for payment of the regular taxes. This is particularly so if entry to a certain country has been closed or where there are also other difficulties with the Alien Police. Many times there is no choice but to resort to the rather unpleasant means of bribing a consular official. I personally consider this completely against my convictions but conditions actually force me to resort to this means. Mr. Menzel is my middleman who helps me obtain visas through this aforementioned means. I have to compensate Mr. Menzel for his efforts, 400 lira for each passport. On occasion I handed him eighteen passports to obtain the necessary visas to Italy."

Here, her attorney turned Switzerland's restrictive refugee policy into an advantage. After all, the government had made it clear that the country was to be used as a temporary transit zone. Recha was simply facilitating their journey so that they could be in and out of Switzerland as quickly as possible. He pointed out that the authorities had in fact given their blessing to her efforts. "A few weeks before Mrs. Sternbuch was arrested and kept in prison," he told the court, "she went to the Alien Police in Bern with sixteen refugee passports. They told her that if she had any difficulties about emigration she should refer them back to Bern. . . . One should also point to the (illegal Aliyah Bet) Palestine transport in the spring of 1939 in which Mrs. Sternbuch took an active part. In these cases, she secured hundreds of Chinese visas, although the real goal of the recipients was to land illegally on the coast of Palestine. These visas were used with the intention of fooling the countries where they passed through, because Italy, for instance, would never give a transit visa unless the final destination was indicated."[25] The court appeared sympathetic to this argument. If Recha had been guilty of violating the letter of Swiss law, then surely her actions were in keeping with the spirit. Her lawyer moved to dismiss all charges, but not before questioning why those charges had been brought in the first place: "There is another question as to whether denunciations of other unknown persons caused this investigation. Unfortunately, in looking over these documents, one has the feeling that Mrs. Sternbuch has been made the scapegoat."[26]

Citing "lack of evidence," the judge dismissed all charges against her. Afterwards, he summoned her to his chambers and handed her an envelope. Inside was a contribution of 100 francs to be used for her rescue operations.[27] It was a poignant gesture—but just one example of the many Swiss who had in their own way rejected their country's hard-hearted policies. When the collective soul-searching began decades after the war had ended, many asked why more Swiss hadn't done the same. Given the horrors that awaited the Jews who were turned away at the border, how could anybody in good conscience have delivered people into the hands of their executioner? Switzerland isn't the only country that found itself asking that question. By the time she was arrested in May 1939, Recha Sternbuch had watched in despair while the Nazis gradually escalated the slow persecution of her people, culminating in the pogroms of Kristallnacht that made her work all the more urgent. Yet—like Paul Grüninger and even Heinrich Rothmund—Recha still had no idea of the unimaginable horrors that lay ahead. Nobody did.

FOUR

STRANGE BEDFELLOWS

B y the time Josef Hell encountered him in 1922, Adolf Hitler, a
failed artist and decorated war veteran, had already seized control of the fledgling National Socialist German Workers' Party
(NSDAP). Hitler's skills as an orator were beginning to attract large
crowds on the streets of Munich, drawn to his blistering denuncia-
tion of the Versailles Treaty, which he claimed had been engineered
by Bolshevik elements controlled by the "Jewish swindle."

Attending one of Hitler's increasingly virulent anti-Semitic
speeches, Hell afterwards asked him what he proposed to do to the
Jews should he one day take power. The retired army major turned
journalist, who would one day become editor of the Catholic weekly
Der gerade Weg, recalled Hitler's unsettling response. "He no longer
looked at me," Hell recalled, "but beyond me into emptiness and made
his next statement in a rising voice; he was seized by a sort of paroxysm
and wound up shouting at me as if I were a large audience: 'If I am ever
really in power, the destruction of Jews will be my first and most
important job. As soon as I have the power, I shall have gallows after
gallows erected, for example, in Munich on the Marienplatz—as many
as the traffic allows. Then the Jews will be hanged one after another,

and they will stay hanging until they stink. They will stay hanging as long as hygienically possible. As soon as they are untied, then the next group will follow and that will continue until the last Jew in Munich is exterminated. Exactly the same procedure will be followed in other cities until Germany is cleansed of the last Jew.'"[1]

Although it is a contemporary account, Hell did not publish Hitler's call for mass murder at the time, and if he had, it likely would have received little attention. Few were paying much notice to the obscure Austrian-born politician in those nascent years of the movement, outside a growing following of fanatical followers. And there is no evidence that he again went as far as advocating liquidation in any of his public pronouncements during these years. Indeed, if Hitler had consistently shared these genocidal musings, those who failed to heed the warning would have had no excuse for ignoring the signs. But by the time Hitler led the failed Beer Hall Putsch a year later, in November 1923, his prescription for what he called the "Jewish Peril" had already taken a very different tone, perhaps out of political expediency, revealing the tactical considerations of a wily political operative with broader electoral ambitions.

In 1924, Hitler was convicted of treason and sentenced to serve five years in Landsberg Prison for his part in the ill-fated coup. Here, he dictated the first volume of the memoir outlining his vision, which would be published a year later as *Mein Kampf.* Its words have been studied by generations of historians seeking clues as to the future dictator's intentions. Many have asked how the world could have so blithely ignored the signs. The closest Hitler comes to advocating genocide in this work, however, is in referencing the mustard gassing that he had experienced during the First World War: "If at the beginning of the War and during the War, twelve or fifteen thousand of these Hebrew corrupters of the people had been held under poison gas, as happened to hundreds of thousands of our very best German workers in the field, the sacrifice of millions at the front would not have been in vain. On the contrary: twelve thousand scoundrels eliminated in time might have saved the lives of a million real Germans."[2]

Some have claimed that the manifesto and its reference to killing Jews serves as a blueprint for the Final Solution. But British historian Ian Kershaw and most other experts disagree. "It was not a prescription for future action," writes Kershaw, "but the thought never left him."[3] The Nationalist Socialist Party platform, adopted in 1920, contained twenty-five points. Only one of these, number four, directly referred to the Jews. "Only those who are our fellow countrymen can become citizens," it declares. "Only those who have German blood, regardless of creed, can be our countrymen. Hence no Jew can be a countryman." The seventh plank in the platform contains a further clue. "We demand that the State make it its duty to provide opportunities of employment first of all for its own Citizens. If it is not possible to maintain the entire population of the State, then foreign nationals (non-Citizens) are to be expelled from the Reich."[4]

By the time Hitler rose to power in January 1933, the NSDAP platform had stood largely unchanged for more than a decade. That month, the German Jewish population stood at just over 520,000, representing less than 1 percent of the country's total populace.[5]

On March 12 that year, two Jewish Americans—a musician and a medical student—were assaulted by Nazis on the streets of Berlin. The same day, the national executive committee of the American Jewish Congress (AJC)—led by the country's most prominent Jewish leader, Rabbi Stephen Wise—convened at New York's Commodore Hotel to discuss how to respond to the events in Germany. During what *The New York Times* described as a "turbulent three-hour session," the committee agreed to recommend a series of protests, including a rally at

Madison Square Garden. A week later, 836 people representing 236 separate Jewish organizations attended an emergency conference at the Astor Hotel to plan a "day of national protest against the mistreatment of Jews in Germany." Nearly 700 more were turned away at the hotel entrance because the meeting room was already overflowing. At this meeting, the group agreed to stage the Madison Square Garden protest on March 27. They also called on President Franklin Roosevelt— inaugurated only two weeks earlier—to rescind America's restrictive immigration laws in favor of German Jews "who may wish to receive a haven of refuge from political or religious persecution."[6] On the same day that Jewish groups were convening in New York, the *Times* German correspondent filed a detailed dispatch describing "atrocities" suffered by German Jews at the hands of the Nazis with reports of the victims "fleeing persecution" in large numbers.

Four days before the rally was scheduled to take place, thousands of Jews and gentiles protested outside the offices of two German shipping lines, calling for a boycott of German businesses and goods. Within days, the lines had experienced a significant number of canceled bookings. After AJC vice-president W.W. Cohen declared that "any Jew who buys German goods is a traitor," two thousand Jewish war veterans paraded to New York's City Hall to deliver the message while ten thousand people lined the route to cheer them on.[7]

On March 27, a mob twenty-three thousand strong—with forty thousand more listening on a PA system set up outside—packed Madison Square Garden to hear a wide variety of speakers denounce the new Nazi regime and urge Americans to raise their voices in opposition. Although the rally had been organized by the AJC, many of the most prominent featured speakers were in fact gentiles. Among them was New York's former Catholic governor, Alfred E. Smith, who had run for president on the Democratic ticket five years earlier.

Accustomed to blaming anti-Nazi reports on the Jews, the regime was clearly taken aback at the escalating criticism leveled by American Christian clergy and churches against the Nazis in the weeks since Hitler had taken power.

On March 29, the Führer publicly announced the regime's response to the "campaign of lies." He decreed that a boycott of Jewish businesses would begin April 1 as a "defensive measure against Jewish atrocity propaganda abroad." Jews must recognize that if the protests and boycotts continued, it would lead to sharp measures against German Jews, he warned. Appointed by the regime to coordinate the boycott was Julius Streicher, editor and publisher of the fiercely anti-Semitic newspaper *Der Stürmer*. Taking up his duties, Streicher issued a directive that the boycott would commence precisely at 10 a.m. on Saturday. In his paper, he compared the coming campaign to a war: "Jewry wanted this battle," he wrote. "It shall have it until it realizes that the Germany of the brown battalions is not a country of cowardice and surrender. Jewry will have to fight until we have won victory. National Socialists! Defeat the enemy of the world. Even if the world is full of devils, we shall succeed in the end."[8]

The day before the boycott was scheduled to begin, Goebbels had delivered a radio broadcast taking up the same theme, "Against the Atrocity Campaign of World Jewry." The Jews were mistaken, he warned, if they believed they could "call upon an international world power" to strengthen their position within Germany. He dismissed anti-Nazi reports circulating abroad as a "campaign of lies and tales of atrocity." In fact, he claimed, the Germans had not "touched a hair" on the head of any German Jew. If the "atrocity campaign" against Germany ceased, he promised that the country would return to "normal circumstances." But if not, the boycott campaign would be escalated to "destroy German Jewry."[9] The following day, Nazi

Brownshirts stationed themselves in front of Jewish-owned businesses throughout the country along with the offices of Jewish professionals. These businesses had been marked the night before with a large Star of David painted in yellow and red along with signs painted with anti-Semitic slogans.

In the end, the Nazis called off the boycott after only a day. Instead, the regime resorted to subtler methods of economic retaliation. Less than a week later, on April 7, the government introduced a law excluding those who were not "of Aryan descent" from the civil service. An edict a few days later clarified that this included Germans who had "particularly Jewish" parents or grandparents. Before the law could be passed, President von Hindenburg forced the regime to introduce a number of exclusions, including an exemption for those who had served in the First World War. Albert Einstein—already the world's most prominent scientist—submitted his resignation to the Prussian Academy of Sciences in Berlin and prepared to emigrate, the first of nine Jewish Nobel Laureates to leave Germany because of Nazi exclusion policies.

On May 10, a month after the civil service law was introduced, pro-Nazi student groups at universities throughout the Reich staged public book burnings of works by Jewish authors and other writers considered "un-German," including Einstein, Sigmund Freud and Bertolt Brecht, a gentile playwright who was widely believed to be a Jew. Even Helen Keller's book *How I Became a Socialist* made it onto the list of those to be destroyed. Watching the Nazis continue to target their brethren only convinced the worldwide Jewish community to step up their tactics. By July 1933, the boycott against German businesses had inflicted so much damage to its bottom line that the chairman and the entire board of the Hamburg-American shipping line were forced to resign. "The disaffection of the outside world toward Germany and the boycott movement are making themselves strongly felt," admitted the company's executive chairman, Max von Schinkel, in submitting his resignation. "This has severely hurt the Hamburg-American's business and is continuing to hurt German shipping generally."[10]

Soon, U.S. imports from Germany had plummeted by nearly a quarter from a year earlier.[11] The German regime was clearly worried about the economic effects of the boycott. In August, 1933, Goebbels told a Stuttgart festival gathering that he longed for the day when the German Reich "will have burst the iron boycott with which the world has encircled us."[12] At the end of the month, the effects were still weighing on the propaganda chief when he arrived to address the first Nuremberg Party rally since the Nazis took power. "We still feel ourselves handcuffed and threatened by this cleverly thought-out plot," he told the party faithful. . . . This boycott is causing us much concern, for it hangs over us like a cloud."[13]

In 1933, less than 10 percent of the Jewish population of Germany would have described themselves as Zionist, while the majority of Jews belonged to liberal congregations similar to the Conservative and Reform movements that were becoming dominant in America during the same period. In Germany, for the most part, these congregations still rejected the idea of a Jewish state even as their American and British counterparts were warming to the idea. Only about 10 percent of German Jews were Orthodox at the time.[14] Overwhelmingly, those in the Jewish community were anxious to distance themselves from the Eastern European *shtetls* and the perceived backwards peasant life that their ancestors had left behind.

"Except for a small Orthodox group, traditional Judaism in Germany had practically disappeared before World War I," writes Israeli historian Shulamit Volkov. "In its place a new and modern Jewish community grew up. Its demographic, professional, and social distinctiveness reinforced the community's cohesiveness and its social and cultural identity, not in the traditional sense, but in a new way." These modern Jews strongly identified themselves as both Jewish and German and most still rejected the Zionist call for a separate homeland.[15]

In 1917, the British foreign secretary, James Balfour, had sent a dispatch to one of Britain's most prominent Jewish leaders, Baron Walter Rothschild, for dissemination to the U.K.'s Zionist Federation. It signaled an important shift in Britain's intentions toward the region five years before it received a mandate from the League of Nations to govern Palestine in 1922. "His Majesty's government views with favour the establishment in Palestine of a national home for the Jewish people," Balfour wrote, "and will use their best endeavours to facilitate the achievement of this object, it being clearly understood that nothing shall be done which may prejudice the civil and religious rights of existing non-Jewish communities in Palestine, or the rights and political status enjoyed by Jews in any other country." This document is known as the Balfour Declaration and would become the basis for Zionists to organize widespread immigration to Palestine—known as Aliyah—to help achieve the goal of a Jewish state.

And while the majority of German Jews still firmly rejected the idea, the Nazis had been paying close attention to the movement for reasons of their own. On August 13, 1920, in the Great Hall of Munich's Hofbräuhaus, Hitler delivered his first ever comprehensive public outline of his anti-Semitic ideology—a two-hour speech entitled "Why We Are Against the Jews." He devoted much of the address to an attack on Zionism: "And so we can now understand why the whole Zionist state and its establishing is nothing but a comedy. Herr Chief Rabbi has now said in Jerusalem: 'Establishment of this state is not the most important; it is far from certain if it will at all be possible.' . . . The whole Zionist state will be nothing else than the perfect high school for their international criminals, and from there they will be directed."

A year before he delivered this speech, Hitler had encountered a worldly Baltic German named Alfred Rosenberg, who had studied both architecture and engineering, earning a Ph.D. at the age of twenty-four. Rosenberg had joined the German Workers' Party—the forerunner of the Nazis—a few months before Hitler, who was immediately drawn to his learned analysis of Germany's problems, especially the Jewish question. Rosenberg would eventually go on to exert an important influence on Hitler's ideological evolution. Even in the nascent years of the movement, Rosenberg's hatred toward the Jewish people was every bit as venomous as Hitler's own anti-Semitism. As an engineering student studying at Moscow's State Technical university in 1917, the young man had first encountered the poisonous anti-Semitic hoax "The Protocols of the Elders of Zion," which passed itself off as the minutes of Theodor Herzl's 1897 Zionist Conference in Basel, in which Zionist leaders supposedly plotted world domination and talked of Jews using the blood of Christian children during Passover. This influential tract—originating in Russia somewhere between 1903 and 1905—would be the basis for many future conspiracy theories involving a Zionist plot. It would also feature prominently in *Mein Kampf.*

The "Protocols" would later gain traction in the United States when Henry Ford regularly featured the hoax as an integral part of the seven-year-long anti-Semitic campaign launched by his weekly newspaper *The Dearborn Independent* between 1920 and 1927.[16] At the time, the paper's toxic Jew-baiting crusade was jarring for America, which had never before experienced its explicitly hateful brand of anti-Semitism. "The Jew is a race that has no civilization to point to, no aspiring religion, no great achievements in any realm," declared one article in Ford's newspaper. "In any country where the Jewish question has come to the forefront as a vital issue, you will discover that the principal cause is the outworking of the Jewish genius to achieve the power of control. Here in the United States is the fact of this remarkable minority attaining in fifty years a degree of control that would be impossible to a ten times larger group of any other race. . . . The finances of the world are in the control of Jews; their decisions and devices are themselves our economic laws." Many future prominent Nazis, in fact, would later trace their anti-Semitism not to Hitler but to reading the German translation of Ford's book, *The International Jew*, first published in Germany in 1921 as a compendium of articles from Ford's newspaper that blamed the Jews for Germany's defeat in the First World War. Ford—who was considered a hero among the working classes for his groundbreaking 1914 introduction of the $5 day at his factories—is in fact the only American mentioned in *Mein Kampf.* Hitler kept a prominent portrait of the industrialist over the desk at his Munich headquarters and would tell a Detroit columnist that he regarded Ford as his "inspiration."[17]

In April 1933, just as the boycott movement in the United States and Britain started to gain traction, the Nazis appear to have come to the realization that their common cause with the German Zionist movement they despised just might prove convenient. Although Nazi policy still favored emigration as the most efficient solution to the Jewish question, German Jews who wished to leave faced significant obstacles. Chief among these was the Reich Flight Tax, which had been implemented two years before the Nazis took power to discourage German capital leaving the country and further crippling the depression-ravaged economy. Emigrants were taxed at a rate of 25 percent of their total assets. When the Nazis took power, they saw the tax—which would eventually reach as high as 96 percent—as a crucial source of revenue for the Reich treasury. Keeping a tight watch on residents they suspected were preparing to leave the country, the regime often blocked bank accounts and took other measures to ensure assets couldn't be transferred out. Many prospective emigrants, in fact, were forced to sell all their belongings just to pay the tax. In addition, they were required to deposit their cash in German currency in a blocked account before they could buy foreign currency at outrageously high exchange rates at a premium as high as 50 percent, amounting to what historian Marion A. Kaplan calls a "further punitive tax."[18]

Although the anti-Nazi boycott had largely started in the United States and Britain, with mixed success, there was one place where it had been embraced wholeheartedly almost from the start. Jews in Palestine—both merchants and consumers—had vowed to choke off the economic engine of the German regime. Posters throughout the small country urged the populace not to buy German. It didn't take long for the boycott to yield results. In a report to Berlin in mid-April 1933, consul Heinrich Wolff reported that German companies were already suffering a major economic blow. Among the hardest hit were the giant film equipment company Agfa, along with German pharmaceutical companies. Of the 652 doctors practicing in Palestine in 1933, roughly two thirds were Jewish and each had stopped prescribing German medicines.[19] Even popular German films were no longer available for viewing in the cinemas of Palestine.

Meanwhile, a small group of German Zionists—well aware of the regime's interest in Jewish emigration—had been discussing the idea of an approach to the German government, which they hoped might be convinced to ease currency restrictions to facilitate passage to Palestine. The British authorities had imposed a requirement of

1000 pounds as a condition for immigration, which presented a significant obstacle to many German emigrants in light of the regime's own restrictions. Negotiations began in earnest in late March, using a go-between named Sam Cohen—a German Jewish businessman with significant financial holdings in Palestine. It didn't take long for Cohen to win a currency exemption. But the Nazis wanted something in return for their endorsement: Zionist support for ending the crippling boycott.

Emboldened by their success, the small group of Zionists envisioned a new plan, one that would facilitate large-scale emigration of German Jews to Palestine while bypassing the effects of the Reich Flight Tax and other deterrents. Soon, an agreement was formalized in which the Reich would permit Jewish emigrants to deposit their assets into a German holding company, the Haavara, with blocked assets used as credit by Palestine to import German goods. When German emigrants arrived in Palestine, they would receive a portion of their capital in the form of goods and the rest in pounds sterling.[20] The benefits for both sides were numerous. First, the agreement would drastically increase German Jewish emigration, fulfilling a central plank of the Nazi Party platform. It would also further the goals of the Zionists, who could help populate Palestine with prosperous settlers whose money could vastly improve the struggling economy. Likewise, the capital purchases of German imports would be a boon for the depression-ravaged German economy at a time when the Nazi regime had promised to return the Reich to economic prosperity.

Although the pact was supported by the Jewish Agency in Palestine, it was fiercely attacked by leaders of the Revisionist Zionist movement and many mainstream Jewish leaders, including Stephen Wise. The Haavara played an undeniable role in diminishing the effects of the international anti-Nazi boycott, though it is not entirely accurate to say it "broke the boycott," as many critics have charged. The campaign—supported by labor unions and many Jews outside of Palestine—was still very much in effect when war broke out in 1939, but its impact had diminished significantly, especially as Nazi rearmament injected new life into the German economy. By the time the Second World War began, tens of thousands of Germans had emigrated to Palestine under the Haavara and more than 35 million dollars' worth of Jewish capital had been transferred from Germany to Palestine.[21] Today, anti-Semites often cite the controversial agreement out of context to discredit Zionism for its supposed historical collusion with Nazis. But in an afterword to the groundbreaking 1984 book *The Transfer Agreement,* Rabbi Abraham Foxman, former director of the B'nai Brith Anti-Defamation League, defends the agreement's legacy. "Unquestionably, without the Transfer Agreement, German Jewry's property—and the people it sustained—would have been completely liquidated by the Nazis," he writes. The book's author, historian Edwin Black, calls the agreement "the first and most effective Holocaust rescue operation."[22] It was also the first time that Jews discovered the Nazis were willing to negotiate with their hated nemesis. It would not be the last.

If the Haavara agreement—and German anxiety over the international boycott—had appeared for a time to provide some respite from Nazi persecution, the introduction of the Nuremberg Laws in September 1935 once again reinforced the reality that Jews no longer had any future in the Reich. They also had a profound impact on Recha Sternbuch's transformation from a traditional housewife to a heroine of rescue.

There would be two separate decrees, one forbidding intermarriage or sexual relations between Jews and Germans, the other depriving Jews of Reich citizenship. Over the course of the next four years, the Nazis would introduce thirteen new laws supplementing the Nuremberg decrees. Many of the most restrictive would be enacted after the 1936 Berlin Olympics—the massive propaganda exercise for which the Reich had deliberately sanitized its image to showcase National Socialism and its achievements to the world.

The Kristallnacht pogroms of November 1938 would finally mark a turning point in the tightening of the noose. If political and economic persecution were not enough to make Germany *Judenrein* (free of Jews), then perhaps the Nazis would have to resort to different methods. Whether or not Kristallnacht was launched in order to expedite Jewish emigration, it wasn't until a meeting of leading Nazi officials two days after the notorious attacks that the regime appears to have turned to a serious evaluation of the issue. Studying the stenographic minutes from the November 12 meeting called by Hermann Göring to discuss the fallout of Kristallnacht, it is clear that the regime had not yet turned to solving the so-called Jewish problem in any meaningful way. Nor was there yet any hint of the monstrous plan to come. At this meeting, held at the Reich Air Ministry, members of Hitler's cabinet, including Goebbels and SD chief Reinhard Heydrich, had gathered to discuss the financial repercussions of the recent anti-Semitic violence in Germany and Austria, especially the impact of the mass destruction of property on the nation's insurance industry.

Göring commenced the meeting by relaying high-level instructions he had received in light of the Paris assassination of the consular official Ernst vom Rath that had served as the excuse for Kristallnacht. "Today's meeting is of a decisive nature," he begins. "I have received a letter written on the Führer's orders by the Stabsleiter of the Führer's deputy Bormann, requesting that the Jewish question be now, once and for all, coordinated and solved one way or another." Heydrich noted his department's efforts to facilitate the emigration of Austrian

Jews and appeared to imply that the recent pogroms had been intended to expedite this process. The terror of Kristallnacht had taken an especially brutal toll on the streets of Vienna, where hundreds of civilians had joined with Brownshirts and uniformed SS members to participate in the violence. Only three months earlier, in August 1938, an ambitious Nazi lieutenant had been assigned by Heydrich to coordinate the Centre for Jewish Emigration in Vienna—an organization tasked with encouraging Jews to leave the Reich and extorting large sums of currency from the community. The official was so efficient at his task that he would soon be given a much more important assignment. His name was Adolf Eichmann.[23]

Otto Adolf Eichmann was born in Cologne, Germany, in 1904, to a bookkeeper and his wife, but when he was nine years old, the family moved to Linz, Austria, where Adolf Hitler had grown up two decades earlier. Eichmann would in fact attend Hitler's former high school, Kaiser Franz Joseph Staatsoberrealschule. A poor student, he failed to complete engineering school and ended up working in a series of sales jobs before encountering a Nazi Party official named Ernst Kaltenbrunner, who introduced the twenty-eight-year-old Eichmann to the ideology of National Socialism. Eichmann officially joined the party in April 1932, just nine months before Hitler took power. Months later, he was let go from the oil company where he worked as a district agent. He would later claim that he had been fired by a Jewish foreman because of his involvement with the Nazi Party. Arriving in Berlin, he received fourteen months of military training before joining the SS, where the corporal was assigned in 1934 to the administrative staff of the Dachau concentration camp outside Munich. Set up a year earlier to house political opponents of the regime, the camp would soon come to be associated with a far more sinister task.

That same year, the SD—the security service arm of the SS that combined the Gestapo and the civilian police apparatus—created a "Jewish desk" under the direction of Leopold von Mildenstein. The Czech-born German nobleman had joined the Nazi Party in 1929 and soon took a strong interest in the Jewish question, especially the still nascent Zionist movement. In the spring of 1933, around the time the Haavara agreement was conceived, von Mildenstein established contact with Kurt Tuchler—one of many German Jews who, like Hitler, had won the Iron Cross for bravery during the First World War. On behalf of the German Zionist Federation, Tuchler had been tasked with convincing the Nazis to promote emigration to Palestine. That April, he and his wife accompanied von Mildenstein via steamship to Palestine. There, the ambitious National Socialist bureaucrat spent six months establishing contacts that would be essential in implementing the soon-to-be-ratified transfer agreement. A year later, von Mildenstein would publish a series of articles about this trip in Goebbels's newspaper, *Der Angriff,* under the title "A Nazi Travels to Palestine."[24]

It appears from this curious chronicle as if the German had come to something of an epiphany when he encountered a Russian Jew named Gurion during his travels. The grizzled settler had already been in Palestine for twelve years, laboring in a *kvutza*—a communal community that was the forerunner of the modern kibbutz. When von Mildenstein asked why he didn't move to Tel Aviv, where he could make a better living, Gurion informed him that he and his comrades were "building our homeland and that it can only be built when everyone is satisfied with little. We don't get our new land on a silver platter. We must work for it." These words came as something of a surprise to the German, who had been steeped in the Nazi ideology, which portrayed Jews as lazy parasites who never did an honest day's work and were loath to get their hands dirty. This, he concluded, was a "new Jew," a Jew at one with the land. "The stocky figure of Gurion stands before us in the moonlight," he later wrote. "He suits the soil. The soil has reformed him and his kind in a decade. This new Jew will be a new people."

In the same vein, he writes about his first trip to Tel Aviv when his car became stuck in a pothole. The driver of a Jewish settler transport had come to his aid, but when the German tourist tried to reward him for the assistance, he "could not move the Jew to accept money for the help."²⁵ A year after von Mildenstein returned to Germany, Goebbels not only saw fit to publish these flattering portraits of Palestinian Jews but even commissioned a medal to commemorate the newspaper series. It sported a swastika on one side with a Star of David on the other.²⁶ The series would eventually prove influential in convincing Nazi officials that the solution to the Jewish problem lay in promoting emigration to Palestine. Reinhard Heydrich was so impressed that in late 1934, he created a new position for von Mildenstein in his SD security apparatus—head of the newly created Section II/112, otherwise known as the Judenreferat (Jewish Section). In this capacity, von Mildenstein energetically advocated for emigration to Palestine as the solution to the Jewish problem. In 1935, he recruited Eichmann, who had been working as an SD file clerk since September 1934 compiling lists of prominent German Freemasons—the secret fraternal society that Nazis believed was plotting with Jews for world domination.

Eichmann was immediately impressed by his new boss, whom he would come to describe as his "mentor" on the Jewish question. "He was different from most superior officers," he recalled during the interrogations that preceded his 1961 war crimes trial. "He didn't have that brusque, clipped way of speaking that overawed you so much that you didn't dare say a word. I was soon on friendly terms with him." Beyond the anti-Semitic propaganda he had absorbed as a young Nazi, Eichmann had little familiarity with Judaism or Zionism when he came to work at his new department. Not long after taking up his new position, he was assigned to read the seminal Zionist treatise *Der Judenstaat* (the Jewish State), by Theodor Herzl. "Von Mildenstein told me to read it through and in the following days I read it carefully," Eichmann told his Israeli interrogators. "The book interested me very much. Up until then, I had no knowledge of such things."[27] Eventually, Eichmann would become so interested in the Jewish question that he would teach himself rudimentary Hebrew and even a little Yiddish. Soon, it appeared, the student had surpassed the master. Although von Mildenstein had been a tireless advocate of emigration to Palestine, the numbers were somewhat disappointing. Only twelve thousand German Jews had emigrated to Palestine in all of 1935, many fewer than the Nazis had envisioned when they implemented the Haavara agreement two years earlier.[28] On July 27, 1936, seemingly disillusioned, von Mildenstein applied for a transfer to Goebbels's Propaganda Ministry. Before he left, he noted in a memo, "The inner political situation of Jewry has achieved hardly any change."[29]

Under the department's new director, Kuno Schroeder, Eichmann faithfully carried on the emigration policy that von Mildenstein had championed. Shortly after being promoted to SS-Hauptführer, the Nazi equivalent of captain, he decided that the task would be made easier if he visited Palestine to familiarize himself with the region. He had been invited by Feivel Polkes, a representative of the Haganah—an underground Zionist paramilitary organization—who had visited Berlin in February to establish contact with Eichmann's department. In October 1937, the self-described "Jewish specialist" set sail with his SS superior Herbert Hagen. Arriving in Haifa, however, the pair were only permitted to stay forty-eight hours by British authorities suspicious of the two Germans, who had avoided official channels in making their travel arrangements. Yet it appeared to be enough time for Eichmann to form a favorable opinion, for much the same reasons von Mildenstein had cited years earlier. "I did see enough to be very impressed by the way the Jewish colonists were building up their land," he later told former SS officer Wilhelm Sassen in a taped 1956 interview about his aborted trip. "I admired their desperate will to live, the more so since I was myself an idealist."[30] The two Nazis soon attempted to enter Palestine again through Egypt, but in Cairo they failed to obtain a visa. Instead, they met with Polkes at a café. The two had also intended to meet with Arab leaders in Palestine, but this plan was thwarted by their subsequent failure to obtain entry, according to evidence presented at Eichmann's trial.[31]

A year earlier, from April to November 1936, a nationalist Arab uprising against British colonial rule had rocked Palestine. Arab leaders—worried about encroaching Jewish settlement in a region where they had until recently outnumbered Jews by four to one—called for a boycott of Jewish goods and violent attacks on Jewish settlers. An estimated ninety Palestinian Jews were killed before the British eventually quelled the revolt. The unrest, however, would severely curtail German Jewish emigration, and it represented a temporary setback for the Haavara agreement. During their time in Cairo, Eichmann and Hagen were said to have established contact with a figure close to the Mufti of Jerusalem—long an ardent opponent of Jewish settlement. But despite this encounter, the Reich's policy encouraging Jewish emigration to Palestine remained largely unchanged. Following the Arab revolt, a report issued by Eichmann's department had reaffirmed the existing Nazi policy. "Any attempt to foster anti-Jewish sentiment among the Arabs in Palestine is strictly prohibited," it stated. "Provoking the Arab against Jewish immigrants only serves to harm the Reich, for the unrest severely hampers our emigration efforts."[32]

On March 15, 1938—just three days after German troops marched in— Hitler formally proclaimed Austria incorporated into the Reich, declaring that the nation would be transformed into a "National Socialist fortress." His first act was to deprive Jews of citizenship, thereby disenfranchising them from the upcoming plebiscite to ratify the annexation. The next day, Reinhard Heydrich assigned Eichmann to Vienna to head a branch office of the Jewish Section, where he had been working for three years. His task was to organize the rapid emigration of Austria's Jewish population in whatever way he saw fit. By August, he had set up the Zentralstelle für Jüdische Auswanderung (Central Office for Jewish Emigration). It was soon clear that the low-level Nazi bureaucrat—who had labored in obscurity for years without much recognition—had finally found his calling. By the time Nazi officials convened on November 12—two days after Kristallnacht—Eichmann's emigration office had been so efficient at the task that it was singled out by Heydrich as a model for dealing with the Jewish question.[33]

Now Heydrich envisioned similar measures in Germany to accelerate the emigration process, although he didn't appear to believe that Eichmann's success could be duplicated among the original Jewish population, most of whom still cherished their German heritage. "As another means of getting the Jews out, measures for emigration ought to be taken in the rest of the Reich for the next 8 to 10 years," he declared. "The highest number of Jews we can possibly get out during one year is 8,000 to 10,000. Therefore, a great number of Jews will remain. Because of the Aryanizing and other restrictions, Jewry will become unemployed. The remaining Jews gradually become proletarians. Therefore, I shall have to take steps to isolate the Jew so he won't enter into the German normal routine of life. On the other hand, I shall have to restrict the Jew to a small circle of consumers, but I shall have to permit certain activities within professions; lawyers, doctors, barbers, etc. This question shall also have to be examined."[34] Göring, who had convened the gathering, agreed with the security chief's prescription, but noted one of its inevitable effects. "But, my dear Heydrich, you won't be able to avoid the creation of ghettos on a very large scale, in all the cities. They shall have to be created."

Heydrich had no ideological objection to this outcome. However, he objected on practical grounds. "From the point of view of the police, I don't think a ghetto in the form of completely segregated districts where only Jews would live can be put up," he said. "We could not control a ghetto where the Jews congregate amidst the whole Jewish people. It would remain the permanent hideout for criminals and also for epidemics and the like. We don't want to let the Jew live in the same house with the German population; but today the German population, their blocks or houses, force the Jew to behave himself. The control of the Jew through the watchful eye of the whole population is better than having him by the thousands in a district where I cannot properly establish a control over his daily life through uniformed agents."

At this point, the Reich minister of finance echoes Heydrich's opposition to Jewish ghettos. Instead, he suggests, "We'll have to try everything possible, by way of additional exports, to shove the Jews into foreign countries. The decisive factor is that we don't want the society-proletariat here. They'll always be a terrific liability for us." Nothing in the discussion to this point indicates that the regime had yet abandoned the idea of emigration as the solution to the Jewish question. But shortly before the meeting concluded at 2:40 p.m., Göring issued a chilling prophecy: "If, in the near future, the German

Reich should come into conflict with foreign powers, it goes without saying that we in Germany should, first of all, let it come to a show-down with the Jews."[35]

Yet, the Luftwaffe chief assured the gathering, such a drastic out-come was unlikely. After all, the Führer had assured him just three days earlier that he had a plan to deal with the problem. "There is no other way," Göring explained. "He'll tell the other countries, 'What are you talking about the Jew for? Take him!'" But tragically, nobody wanted him. This reality had already become painfully evident only four months earlier when the nations of the world convened in Évian, France, to decide how to address the issue of German and Austrian Jews. On March 18, 1938, only a week after the Anschluss, President Roosevelt had convened a meeting of his cabinet to discuss how to aid Austrian "political refugees." Present at this meeting was FDR's secretary of the interior, Harold Ickes, who recorded the president making the case for an increase in refugee quotas to accommodate the persecuted Austrians. Not for the first time, FDR failed to explicitly note the religion of these refugees, which Ickes believed was a calculated move designed to avoid an anti-Semitic backlash. In his diary, the president's treasury secretary, Henry Morgenthau—the only Jew in the cabinet—recorded the president telling the gathering, "After all, America had been a place of refuge for so many fine Germans in the period of 1848 and why couldn't we offer them again a place of refuge at this time."[36]

One obstacle to the president's proposed humanitarian gesture was the United States' insufficient German immigration quota, ori-ginally set in 1924 at 25,000 immigrants per year and unchanged since that time, though the country had never come close to meeting even this quota before 1938.[37] Now that Austria was part of Germany, Roosevelt proposed, the quotas of both countries could be combined for a total of 27,340—still much too low to meet the burgeoning demand.[38] There had already been reports of thousands of Austrian Jews lining up at U.S. consulates since the Anschluss. But when Roosevelt enquired about the idea of asking Congress to increase the quotas, he was met with a sobering response from his vice-president, John Nance Garner, who mused that if Congress had a secret ballot, they would likely eliminate immigration altogether.[39]

In the days following his initial announcement about an international committee, Roosevelt had been bombarded with a slew of letters and telegrams—some in support of the proposed conference, others filled with Jew-baiting diatribes. Roosevelt had become accustomed to these kinds of anti-Semitic attacks. Almost from the moment he took office in 1933, hate propaganda circulated, labeling the president's policies as "the Jew Deal" and spreading the fiction that his real name was "Rosenfeld." But those fringe groups—many formed during Henry Ford's anti-Semitic campaign a decade earlier—represented a relatively tiny portion of the population. The fiercely anti-Semitic radio priest Father Coughlin had a large following of mostly rural Americans, reaching more than three million listeners per week. His broadcasts frequently referenced what was happening in Nazi Germany, acknowledging the persecution of the Jews but stating that they deserved no pity because they "had shown no sympathy for the persecuted in their own lands." On occasion, Coughlin's sermons sounded not much different from the anti-Semitic tirades frequently heard in Germany during those years.

As early as 1937, 46 percent of Americans polled by Gallup had said they would be willing to elect a Jewish president, though 47 percent said they would not. In contrast, 60 percent of Americans in the same poll said they would vote for a Catholic president even though anti-Catholic sentiment was also rampant in some quarters.[40]

In July 1938, when *Fortune* magazine conducted a much-cited national poll asking Americans, "What is your attitude toward allowing German, Austrian, and other political refugees to come to the U.S.?," 67.4 percent of respondents chose the category "With conditions as they are, we should try to keep them out." Only 4.9 percent agreed that the U.S. "should encourage them to come even if we have to raise our immigration quotas."[41] In a nation still ravaged by the Depression and high unemployment, however, much of this opposition was almost certainly motivated as much (or more) by economic considerations as by hostility to Jews. While anti-Semitism was an undeniable force in America at the time, there is no strong evidence that it was a pervasive trend or that it rose to the levels of overt extreme hostility except among relatively fringe elements.

Like many Americans of his social class, Roosevelt undeniably harbored social prejudices against the Jews. As a member of the Harvard University Board in the 1920s, he had supported a quota to limit the number of Jews admitted to the university. In 1941, he is known to have told cabinet colleagues that there were too many Jewish federal employees in Oregon.[42] *New York Times* publisher Arthur Sulzberger would later relate a secondhand anecdote he claims he had heard from reliable sources to whom Roosevelt described a tax maneuver employed by Sulzberger's predecessor, Adolph Ochs, as a "dirty Jewish Trick."[43] Notwithstanding these anecdotes, Roosevelt's own failures to do more for Jews appear to have been influenced by a misguided sense of political expediency rather than by his own anti-Semitism. Roosevelt would remain acutely sensitive to a potential anti-Semitic backlash throughout his presidency, and these fears would continue to exert a profound influence on both his foreign and domestic policies.

At the April 13 White House meeting, attended by ten faith leaders as well as Secretary of State Cordell Hull, among other cabinet members, Roosevelt described Hitler as a "maniac with a mission."[44] He informed the gathering that he intended to convene an international conference in July on the shores of Lake Geneva in Évian, France, with the goal of creating temporary or permanent havens for Austrian and German refugees fleeing the Reich. But if some had believed America would lead the way on the issue, they would soon be disabused of that notion. The first hints appeared when it became clear that neither the secretary of state nor any high-level administration figure would be attending the conference on behalf of the United States. Instead, FDR had designated Myron C. Taylor—a former steel tycoon and a generous contributor to the Democratic Party—as his special ambassador.[45] It was not a good omen for success. Neither was Roosevelt's assurance that "no country would be expected to receive a greater number of immigrants than is permitted by its existing legislation."[46] With this caveat, it was immediately obvious that the conference was built to fail because it gave tacit permission for countries, including the United States, to maintain their existing restrictive immigration quotas.

Sure enough, as the conference got under way on July 7 at the posh Hotel Royal in the French resort town of Évian-les-Bains, it didn't take long for Taylor and the U.S. delegation to conclude that they were on a fool's errand. Thirty-two countries had agreed to attend the conference, along with representatives of various Jewish organizations and private agencies who attended as observers. As the delegates met, they could look out the window and get a spectacular view of Switzerland on the other side of Lake Geneva. The Swiss had been offered the chance to host the conference, but Heinrich Rothmund had convinced his government to decline, for fear that it would put pressure on Switzerland to accept more Jews. He did, however, attend as the head of the Swiss delegation. The attitude of the other countries present underscored the fact that Switzerland was not the only country whose restrictive refugee policies were guided by anti-Semitism.

Arriving at Évian, Taylor had harbored hopes that the Latin American countries—which historically welcomed large numbers of immigrants—would open their borders to Jews fleeing the Reich. But he quickly hit a brick wall. One by one, the leaders of the international delegations rose to express their sympathy with the plight of the Jewish refugees and then just as quickly offered excuses why their countries couldn't offer refuge. As one Brazilian delegate later observed, "All the South American republics made it clear at Évian that they were repulsed by Jewish immigration [and would never] receive these subversive elements who bring social disorder."[47] While most of the delegates expressed sympathy for the persecuted Jews, some were brutally honest about why they wouldn't be opening their borders. Australia's minister for trade and customs, Thomas White, was one of these. "It will no doubt be appreciated also that as we have no real racial problem, we are not desirous of importing one by encouraging any scheme of large-scale foreign migration," he told the delegates.[48]

Canada was among the many countries attending the Évian conference that conspicuously turned their backs on the Jews, and whose refugee policy before and during the war still casts a dark shadow over the country's legacy. This record is well documented in Irving Abella and Harold Troper's landmark 1983 chronicle, *None Is Too Many*.[49] The title refers to the infamous words of a government official who uttered the phrase when asked how many Jews Canada would be prepared to admit after the war. The official remains unidentified, but his attitude was merely a reflection of the anti-Semitic views of both the country's prime minister, Mackenzie King, and especially its powerful immigration official, Frederick Blair. The son of Scottish immigrants, Blair was described by colleagues as a "holy terror" who ran his department with an iron fist. As the head of Canada's Immigration Branch since 1936, he had put in place every possible barrier to Jewish immigration. His private correspondence makes it clear that his hostility toward Jews guided every aspect of the country's immigration policies, imposing a series of restrictions designed to keep Jews out unless the prospective immigrant could demonstrate agricultural proficiency—a trait unlikely to be found among German and Austrian refugees. "To Blair, the term refugee was a code word for Jew," note Abella and Troper.[50] In one 1938 letter to the prime minister, Blair noted, "Pressure by Jewish people to get into Canada has never been greater than it is now, and I am glad to be able to add that, after 35 years of experience here, that it has never been so carefully controlled."[51]

For his part, King was happy to allow Blair free rein, and appeared to endorse the restrictions limiting Jewish immigration. When Canada received its invitation to attend the Évian conference, King privately lamented that his country would be expected to increase its refugee quotas, as his diary entry from March 29 makes clear: "A very difficult question has presented itself in Roosevelt's appeal to different countries to unite with the United States in admitting refugees from Austria, Germany, etc. That means, in a word, admitting numbers of Jews. My own feeling is that nothing is to be gained by creating an internal problem in an effort to meet an international one."[52] In contrast to Roosevelt and his comparatively mild prejudices, King's private diaries reveal that the Canadian prime minister was in fact a racist and that his government's neglect of refugees was likely influenced by his racial views. "We must . . . seek to keep this part of the Continent free from unrest and from too great an intermixture of foreign strains of blood, as much the same thing as lies at the basis of the Oriental problem," King wrote in a 1938 diary entry discussing potential Jewish refugees.[53]

King had in fact met personally with Hitler for an hour on June 29, 1937, when he visited Berlin to see for himself the much-heralded economic progress and political stability that the Nazis were said to have achieved. Afterwards, the prime minister described his impressions of the Führer. "He smiled very pleasantly, and indeed had a sort of appealing and affectionate look in his eyes. My sizing up of the man as I sat and talked with him was that he is really one who truly loves his fellow man and his country . . . his eyes impressed me most of all. There was a liquid quality about them which indicated keen perception and profound sympathy (calm, composed)—and one could see how particularly humble folk would come to have a profound love for the man. . . ."[54] The Canadian leader—a bachelor who dabbled in the occult and held séances at the prime minister's residence—was particularly impressed by how much he had in common with the German leader: "As I talked with him, I could not but think of Joan of Arc. He is distinctly a mystic. . . . He is a teetotaller and also a vegetarian; is unmarried, abstemist in all his habits and ways." Hitler, he added, came across as "a reasonable and caring man . . . who might be thought of as one of the saviors of the world."[55]

Still, there is no indication that he shared Hitler's extreme prescription for the Jewish problem. Like Roosevelt, King let it be known that his reluctance to open the borders to Jewish refugees was influenced more by his fear of the political fallout than by his own anti-Semitism. He appeared especially worried that increasing immigration would incite riots in the province of Quebec, where the powerful Catholic Church had a long history of hostility toward Jews. Influential clerics such as the Abbé Lionel Groulx—a rabid anti-Semite—strongly supported the "Achat Chez Nous" movement, which encouraged Quebeckers to boycott Jewish businesses. As the Québécoise historian Esther Delisle noted in her controversial 1992 work *The Traitor and the Jew*, hostility toward Jews in the province was more common among the writers, intellectuals and opinion-makers—many of whom were also open admirers of Franco and Mussolini—than among the everyday Quebecker. Those who revolved around Groulx and his circle, she writes, shared "the same wish at heart: via dictatorship, by the re-education of the Traitor and the expulsion of the Jew, the chaos and decay which surround us will end."[56]

While these sentiments were at the extreme end of popular opinion, a large segment of the Quebec media had picked up on some of these same themes, as Abella and Troper note. "Why allow Jewish refugees?" asked the influential *Le Devoir* newspaper in 1938. "The Jewish shopkeeper on St. Lawrence Boulevard does nothing to increase our natural resources."[57] In the days leading up to the Évian conference, Blair warned King that he believed the conference was in fact a backdoor attempt by the Americans to pressure Canada to let in more Eastern European Jews. "We will not satisfy Canadian Jewry by a special effort limited to the Jews of Germany and Austria," he cautioned the prime minister. Canada's delegate to the Évian conference, Hume Wrong, was instructed to oppose any specific American proposals to address the refugee problem, but was also advised not to appear "obstructionist."[58] Rising to address the conference on July 7, the Canadian delegate expressed the "sympathy and concern of the Canadian Government for the victims of changes of regime and of racial and class conflict" but quickly made his instructions clear, choosing to cite the toll that the Depression had taken on the Canadian economy as his excuse for Canada's refusal to welcome Jewish refugees. "Unfortunately, the continuance of serious unemployment and of economic uncertainty and disturbance still limits severely Canadian power to absorb any considerable number of immigrants," he told the delegates.[59]

Attending the Évian conference as an observer representing Palestine, Israel's future prime minister Golda Meir would later recall the despair she felt watching the proceedings: "Sitting there in that magnificent hall and listening to the delegates of thirty-two countries rise, each in turn, to explain how much they would have liked to take in substantial numbers of refugees and how unfortunate it was that they were not able to do so, was a terrible experience. I don't think that anyone who didn't live through it can understand what I felt at Évian—a mixture of sorrow, rage, frustration and horror."[60]

When the White House originally heralded the Évian conference as a forum to create a haven for German refugees, Adolf Hitler seemed thrilled that a solution to the Jewish question appeared to be at hand. "I can only hope and expect that the other world, which has such deep sympathy for these criminals [Jews], will at least be generous enough to convert this sympathy into practical aid," he declared in a speech at Königsberg about the prospect of the world taking the Jewish population off his hands. "We, on our part, are ready to put all these criminals at the disposal of these countries, for all I care, even on luxury ships."[61]

By the time the conference ended in failure, the Führer surely couldn't help but notice the painful reality that was becoming clearer by the day. Nobody, it seemed, cared what happened to the Jews.

FIVE

THE REICHSFÜHRER-SS

I n the early hours of the morning on September 1, 1939, 1.5 million German troops surged over the Polish border to stage the most ferocious military assault the world had ever seen. From land, sea and air, the Germans bombarded the hapless central European nation into rapid submission in what the West would label "Blitzkrieg," but which Hitler described as a "defensive action" against a Polish attack. In a speech to the Reichstag only an hour after the invasion commenced, the Führer described Germans in Poland who had been persecuted with "bloody terror." He vowed that "force will be met by force."[1] Two days later, England and France—bound by a treaty with Poland—declared war on Germany.

Although Switzerland immediately affirmed its historic neutrality, the country's press was rife with speculation that Hitler entertained designs to add the mostly German country into the greater Reich. The Führer would in fact later ask his generals for a plan—code-named Operation Tannenbaum—to invade the country that he derisively referred to as a "pimple on the face of Europe." Recha Sternbuch—arrested only four months earlier for her underground refugee smuggling operation—was mostly preoccupied with her upcoming trial. But the Sternbuchs watched the developments in Europe with trepidation. "She would often wonder what would become of the Jews if Hitler invaded Switzerland," recalls her daughter Netty.[2] As it turned out, the Germans' conquest of Poland would bring the Sternbuchs into contact with a heroic contingent of Poles who would provide Isaac and Recha with their most valuable allies.

Remarkably, even the start of the Second World War did not at first appear to change the Nazis' long-stated solution to the Jewish question—emigration. Following the invasion of Poland, however, the Reich Flight Tax was raised to 96 percent. Jews wishing to flee would now have to give up virtually all their possessions. Still, at least 13,000 additional emigrants would manage to get out between September 1939 and Germany's official emigration ban in October 1941.[3] That left some 250,000 Jews in the old German and Austrian Reich—many of them elderly or sick—and millions more soon to come under Nazi control.

On October 23, 1941, more than two years after the start of the war, the regime put an end once and for all to the policy that had been the officially stated solution to the Jewish question for more than a decade. "The emigration of Jews is to be prevented, taking effect immediately," it decreed.[4] The man who issued the order happened to be the same figure whom Hitler had entrusted with implementing the horrifying solution that replaced it: Heinrich Luitpold Himmler. The Führer had dubbed the solution "Evacuation to the East."

It is difficult to imagine that the monster who oversaw and executed the horrors of the Final Solution could have played any role at all in the dramatic events that led to the beginning of its end. If Heinrich Himmler has gone down as one of history's greatest villains—second only to his Führer—he is also one of its greatest enigmas. Himmler was born at the dawn of a new century that he would help shape, on October 7, 1900, the second son of a grammar school teacher, Gebhard, and his wife, Anna, daughter of a prosperous Munich businessman. Anna, like Gebhard, had been raised Catholic, but was considerably more devout than her husband. They were, at first glance, a typical middle-class Bavarian family. But Gebhard Himmler's life was anything but ordinary. Before settling down in Munich after his studies, he had spent several years in St. Petersburg, Russia, which, before the revolution, had been home to a sizable German colony. There, he attained work as a private tutor for the children of Freiherr von Lamezan, the honorary German consul, a position that soon brought the ambitious Gebhard into contact with the Wittelsbachs, the Bavarian royal family. Returning to Munich in 1897 to take up a position teaching Greek and Latin and to raise a family, he resolved to pay tribute to his brief flirtation with royalty. When his second son came along three years later, the boy was named Heinrich Luitpold after the two Bavarian princes whom Gebhard had tutored.

His father had high ambitions for little Heinrich, and, as it would turn out, these connections to German nobility would one day prove very useful. Gebhard took his sons' education seriously, rigorously preparing them for entry into the *Gymnasium*—an academically selective high school that would determine the course of their lives and careers. He and his wife introduced their sons to modern languages, music, drawing and shorthand, but above all, the boys were raised to cherish their heritage. A notation from Gebhard's diary from this period contains a hint of the values he wished to instill in his children. "As we have already done, continue to bring up my dear children according to our way of thinking, strictly but with love, with religion, but not to excess, to be really German-minded men."[5]

Describing the young Himmler, historian Richard Breitman points to his undistinguished physique as a reason why many people later underestimated him. He was "short, pudgy and un-athletic. He was very near-sighted and the pince-nez or the thick glasses he wore did little for his appearance." That would continue to be true into adulthood: "Contemporaries who looked at this flabby, balding man could see nothing of the Nordic ideal to which he was so devoted."[6]

Thanks in part to a reference from the prince regent—who remained close to the Himmler family—Heinrich was admitted into the prestigious Royal Wilhelm Gymnasium. Although he excelled at academic pursuits, the boy had no aptitude for athletics. George Hallgarten, whose father taught at the school Himmler attended, would later publish a pamphlet describing his recollections of young Heinrich and noting his "pathetic determination to succeed at sport" even though he was hopeless at it, unable to complete a single pull-up.[7] According to Hallgarten, the teenage Heinrich was regularly terrorized in school by his phys ed instructor, Carl Hagenmuller. Still, as historians and biographers later combed through his childhood, they found little hint of any lingering early psychological scars that would explain the monster Himmler later became.

His biographers Roger Manvell and Heinrich Fraenkel interviewed a number of his early acquaintances as well as his older brother, Gebhard, who together paint a vivid portrait of the young adolescent. "He is remembered as being meticulous in his studies and awkward in his social relationships," they write. "He wore his rimless pince-nez even when dueling, he recited Bavarian folk poetry rather badly, he avoided association with girls except those who expected to be treated with formality and politeness." According to Gebhard, Heinrich vowed to remain "chaste until marriage, however much he might be tempted."[8] His father was a faithful diarist who encouraged his sons to keep a journal of their day-to-day thoughts and activities. Some of the surviving passages reveal that Heinrich frequently used his journal to assess his own character. In one passage, he notes that he talks too much, that he is too "warm-hearted" and that he lacks self-control and a "gentlemanly assurance of manner."[9]

When war broke out in 1914, the fourteen-year-old was largely unaffected at first. Like most of his peers, he followed news from the front with great interest but assumed the war would be over long before he was old enough to fight. Still, he yearned for action. When his brother turned seventeen on July 29, 1915, and joined the army reserve, Heinrich recorded his jealousy in that day's diary entry: "Oh, how I wish to be as old as that, and so able to go to the front."[10] Two years later, he thought he would finally get his chance. But his father appears to have used his royal connections to ensure that his youngest son could instead attend an officer-cadet program while completing his studies. Himmler would later falsely claim that he led men in battle, but the war had in fact ended before he could see any action.

Perhaps because he didn't serve, there is no immediate sign that Himmler felt the bitterness of defeat and the subsequent humiliation of Versailles that would help form the character of many of his future comrades, especially Hitler. Instead, he soon turned his attention to his place in the postwar world. The young man had expressed an interest in becoming a farmer. It was an unusual ambition for the son of a classics teacher, but he told his father that he was drawn to the land. He even took up a position as a farm apprentice in Ingolstadt, a rural community on the Danube, but the stint was cut short when he developed paratyphoid fever in September 1919. Doctors prescribed a year away from the farm, but he hadn't given up on his dream. When he graduated from the *Gymnasium* the same year, he promptly enrolled in an agricultural program at the University of Munich.

Although he had no proficiency for most athletics, the teenage Himmler had taken to fencing—a pursuit associated with the virtues of honor and patriotism that his father had instilled as distinctly German values. Fencing was considered one of the best ways for the country's youth to pass on these values to society, giving rise to hundreds of fraternities dedicated to the sport. When a friend sponsored him for the university's most prestigious fencing fraternity—the League of Apollo—he happily accepted. It is during this period that we get the first hint of young Himmler's attitudes toward Jews.

Near the end of the nineteenth century, most fencing fraternities throughout Europe had excluded Jews from participating in duels. This gave rise to the formation of a number of Jewish fencing clubs, which counted among their members a young Theodor Herzl. By the time Himmler joined the League of Apollo, a debate was raging about whether to exclude Jews from membership. At the time, Himmler, like his mother, was still a devout Catholic, attending church most Sundays. In his diary entry of December 15, 1919—written shortly after joining the fencing league during his first semester at university—Himmler refers to Jews for the first time. "After dinner, I had a conversation . . . about Jewishness, questions of honour and so on. A very interesting discussion. I was thinking about it on the way home. I think I am heading for conflict with my religion. Whatever happens I shall always love God and pray to him, and belong to the Catholic Church and defend it, even if I should be excluded from it."[11] It's uncertain from the entry how he believes the subject of Jews affects his faith. A few months later, in April 1920, he notes that he has just finished reading Arthur Dinter's novel *The Sin Against Blood*—an influential anti-Semitic work that had been published three years earlier and had taken Germany by storm, selling more than 250,000 copies. Dinter would eventually become a leading Nazi figure. Reading the book as a nineteen-year-old, however, Himmler hints in his diary entry that he isn't entirely sold on its radical message: "A book that gives a startlingly clear introduction to the Jewish question and makes one approach this subject extremely warily but also investigate the sources on which the novel is based. For the middle way is probably the right one. The author is, I think, somewhat rabid in his hatred of the Jews."[12] Like many future Nazis, Himmler was also deeply influenced by Henry Ford's tract *The International Jew*—translated into German in 1921—which he would later describe as a "revelation" that helped him open his eyes to the "Jewish danger."[13]

His politicization, and his anti-Semitism, would evolve rapidly. At a meeting of the Freiweg Rifle Club on January 26, 1922, Himmler encountered Captain Ernst Röhm, who would introduce him to his life's calling. Fourteen years Himmler's senior, Röhm had distinguished himself in the First World War and had been awarded the Iron Cross for bravery. After the war, he helped crush the short-lived communist inspired republic that attempted to break away from the new Weimar Republic in the spring of 1919. Embittered by the terms of Versailles, Röhm joined the German Workers' Party shortly before Hitler. After Hitler took control of its successor, the National Socialist German Workers' Party, the two men formed a strong personal bond, and Röhm would become one of the key players in the party's rise to power. William Shirer describes him as a "stocky, bull-necked, piggish-eyed, scar-faced professional soldier . . . with a flair for politics and a natural ability as an organizer. Like Hitler, he was possessed of a burning hatred for the democratic Republic and the November criminals (who had signed the Versailles Treaty) he held responsible for it."[14]

Röhm, like the men he commanded, had already acquired a reputation for ruthlessness, though he had not yet taken control of the SA—the embodiment of Nazi terror that would soon become known as the Storm Troopers. The first time Himmler encountered him, however, he described the rifle club leader in his diary entry as "very friendly."[15] Most of Himmler's diaries from the years 1922 to 1924 have never surfaced, so comparatively little is known about his life and political evolution during this time. Shortly after graduating from agricultural school in 1922, he landed a somewhat unsatisfying office job in a fertilizer factory outside Munich. Little else survives from this period.[16] It is an unfortunate void, since this is when Himmler would first encounter Adolf Hitler and his fledgling movement. Röhm certainly played a central role, for it is he who recruited the twenty-three-year-old Himmler into a right-wing paramilitary organization called the Bund Reichskriegsflagge (the Reich War Flag). And in August 1923, four months before the Beer Hall Putsch, Himmler became Nazi Party member number 14,303.

Although he must have come into contact with Hitler at some point—or at least seen him speak at a party rally—there is no record of any contact between Himmler and his future Führer or any of the later Nazi high command, other than Röhm, by the time Hitler embarked on his December march through Munich during the Beer Hall Putsch. The Bund Reichskriegsflagge, led by Röhm, had been instructed to occupy the offices of the army headquarters on the site of the former War Ministry—the destination of Hitler's marchers. Since dawn, the unit had established itself in front of the government building, awaiting action. The one known photo of his contingent shows Himmler standing behind a barbed-wire barricade bearing the war flag while surrounded by government troops waiting for the marchers to arrive.[17] But Hitler and his followers never made it as far as the ministry. Instead, they were stopped by armed police a mile from their destination. Shots were fired, including one that severely injured Hermann Göring, and the marchers were soon dispersed. Himmler and his cohorts escaped arrest, though Röhm would be detained two days later for his part in the failed coup and, like Hitler, charged with high treason. With the Nazi Party banned and its members now pariahs, Himmler was let go from his job at the fertilizer factory.

Rudderless, he appeared to harbor no regrets about his participation in November's momentous events. On February 15, Himmler wrote the Bavarian Ministry of Justice asking for permission to visit Röhm at Standelheim Prison, where he was being held while he awaited trial. Driving to the prison on his motorbike days later, he brought with him oranges and a copy of the party newspaper *Grossdeutsche Zeitung*.[18] Losing his job because of his participation in the *putsch* had not appeared to dissuade Himmler from political activity. If anything, it increased his resolve. Officially banned, and with its leader in prison, the Nazi Party would fall into disarray for at least the next year, but Himmler soon sought out other nationalist forces as he became increasingly radicalized on a number of issues, especially the Jewish question. Starting in 1923, in fact, anti-Semitic literature appears to form the core of his reading material. In one diary entry, after reading a book on German criminal culture, he notes his disapproval of the book's tone since its author was "evidently someone patronized by Jews and in any event not a Jew hater." In 1924, he read a conspiracy tract titled *In the Power of Dark Forces*. His diary entry indicates that he doesn't necessarily subscribe to the "paranoia" of the author's argument except in one respect: "Description of the Jewish system which is designed to condemn people to a moral death. It's conceivable that there's a persecution complex involved in all this to a certain degree. But the system undoubtedly exists and the Jews operate it."[19]

The only time he briefly appears to soften his attitude during this period is when he encounters a young Austrian Jewish girl at a nightclub while out with a friend. The girl had "nothing of the Jew in her manner, at least as far as one can judge. At first I made several remarks about Jews; I absolutely never suspected her to be one."[20] The first time Hitler is mentioned in Himmler's surviving diaries comes in 1924 after he read two party pamphlets containing Hitler's speeches. "He is truly a great man and above all a genuine and pure one," he writes in January 1924 while Hitler was awaiting trial. "His speeches are marvelous examples of Germanness and Aryanness."[21]

While Hitler was in Landsberg, and the party moribund, Himmler began to work with Gregor Strasser, the leader of a right-wing paramilitary unit, who had been arrested for his part in the 1923 *putsch* but who had not yet joined the Nazi Party. Upon his release from prison in May 1924, Strasser enlisted Himmler as his adjutant— recruiting for an organization called the Nationalist Socialist Freedom Movement, which would eventually merge with the newly revived Nazi Party after Hitler's release from Landsberg. During this period, Himmler emerged as an effective speaker and organizer, delivering rousing speeches about the pervasive effects of Jewry while recruiting new party members. He also became a frequent contributor to the party newspaper, in which he wrote articles warning of the close links between Freemasonry and the Jews.

The same month that Hitler was released from Landsberg, Strasser was elected to the Reichstag under the banner of the German Völkisch Freedom Party. The Nazis were still forbidden from fielding candidates because of the ban, but when the party was re-formed two months later, Strasser was appointed by Hitler as the first *Gauleiter* (party leader) for Lower Bavaria. For his deputy, Strasser chose Himmler, who had distinguished himself with his tireless organizing abilities while the party was still underground. Among his tasks as deputy, he volunteered to help edit a small Lower Bavarian daily, the

Kurier für Niederbayern, which billed itself as a "paper for national and social politics."²² Himmler, however, appeared determined to turn the paper into a propaganda vehicle. At first, it simply functioned as a forum for party announcements and meeting notices, but it was soon evident that he had more in mind for the publication that he would later describe as a local "folk journal."

In 1925, he wrote a letter to Kurt Ludecke, a prolific Nazi Party fund-raiser who was about to embark on a trip to the United States to solicit money from Henry Ford because of the auto magnate's ongoing anti-Semitic campaign in *The Dearborn Independent.*²³ Perhaps because he envisioned parallels between the *Kurier* and Ford's paper, he apprised Ludecke of his plans. "For some time I have entertained the project of publishing the names of all the Jews, as well as all the Christian friends of the Jews, residing in Lower Bavaria. . . . I would be very indebted to you if as soon as possible you would give me your view, which for me is authoritative, thanks to your great experience in the Jewish question and your knowledge of the anti-Semitic fight in the whole world." Ludecke would later recall that Strasser "laughed" when he learned of his deputy's letter, noting that Himmler was getting fanatical about the Jews.²⁴

But, although he would serve for a time under Strasser as the party's deputy propaganda chief, it was clear that propaganda wasn't his true calling. Instead, Heinrich Himmler appears to have finally discovered his purpose when he signed up for a new task, joining a small elite party unit founded in 1922 to act as Hitler's bodyguard. The unit had been known as the Stoßtrupp (Shock Troops) until it gained a new name shortly after the *putsch.* In late 1925, Heinrich Himmler was accepted for membership as the one hundred and sixty-eighth member of the Schutzstaffel, a unit that had come to be known by its abbreviation, the SS. When Hitler named him

Reichsführer-SS in 1929 after serving as second-in-command for two years, Himmler considered the promotion the pinnacle of his career. He was no longer anybody's deputy. He now commanded three hundred men. That was enough for now.

In the same year, Recha Sternbuch discovered she was pregnant with her first child less than a year after her arrival in Switzerland. Overjoyed at the news, she looked forward to the *mitzvah* of providing a house full of children, fulfilling the words of the *midrash* that she could recall her father reciting with great passion in Antwerp: "Bearing children in a world inimical to Jewish survival is perhaps the highest form of righteousness." Little did she know that she would soon be entwined with the new Reichsführer-SS in a monumental struggle for Jewish survival.

SIX

EVACUATION TO THE EAST

O n June 22, 1941—exactly a year to the day after the fall of France—German forces launched Operation Barbarossa, the first step toward fulfilling the only one of Hitler's goals that rivaled his obsession with the Jewish question. He had long dreamed of crushing the leaders of Bolshevism whom he had labeled in *Mein Kampf* as "common blood-stained criminals . . . the scum of humanity." Now, as his troops turned east—shattering the Nonaggression Pact signed a year earlier—it appeared all the pieces were finally in place to establish his Thousand Year Reich. Coincidentally or not, June 22 happened to be the anniversary of the day another dictator also chose to invade Russia and send his troops to take Moscow. A leader with only a tenuous grasp on history, Hitler did not foresee that his forces would inevitably meet the same fate Napoleon had 127 years earlier. His decision to invade the Soviet Union would eventually lead to the destruction of his Reich. It would also mark the beginning of the end for European Jewry.

What we know today as the Final Solution—the decision by the Nazis to completely exterminate the Jews of Europe—would only be formalized at the beginning of 1942. But although the terms are often used interchangeably, it's probably safe to say that the Holocaust began with Operation Barbarossa in the summer of 1941.

In the chaotic weeks and months after the invasion of Poland in 1939, Himmler had largely concerned himself with the reorganization of the territory along ethnic divisions—faithfully fulfilling Hitler's vision of *Lebensraum*—living space for the German people. In the years since he had helped to ruthlessly crush the SA during the Night of the Long Knives in 1934 that saw his former mentor Röhm executed on concocted charges of plotting against Hitler, the Reichsführer had built his SS into a force that exceeded even the immense power that Röhm's Storm Troopers had once enjoyed. In 1936, Hitler had given Himmler complete control over the nation's police forces, naming him chief of the German police to add to the authority that he had been granted over all political police departments. In addition, the SD—the all-powerful intelligence service commanded by Reinhard Heydrich—functioned as an agency of the SS. By 1939, in fact, Heydrich's SD enjoyed more influence than even its supposed sister organization, the Gestapo, which had been founded by Hermann Göring but which had been folded into the SS in 1936. While Hollywood movies would later portray the Gestapo as a massive, all-pervasive element of the totalitarian police state, its reach was in fact constrained by its relatively limited resources and manpower.

As an instrument of Nazi terror, the SD was far more effective and its methods more sinister than those that many still associate with the Gestapo. The war would allow Heydrich to add to his already immense power when Himmler created a new agency, the Reich Main Security Office (RSHA), four weeks after the invasion of Poland, appointing Heydrich as its head. The new agency merged the SD with the old security police force, granting Heydrich authority over both the criminal police and the Gestapo. The latter agency would be headed by an ambitious SS veteran named Heinrich Müller, who had once referred to Hitler as an "immigrant unemployed house painter" before the Beer Hall Putsch, but who later gained favor with Heydrich.[1] Among Müller's subordinates was Adolf Eichmann.

With Heydrich's newly acquired powers, he would effectively function as Himmler's second-in-command and gain crucial authority in an area in which he had long taken an obsessive interest—the solution to the Jewish question. Like Heydrich, Himmler too would use the war as an opportunity to consolidate his powers. Although the Reichsführer answered only to Hitler, his SS would for a time nominally function as a subordinate agency to the armed forces, perhaps because Hitler was wary of Himmler's vast powers just as he had eventually grown suspicious of Röhm and the SA years earlier. Until at least 1942, Göring arguably exerted more influence over the Führer, who would eventually designate him as his preferred successor. As propaganda chief, Goebbels enjoyed a more intimate relationship with Hitler but had no power base of his own beyond the acolytes he had carefully cultivated.

According to Albert Speer, who would serve as minister of armaments during the war, the three powerful Nazis kept a wary eye on each other while building up their influence within the party. "After 1933 there quickly formed various rival factions that held divergent views, spied on each other, and held each other in contempt," he wrote in his 1970 memoir *Inside the Third Reich*. "A mixture of scorn and dislike became the prevailing mood within the party. Each new dignitary rapidly gathered a circle of intimates around him. Thus Himmler associated almost exclusively with his SS following, from whom he could count on unqualified respect. Göring also had his band of uncritical admirers, consisting partly of members of his family, partly of his closest associates and adjutants. Goebbels felt at ease in the company of literary and movie people. . . . Göring considered neither the Munich philistines nor Goebbels sufficiently aristocratic for him and therefore avoided all social relations with them; whereas Himmler, filled with the elitist missionary zeal of the SS, felt far superior to all the others."[2] The war would give the rivals an ideal opportunity to consolidate their power bases. Himmler was especially determined not to let this opportunity go to waste.

It took only days after the invasion of Poland for him to send a message that his security services would play a central role in the conflict ahead. On September 3, Heydrich was tasked with eliminating the "leading elements in Polish society" who might interfere with Germany's plans for the territory.[3] The security chief began organizing *Einsatzgruppen*—mobile task forces of between 2500 and 3000 commandos who would be given responsibility for the elimination of political enemies. The Nazis had compiled lists of up to 30,000 Polish opponents to be targeted for arrest even before the invasion. In the weeks and months after September 1, Heydrich's units began rounding up the names on the list, many of whom would eventually be executed. When the Germans began to implement Heydrich's plan to herd Polish Jews into ghettos in December 1939 and throughout much of 1940, the Einsatzgruppen would be enlisted for the job. It was only after the invasion of the Soviet Union that they would be given the task for which they would become infamous.

As the German high command secretly planned Barbarossa, Himmler had already staked his claim to ensure the participation of the SS, thus expanding his already immense domestic powers into the military sphere. In advance of the invasion, he established four *Einsatz* groups (task forces)—each consisting of multiple units. One would operate in the Baltic states, a second would follow the German invaders toward Moscow, another would make its way to Kiev, while the fourth would be responsible for southern Russia.[4] During the first week after the launch of Barbarossa, these units had carried out a number of massacres of Jews along the German–Lithuanian border. On June 27, up to two thousand Jews were killed in Bialystok, including five hundred men, women and children who were herded into a synagogue and burned alive.[5] For weeks, similar massacres occurred throughout Lithuania, although they were usually passed off as purported attempts to "cleanse" political opponents and other undesirable elements or as retaliation for alleged Jewish plundering or attacks on German troops.[6] Often, the Einsatzgruppen would follow Wehrmacht divisions as they routed the Red Army, executing Jews, Gypsies and so-called saboteurs once the army had passed. There had not yet been any explicit order to liquidate Jews. Instead, the terror inflicted by the Einsatzgruppen was designed to send a message to the Soviet population. On July 23, Wehrmacht commander Wilhelm Keitel issued a directive calling for his troops to keep order by applying "draconian measures."[7]

As German forces swept into Ukraine in the late summer of 1941, it soon became clear what these measures were. The region—home to the majority of the Soviet Union's Jewish population—had once witnessed the worst pogroms of the czarist era. But the brutality of the nineteenth-century Cossacks paled in comparison to the terror now inflicted by the Einsatzgruppen as they followed the Wehrmacht into Ukraine. By the summer of 1942, more than a million Jews had been killed by the mobile killing units—often with the willing assistance of local accomplices. In a letter to SS General Gottlob Berger dated July 28, 1942, Himmler indicates that orders for the systematic genocide had come from above. "The occupied eastern territories will become free of Jews," he writes. "The Führer has placed the implementation of this very burdensome order on my shoulders. Nobody can relieve me of this responsibility."[8]

When Allied forces eventually liberated Germany in the spring of 1945—as the world was waking up to the true extent of the monstrous crime that would soon be known as the Holocaust—the liberators were under strict orders to capture and preserve the evidence that would be used to bring the perpetrators to justice. It was widely assumed that this evidence would include a smoking gun directly linking Hitler to the order to launch the mass genocide. Seven decades later, no such document has ever been found. As a result, there is no clear consensus about exactly when the decision was taken and what constitutes the beginning of the Final Solution. Most historians, however, agree that the liquidation of European Jewry begins with the killing spree of the Einsatzgruppen during the summer of 1941. There is unanimity on only one other point. No matter when Hitler gave the green light to extend the murder of Soviet Jewry to the rest of Europe, there is one figure whom he entrusted to carry out the vision that he had first shared with Josef Hell in 1922. Thus, history will forever remember Heinrich Himmler as the architect of genocide.[9]

On January 30, 1942, Himmler's top deputy Reinhard Heydrich convened a meeting of high-ranking Nazi officials at a lakeside villa outside Berlin to formalize the extinction of European Jewry. But by the time the participants arrived for the ninety-minute meeting—known to history as the Wannsee Conference—the Final Solution was already well under way.

As the mass killings continued in the Soviet Union, Himmler received a number of reports from his subordinates about the "brutalizing effects" on the SS personnel carrying out the executions and the "adverse effects on troops" who had come into indirect contact with the activities of the mobile killing units.[10] On August 14, 1941, he traveled to Minsk—the largest city in Belorussia—where Einsatzgruppe B had already murdered thousands. There, he requested the unit commander, Arthur Nebe, to arrange for him to witness an *Aktion*. Nebe proceeded to round up between 120 and 180 partisans and Jews, who were brought to a trench that had been specially dug for the occasion. One group at a time were made to lie facedown in the mass grave. While Himmler looked on, Nebe's men trained their machine guns from the top of the trench and quickly finished them off. After the corpses were covered with earth, the next group—kept a distance away so as not to witness the killings—were brought in and the exercise repeated until all were dead.[11] One of the people present that day was Nebe's commander, SS General Erich Von Dem Bach-Zelewski. He would later testify at the Eichmann trial about what he had witnessed. "Himmler himself was present at the executions," he recalled in 1961. "*Obergruppenfuehrer* Wolff and I were also present. He had accompanied Himmler from Baranovichi to Minsk. Himmler was very pale during the executions. I think that watching it made him feel sick. The executions were carried out by shooting with carbines."[12]

Others present that afternoon recalled that when the liquidations were completed, Himmler gathered the men of the killing unit and delivered a short speech. He assured them that the orders for such actions had been personally handed down from the Führer. They were merely carrying out a "repulsive but necessary" duty, he informed them. Combat was a "law of nature" and human beings had to defend themselves against "vermin."[13]

If watching the executions that day in Minsk had bothered Himmler, or caused him to rethink the mass killings, it wasn't evident in the later testimony of an SS member of Nebe's unit. "On the day after Himmler's visit, we were told that he had ordered that now not only men but also women and children, that is the entire Jewish population, was to be seized. We were told that if left alive the young ones could later take revenge. From this day on then, women and children of every age were also shot."[14]

A year earlier, Himmler had supported the idea of mass

resettlement of Jews while appearing to reject the idea of mass genocide. Out of "inner conviction," he wrote in a memorandum about the plan, he rejected the "physical extermination of a race through Bolshevik methods" as "un-Germanic and impracticable."[15] By the summer of 1941, it appears, he no longer had any such qualms. On the same day as Himmler witnessed the executions, the Reichsführer-SS had accompanied Nebe to a mental institution in Novinki just outside of Minsk, where he ordered the inmates liquidated. But having witnessed the mass executions earlier in the day, Himmler had now apparently concluded that shooting was not the most "humane method." Sharing his reservations with Nebe, the SS commander at first suggested dynamite as an alternative. But explosives weren't the most practical method for what Himmler had in mind.[16]

On July 31, only two weeks before Himmler's visit to Belorussia, Heydrich had presented a document to Hermann Göring for his signature. It authorized him—Himmler's security chief—to make "all necessary preparations" for a "total solution of the Jewish question" and to submit a "comprehensive draft" for the "Final solution to the Jewish question."[17] Two years earlier, on January 24, 1939, Göring had first instructed Heydrich to develop a "solution to the Jewish question." At that time, however, the solution he had in mind was apparently still forced emigration. Now, as Himmler sought a "humane" alternative to shooting as a method of liquidation, it appears almost certain that he was already making plans to implement the solution for which his security chief had just received official authorization. Whether or not this yet meant total extermination, within days of Himmler's return from Minsk the SS had already begun to devise such an alternative method. Humane it was not. But it was arguably more efficient than bullets, especially if the goal was to exterminate human beings on a mass scale.

During the week of Himmler's Minsk visit, Bach-Zelewski summoned Herbert Lange, the head of an Einsatzgruppe unit, who had considerable experience in developing alternative liquidation methods. Shortly after the war began, the Nazis had extended to Poland the German T4 program, which, since 1939, had put to death tens of thousands of German so-called physical and mental defectives. In the German euthanasia centers, chemists had devised a way to eliminate undesirables in gas chambers. They had experimented with a number of methods and had decided that bottled carbon monoxide was the most efficient for liquidating patients en masse.[18] After the war began, a similar method was devised to deliver the carbon monoxide into vans crammed with inmates. The first "gas van"—disguised with a sign for "Kaiser's Coffee Company"—was operated in Poznan under the command of Lange, who would later serve as commandant of the Chelmno death camp. Thousands of mental patients met their fate suffocating on the carbon monoxide fumes fed into the van through a nozzle fitted through a two-inch hole in the rear compartment. Eventually, the gas vans were also used to eliminate Poles designated by the Nazis as "undesirable."

Now, apparently, Himmler's men wished to duplicate the Poznan method on a larger scale. By October 1941, around the time Himmler ordered the end of the Nazis' emigration policy, planning had begun for the construction of the first two German death camps in Poland. The first was Chelmno, built fifty kilometers north of Łódź, where hundreds of thousands of Jews from the region had been herded into a massive ghetto the previous February. Starvation and disease were already rampant. So when word spread in September that twenty thousand Jews would be transported to Łódź from the old Reich, no one could conceive how a ghetto stretched to its limit could accommodate twenty thousand more. A month later, another five thousand arrived—Roma (or "Gypsies") who had been targeted for racial cleansing. When the order was given to begin clearing out the inhabitants of the ghetto some months later, Chelmno was the destination. In this first extermination camp, thousands would die an agonizing death in the vans.

Meanwhile, experiments were continuing on devising methods more efficient than carbon monoxide, which resulted in slow death by poisoning over a period of twenty or so minutes, rather than quick suffocation, as the Nazis preferred. At a camp in southern Poland originally built in 1940 to house Polish political prisoners, the commandant had already been testing a chemical fumigant known as Zyklon-B, developed by the German industrial giant IG Farben, on Soviet prisoners of war. The substance had been condensed into crystal pellets. Delivered to an airtight chamber—later disguised as shower rooms—through a small opening, the pellets immediately turned into poison gas once exposed to air. The camp's commander, Rudolf Höss, apparently had good reason to be looking for efficient ways to liquidate large numbers of inmates. He had recently met with his superior to discuss a secret plan in which his camp would soon play an instrumental role.

In advance of his 1947 war crimes trial, Höss provided written evidence of his conversation with Himmler about what he had in mind for his camp, named for the nondescript town of Oświęcim, where it was located, but better known by the German translation, Auschwitz: "In the summer of 1941, I cannot remember the exact date, I was suddenly summoned to the Reichsführer-SS, directly by his adjutant's office. Contrary to his usual custom, Himmler received me without his adjutant being present and said in effect: 'The Führer has ordered that the Jewish question be solved once and for all and that we, the SS, are to implement that order. . . . If we cannot now obliterate the biological basis of Jewry, the Jews will one day destroy the German people.'"[19]

As the Wannsee Conference convened on January 20, 1942, the fate of European Jews had already been sealed. All that remained were the details. Each of the participants invited by Heydrich had already played some role in the regime's escalating persecution of the Jews. Now, Himmler's deputy gathered the personnel who would be instrumental in carrying out the final phase. Among those who would arguably bear the most personal responsibility for carrying out the gruesome task ahead was Adolf Eichmann, who had been laboring in the RSHA since the beginning of the war as a "special expert" on the resettlement of the Reich's remaining Jewish population. It was he whom Heydrich had assigned to coordinate the minutes of the meeting. And as would become standard practice during the Final Solution—to the frustration of future historians—the senior Nazis ensured that their diabolical mission was always couched in euphemisms whenever something had to be put in writing. Thus, after Heydrich shared the new policy of annihilating the remaining Jews of Europe, the minutes reflected that the Nazis merely intended "evacuation of the Jews to the east"—a veiled reference we now know refers to the plan for internment in concentration camps followed by extermination.[20]

Heydrich informed the participants that he and Himmler had been "entrusted with the control handling of the final solution of the Jewish question without regard to geographic borders." Approximately "eleven million Jews will be involved in the final solution of the European Jewish question," he revealed before providing the group with an enumeration of the Jewish population of every European country, including many that had not yet come under Nazi control, including England and Switzerland. Only one country, Estonia, had no Jewish population listed. The Einsatzgruppen had been so efficient in their task that, according to the list provided, the Baltic nation was already "free of Jews." The protocol contained a directive for what would happen to the remainder.

"The evacuated Jews will first be sent, group by group, to so-called transit ghettos, from which they will be transported to the East," the minutes reveal before defining what categories the Nazis deemed would qualify for evacuation and who would be exempt, including those Jews descended from "mixed blood" who were married to Aryans. The protocol decreed that even those lucky few would be subject to forced sterilization to ensure that they didn't produce offspring who might pollute the German race. It also addressed a recurring question that had not yet been resolved among the various factions of the high command: some advocated for the complete extermination of Jewry while others argued that able-bodied Jews could be a valuable source of slave labor useful for the war effort. The minutes indicate that the latter option had been settled on—at least for now. "Jews who are working in industries vital to the war effort, provided that no replacements are available, cannot be evacuated," the protocol dictated. This would ensure that many of the concentration camps already being planned would function as labor camps rather than strictly extermination facilities or, like Auschwitz-Birkenau, a combination of the two.

At the conclusion of the formal meeting, orderlies served cognac while participants continued the discussion. During this phase of the conference, participants discussed methods to be used to carry out the complex task that they had just been assigned. On Heydrich's instructions, the minutes did not include those details. They simply stated, "Different types of possible solutions were discussed." But at his 1961 war crimes trial, Eichmann recalled the solutions he heard proposed that afternoon. "There was talk about killing and eliminating and exterminating," he told his inquisitors.[21]

SEVEN

SAVING THE GUARDIANS
OF THE TORAH

A s preparations for the Final Solution were being shaped in
Poland, Recha and Isaac Sternbuch and their three children
relocated in 1940 from St. Gallen to Montreux, a scenic town
nestled at the foot of the Swiss Alps. It was an area known as the Swiss
Riviera because it lies on the shores of Lake Geneva, and it had once
been the home of such literary giants as Voltaire, Lord Byron,
Rousseau, Tolstoy and, later, Nabokov. Journeying to Montreux in
1931 to visit the Nobel laureate Romain Rolland, Mahatma Gandhi
reflected on Swiss neutrality, hoping it would inspire the rest of
Europe. In Hemingway's First World War classic *A Farewell to Arms*,
the American ambulance driver Frederic Henry escapes France with
his lover, Catherine Barkley, rowing all night across Lake Geneva
before reaching Montreux, where they vow to forget the war still
raging across its waters. But it wasn't its storied reputation that
brought the Sternbuchs to Montreux. Instead, they moved there so
that their oldest son, Avrohom, could attend the famed Etz Chaim
Yeshiva, founded in the 1920s as a Talmudic academy for Orthodox

Jewish boys, the first such school in Switzerland. Ruth—the niece that Recha informally adopted after the death of her mother in 1928—had returned to Antwerp shortly before the war to live with her father. She would eventually escape to England on the last ship before Belgium fell to the Nazis.[1]

Since her arrest in May 1939, Recha had been forced to curtail her activities. She now found herself firmly in the crosshairs of Swiss authorities, who had dealt a significant blow to her rescue network with the dismissal of Paul Grüninger as chief of the cantonal police. Her frenetic underground activities had also taken a severe personal toll. Two of her babies were stillborn, and a third, born in 1938, lived only eight months. Her devout religious faith helped get Recha through those tragedies. It also compelled her to resume the work that she would always describe as her moral duty.

When they lived in St. Gallen—close to the German and Austrian borders—the Sternbuchs had found themselves in an ideal location to effect the rescue work that saw them smuggle hundreds of refugees over the border to safety during the thirties and eventually landed Recha in jail. In contrast, Montreux was located hundreds of kilometers away from the nearest Reich border, leaving little opportunity for such activities. That would soon change.

Within weeks of the Sternbuchs' arrival in Montreux, two cataclysmic events conspired to send Recha embarking on the mission for which she would be remembered. With the fall of France to the German army in June 1940, the terms of the armistice signed in the Compiègne forest divided the country into two zones. Northern France, encompassing roughly two thirds of the country, including Paris, would be occupied by German troops. Meanwhile, the southern region would be designated as the *zone libre*—the free zone—which would remain under autonomous French control, with its capital located in the resort town of Vichy. Its leader, Marshal Philippe Pétain, had distinguished himself as the country's greatest hero during the First World War, leading French forces to victory over Germany during the Battle of Verdun—the ten-month-long battle that saw nearly a million casualties and marked the beginning of the end for the Kaiser's troops after Germany was forced to retreat. Pétain had vowed that Vichy France would remain autonomous, but it soon became clear that he was little more than a Nazi lapdog as he implemented fascist and anti-Semitic measures designed to ingratiate himself with his German masters. From July 1940 on, Montreux found itself only an hour or so from the border of Vichy France, which lay just on the other side of Lake Geneva—known to locals as Lac Léman.

Meanwhile, in Poland, work had begun in April on the first walls of a ghetto meant to house the 375,000 or so Jews living in the Polish capital of Warsaw and its environs. The prospect of resettlement in Madagascar had resulted in a brief hiatus in building the ghetto, as Hans Frank believed the Reich had found a solution to its Jewish problem, but by the end of the summer of 1940, it was apparent that the Germans had already lost interest in the dubious scheme.

A year earlier, as the first German troops occupied her city, a fifteen-year-old Jewish girl named Mary Berg had begun compiling a diary to chronicle her daily life in Warsaw. Her entry from January 4, 1941, described the bleakness of her surroundings: "Wherever I go, I find people wrapped up in blankets or huddling under feather beds, that is, if the Germans have not yet taken all these warm things for their own soldiers. The bitter cold makes the Nazi beasts who stand guard near the ghetto entrances even more savage than usual. . . . For instance, they choose a victim from among the people who chance to go by, order him to throw himself in the snow with his face down, and if he is a Jew who wears a beard, they tear it off, together with the skin, until the snow is red with blood."[2]

The Germans had introduced ration cards entitling each resident to a quarter pound of bread a day, along with one egg and two pounds of jam a month. For those with money, a thriving black market supplemented these meager foodstuffs. Flour, sugar and cereal were smuggled in every night through sewer pipes, often by enterprising children who could sneak in and out without detection. But for those without means, the specter of starvation became a daily reality. Hundreds died from hunger that winter, 858 in January alone, and thousands more from a typhus epidemic that remained untreated for lack of medicines. By February, Warsaw's original population of 138,000 Jews had grown to an estimated 450,000 as the Germans emptied Jewish villages from the surrounding countryside, along with thousands of Gypsies who had been added to the ghettoization decree.[3] Before long, children of the ghetto were reciting a grisly rhyme:

When we have nothing to eat,
They gave us a turnip, they gave us a beet.
Here have some grub, have some fleas,
Have some typhus, die of disease.[4]

News of the plight of Poland's Jews and the creation of ghettos had trickled out in the months since the invasion, but the first reports of life inside the ghettos would not start to reach the world until the spring of 1941, when *The Saturday Evening Post* published the first eyewitness account. Demaree Bess, a Swiss-born journalist, had previously served as the Russian correspondent for *The Christian Science Monitor*, before being appointed associate editor for the popular American magazine. For his first major piece, Bess secured permission to visit the ghetto from Reichsamtsleiter Waldemar Schön, coordinator of the Warsaw resettlement division for Hans Frank's Generalgouvernement, who arranged for him to be driven through the area by an "escort." It is apparent from the tone of his coverage that the visit had been carefully stage-managed by Schön who tells Bess that he is in the process of arranging employment inside the Jewish Quarter for sixty thousand workers who would receive "four fifths of the Polish wage scale." Although the ghetto residents had long since been conscripted for slave labor, this fiction was dutifully reported by Bess, whose piece in the *Post* purported·to be the first eyewitness account of the ghetto, yet merely served as propaganda for the regime. Only through a chance encounter in the summer of 1941 with a Polish Jew named Julius Kühl would Recha learn the horrifying truth and forge an alliance with a supremely important Polish network that would prove instrumental in the dramatic rescue operation to come.

Kühl had been born to a Polish Chassidic family in 1913 and grew up with his widowed mother and sister. By the time young Julius reached bar mitzvah age, his mother feared that he would be influenced by what she described as the "number of irreligious youth" in Sanok, the Galician town where they lived.[5] By then, the Chassidim were outnumbered by a growing population of liberal secular and assimilated Jews. Her sister Ginendel had settled in Baden, Switzerland, before the war—less than two hours from Montreux. A prominent Chassidic rabbi, Moshe Bunim Krausz, had established a small yeshiva in the town, where Orthodox boys without means could study at no cost. There, Julius would spend two and a half years receiving a religious education before he decided that he wasn't cut out to be a rabbi.

When he turned seventeen, Julius won a full scholarship to the University of Bern, where he studied political economy. There, he discovered religious Zionism—a movement that was still widely frowned upon by his Orthodox peers in Switzerland and considered thoroughly heretical among much of his community back home in Poland. Upon graduating, he became a regular contributor to the Jewish Swiss weekly magazine *Israelitisches Wochenblatt*, writing passionately about Zionism. He also delivered regular lectures about Palestine to the small Jewish community of Bern, and gave at least one well-received radio broadcast on the same subject in 1937. That same year, Kühl returned to Sanok for the last time, to visit his ailing mother. During this brief sojourn, he was shocked at the pervasive anti-Semitism that had taken hold among the Polish gentiles since he was last home.[6] Returning to Bern to pursue his doctorate, he chose Swiss-Polish trade relations as his dissertation topic. For his research, he spent hours every day at Poland's embassy in Bern, whose staff provided the use of its library and extensive documentation. With the invasion of Poland in 1939, much of the country's political and military leadership fled to Angers, France. There, Władysław Raczkiewicz—formerly speaker of the Senate—was appointed prime minister of the new government-in-exile. It would remain in the French city until June 1940, when the Free Polish forces fled to England ahead of the Nazi invaders.

The embassy in Bern became a crucial European outpost for the government of the Republic of Poland in exile. Its ambassador remained Alexander Lados—originally appointed in 1938 by the old regime—whom Kühl had come to know very well during his doctoral research. With the fall of Poland, thousands of troops managed to escape through Hungary and Romania, though the vast majority were either killed or taken prisoner. Those who escaped formed military units that would fight valiantly with the French army in the Battle of France in May 1940 against the Nazi invaders who had decimated their homeland. When the French capitulated a month later, more than twelve thousand Polish troops made their way to Switzerland to avoid capture.

If Switzerland had been inhospitable to refugees in the years leading up to the war, it was now faced with a crisis that would force the country to reluctantly accommodate a new influx. During the First World War, the country had become known for its generous refugee policy, sheltering tens of thousands of civilians and deserting soldiers fleeing from France, Belgium and Russia. Among the refugees who were welcomed during this period was the political agitator Vladimir Ulyanov, who spent three years in Switzerland before returning to Russia to lead a revolution at the end of the war under his better known name—Lenin. But during those years, the majority of the refugees fleeing their countries weren't Jews, and this new dynamic would have a profound effect on the country's recently crafted policies.

In the years after Hitler took power in Germany, Swiss policy—even for the lucky ones who weren't turned away at the border—dictated that refugees could only stay for a short period since Switzerland had been formally declared a "transit country." But with the advent of the war, Jewish refugees already in Switzerland now had nowhere to go. It was no longer realistic for them to move along as quickly as possible. Those cases would be dealt with later. For now, the Federal Council feared a massive new wave of Jews and Poles fleeing from the Nazi invasion in the east. On October 17, 1939, the Council passed Article 9, which decreed that any foreigner entering Switzerland illegally could be expelled immediately without due process. At the same time, it passed a supplementary law—Article 14—which dictated that those who could not be deported, including stateless refugees, would be interned for the duration of the war.[7] At that time, the government estimated that there were somewhere between seven and eight thousand immigrants in the country—at least five thousand of whom were Jews.[8]

Debating what to do about the existing numbers, the lawmakers came to a decision. Existing refugees would be interned in "civilian work camps." The wealthiest among them would be forced to pay a tax to finance their upkeep—a levy that would later be described in some circles as a "Jew tax."⁹ The situation was further complicated by Swiss neutrality laws, which obligated the country to shelter soldiers who might otherwise be captured by belligerent forces.

The fall of France in June 1940 further swelled the refugee ranks. During a two-week period ahead of the armistice, a total of 42,600 soldiers—mostly French and Polish—were allowed into Switzerland. In the beginning, the Poles were billeted throughout the country, many with private families who celebrated their storied heroism for volunteering to defend France from the Nazis even after their own country was defeated. But in July, Swiss military authorities decided to set up a detention camp at Büren an der Aare—a small village outside Bern—where six thousand Poles would be forced to spend the remainder of the war.¹⁰ Announcing the decision, the army high command called the facility a "Concentration Camp." As news of a different sort of camp filtered out of Nazi Germany later in the war, the designation would eventually be quietly changed to "Polish Detention camp."¹¹

With the internment of thousands of its soldiers in July, the Polish embassy established a new department to provide relief to its compatriots in the camp and those who were still scattered around the country. Among the exiled military forces were some two hundred Jews. It was at this point that the ambassador, Alexander Lados, offered Kühl the position of consul, designated "ambassador's assistant for Jewish affairs."¹² His duties were at first confined to attending to the needs of the Polish Jews—including the soldiers but also the hundreds of civilian Jewish Poles interned in the dozens of spartan camps throughout the country. There, refugees were often forced to sleep in unheated barns and forced to haul logs or dig ditches.[13]

During this period, the Bern embassy was in close contact with the Polish Underground State (PUS), which functioned as a civilian and military resistance movement in occupied Poland as well as a valuable intelligence network. It was from dispatches smuggled by the network out of occupied Poland that the embassy and Kühl first learned of the increasingly grim conditions in the Warsaw Ghetto. Through various political and social circles, Kühl had become acquainted with Isaac Sternbuch's brother, Eli. In the spring of 1939, only a few months before the war, Eli had journeyed to Warsaw to meet a young woman who, through Orthodox circles, had been suggested as a possible *shidduch*—a match for a suitable Jewish marriage. As per custom, he first sought permission from Rabbi Yehuda Orlean, who headed the Beis Yaakov movement, which ran a series of schools for Orthodox Jewish girls. Gutta Eisenzweig had graduated from one of these academies and had recently completed her *magister*—teaching credentials similar to a master's degree in the liberal arts. With the rabbi's blessing, Eli traveled to Kraków to meet Gutta's parents and grandfather, who also gave their approval. When it was time to meet Gutta, however, it took less than an hour for her to veto the prospective match. "Eli wasn't the prince on a white horse that I had been dreaming of," she later recalled.[14] Instead, she chose to pursue a doctorate, and Eli returned to Switzerland, disappointed. But he had not forgotten her and vowed that she would one day be his wife.

When Julius Kühl informed Eli about the increasingly desperate plight of Warsaw's Jews, he thought immediately of Gutta. Like Recha and Isaac, Eli had actively saved many refugees before the war. Now, he became determined to alleviate the plight of those in the Warsaw Ghetto. Days later, he introduced Recha to the man who would prove to be an invaluable connection in the rescue network, which had been largely dormant since her 1939 arrest. Within minutes of hearing the ugly news out of Poland, she vowed to revive it. Kühl, in turn, introduced Recha to the ambassador, Alexander Lados, who promised to put his embassy and its resources at her disposal.

The first priority was relief. Reports from the ghetto indicated that food staples and medicines were desperately needed. Recha organized hundreds of food packages—sardines, flour and saccharine—while Eli used a contact at a Zürich pharmaceutical concern to secure medicines. Meanwhile, Isaac arranged for regular provisions to be directed to Gutta and her family.

Occasionally, the deliveries comprised more than just food and medicine. For the Jewish harvest festival of Sukkot in September 1941, the Sternbuchs sent three sets of important Jewish ceremonial symbols for ghetto residents to celebrate. "The line of people wanting to make use of a *lulav* and *etrog* were longer than the lines for getting water," Gutta later recalled.[15] The Sternbuchs had also apprised the Agudath Israel about the dire conditions. The Orthodox network would eventually arrange for thousands of packages to be delivered to religious residents of the ghetto. For the first year, anybody residing in the Jewish quarter could still receive packages and correspondence through a post office on the Aryan side, which then forwarded the mail to a depot inside the ghetto. But the Sternbuchs deemed this delivery method too risky because of the thriving black market, which more often than not saw deliveries looted of food and valuables. To avoid racketeering, the Polish underground had drawn up lists of recipients for whom the packages would do the most good. Thousands of lives were saved through these deliveries. Yet it was never enough.

In the fall of 1941, word reached the Sternbuchs that an Orthodox Jewish resident of the ghetto named I.M. Domb—who possessed a

Swiss passport—had been granted a level of protection not enjoyed by other ghetto dwellers. He was not required, for example, to wear the blue Star of David armband compulsory for all Polish Jews, and he was permitted to travel to the so-called Aryan side during the day. The Nazis had formally banned Jewish emigration, but there was some indication that this policy would be relaxed for those holding foreign citizenship. In the years before her arrest, Recha had found that Latin American papers could be easily obtained through bribery. As revealed at her trial, she had secured hundreds of Cuban and Chinese passports this way from corrupt middlemen, allowing refugees to make their way to Palestine in 1939 through the illegal Aliyah Bet network. But those contacts had long since been shut down by Swiss authorities, who cracked down heavily on smuggling following the dismissal of Paul Grüninger in May 1939. Eli wasted no time in finding a new middleman. Through Kühl, he was put in contact with the honorary consul of Paraguay, Rodolphe Hügli, who agreed to supply forged identity documents at a very reasonable rate, although the quantity Eli had in mind would not come cheap. He was willing to supply a thousand passports at a cost of 100 francs each. Fortunately, the Sternbuch brothers had each started his own textile company, and by this time each was thriving. In November 1941, Gutta received a package from Eli along with two tins of sardines, 100 saccharine pills and a note:

> *Dear Gutta. I'm sending you a few things that might be useful in this hard time. I'm constantly trying to arrange your coming to Switzerland. Elias.*[16]

Inside the package was a brand-new passport. It was accompanied by a document from the Paraguayan consul in Bern: "It is hereby certified that Gitla Mariem Eisenzweig is a citizen of

Paraguay. Nov. 3, 1941, Bern, Switzerland." From the moment she received the passport, her position in the ghetto was radically transformed, as Gutta discovered when she registered the document with the Gestapo as required. "I was still Polish but born in South America," she later recalled. "I became a citizen of the Americas. Citizens of the Americas were treated differently by the Nazis than Polish people."[17] Believing that these "protective papers" were now the single most effective means of rescuing the Jews of Warsaw, the Sternbuchs would devote the next year and much of their financial resources to bribing other Latin American consular officials to provide similar forged documents. By the autumn of 1942, they had secured more than 2500 passports from the embassies of Paraguay, Honduras and El Salvador. Using middlemen connected to the British Embassy, Recha also managed to secure 260 entry certificates for Palestine. Only the Salvadoran first secretary, George Mantello (a Jew whose real name was Mandel), agreed to provide these papers for strictly humanitarian reasons. The others charged as much as 700 francs per certificate—an enormous sum equivalent to approximately 170 U.S. dollars at the time.[18]

Meanwhile, though she never stopped working to help the residents of the Warsaw Ghetto, Recha had become aware of another group of Jews who needed her help on the other side of the world.

When Germany invaded Poland on September 1, 1939, the assault would have a tragic and far-reaching effect for millions of Jews. Less attention has been paid to another invasion the same month, when the Soviet Union moved into eastern Poland as part of the secret pact the Germans and the Soviets had forged a month earlier. The incursion would have a profound impact on the Sternbuchs and would eventually provide a new mission for their rescue work.

Although many Polish Jews greeted the Soviets as liberators at first, the Orthodox were not among this group. Stalin had for years brutally persecuted the leaders of the *yeshivot* (Orthodox schools) in Russia. The rabbis and scholars of eastern Poland had no doubt that the same fate would befall them and their religious institutions once they came under Russian jurisdiction. As they feared, the student bodies of several *yeshivot* were rounded up within a month of the Soviet occupation. Panicked, hundreds of others who had so far evaded the authorities fled to Vilnius—known before the war as the "Jerusalem of Lithuania."[19] As winter approached, the city was swelling with refugees. The newly arrived rabbis and Torah scholars were forced to sleep in unheated synagogues. Food was scarce and disease spread quickly through the city. As word of their plight reached the Orthodox community in New York, and the Sternbuchs in Switzerland, the devoutly religious Jews agonized about "the fate of the Torah." An emergency meeting was called in New York in November 1939, presided over by many of America's leading Orthodox rabbis, determined to help their brethren in Lithuania. The gathering voted to establish a new organization that would raise money to rescue the students and rabbis who had fled to Vilnius and to lobby for a haven that would provide refuge for the Polish Torah scholars. The new group would be called the Emergency Committee for War-Torn Yeshivot, but it would become better known by its Hebrew name—the Vaad ha-Hatzalah (literally, Rescue Committee).

Within weeks, tens of thousands of dollars were raised by the Vaad and dispatched to Vilnius. By the beginning of 1940, the *yeshivot* were once again thriving. That brief respite, however, ended in June 1940, when the Soviets occupied Lithuania and imposed a Communist government. The rabbis knew it was only a matter of time before the new regime introduced measures to suppress the Jewish religious schools. They had to leave, but where could they go?

Help came from an unlikely source when the Japanese consul in Kaunas, Chiune Sugihara, agreed to issue papers allowing the religious Jews to emigrate to his country. Within three weeks, he had issued 3500 transit visas permitting them to travel through Japan. In this, he was aided by the Dutch consul, Jan Zwartendijk, who issued papers that permitted more than 2000 Jews to pretend they were traveling through Japan to Curaçao in the Dutch Antilles.

That still left the problem of securing Soviet permission to leave Lithuania. Meanwhile, the Vaad leadership had seized on the unlikely idea of transferring the *yeshivot* to the United States to ensure their permanent survival. Considering Roosevelt's doomed and ineffectual efforts to bring in Jewish refugees fleeing from the Reich in 1938, the delegation of rabbis who traveled to Washington to pursue the idea must have believed they were on a fool's errand. The man who agreed to meet them, Undersecretary of State Breckinridge Long, would later be identified as one of the prime obstacles to the rescue of European Jews. It was all the more surprising, then, that Long appeared open to the rabbis' plea. The leadership was jubilant when they received the news on September 18, 1940. Seven hundred and thirty-two "alleged leaders of the intellectual thought of the Jewish religion and leading exponents of the Talmudic schools and colleges together with their families" were granted visas to immigrate to the United States.[20]

It was a watershed moment, yet it still left thousands stranded in Lithuania. The Soviets had finally permitted the scholars to leave for Asia, but the Japanese weren't at all happy about the sudden influx—especially since the decision to let them in had been granted by a rogue diplomat, Sugihara, against Tokyo's expressed orders. Only after the American consul in Moscow assured the Japanese that the Jews would likely soon be allowed to emigrate to the United States did the Imperial government relent and grant entry visas. But when no such visas appeared forthcoming, the Japanese threatened to send the scholars and rabbis back to Russia. The Imperial government sent word to the Western diplomatic corps that the Jewish scholars would soon be expelled unless their nations agreed to take them.

The Vaad leadership knew they had to act fast to find an alternative settlement before Japan moved to deport the scholars. Because Shanghai was one of the rare places with few restrictions on Jews, it was the obvious choice. Yet the logistics were complicated. At the time, the Chinese city was designated as an international settlement, governed through a municipal council controlled by a number of foreign powers that used its port. These included Japan, England and the United States. Before 1938, the city had already boasted a small Jewish community made up of Jews who had fled the Russian revolution two decades earlier. When the world closed its doors to Jewish refugees, almost ten thousand ended up seeking refuge in Shanghai. A month before the war began, in August 1939, the Japanese authorities argued that the city could no longer sustain unlimited immigration and imposed the first restrictions. But since Japan was anxious to unload the recent influx of Jewish scholars, the Imperial government granted permission for the Jews to settle. By November 1941, some 860 Polish Jews had settled in Shanghai, including about 500 rabbis and yeshiva scholars. They would be the last.[21]

When the Japanese bombed Pearl Harbor on December 7, 1941, it would mark a crucial turning point in the war. It also meant that the Jewish scholars of Shanghai were now stranded in the port city, which, within days, fell under Japanese occupation. The U.S. Joint Distribution Committee had been sustaining the scholars since their arrival in Shanghai, but now, because of trading-with-the enemy laws, the committee was forbidden from transmitting funds to enemy-occupied territory. The U.S.-based Vaad ha-Hatzalah was also prohibited from sending aid. Funds could only come from a neutral country such as Switzerland.

Since its founding two years earlier, the Vaad had established strong ties with Agudath Israel—the political wing of Orthodox Judaism co-founded by Recha Sternbuch's father at the turn of the century. It was through the Swiss wing of the Agudah that Recha Sternbuch learned of the plight of Shanghai's Torah scholars. She knew she had to act. The Sternbuchs' financial resources were already stretched thin thanks to the considerable sums expended to assist those in the Warsaw Ghetto. They could not also sustain the Shanghai scholars from their own pockets. For the first time since she embarked on her rescue work eight years earlier, Recha sought outside assistance. In the winter of 1942, notices began to appear in synagogues throughout Switzerland:

If someone saves one Jewish life, it's as if he saved the entire world. 400 young men and many rabbinic families from Mir, Telser and Lubline, etc. are detained in Shanghai en route to America, and are studying Torah. Their last telegram reads, "Save us from starvation!" No Jewish heart should, or could, be closed to this call. Please save our hungry brothers in Shanghai! Every contribution for this purpose, during the reading of the Torah, contributes to saving a most noble Jewish human life.

Signed,
Relief Association for Jewish Refugees in Shanghai.
Secretary:
Recha Sternbuch, Montreux[22]

It was the beginning of the organization that would be known as HIJEFS, the acronym of its German name, Hilfsverein für Jüdische

Flüchtlinge in Shanghai (Aid Society for Jewish Refugees in Shanghai). It was also one of the last times Recha Sternbuch's name would ever officially appear on any document or correspondence in connection to the rescue work for which she never sought any credit. For months, Recha traveled the country raising thousands of francs for the Shanghai scholars. Later, her cousin Hermann Landau, who eventually took on the position as HIJEFS secretary, would explain why she threw herself as passionately into saving the Shanghai scholars as she had rescuing refugees from the Reich before the war. "The [Polish scholars in Lithuania] were the lifeline of Judaism," he recalled. "They were the guardians of the Torah. If the Yeshivas were destroyed, it was as if Judaism would no longer exist. That's what the Nazis were trying to do, to exterminate Judaism from the face of the earth. Recha Sternbuch was a very devout woman. It was very important for her, for all of us, that the Torah be kept alive, that the Yeshivas continue to operate, so that Judaism could also continue."[23]

In fact, Recha had felt so strongly about the importance of a yeshiva education that the whole family had uprooted from St. Gallen to Montreux so that her son Avrohom could attend the famed Talmudic academy Etz Chaim. As a result, Isaac could no longer commute to his factory, Helco AG, in Zürich—less than an hour from St. Gallen—where he manufactured women's clothing. Now, he was forced to stay in Zürich during the week and only return home to Montreux on weekends. But an Orthodox education was important enough that it seemed a small sacrifice.

A bar mitzvah in the 1940s wasn't the lavish occasion it has become in recent years, but it was celebrated then, like now, as an immensely important step in a boy's journey into adulthood. For Orthodox Jews, it represented an especially momentous religious transformation that

marked the stage in a boy's life when he would observe God's com-
mandments. The ceremony for Avrohom was to take place in the
spring of 1942 at the Sternbuch residence, presided over by the Rabbi
Eliyahu Botchko, who was married to Isaac's sister Rivkah.[24]

After the fall of France in June 1940, Montreux found itself just
across the lake from Vichy France, where Philippe Pétain had established his own fascist state, purportedly autonomous from Nazi-
occupied France. But if the Jews of Vichy presumed they were safe
from the inevitable fate of those living in the Nazi-occupied zone, they
were proved wrong when the Vichy government introduced a series of
anti-Semitic measures in October 1940. The Statut des Juifs was just
the beginning of a gradually escalating persecution that would eventually see thousands of Jews sent to extermination camps. The Vichy
regime would reserve its harshest measures for "foreign Jews."[25]

In the first eighteen months after Swiss authorities passed Article
9 in October 1939—giving cantons the power to deport refugees—
the law was seldom enforced. Instead, those civilians and soldiers
fleeing the war were usually interned in work camps, where they were
forced to stay for the duration of the war. Still, they were safe from
the Nazis. But in 1942, as thousands of French refugees—many
Jewish—made their way to sanctuary in Switzerland, the government
formally sealed the Franco–Swiss border and often sent back those
fleeing persecution to face their grim fate. No accurate statistics exist
documenting how many refugees were turned away during this
period, but estimates range from 2600 to 3500 in 1942.[26] It is this
period that would later give rise to the infamous name applied to the
Swiss refugee policy after the war, *réfoulement*—the French expression for the forcible return of refugees.

As the Sternbuchs excitedly prepared for the bar mitzvah of their
son, three young men were nearing the completion of their own

journey. The three brothers had escaped westward from the city of their birth, Vienna, to Brussels, following the Anschluss in 1938. They were preparing to start a new life when Belgium fell to the Germans in May 1940. On the move again, they reached safety in Lyons, in the *zone libre*, far from Nazi-occupied France. But as the Vichy regime stepped up its anti-Semitic persecution, it became apparent that "foreigners of the Jewish race" were especially unwelcome.[27] Many had already been interned. The three brothers concluded that Switzerland was their only possible refuge. As Orthodox Jews, they had heard of a famed yeshiva located in Montreux, about three hundred kilometers from Lyon. For a price, their French landlord agreed to drive them to the well-guarded Franco–Swiss border in the back of his truck. Scouting out a safe passage, they eventually emerged in the Swiss town of Port Valais. From there, the three hailed a taxi to Montreux, about fifteen kilometers away from the yeshiva where they had hoped they would be offered refuge.

Unbeknownst to the three bedraggled refugees, the taxi driver drove immediately to the local police station and reported the three foreign Jews he had just transported. When the phone rang at the Sternbuch household less than an hour later, the Shabbat service was already underway. When the rabbi was finished his portion of the Torah reading, Aviohom would be called to the podium to read the *haftarah* that would make him *bar mitzvah* and Isaar would pronounce the blessing—"*Baruch Sh'petarani M'onsho Shel Zeh*—praising God for relieving him of responsibility for his son's conduct.

Orthodox Jews are forbidden to answer the phone on the sabbath. But the Sternbuchs had long since ignored this rule, along with countless other religious prohibitions. "Rescue always came first," recalled their daughter Netty. "That wasn't even something they thought about any longer. If they could save somebody, they would work, they would drive, whatever needed to be done. Religious law recognized this principle." In fact, the Torah commandment of *Pikuach Nefesh*—saving a life—is said to take precedence over all Jewish law. So when Isaac answered the phone to discover from a contact that three Jewish refugees had been picked up and were in danger of being deported to Vichy France, the Sternbuchs didn't hesitate.

Isaac's contact informed him that the boys were to be taken for processing in Lausanne. He and Elias left immediately to try to intervene. Meanwhile, Recha started making phone calls, as did Julius Kühl who had been invited by the family to mark their son's special day.[28] Meanwhile, despite the commotion, the rabbi continued with the service and Avrohom waited his turn at the Torah. His sister Netty, eleven years old at the time, remembers the turmoil of the occasion. "I think I was too young to know what was going on," she recalls, "but I remember that it was about saving three boys and that my mother and others were on the phone the whole time the ceremony was going on in the other room."[29]

In the end, the boys were freed when Kühl received permission from the ambassador to guarantee the refugees the protection of the Polish government. By the time the boys were saved that afternoon, Avrohom's ceremony was over. Isaac never had the chance to deliver the blessing he had been waiting thirteen years to bestow upon his only son. Recha, too, had missed the boy's *haftarah*. It was left to Shaul Weingort, the son of the rabbi, to console his cousin Avrohom about his parents' absence from the most important event of his young life to date: "You have received the most precious Bar Mitzvah gift a Jewish boy could get in these days—the lives of three Jews!"[30]

EIGHT

THE STERNBUCH CABLE

History records 1942 as the birth of the Final Solution, a measure that saw Hitler's killing apparatus begin the extermination of a people the world had abandoned. To this day, however, little attention has been given to the central role the Sternbuchs played in alerting the world to the unfolding tragedy.

On January 30, 1942, only hours after the Wannsee Conference had formalized Hitler's genocidal plans, the Führer strode to the podium of the Berlin Sportpalast to mark the ninth anniversary of his rise to power. "We should be in no doubt that this war can only end either with the extermination of the Aryan peoples or with the disappearance of Jewry from Europe," he told members of the Reichstag and the party faithful. "For the first time, the ancient Jewish rule will now be applied: '"An eye for an eye, a tooth for a tooth."'"[1]

Three months earlier, Himmler had met for two hours with the Lublin SS and police leader Odilo Globocnik and another SS official. Globocnik had recently requested urgent permission of the Reichsführer-SS to discuss the "removal" of alien populations of the Generalgouvernement (German zone of occupation)—home to more than 2.2 million Polish Jews. At the meeting of October 13,

Himmler authorized the construction of the first Nazi death camp, to be located at Bełżec in the Lublin district.[2]

Soon afterwards, according to his own 1961 war crimes trial account, Eichmann was summoned by Reinhard Heydrich, who told him, "The Führer has ordered the physical destruction of the Jews. . . . Go to Globocnik, the Reichsführer has already given appropriate instructions, and see how far he has progressed in his objective. He uses, so I believe, Russian tank trenches for the extermination of the Jews."[3] Arriving in Lublin, Eichmann revealed, he witnessed Jews being liquidated with engine exhaust from trucks diverted into three sealed huts—testing the methods that were about to be used on a larger scale.

The eastward deportation of Jews from the old Reich—Germany, Austria and the Czech protectorate—had commenced in November 1941. The long-delayed task of removing the 300,000 who remained had begun. The destination of the first batch—some 20,000—was the Łódź ghetto, second in size only to Warsaw but already stretched to full capacity. To make room for the new arrivals, 6500 Wartheland Jews from the ghetto were transported to Chelmno, where they were liquidated, beginning on December 8, 1941.[4] Those victims would represent the first systematic exterminations of the Final Solution. By March 1942, Bełżec was ready to begin its own grisly task. Located only five hundred meters from the local railway station, the camp itself—situated on the grounds of a run-down castle—was surrounded by trees planted along the perimeter of a barbed-wire fence to conceal what went on inside. Trains carrying between 3000 and 6000 prisoners would unload their human cargo at a reception center, where the new arrivals were instructed to hand over their valuables and undress. They were then herded along a narrow path known as the "tube," which led to the recently completed gas chambers.

Between January 12 and 19, 1942, an additional 10,103 Jews were deported to Chelmno, where they were gassed on arrival. By April, 34,000 more would join them, along with approximately 4400 Gypsies.[5] Soon, a third death camp was completed at Sobibór. Rudolf Höss had not yet completed the task assigned him by Himmler—building a camp at Birkenau that would accommodate 100,000 people to join the *Stammlager* (main camp) at Auschwitz, which had originally been used to house Soviet prisoners of war. Here, construction of a new crematorium had commenced in October 1941. The first mass gassings would begin in March 1942, with the arrival of transports from Upper Silesia, though these bodies were buried in a nearby meadow since there was not yet an efficient means of disposal. By May, with the completion of the crematoria, Auschwitz-Birkenau could start the mass exterminations that would lend it infamy as history's largest killing operation. Also in May, 2400 Jews arrived at Sobibór, where they were gassed upon arrival.[6] The Final Solution was well under way by the time its most ardent proponent met his fate later the same month.

On the morning of May 27, 1942, Reinhard Heydrich was driving from his home in the Czech protectorate village of Panenské Břežany to his headquarters at Prague Castle when Czech commandos ambushed him, tossing an anti-tank grenade that sent shrapnel through the green Mercedes and Heydrich's body. He succumbed to his wounds nine days later. Himmler's most faithful henchman had been eliminated. His death also gave a name to the extermination of Polish Jews in the Generalgouvernement that had begun months earlier. Henceforth, the liquidations would be referred to as Operation Reinhard—its horrors significantly accelerated in the days and weeks after Heydrich's assassination.

And yet, though the ghettos were being cleared and hundreds of thousands of Jews had already been sent to their deaths, the world was still mostly unaware that a holocaust was under way. By the spring of 1942, as the ghettoes of Poland were being emptied, stories of terrible happenings were beginning to trickle out, but most ghetto residents appear to have dismissed such stories as unfounded rumors. On May 13, the world finally awoke to the reality of the Warsaw Ghetto, when the Jewish Telegraphic Agency published an eyewitness account describing the deteriorating conditions: "The prevailing elements in Ghetto life are misery and hunger. Every parcel arriving from abroad saves people from actual starvation. The Jewish physicians, who were compelled to move into the Ghetto, are overwhelmed with work. Hundreds of people die daily from exposure and hunger. . . . Life in the Ghetto is a veritable hell on earth."[7]

Two months later, *The New York Times* ran a small piece buried on page six about a report received by the Polish government in exile about the "slaughter" of up to 700,000 Jews in German-occupied territories. The report—which we know today was compiled by the Jewish socialist Bund party—called on the Allies to adopt a "policy of retaliation" to force the Germans to cease the killings. The article also reported a "blood bath" that had been perpetrated in the Warsaw Ghetto on April 17, when homes were "visited by the Gestapo and Jews of all classes were dragged out and killed." The unnamed authors of the report cite these incidents as evidence of Nazi barbarity. "This shows that the criminal German government is fulfilling Hitler's threat that, whoever wins, all Jews will be murdered." The *Times*, however, appears to dismiss the report as exaggerated: "Its figure of 700,000 Jews slain by the Germans since the occupation—one fifth of the entire Jewish population of Poland—probably includes many who died of maltreatment in concentration camps, or starvation in ghettos or of unbearable conditions of forced labor," writes the paper's unnamed correspondent.[8] This marks only the first example of the

Jewish-owned *Times* intentionally burying or downplaying credible evidence of the Holocaust. If the influential "paper of record" had chosen to run the same article on the front page with a banner head-line, it might have had a marshaling effect on world opinion and forced Allied leaders to respond. In 2001, *Times* executive editor Max Frankel would look back on what he called "the century's bitterest journalistic failure," writing in the *Times*, "Then, too, papers owned by Jewish families, like *The Times*, were plainly afraid to have a society that was still widely anti-Semitic misread their passionate opposition to Hitler as a merely parochial cause. Even some leading Jewish groups hedged their appeals for rescue lest they be accused of wanting to divert wartime energies."[9]

The *Times* report was echoed by a leader of the Bund named Szmul Zygielbojm, who had recently escaped from the Warsaw Ghetto and made his way to London, where he joined the parliament of the Polish government in exile. As an eyewitness to the brutalities in Poland, Zygielbojm delivered an address to the BBC asking listeners to "ponder over the undiluted horror of the planned extermination of a whole nation by means of shot, shell, starvation and gas. It will really be a shame to live on, a shame to belong to the human race, if means are not found at once to put an end to the greatest crime in human history."[10] The warning, however, appeared to fall on deaf ears as no other media picked up on these accounts.

A few weeks after the *Times* reported the slaughter of 700,000 Jews—to no discernible effect—a thirty-year-old consul working in the Geneva office of the World Jewish Congress made the acquaintance of a German industrialist named Eduard Schulte. Chief executive of Europe's largest zinc producer, Schulte had frequent dealings with the Nazi regime as well as with prominent military officials with whom his firm did business. His deputy, Otto Fitzner, was a member of the

Nazi Party, but Schulte was a committed anti-Nazi who believed Hitler was destroying the country he loved. Since the beginning of the war, he had passed on valuable intelligence—including a warning about the German invasion of Russia—to an Allied intelligence agent working for the Polish government-in-exile.[11] A year into the war, Fitzner had introduced Schulte to a man named Karl Hanke, the *Gauleiter* (party leader) of Lower Silesia, whom Hitler often called "the very best of our Gauleiters."[12]

Through Hanke, Schulte had gotten wind of Himmler's intention to liquidate the Jews of Europe,[13] and the industrialist made the decision to alert the world to the monstrous crime in progress. For this task, he enlisted a Jewish Austrian investment banker based in Switzerland named Isidor Koppelman, who connected him with Benjamin Sagalowitz, a journalist with an encyclopedic knowledge of Nazi Germany. When Sagalowitz heard what Koppelman had to tell him, he thought immediately of the man who needed to hear the dire news: a young Jewish lawyer named Gerhart Riegner.

After studying international law in Berlin and Paris, Riegner had moved to Switzerland, where he was offered a job with the recently created World Jewish Congress, founded by Stephen Wise. It was based in New York but had a small office in Geneva, headquarters of the League of Nations. Riegner's expertise in international law made him an ideal candidate to keep New York apprised of the League's activities, especially its mandate to protect the rights of minorities around the world.[14] By the time Sagalowitz passed on the news, Riegner had already heard a number of reports about the Nazis' "lethal experiments with gas and injections" carried out in sealed trucks. Occasionally, he recalled, the same news would reach the WJC offices from multiple sources. "The first time we would ask ourselves whether such things were possible," he wrote in his 1998 memoir. "But when it was repeatedly communicated from different locations, we began to believe it. We were convinced the situation was growing worse with each passing day."[15] Still, news that the Nazis planned to exterminate European Jewry now shook the WJC counsel to his core.

Over a five-hour lunch in Lausanne in late July, Sagalowitz filled Riegner in on what he had learned of Hitler's plans. One of the most horrifying details that Schulte had passed on was the supposed plan to exterminate Jews in a gas chamber using prussic acid—the key ingredient of Zyklon-B, which Himmler had seen demonstrated in Auschwitz two weeks earlier while he observed an extermination in progress.

The source was credible enough, they agreed, that the news had to be transmitted to the United States as soon as possible. On August 8, 1942, Riegner crafted a Western Union cablegram. Instead of sending it directly to New York, he visited the U.S. consulate, where he was received by the vice-consul, Howard Elting Jr. Recalling this meeting, Elting would later describe Riegner as being in a state of "great agitation."[16] Riegner requested three things of the diplomat: "I am asking you to inform your government. Second, you have a secret service; I do not. Have your secret service verify the accuracy of these affirmations. Third, send the telegram to Stephen Wise, president of the World Jewish Congress in the United States. He is a well known figure and a personal friend of President Roosevelt's."[17]

Elting was at first skeptical of the news. Riegner had declined to name his informant, but after a lengthy discussion the diplomat was convinced of the veracity of the information.[18] In a covering letter to the State Department, he explained that the news at first "seemed fantastic to me," but Riegner's report that mass deportations had been taking place since July 16 appeared credible. "It was always conceivable that such a diabolical plan was actually being considered by Hitler," Elting wrote to Washington. Advising that the report should be passed on to the State Department, he prepared to transmit the cable Riegner had drafted, though it would not be sent to Washington until three days later. The original cablegram read:[19] "Received alarming report stating that, in the Fuehrer's headquarters, a plan has been discussed, and is under consideration, according to which all Jews in countries occupied or controlled by Germany numbering 3½ to 4 millions should, after deportation and concentration in the east, be at one blow exterminated, in order to resolve, once and for all the jewish question in europe. Action is reported to be planned for the autumn. Ways of execution are still being discussed including the use of prussic acid. Transmit this information with all the necessary reservation, as exactitude cannot be confirmed by us. Our informant is reported to have close connexions with the highest German authorities, and his reports are generally reliable."[20]

Then, uncertain whether the cable would be passed on to Wise as requested, Riegner paid a visit to the British consulate, where he was again received by a vice-consul. This time he requested the telegram be transmitted to the prominent Labour MP Sydney Silverman, who was also chair of the British section of the WJC. The text of the telegram was the same as what he had handed to the U.S. Consulate, except for one addition at the end: "Please inform and consult New York."[21]

As it turned out, Riegner had good reason to be skeptical. Although Elting had affirmed his belief in the "utter seriousness of my informant," his superior, the ambassador Leland Harrison, had added a dismissive notation of his own in the report dispatched to Washington: "Legation has no information which would tend to confirm this report which is however forwarded in accordance with Riegner's wishes," he wrote. "In conversation with Elting, Riegner drew attention to recently reported Jewish deportations eastward from occupied France, protectorate and probably elsewhere. The report has earmarks of war rumor inspired by fear and what is commonly understood to be the actually miserable condition of these refugees who face decimation as result physical maltreatment persecution and scarcely endurable privations malnutrition and disease."[22]

When Riegner's cable was received, it was forwarded to the Department of European Affairs, where a debate ensued among the mid-level department officials as to whether it should be passed on to Wise. The department's assistant chief, Paul Culbertson, worried about the consequences of withholding such news. "I don't like the idea of sending this on to Wise but if the Rabbi hears later that we didn't let him in on it, he might put up a kick. Why not send it on and add that the Legation has no information to confirm the story," he wrote in a memo.[23]

Meanwhile, when the British Labour MP Sydney Silverman finally received the Riegner cable a full ten days after its transmission, he immediately sought permission from the Foreign Office to telephone Wise, but was refused. Strict wartime censorship prohibited overseas contact without prior authorization, and British government officials clearly saw no reason to pass along what they regarded as fear-mongering. Anxiously waiting for a reaction to his dire warning, Riegner was shocked to be informed by the U.S. consul on August 24 that his telegram had not been passed on to Wise because of its "unsubstantiated character"; but, the consul assured him, the "substance" would now be transmitted.[24] That same day, Silverman was finally able to send a cable to Wise, which arrived on August 29—a full three weeks after Riegner had composed his warning. "Three weeks during which thousands of Jews were massacred daily," he later wrote. Shaken by the revelations, Wise immediately contacted Riegner and asked whether he was absolutely sure that "deportations" meant "extermination."[25]

Unaware that the State Department had been sitting on the Riegner cable for weeks, Wise contacted the U.S. undersecretary of state, Sumner Welles, to alert him to the German plan. According to Wise, Welles asked him not to share the information until the State Department had a chance to verify it.[26] And so the world remained unaware of the ongoing European catastrophe. But not for long.

By the time Riegner was preparing to share the news on August 8 about the Final Solution, which he still believed had not yet begun, the Sternbuchs were aware of the terrible plight of Warsaw's Jewish population. But, like most of the ghetto dwellers themselves, they had not yet heard of Hitler's monstrous plan.

Recha and Elias had continued their activities for months, securing forged passports for the residents of the Warsaw Ghetto. By July, they had dispatched hundreds of documents obtained from the embassies of Paraguay, El Salvador and Honduras, as well as more than two hundred entry visas for Palestine. Unbeknownst to them, the recipients of these foreign passports had already been rounded up by the Germans on July 17 and brought to Pawiak Prison, the Gestapo headquarters that also served as a political prison. From there, the "passport Jews" would be sent to two internment camps—one a luxurious spa in Vittel, France, the other a camp in Bergen-Belsen in northern Germany. In both facilities, the new arrivals at first enjoyed special privileges—likely because the Nazis were planning on using the foreign Jews for bargaining purposes. Among the group deported to Vittel was Gutta Eisenzweig, the recipient of the very first Paraguayan passport smuggled in by Elias Sternbuch eight months earlier. As the Sternbuchs continued to send forged passports to the ghetto, they remained unaware that for weeks most of the documents had no longer been reaching their intended recipients, many of whom were already dead of starvation or disease.

On July 22, five days after Gutta and the others were brought to Pawiak, the leadership of the Judenrat was given an ominous notice by Hermann Höfle, an SS officer who served as Odilo Globocnik's chief of staff in Operation Reinhard, coordinating the extermination of Polish Jewry: "All Jewish persons living in Warsaw, regardless of age and sex, will be resettled in the East."[27] The notice provided a number of exclusions, including employees of both the Judenrat and Aryan businesses, as well as the staff of Jewish hospitals. The deportations—described as "resettlement"—were scheduled to commence at 11 a.m., according to the notice. A new extermination camp had opened the very same day in a village northeast of Warsaw known as Treblinka. This would be the destination for more than 250,000 ghetto residents over the next two months in an operation that had already been labeled by the Nazis as Grossaktion Warschau. Residents were instructed to report to a central assembly point for processing. To avoid suspicion, the Germans permitted each evacuee to bring fifteen kilograms of property, all valuables and three days' worth of food. On the day the deportations began, five thousand were brought by train to Treblinka, where they were exterminated upon arrival. Most of the residents left behind at first believed the official version—that the Jews were simply being sent into "exile" at labor camps. Adam Czerniaków, head of the Judenrat, was under no such illusion. The day after the deportations began, he took his own life by swallowing a cyanide pill. The final entry in his diary read, "I am powerless, my heart trembles in sorrow and compassion. I can no longer bear all this."[28]

The Sternbuchs received the first word about the deportations at the end of July, but, like the residents, they still had no idea about the fate of the evacuees. It wasn't until early September that the first gut-wrenching reports reached Elias in the form of two coded letters from an Orthodox ghetto resident, I.M. Domb, who shared the horrifying news through the Polish Underground.[29] Each was innocuous on its surface but contained a code based on a combination of Hebrew and German words and Torah passages. The first read: "I spoke to Mr. Jäger. He told me that he will invite all relatives of the family Achenu (with the exception of Miss Eisenzweig from Warsaw) to his countryside dwelling Graber. I am done here. I feel lonely. As to the citrus fruit, I hope I shall receive them in time but I do not know whether I shall then find anybody of my acquaintance. I feel very weak. A week ago I spoke to Mr. Orleans. Mrs. Gefen telephones very often. Uncle Gerusch works also in Warsaw; he is a very capable worker. His friend Miso works together for him. . . . Please pray for me."[30]

Each of the key words represented a code easily decipherable to an Orthodox Jew. "Jäger"—the German word for hunter—refers to the Nazis. The "family Achenu" signifies Jewish brethren. "Graber" is a grave. The "citrus fruit" refers to the *etrog* used in the festival of Sukkot at the end of September. "Friend Miso" refers to his "friend Death" while "Onkel Gerusch" (Uncle Gerusch) refers to deportations.[31] In 1980, Elias Sternbuch revealed how he and Recha deciphered the code and immediately understood its meaning: "All Jews of the Warsaw ghetto were being deported to be killed in the countryside. By the end of September, the ghetto will be empty."[32]

The coded letter contained more details, including the numbers of Jews already deported. The reference to "the exception of Miss Eisenzweig" is an allusion to Elias's prospective prewar lady friend Gutta Eisenzweig, who had been sent to the Pawiak political prison on July 17 and was thus spared from the deportations that began five days later (along with her mother—whose maiden name was Gefen—another recipient of a Paraguayan passport from Eli Sternbuch).[33]

When Recha and Isaac deciphered the code, they knew immediately what had to be done. They contacted Julius Kühl, who had offered to put the diplomatic pouch and communication network of the Polish embassy at their disposal. On September 3, Jacob Rosenheim, president of Agudath Israel, received a telegram in New York from Isaac Sternbuch, transmitted through the embassy:

> According to recently received authentic information, the German authorities have evacuated the last Ghetto in Warsaw, bestially murdering about one hundred thousand Jews. Mass murders continue. From the corpses of the murdered, soap and artificial fertilizers are produced. The deportees from other occupied countries will meet the same fate. It must be supposed that only energetic reprisals on the part of America could halt these persecutions. Do whatever you can to cause an American reaction to halt these persecutions. Do whatever you can to produce such a reaction, stirring up statesmen, the press, and the community. Inform Wise, Silver, Lubavitcher, Einstein, Klatskin, Goldman, Thomas Mann and others about this. Do not mention my name. Please acknowledge receipt of the present dispatch.[34]

Days later, Elias Sternbuch received another coded message from his informant that wholesale gassing of Polish Jews had already begun. Rosenheim immediately heeded Sternbuch's call to cause an "American reaction." The same day, he cabled President Roosevelt in Washington with the dire news. "I dare in the name of Orthodox Jews all over the world to propose for consideration the arrangement by American initiative of a joint intervention of all the neutral states in Europe and America expressing their moral indignation."[35] Worried that the communiqué would be kept from FDR, he arranged for a copy to be sent to Eleanor Roosevelt and Felix Frankfurter—the

Jewish Supreme Court justice who enjoyed close ties with the president—asking him to consider passing it on to "the Chief."[36]

In addition, Rosenheim contacted all the prominent figures Sternbuch cited in the cable, including Albert Einstein and the great anti-Nazi German novelist Thomas Mann, urging them to inform the world about the plight of European Jewry. Three weeks later, on September 27, Mann would use his German-language BBC broadcast to inform his listeners: "Now one has arrived at extermination, the maniacal decision to completely stamp out European Jewry. . . . there is available an exact and authentic report about the killing of not less than 11,000 Polish Jews with poison gas."[37] Less than two weeks after this broadcast, on October 9, Anne Frank—hiding from the Nazis in the Amsterdam annex—lamented in her diary the fate of the deported Jews: "If it's that bad in Holland, what must it be like in those faraway and uncivilized places where the Germans are sending them? We assume that most of them are being murdered. The English radio says that they're being gassed. Perhaps that's the quickest way to die."[38]

The Sternbuchs had not been the first to sound a warning about the unfolding catastrophe, but they were unquestionably instrumental in waking the world up to the horror of the death camps—at least for those willing to listen.

Although the information in Sternbuch's cable—like Riegner's before it—had proven remarkably accurate, it unfortunately repeated a rumor that had been circulating in Poland for some time. "From the corpses of the murdered, soap and artificial fertilizers are produced," Sternbuch wrote on September 3. This cable may in fact be the source of the oft-repeated story that many still believe to this day—that the Nazis manufactured soap from the corpses of Holocaust victims. It is a falsehood long since discredited by Israel's Yad Vashem

Holocaust research institute and most other experts.[39] Nor is there any evidence that the ashes of Jews were ever used for fertilizer.

By the time news contained in the Sternbuch report reached Himmler, the SS chief had already personally authorized operations resulting in the genocide of more than three million Jews, Gypsies and Slavs. He had even ordered the mass shootings of children lest the young ones one day "take revenge." Yet, according to the historian Richard Breitman, Himmler was enraged by the report that soap was allegedly being manufactured from the remains of Jews. "Himmler knew that no one was supposed to be manufacturing fats or artificial fertilizers of corpses," Breitman writes. Consequently, he wrote to Gestapo chief Heinrich Müller—whom Himmler had recently entrusted with overseeing many of the logistics of the Final Solution— demanding a "guarantee" that the corpses were not being "misused."[40]

Such was the twisted morality of the Reichsführer-SS at the height of the Holocaust.

NINE

MARCH OF THE RABBIS

O n December 13, 1942, Nazi propaganda chief Joseph Goebbels sat down to record his thoughts in the diary that he had painstakingly maintained since just before his twenty-seventh birthday, when he was still an unemployed writer living with his parents in Rheydt. His entry that day provides a telling insight into the thoughts of the Nazi leadership a year after Hitler had authorized the total destruction of European Jewry: "The question of Jewish persecution in Europe is being given top news priority by the English and the Americans. . . . At bottom, however, I believe both the English and Americans are happy that we are exterminating the Jewish riff raff."[1] Goebbels could hardly be blamed for coming to this conclusion.

Less than three weeks earlier, Sumner Welles had summoned Stephen Wise to the State Department for an urgent meeting. Wise had still not shared Riegner's ominous warning with his colleagues. Instead, he accepted Jacob Rosenheim's demand on behalf of the Agudah that he call an emergency meeting of Jewish leaders to discuss the alarming contents of Isaac Sternbuch's September 3 cable. On September 5, Wise invited the leaders of thirty-five major Jewish organizations to gather at the offices of the World Jewish Congress.

The somber tone of his telegrammed invitation underscored the urgency of the meeting:

> HORRIFYING NEWS OF MASS MASSACRES OF JEWS
> HAS JUST RECEIVED US [sic]. INFORMATION SO
> APPALLING AND IMPLICATIONS FOR FUTURE SO
> GRAVE THAT WE ARE CALLING SPECIAL MEETING OF
> LEADING JEWISH BODIES TO CONSIDER TOGETHER
> ACTION WHICH CAN AND SHOULD BE TAKEN.[2]

The next day, representatives of all but one of the major organizations crammed into the WJC board room to hear Wise share the news.[3] At this meeting, America's most prominent Jewish leader chose not to mention the Riegner telegram, which he had promised Welles he would not disclose until the State Department could verify its contents. Instead, he shared the contents of the Sternbuch cable. But rather than urging the assembled leaders to take action, he made them promise to keep silent about its contents until further notice. Some Orthodox leaders emerged from the meeting with the feeling that Wise had disparaged Sternbuch's information and implied that it was a result of the Orthodox spreading *gruelmarchen*, or atrocity myths.[4]

One has to wonder, in fact, whether Wise at this point still doubted the contents of the Riegner cable that he had personally passed on to the State Department days earlier. If he continued to suspect at this stage that the horrifying stories out of Europe were exaggerated, his skepticism may not have entirely been unfounded. Everyone in the room was old enough to remember the so-called atrocity propaganda—long since discredited—that featured prominently in the Allied war effort during the First World War, used to whip up hatred against Germany. In his 2003 book *Propaganda and*

Persuasion, historian Nicholas John Cull documents the widespread use of this technique, especially by the British. "Tales of the spike-helmeted German 'Hun' cutting off the hands of children, boiling corpses to make soap, crucifying prisoners of war, and using priests as clappers in cathedral bells were widely believed by the British public," he writes.[5] As hundreds of stories about the Holocaust began to circulate in American media throughout the war—meticulously documented in Deborah Lipstadt's important 1993 book *Beyond Belief*—it is clear that most Americans didn't begin to fully believe these stories until at least 1944. The same can't be said, however, of the Allied governments.

The Sternbuchs had forwarded both coded cables to Riegner, who sent them on to Washington, where they would prove instrumental in confirming news of the Final Solution. When I interviewed Riegner in 2000, a year before his death, the WJC official—still working out of the Geneva office at the age of eighty-eight—told me that he had a "vague" knowledge of the Sternbuchs and their activities, but that their paths had not formally crossed at the time that he had prepared his cable. Although Riegner always remained tight-lipped about his sources, he once revealed that he had received the coded cables confirming details of the Final Solution from "friends in St. Gallen." Later, documents in WJC archives confirmed that Elias Sternbuch was, in fact, his source.[6]

On November 24, almost a full three months after Wise forwarded Riegner's telegram to the State Department, Sumner Welles summoned him to a meeting. In his 1998 memoir, Wise recalled what happened next: "In the office of Mr. Welles, we took our places and I shall never forget the quiet but deeply moving way in which he turned to us and said, every word etching itself into my heart, 'Gentlemen, I hold in my hands documents which have come to me from our legation in Bern. I regret to tell you, Dr. Wise, that these confirm and justify your deepest fears.' He handed me the original documents from Bern which confirmed our dreadful apprehensions. The documents' red seals suggested the blood of my people pouring forth in rivers. Mr. Welles added, 'For reasons you will understand, I cannot give these to the press, but there is no reason why you should not. It might even help if you did.'"[7]

Thus, we know for a certainty that the Roosevelt administration had by November 1942 verified Hitler's plan to exterminate the Jews of Europe. Yet rather than the president going on the radio or holding a press conference to announce the Nazis' barbaric plan, it was left up to Wise—a rabbi with little credibility or profile outside the American Jewish community—to deliver the news. The WJC president immediately called two press conferences—one in Washington later the same day and one in New York scheduled for the following day—to alert the media.

In front of the Washington press corps a few hours later, Wise revealed that Hitler had ordered the annihilation of all Jews in Europe by the end of the year. "This news is substantiated in documents furnished to me by the State Department this afternoon," he said. "It is one of the last mad acts of destruction which Hitler will perpetrate before he is called to judgment." At this conference, he still makes no mention of the Riegner telegram, which would prove to be remarkably accurate and correctly reported that the Nazis planned to use prussic acid (Zyklon-B) to carry out the exterminations. Instead, he makes reference to the inaccurate information contained in the Sternbuch cable along with another rumor circulating about German killing methods: "The Nazis have used various means of killing off large portions of the Jewish population, including poison and asphyxiation, but have now found that the most efficient method is for a doctor to inject an air bubble into the victims' veins," he revealed. "In this way a single doctor can kill 100 persons in an hour." He added that the Nazis had set a value of about ten dollars for each corpse and are "reclaiming them for soap fats and fertilizer."[8]

The sensational revelation was covered by a number of news outlets, but few gave the story prominent placement. Characteristically, *The New York Times* ran only a small piece buried on page ten.[9] However, Wise and other Jewish leaders were now determined that the world must respond to the tragedy, and so launched an intense lobbying effort. Wise had already repeatedly pleaded with the Roosevelt administration to urge the Vatican to use its influence to stop the genocide. At his New York press conference on November 25, he explained that his aim in publicizing the exterminations was to "win the support of a Christian world so that its leaders may intervene and protest the horrible treatment of Jews in Hitler Europe."[10] And yet it seemed that outside the Jewish press, there was little public outcry at the unfolding catastrophe—a tragedy that could no longer be dismissed as rumor-mongering.

On December 2, Jewish organizations called for a day of prayer and mourning for the "victims of Hitlerism."[11] A week later, on December 8, President Roosevelt met at the White House with a delegation led by Wise. Afterwards, the group reported that the president had promised "we are doing everything possible to determine who are personally guilty" for the deaths of two million Jews to date in Nazi-occupied Europe. He had also given his assurance that the United Nations—the term that FDR had recently coined to refer to the countries allied against Germany—are prepared to "take every possible step" to end the Nazi massacres of Jews in Europe. "The mills of the Gods grind slowly, but they grind exceedingly small," Roosevelt told the group.[12] Eight days later, it appeared that the president had kept his pledge for United Nations intervention when eleven UN countries, including the United States, issued a joint declaration condemning Germany's "bestial policy of cold-blooded extermination of Jews."[13] But while British foreign minister Anthony Eden delivered this declaration on the floor of the House of Commons in London, neither U.S. secretary of state Cordell Hull nor President Roosevelt chose to utter these words out loud. Instead, Washington released its position via a State Department press release. Still, its coverage the next day marked the only time in all of 1942 that *The New York Times* would mention the extermination of Jews on its front page. As 1943 dawned, American Jewish leaders had renewed hope that their government and the civilized world would intervene to stop the genocide. The next fourteen months would see those hopes cruelly and repeatedly shattered.

At the Bermuda Conference of April 1943—convened by the United States and Britain to address the issue of Jewish refugees—delegates from both countries agreed that "no approach be made to Hitler for the release of potential refugees in Germany or German-occupied territory." Instead, the countries would seek neutral shipping lines for the potential evacuation of the refugees if such a possibility arose.[14] The toothless declaration again underscored the unwillingness of the Allied powers to launch any meaningful rescue operation. From that point on, official policy appeared to hold that the only way to save Jews from Hitler's ovens was for the Allies to win the war as quickly as possible.

As conference delegates were meeting in Bermuda, the underground Polish radio station SWIAT broadcast an urgent SOS: "Death sentence has been proclaimed on the last 35,000 Jews in the Warsaw ghetto. Gun salvoes are echoing in the streets of Warsaw. Women and children are defending themselves with bare hands. Save us. . . ."[15]

By the eve of Passover, April 19, 1943, three hundred thousand residents of the Warsaw Ghetto had already been transported to Treblinka, leaving a fraction of the original population. The remaining Jews no longer believed the Nazi fiction that their brethren had been sent to labor camps. News of Treblinka's ovens had long since reached the ghetto, and its dwellers had vowed to resist any new deportation. Socialist, communist and Zionist factions put aside their political differences to form the Jewish Fighting Organization (ZOB), while the Revisionists formed a paramilitary force of their own, bringing the total of fighting units to twenty-two. Now, the resistance prepared for a battle, smuggling in weapons and training for a confrontation. When residents got word on April 18 that the final liquidations would commence the next day, the entire ghetto mobilized. When SS units arrived the following morning to round up Jews for deportation, they found the streets empty. Thousands had retreated into underground bunkers and hiding places. Within minutes, the Germans were ambushed by hundreds of armed fighters, including Polish communists and partisans who had joined them from the Aryan side. The unexpected assault caused the SS to retreat. The same scene was repeated for days until the Nazis changed tactics and decided to smoke out the fighters by setting fire to each dwelling. Still, the fighting persisted as the small band held out heroically for weeks against overwhelming odds. Finally, the Germans cornered the last of the resistance in their headquarters at 18 Miła Street, where most of the leaders met their end. By May 16, twenty-eight days after the Warsaw Ghetto Uprising began, 56,065 Jews had perished.[16] All likely went to their deaths believing the world had abandoned them.

Meanwhile, as Stephen Wise continued to place his faith in the Roosevelt administration with minimal results, two distinct factions were becoming increasingly dissatisfied with the failure of the Jewish establishment to call for a concerted rescue of European Jewry. The leadership of the Vaad ha-Hatzalah had since 1942 been working closely with the Emergency Committee, despite the committee's preponderance of liberal and Zionist Jews. When Rabbi Aron Kotler was criticized by some of his Orthodox colleagues for working with Stephen Wise, a Reform rabbi, he responded that he would "work with the Pope if it would save even the fingernail of one Jewish child."[17] The Vaad representative Isaac Lewin was one of the few who had expressed any dissent over the consensus after Wise asked the group to keep silent about the Sternbuch cable in September 1942. Lewin had openly called on the leadership to publicize news of the exterminations in the Jewish press in order to mobilize the community. When the Orthodox leadership disagreed with his position, he wrote his own article in a small Yiddish paper with a call to action. "We must not forget for a minute our brothers and sisters in the Nazi hell," he wrote. "We ask the leaders of the American Jewish organizations, 'What will you answer on the "day of retribution?" What will you answer should someone some day request an accounting of what you did at a time when the blood of your brother flowed in rivers?"[18] Few paid attention.

By March 1943, dozens of new and credible reports had circulated from occupied Europe confirming the unfolding Final Solution in graphic new detail. As Jewish groups clamored for a response, Wise reconvened the temporary committee under a new name, the Joint Emergency Committee on European Jewish Affairs.[19] Meanwhile, as mainstream Jewish leaders struggled to respond to the ongoing European tragedy, one organization had already been advocating more radical solutions for some time.

The Committee for a Jewish Army of Stateless and Palestinian Jews had formed as a wing of Ze'ev Jabotinsky's Revisionist Zionist movement under the leadership of a Lithuanian Zionist named Hillel Kook. Kook had accompanied Jabotinksky to the United States in 1940 and remained there after his mentor died of a heart attack soon afterward. He had taken the name Peter Bergson so as not to cause embarrassment to the legacy of his uncle Abraham Isaac Kook, who had been the Ashkenazi chief rabbi of Palestine—the man who had stayed with the Sternbuch family in Switzerland during most of the First World War. Bergson's goals were twofold. Like all Zionist leaders, he advocated for the creation of a Jewish state in Palestine. But since 1941, he had also sought to mobilize a Jewish army that would fight separately for the Jewish cause.[20] His organization was in fact an offshoot of the Irgun—the underground paramilitary organization that would soon engage in armed resistance in Palestine under the leadership of the future Israeli prime minister Menachem Begin and others.

At the very first meeting of the newly formed Emergency Committee on March 15, 1943, participants debated whether to include Bergson's Committee for a Jewish Army, but decided that the group's radical approach was not to their taste. They informed Bergson that the presence of the group on their committee was "not desirable."[21] At each successive meeting, participants were apprised of the worsening situation in Europe. Their initial response was to form two sub-committees. One would be delegated to organize "mass meetings throughout the country," similar to the AJC-sponsored "Stop Hitler Now" rally that had taken place at Madison Square Garden on March 1. The organizers proposed an eleven-point plan to save the Jews of Europe.[22] The other committee would handle "Public Relations," with a mandate to make the country "more aware of Nazi atrocities and stimulate action by the government through the press."[23]

But by 1943, the Vaad leadership had grown restless. Lewin and a few others had for some time grown more vocal in calls for rescue.

Through the Agudah, members of the Orthodox leadership were in contact with the Sternbuchs in Switzerland and other European rescuers but had not yet designated Recha and Isaac as official representatives of the Vaad—in part because the Sternbuchs were not working exclusively to save the Orthodox.

In January 1943, the president of B'Nai Brith, Henry Monsky, invited most of the major Jewish organizations to a conference in Pittsburgh to discuss postwar policy and strategy around Palestine. Although most of the Orthodox leadership was firmly anti-Zionist, it sent three representatives to the conference.[24] But although Lewin and other Orthodox leaders pushed to make rescue a major agenda item, the gathering was not so inclined. A month later, Orthodox organizations including Agudath Israel formed their own committee, the Council of Jewish Organizations for the Rescue of Jews in Europe.

Meanwhile, Peter Bergson had also become increasingly fed up with the Jewish establishment and its lack of a cohesive strategy for confronting the unfolding European calamity. Dismayed at the failure of the Bermuda conference, he resolved to organize a conference of his own dedicated to rescue. In July 1943, he announced the formation of the Emergency Conference to Save the Jewish People of Europe. When the conference convened at New York's Commodore Hotel on July 23, a plethora of celebrities and political figures from both the left and right attended, including the press baron William Randolph Hearst and former Republican president Herbert Hoover. Roosevelt's interior secretary, the fiercely anti-Nazi Harold Ickes, also played a prominent role. The president sent a message of greeting to the delegates. "The government of the United States is greatly interested in the plight of the Jews in Europe and will not cease its attempts to save those who can be rescued until the Nazi power is forever crushed," Roosevelt declared.[25]

Addressing the delegates, Congressman Will Rogers Jr. called for the creation of a United Nations agency to "assist in getting the Jewish people out of Europe at once."[26] A sub-committee focusing on relief and transportation issued a report revealing the possibility of transferring fifty thousand Jews every month from the Balkan countries to Palestine or any other Mediterranean port in the Middle East without using United Nations ships. They had confirmed the availability of Portuguese and Swedish vessels that could be mobilized for the task without interfering with the war effort. This had in fact been a crucial precondition cited by the participants of the Bermuda Conference two months earlier. What the delegates didn't know, however, was that neither Britain nor the United States had any interest in any such rescue operations. The reasons—as uncovered in great detail by the American historians Monty Penkower, Arthur Morse and David Wyman in their landmark research—would have horrified those gathered. It was not the unworkability of such a rescue operation that doomed the idea, but rather the fact that it might have succeeded.

Indeed, U.S. secretary of state Cordell Hull had brought up the plight of the eighty thousand Bulgarian Jews facing extermination with British foreign secretary Anthony Eden when he visited Washington in March 1943. According to the notes of FDR's aide Harry Hopkins, Eden was reluctant to set a precedent that could have implications for similar rescues in the future. "The whole problem of the Jews in Europe is very difficult and we should move very cautiously about offering to take all the Jews out of a country like Bulgaria," Eden replied. "If we do that, then the Jews of the world will be wanting us to make similar offers in Poland and Germany. Hitler might well take us up on any such offer and there simply are not enough ships in the world to handle them."[27]

Like the Roosevelt administration, Britain appears to have done an about-face from what at first appeared a genuine commitment to stop the genocide. In 2012, the BBC's official historian, Professor Jean Seaton, studied the reaction to early broadcasts about Nazi atrocities, which had ensured Britons were much better informed than the American public about the plight of Jews in occupied Europe. She believes that as the government monitored public reaction to the news, they "backfooted" their response to the Holocaust. "There was dramatic evidence that the more the BBC talked about Jews, the more the public thought the war was [solely] about Jews," she concluded.[28]

Many historians believe that Roosevelt's continuous reluctance to act was motivated by the same fear. In fact, Undersecretary of State Breckinridge Long—the man many historians cite as the most obstructionist American official—penned a telling entry in his diary on April 20, 1943, about the "assiduous" lobbying of Stephen Wise and American Jewish groups. "One danger in it is that their activities may lend color to the charges of Hitler that we are fighting this war on account of and at the instigation of Jewish citizens," he wrote.[29] In their relatively sympathetic 2013 book *FDR and the Jews*, historians Richard Breitman and Allan Lichtman acknowledge that these same fears may have influenced Roosevelt's continual reluctance to publicly address first the persecution and then the genocide of the Jews. "Roosevelt did not easily succumb to outside pressure," they write. "He would have shunned any actions that gave the impression that the United States was fighting a Jewish war regardless of views expressed by Jewish advocates either within or outside his circle of advisers."[30]

The charge that America was abetting a so-called "Jewish War" was one that Roosevelt had been battling since long before Pearl Harbor. For more than two years after the start of the war in Europe, FDR had faced an avalanche of opposition from the isolationist movement led by Charles Lindbergh. Once America's most celebrated hero for his unprecedented solo flight across the Atlantic in 1927, Lindbergh's popularity and the platform it provided had vaulted him to the forefront of the forces attempting to keep the United States out of the war—exploiting Americans' strong reluctance for a repeat of the brutal and unnecessary bloodbath of the First World War. The flier had taken several trips to Nazi Germany during the 1930s and came back each time with increased admiration for Hitler and what he had achieved for the Third Reich. Recognizing his influence, the Nazis had unwittingly duped him into returning to America with wildly exaggerated reports about the size of Germany's Luftwaffe air force—which, unbeknownst to Lindbergh, was comparably tiny and ineffectual at the time.

Lindbergh's reports about Germany's terrifying air arsenal would, in fact, play an important role in the decision to appease Hitler at Munich in October 1938 as British and French officials cited Lindbergh's inflated air estimates to argue it would be "military suicide" to stand up to Hitler at the time.[31] In gratitude for his support, the Nazis awarded Lindbergh their highest civilian decoration, the Order of the German Eagle, only three weeks after the Munich agreement was signed (though there is no evidence that he ever deliberately passed on false military data).

While Roosevelt attempted to rally Americans against Hitler and marshal support for the beleaguered British island after the fall of Western Europe in 1940, he found Lindbergh at first to be a daunting and effective obstacle. FDR's secretary of the interior, Harold Ickes, described the flier in April 1941 as America's "number one Nazi fellow traveler." Roosevelt's assessment was even harsher. "If I should die tomorrow, I want you to know this," he told Treasury Secretary Henry Morgenthau in May that year. "I am absolutely convinced that Lindbergh is a Nazi."[32]

Lindbergh's credibility as a spokesperson for the isolationist movement, however, would come to a crashing halt on September 11, 1941, only three months before the Japanese attack on Pearl Harbor. On that day, speaking at a rally in Des Moines, Iowa, he delivered his standard speech arguing against American intervention in the European war. But on this occasion he uttered the fateful sentiments that he had heretofore only shared in private correspondence and with close associates: "Tolerance is a virtue that depends upon peace and strength. History shows that it cannot survive war and devastations. A few far-sighted Jewish people realize this and stand opposed to intervention. But the majority still do not . . . Their greatest danger to this country lies in their large ownership and influence in our motion pictures, our press, our radio and our government . . . Instead of agitating for war, the Jewish groups in this country should be opposing it in every possible way for they will be among the first to feel its consequences. . . ."

When his speech was reported the next day—with his emphasis that the Jews were attempting to push America into the war—it sparked a massive national outcry. Politicians from both parties attacked his anti-Semitic polemic, and editorials in all the major newspapers condemned his words. The former Republican presidential candidate Wendell Wilkie, for whom Lindbergh had voted a year earlier, described the speech as "the most un-American talk made in my time by any person of national reputation." The *San Francisco Chronicle* charged that "the voice is Lindbergh's but the words are Hitler's." With that one speech, Lindbergh went from a widely admired national hero to an overnight pariah, a descent from which his reputation would never recover. Even the isolationist America First Committee—which was littered with extremist members and far-right organizations—moved quickly to distance themselves from their spokesman as resignations poured in from all over the country and the committee came close to collapse.[33] In a nation where anti-Semitic attitudes were still prevalent, overt intolerance was clearly not acceptable. Perhaps the outpouring of revulsion toward Lindbergh's address should have convinced Roosevelt that America was more tolerant than he had assumed. Were FDR's fears, then, unjustified? Would Americans really have failed to unite around the war effort if they believed it was a "Jewish war"? There is no easy answer to that question.

Fast-forward to the spring of 1943, by which time the U.S. government was already fully aware of the Final Solution. In response to calls for the Allies to negotiate with Germany for the release of Jews, State Department official R. Borden Reams cautioned against a wholesale rescue of the Jews. "There was always the danger that the German government might agree to turn over to the United States and Great Britain a large number of Jewish refugees at some designated place for immediate transportation to areas under control of the United Nations." If that happened and the U.S. admitted it couldn't facilitate such a handover, he argued, "The onus for their continued persecution would have been largely transferred from the German government to the United Nations."[34] Since policy-makers in both the U.S. State Department and the British Foreign Office viewed the escape of Jews from certain extermination as a "burden" or a "danger," writes Wyman, "It is hardly surprising that they looked upon the rescue of Jews as something to avoid rather than to strive for."[35]

Washington had never seen anything like it. As four hundred rabbis sporting long beards and clad in black hats made their way through the capital, passersby gawked at the unusual spectacle. Some jeered. But the Orthodox marchers were undaunted. They were on a mission inspired by an unlikely ally. The genesis of the Rabbis' March of October 1943 dates back to a meeting that spring in the Capitol Hill office of Henry Wallace. Roosevelt's left-leaning vice-president had been moved by a number of full-page newspaper ads placed by Peter

Bergson's group attempting to rouse the government to stop the ongoing extermination of European Jewry. Among these was an ad that ran in hundreds of papers after the futile Bermuda Conference in April. "To 5,000,000 Jews in the Nazi Death-Trap, Bermuda Was a Cruel Mockery," it complained.[36] The ad, and many like it, called on the Roosevelt administration to establish an agency to rescue the victims of Hitler. When Wallace invited Bergson and his group's chief Washington lobbyist, Baruch Rabinowitz, to a meeting to hear their proposal, they were met by the vice-president's assistant, Harold Young, who offered a suggestion. They should bring five hundred thousand people to the White House gates and refuse to leave until the administration agreed to save the Jews. Bergson was reticent. He questioned whether that many people could make their way to Washington on trains, given wartime travel restrictions. "That's the trouble with you Jews," Young told him. "You always want to appear as gentlemen."[37]

Bergson's group had long since alienated themselves from the mainstream Jewish establishment who disapproved of their militant tactics. Yet they had also gained a number of powerful allies, including William Randolph Hearst, who used his national chain of papers to galvanize public demand for rescue. "REMEMBER Americans, THIS IS NOT A JEWISH PROBLEM. It is a HUMAN PROBLEM," stated one Hearst editorial. Bergson even managed to convince Eleanor Roosevelt to use her influential syndicated column, "My Day," to discuss the "hardships and persecution" of European Jews.[38] Her husband, however, continued to stall on his promise to do anything he could to stop the massacres.

Stephen Wise and most other mainstream Jewish leaders continued to place their faith in the Roosevelt administration, at least publicly. Only the Vaad were beginning to forcefully break with the consensus and demand rescue. Bergson had rejected the idea of bringing hundreds of thousands of people to the White House as unworkable. Instead, he seized on an idea nearly as dramatic. If three hundred or more rabbis were to march on the White House to demand a meeting with the president, he concluded, it couldn't help but get the attention needed to galvanize public and political support for a rescue agency.

Despite his lineage, Bergson was not at all observant. He was, however, a militant supporter of a Jewish state. The Vaad leadership and its devoutly Orthodox membership were almost exclusively anti-Zionist, or at least opposed to the strongly secular and anti-religious direction of the 1940s Zionist leadership. Yet when Bergson approached the rabbis with his idea, the group seized on their common ground.[39] "The religious, Orthodox people really cared," Bergson later recalled. "They were emotionally involved and they cooperated with us to the full extent."[40] Both groups were dedicated to rescue, and now, confronted with the greatest crisis that world Jewry had ever faced, nothing else mattered.

On October 6, 1943, three days before Yom Kippur, almost four hundred rabbis—led by Rabbi Eliezer Silver of the Vaad—made their way from Washington's Union Station toward the White House accompanied by members of the Jewish War Veterans of America. They had been hoping for a meeting with Roosevelt to present a petition organized by Bergson's committee with thousands of signatures calling for the creation of a rescue agency.[41] But since news of the rabbis' march was announced a week earlier, Stephen Wise and Jewish members of Congress had been furiously working to prevent the action, fearing it would embarrass the president. FDR's senior adviser, Samuel Rosenman, who was Jewish, advised the president that the group behind the march was "not representative of the most thoughtful elements in Jewry" and noted that the "leading Jews of his acquaintance" opposed the action. He told Roosevelt that he had done everything he could to "keep the hordes from storming Washington."[42]

Despite these efforts, the march went ahead on a crisp October day. "Clear the way for the rabbis," blared the stationmaster as they set off from Washington's Union Station. When the group reached the Lincoln Memorial, they led a mourner's kaddish (Jewish prayer for the dead) for the Jews of Europe and prayed for the president before singing "The Star-Spangled Banner" in Hebrew.[43] On the Capitol steps, Vice-President Wallace greeted the group and heard them read their petition in Hebrew and English. But when they reached their destination, they were met not by the president but by his secretary, who informed the rabbis that Roosevelt was unavailable "because of the pressure of other business." The official presidential calendar would later reveal that Roosevelt in fact had nothing scheduled between 1 and 4 p.m. that day.

The next day, not a word of the rabbis' march appeared in *The New York Times*, although its front page prominently featured a Yankees playoff loss to the St. Louis Cardinals. But a newsreel crew had followed the marchers through the nation's capital and within days, moviegoers throughout the country would view footage of the unprecedented event. Yet the march was only the first phase of Bergson's plan. His group had already drafted a congressional resolution calling for the establishment of a refugee rescue agency. On November 9, less than a month after the march took place, the joint Congressional resolution was introduced on the floor of the Senate by a Democrat, Guy Gillette, and a Republican, Robert Taft, recommending the creation of the agency. When public hearings commenced ten days later, an impressive array of supporters—including popular New York mayor Fiorello La Guardia—lined up to defend the resolution. Though party whips had predicted swift passage, opposition to the bill soon came from some surprising quarters. Stephen Wise criticized the resolution as "inadequate" because it didn't call for Jewish refugees to be brought to Palestine. His opposition was especially ironic since the initiative came from Bergson, a militant Zionist. But the Emergency Committee and its supporters had deliberately refrained from naming Palestine because it feared that many congressmen would hesitate to support a resolution that challenged official British policy.[44]

Meanwhile, State Department official Breckinridge Long was also working furiously behind the scenes to defeat the resolution. In secret testimony before the committee on November 26, Long argued that a rescue agency was unnecessary because the administration had already "taken into this country since the beginning of the Hitler regime and the persecution of the Jews, until today, approximately 580,000 refugees."[45] When news of his testimony was leaked three weeks later, the statistic would appear on the front page of *The New York Times*. But New York Democrat Emanuel Celler immediately took issue with both the grossly inflated figure and Long's assurances. "In the first place these 580,000 refugees were in the main ordinary quota immigrants coming in from all countries. The majority were not Jews. The tears he sheds are crocodile," Celler told his fellow House members. "I would like to ask him how many Jews were admitted during the last three years in comparison with the numbers seeking entrance to preserve life and dignity. It is not a proud record." Celler then went on to level a fateful accusation: "Frankly, Breckinridge Long, in my humble opinion, is least sympathetic to refugees in all the State Department. I attribute to him the tragic bottleneck in the granting of visas."[46]

Celler wasn't the only official who suspected Long of sabotaging efforts to rescue Jews. Roosevelt's treasury secretary, Henry Morgenthau Jr.—the only Jewish member of FDR's cabinet—had for some time been uneasy about his government's response to the plight of European Jewry. Morgenthau had always walked on eggshells around issues involving his faith, conscious that he might be accused of bias if he was seen pushing a "Jewish agenda."

But in the fall of 1943, Morgenthau finally threw himself into a cause for which he had shown little previous interest. He learned of a license that had been issued by the Treasury in July to facilitate the evacuation of thousands of Jewish children from Romania and France to North Africa and Spain—an initiative that had been conceived by Gerhart Riegner in the spring of 1943. Treasury counsel Randolph Paul reported that the State Department had delayed acting on the license for months, and when confronted about the delays, Secretary of State Cordell Hull had blamed the Treasury for "failing to formulate a workable proposal for financing such a program" and for failing to clear the proposal with the British, who had raised strong objections to the evacuation.[47]

On December 18, Morgenthau gathered his top officials to get to the bottom of why the administration had failed to act on Riegner's proposal. On the same day, a young Treasury Department lawyer named Josiah E. DuBois Jr. issued a confidential memo to Morgenthau alerting him to the State Department directive from the previous February addressed to the U.S. ambassador in Bern in response to Riegner's information about the Final Solution:

IT IS SUGGESTED THAT IN THE FUTURE, REPORTS
SUBMITTED TO YOU FOR TRANSMISSION TO PRI-
VATE PERSONS IN THE UNITED STATES SHOULD
NOT BE ACCEPTED UNLESS EXTRAORDINARY
CIRCUMSTANCES MAKE SUCH ACTION ADVISABLE.[48]

Morgenthau was shocked at the callous directive. He met personally with Breckinridge Long to determine who was responsible and to request the exchange of correspondence leading to this communication.

Morgenthau had been given a copy of Riegner's original cable detailing the plight of Romanian Jews in Transnistria. So when Long failed to hand over the cable as part of the paper trail, the treasury secretary realized that it had been deliberately withheld in an attempt to deceive the Treasury Department. Morgenthau was infuriated. Suspicious that the incident was merely part of a larger pattern of State Department obstruction, Morgenthau resolved to get to the bottom of the matter. DuBois, the diligent young lawyer who had once worked for the Secret Service, was given the opportunity to put his investigative skills to work. Three weeks later, on January 13, 1944, DuBois forwarded his conclusions to the secretary in a memorandum entitled, "Report to the Secretary on the Acquiescence of This Government in the Murder of Jews."

In this unprecedented document, DuBois devotes eighteen pages to a detailed and devastating indictment of State Department efforts to obstruct rescue efforts. Its harshest words are reserved for Breckinridge Long, whom DuBois accuses of a "cover-up." The report called for immediate and drastic action: "One of the greatest crimes in history, the slaughter of the Jewish people in Europe, is continuing unabated. This Government has for a long time maintained that its policy is to work out programs to serve those Jews of Europe who could be saved. . . . Unless remedial steps of a drastic nature are taken, and taken immediately, I am certain that no effective action will be taken by this government to prevent the complete extermination of the Jews in German-controlled Europe, and that this Government will have to share for all time responsibility for this extermination."[49]

The withering report set the stage for an extraordinary meeting convened by Morgenthau on January 15, in which senior Treasury Department staff discussed how to present the shocking findings to Roosevelt. During that meeting, in fact, the officials revealed that the president had been deliberately kept in the dark about various opportunities for rescue and that, in some instances, State Department officials had sabotaged his own directives concerning refugees. At one point, Morgenthau—always loyal to the man who appointed him—pointed to the example of FDR's support for bringing in thirty thousand refugee children: "I think when the facts are known, and I know that Mrs. Roosevelt brought it to the President's attention very, very forcibly, this question of bringing in children—everything the President tried to do was turned down."[50]

At this historic meeting, Morgenthau and his staff refined two documents that had been prepared in advance. The first was a "Personal Report to the President" summarizing DuBois's findings and describing the "utter failure of certain State Department officials" to take any effective action "to prevent the complete extermination of the Jews in German-controlled Europe."[51] The second and most significant order of business was the presentation of an executive order establishing a rescue agency.

The next day, Morgenthau met with FDR to present the report. He was blunt. "These are the facts, Mr. President, the most shocking thing I have found since I have been in Washington. Here we find ourselves aiding and abetting Hitler."[52] Roosevelt appears to have taken the admonition to heart. After ignoring for eighteen months the most heinous crime the world had ever known, the president issued an executive order on January 22, 1944, creating the War Refugee Board dedicated to the "immediate rescue and relief of the Jews of Europe and other victims of enemy persecution."[53]

TEN

THE RESCUE COMMITTEE

From the moment they learned of Hitler's plan to exterminate the Jews of Europe, the Sternbuchs rededicated themselves to the mission that had been severely curtailed since Recha's arrest in May 1939. But whereas the couple's previous rescue efforts had focused on saving Jews from Hitler's persecution, they were now fully cognizant that the fate of their people was far more dire. And while Jewish leaders in the United States and Britain would spend more than a year lobbying for political and diplomatic solutions, Recha and Isaac Sternbuch knew immediately that the plight of European Jewry required only one response. "Almost from the second they learned of the death camps, they threw themselves into rescue," recalls Recha's cousin Renée Landau. "Every waking moment was devoted to saving the European Jews. They neglected their children, they neglected their business. They said the Torah required nothing less."[1]

Until September 1942, their activities had primarily focused on two areas. Recha and her brother-in-law Elias Sternbuch had worked to secure forged Latin American passports to send to the Warsaw Ghetto, an effort that saved hundreds, perhaps thousands, from the death camps when the deportations began in June 1942. And for

months, HIJEFS—the committee founded by Recha—had been raising relief funds for the Polish rabbis and scholars stranded in Shanghai.
Now the committee was reconstituted with a new name and a new
mission dedicated to the rescue of all European Jews threatened with
Nazi persecution and liquidation. The group now became known as
Schweizerischer Hilfsverein für Jüdische Flüctlinge (the Relief
Association for Jewish Refugees in Foreign Lands). Julius Kühl, still
employed at the embassy of the Polish government-in-exile, was invited
to join the new rescue committee. His diplomatic contacts would play
an instrumental role in the Sternbuchs' renewed activities.

Long before the formation of HIJEFS, Recha's role in leading an
extensive underground network was already undeniably extraordinary. But now, as she assumed leadership of a formal organization, it
hardly escaped notice that a woman had taken command over a
group of men. Such an arrangement was almost unheard of in the
1940s, let alone in Orthodox Jewish circles, where gender roles were
rigidly defined. However, according to Renée Landau, those around
her never balked at her leadership: "Recha was such a towering force
that she commanded immediate respect from all those around her
and almost everybody with whom she came in contact. Nobody
seemed to be bothered by the fact that she was a woman. She did not
issue orders but when she spoke, she was listened to. Isaac was also
very impressive. He was not a meek figure who took a back seat to his
wife. In Orthodox homes, the woman was always a powerful figure
in the household so that may have been a factor."[2]

Before her arrest in 1939, Recha had focused her efforts primarily
on smuggling Jews fleeing Nazi Austria—its frontier just a short distance from her home in St. Gallen. Since relocating to Montreux, she
had occasionally intervened to prevent the deportation of Jews who
had made their way illegally over the Swiss border from Vichy France.

In these efforts—notably the rescue of the yeshiva boys on the day of her son's bar mitzvah—Kühl's intervention had proved invaluable. But the revelations from Poland now drove home a horrific realization. The Jews being turned away at the Franco–Swiss border under the Swiss policy of *réfoulement* were not simply facing anti-Semitic persecution if they were sent back. They were almost certainly facing deportation to death camps. In their 1981 book *Vichy France and the Jews*, historians Michael R. Marrus and Robert O. Paxton explode a number of myths about the fate of Jews in Vichy, most importantly the long-held belief that it was the Germans who forced brutal anti-Semitic policies on Pétain's government. Accessing wartime archives, they demonstrate beyond doubt that it was, in fact, French anti-Semites who were responsible for Vichy's policy toward the Jews early on. "Vichy's anti-Jewish program was neither new nor limited to a small minority on the far right. It fed upon a decades-long obsession with the alien menace," observed Marrus and Paxton.[3] At the same time, however, the authors establish that many of the worst excesses were directed at so-called foreign Jews. Nevertheless, "Vichy France became in August 1942 the only European country except Bulgaria to hand Jews over to the Nazis for deportation."[4] Over the next two years, more than seventy-six thousand Jews would be deported, most of whom would perish in Auschwitz, according to a 2009 judicial finding by France's Council of State.[5]

Among the foreign Jews who had taken refuge in France and who now faced deportation were thousands who had fled Belgium as the Nazis marched in during the spring of 1940. These included many of Recha's own relatives who had fled Antwerp in 1940 to settle in what would become unoccupied France. Others waited until the deportations began in 1942. Hermann Landau had been a member of the Belgian Judenrat when he received a letter from the Germans ordering Jews to report to a purported work camp in Malines. Fearing the worst, he made the decision to flee to France, hoping to take refuge in Switzerland later with the assistance of his cousin Recha. In August, Landau set out with his wife, his brother and sister-in-law, his niece Renée and three members of his wife's family. The group paid a *passeur* (smuggler) to spirit them safely over the Swiss border as Recha had advised. Renée Landau, only eleven at the time, recalls what happened next: "We made it into Switzerland without detection and soon found a phone to call Recha to come fetch us. When Hermann gave her our location, she told him she would soon come to pick us up. At exactly that moment, a voice interrupted the call. It was a Swiss police official monitoring her phone calls. He said, 'Stay where you are. We will come get you.'"[6]

Because the group was traveling as a family, they were permitted to stay, but, under a Swiss policy that had been in place since the start of the war, the group of Belgian Jews were subject to immediate internment. While the women were sent to an intake camp for female refugees, the men were designated to perform forced labor in one of a hundred refugee camps that had been established throughout the country. Because most of those camps were already full, Hermann Landau and his brother were instead confined to a general prison, Bellechasse, where they were forced to live for months.

Recha asked Julius Kühl to intervene on behalf of her cousin and some other Jewish refugees. In a family memoir he prepared for his grandchildren, Kühl recalled, "I was shocked to discover that [Jewish internees] were placed in a jail for hardened and dangerous criminals. . . . The first meeting I had there was with a 13-year-old boy from Belgium named Popafski. He cried as he told me that the Swiss police had sent his father back to France where the Germans had hung him. The boy requested to be removed from jail. After all he had not committed any crime. The next meeting I had was with two brothers named Landau, from Belgium. I was so distressed by what I had seen that I could not continue visiting other camps that day."[7]

Within days of Kühl's visit, Landau was released and could now live freely under the protection of Polish citizenship bestowed by the Bern embassy. He would soon join HIJEFS, serving as the committee's secretary and playing an instrumental role in the Sternbuchs' rescue operations for the remainder of the war. Although on this occasion Recha had used Kühl to help her cousin, it was an avenue of rescue that could be used only sparingly, since the Polish government had to be careful about incurring the wrath of Swiss authorities. The ambassador, Alexander Lados, needed to authorize each visa or passport personally, and Kühl was anxious to avoid being seen as abusing the privilege. He would later recall how he curried favor with his boss. "He loved to play chess and I used to play him every Sunday, trying hard not to win to make sure that he would be well-disposed of me," Kühl wrote.[8] Lados, he recalls, was "very highly impressed with Recha and did his utmost to be of service to her, using all his influence in the Swiss diplomatic service as well as with the Polish Government-in-Exile in London. For example, he made sure to approve all the Polish passports that I made out at the request of the Sternbuchs and other Jews."[9]

The Swiss, it appears, were well aware of Kühl's activities and were not happy with the influx of Jewish refugees that flooded their country as the result of his diplomatic interventions. Occasionally there were repercussions. He recalls being summoned to meet with Lados after he intervened on behalf of a Jewish refugee couple who faced deportation: "The Ambassador informed me that the Swiss authorities had contacted him, questioning, 'Who's the boss here—the Swiss authorities or Kühl?'" Nevertheless, Lados remained steadfast in his support for Recha's activities even after Heinrich

Rothmund attempted to have him removed from his post. In 1944, Recha would write in a letter to Agudath Israel president Jacob Rosenheim in New York, "Without the help of Ambassador Lados, hardly a solitary soul would have been rescued."[10]

On occasions when even his diplomatic ties weren't enough to help with her rescue operations, however, Recha turned to a contact who would prove to be equally important—Archbishop Filippo Bernardini, the papal nuncio (ambassador) in Bern. As nuncio, Bernardini was regarded as the dean of the diplomatic corps in Switzerland, and as such was very influential. "I introduced him to Recha," recalled Kühl, "and he too fell under her spell."[11] With Lados, he had regularly played chess to get into the ambassador's good graces. But the archbishop's chosen sport was Ping-Pong, and the two spent hours playing at the nuncio's residence while Kühl enlisted his support for rescue efforts on behalf of his people. Bernardini would become an important ally of the Sternbuchs and an eventual conduit in convincing the Vatican to intervene on behalf of the remaining European Jews. Although most of the cleric's interventions took place behind the scenes, Kühl recalls one incident in 1943 when Bernardini took the unusual step of aiding Recha's efforts in a very public manner:

The Swiss used to allow families to enter as a unit, but would return single people or couples. Recha always used to help groups of refugees create "families" so that they would be allowed entry into Switzerland. When the Swiss inspectors once noticed that such "families" were no longer living together in the refugee camp, they began to suspect the truth. When Recha found out that the angry Swiss authorities were ready to send them all back over the French border into German hands, because of this "treacherous hoax," she quickly ran to the Nuncio. To him she poured her heart out and begged him to do something to save the people. The kind-hearted Nuncio promised to do something— and he did so promptly. He announced on radio that the "hoax" pulled by the refugees was perfectly moral, since their lives were in danger, and he convinced the Swiss not to condemn these helpless refugees to certain death by sending them back.[12]

Although these high-ranking contacts repeatedly proved invaluable to Recha's rescue efforts, there were times when no amount of diplomatic intervention would be sufficient to rescue Jews in peril. The *Haredim* often view danger differently than their secular peers, convinced that HaShem—God—is looking out for them at all times. There is no other explanation for a rescue operation in 1943 that witnessed Recha throwing herself headlong into the jaws of the Nazi beast. In later years, she rarely discussed her wartime activities, even with her own family. But toward the end of her life, she did share a notable anecdote with one of her nieces. Her sister-in-law Gutta Sternbuch would later recount the extraordinary story to a biographer and a documentary film crew. "Never did I hear her speak about herself, of her experiences, and her acts of bravery," Gutta recalled. "She nagged herself constantly with feelings of inadequacy—perhaps this is what made it impossible for her to talk about herself. Only once did she break her silence. It happened when I, with my daughter, spent a night in her house. My daughter would not stop asking her to tell us one of her experiences. 'Only one,' she begged, until Recha finally gave in."

According to the account, Recha one night received a call from a contact in a border town informing her that a group of Jews— including men, women and children—had been apprehended by

Swiss border guards and sent back to the Reich, where they faced imminent deportation to a concentration camp. Soon, Recha made her way across the border in a motorcycle sidecar accompanied by an accomplice with a truck. On a side street near the frontier, she met with her contact, who informed her that the group was in the hands of the Gestapo. Her contact warned her that it would be futile and very dangerous to intervene. Once in the hands of the Gestapo, their fate was sealed, he assured her. But Recha was undaunted by this warning. Returning to the no-man's-land detachment where the Jews were confined, she was immediately flooded by lights and confronted by three border guards in German uniforms, accompanied by barking dogs, who took her to see the officer in charge. Gutta's account described what happened next:

> She was so repelled by the sight of the middle-aged man sitting at his desk, his bloated face masked with a cold heartless expression, that for a moment she withdrew. On his chest rows of medals shone, while at his side sat a huge dog. "What do you want?" he asked curtly, in threatening tones. She pulled herself together and answered, "I am Swiss. These Jews came upon my initiative. I am responsible for them. I would like to ask you to turn them over to me. I am taking them into Switzerland." His eyes reddened with fury. He seemed as though he were ready to explode. But then he regained his composure, took several steps forward, planted himself directly in front of her and hissed into her face. "What do you dare ask for? I'll send you away with these dirty Jews. You cursed Jewish woman. I'll rip up your Swiss passport if you don't disappear from here this minute . . ."
>
> "I'll voluntarily join them if you don't turn them over to me. I am responsible for them," she said quietly, even though her

heart was quaking. It became quiet. A fearful silence, and then the unbelievable happened. "Take your twelve Jews and be gone immediately," he shouted. "But at once. Otherwise I'll change my mind."[13]

The story may have been exaggerated in the telling but we know from HIJEFS members, including Hermann Landau, that Recha did travel to Nazi Austria and Vichy France on more than one occasion to intervene on behalf of Jews captured or turned away at the Swiss border. But from late 1942 until mid-1944, these efforts and those of her committee had focused almost exclusively on rescuing individuals. It is impossible to estimate how many were saved as a result of these interventions, but the number was certainly substantial. Still, her activities and similar rescue operations carried out by various underground and partisan networks throughout Europe appear almost insignificant while millions perished in the camps. Each Jew rescued from the clutches of Hitler was deeply satisfying to members of the rescue committee. But Recha and Isaac continued to despair as reports reached them of the imminent extinction of their people. Like their brethren in the United States, they were often overwhelmed by a feeling of helplessness in the face of the catastrophe. But even as HIJEFS labored to save a tiny remnant of European Jewry, events were beginning to unfold elsewhere that offered a glimmer of hope for the masses of Jews whose lives had not yet been extinguished.

The beginning of the end of the Final Solution had its roots in a ransom scheme conceived in the tiny republic of Slovakia. Of those who fell victim to the Final Solution, the Jews of Slovakia were unique. While the majority of the six million or so who died at the hands of the Nazis were deported to their fate by the bureaucratic killing machinery of the

SS, it was in fact the Slovaks—not the Germans—who made the decision to cleanse their country of its Jewish population.

The Slovak state had only come into existence as an autonomous region inside the former Czechoslovakia in March 1939, when Hitler invited the deposed former prime minister—a Catholic monsignor named Jozef Tiso—to form an independent state under the "protection" of Germany. For much of the war, Slovakia functioned as a fascist client government with nominal autonomy from Germany. The population of the new republic numbered 2.6 million in 1940, of which about eighty-nine thousand were Jews.[14] A mere month after independence, Tiso implemented a series of anti-Semitic laws. These were stepped up considerably following a meeting between Hitler and the Slovakian regime in July 1940, during which the Führer demanded the Slovaks take radical action on the Jewish question.[15] A month later, Adolf Eichmann's deputy, Dieter Wisliceny, arrived to take up the post as "adviser" on Jewish affairs at the German embassy. Wisliceny, who had studied theology with the ambition of entering the Protestant clergy, had originally joined the Nazi Party in 1931. Three years later, he became a member of the Gestapo at around the same time as Adolf Eichmann. The two became very close and Eichmann would eventually recruit Wisliceny to work under him at Section IVA4—the so-called Jewish department of the SS.[16]

Although Eichmann would almost certainly have turned his sights eventually on Slovakia's Jews for deportation, the apparatus of the Final Solution was still in its formative stages at the time. The death camps were not yet even up and running. Still, Slovakian Jews could be put to use in Poland building the additional camps that would soon be required for the grisly task to come.

On March 27, 1942, the German Foreign Ministry notified its ambassador in Bratislava that Himmler himself had accepted a Slovak proposal to deport the remainder of the Jewish population and "thus free Slovakia of Jews."[17] There is no firm evidence, however, that the Slovak regime knew at this point that its Jews were slated for liquidation. At Nuremberg, Wisliceny testified that Eichmann had assured the government that "these Jews would be humanely and decently treated in the Polish ghettos."[18] He claims that several months later, the Slovaks even requested to send a delegation to the areas where the Jews had been settled to check on their treatment after rumors of unspeakable horrors began to circulate out of Poland that summer.

Meanwhile, others had also heard the rumors of extermination. The Vatican had protested the impending deportations of Slovakia's Jews, insisting that such an act violated the teachings of the Church, especially in a country whose head of state, Tiso, was a Catholic priest.[19] Despite these protests, the Slovak church hierarchy—in a pastoral letter from its bishops—appeared to support the idea of ridding the country of its Jews because of their "pernicious" nature.[20] The first transports left for Poland on March 26, 1942, carrying a trainload of women over the age of sixteen.

By July, nearly fifty thousand Slovaks had been deported, most destined for extermination at Majdanek, Bełżec and Auschwitz. Their property was confiscated and redistributed to Slovak gentiles. Meanwhile, the regime had forced the creation of the Jewish Center— the UZ—to act as an intermediary between the Jews and the regime, much like the role played by the Judenrat in areas under Nazi occupation. The Orthodox community was designated to staff and run the center. Among its functions, the UZ would run Jewish schools and relief organizations. It was also responsible for the administration of three Jewish "labor" camps set up at the behest of Wisliceny. As a result, a disparate cross-section of Slovakian Jewry would cross paths at the center.[21] Among these were two unlikely allies who would play a central role in the events to come.

Under ordinary circumstances, Rabbi Chaim Michael Dov Weissmandl—the fiercely anti-Zionist ultra-Orthodox figure known as the "partisan rabbi"—likely would not have crossed paths with a secular Zionist leader named Gisi Fleischmann. But the two were distantly related. And like the rabbi, who was studying Hebrew manuscripts at Oxford in 1939, Fleischmann was in England when war broke out. She immediately returned to Slovakia, where she had been raised by Orthodox parents in Bratislava, the Slovakian capital sometimes known by its Germanized name, Pressburg. One of Europe's most prominent Zionist women's leaders, Fleischmann trained as a social worker and specialized in helping to resettle German Jewish refugees who fled to Slovakia after Hitler's rise to power. Raising money for refugee relief brought her into contact with the Joint Jewish Distribution Committee in Paris and Prague, and she was soon asked to represent the Joint in Slovakia.

At the outbreak of the war, she had been in London lobbying the British government to accept more Jewish refugees. Back in Bratislava, she was assigned a position at the Jewish Center in the immigration department of HICEM (the Hebrew Sheltering and Immigrant Aid Society).[22] There, she came into frequent contact with a number of figures who in early 1942 began working to smuggle Slovakian Jews into Hungary in an operation guided largely by the Orthodox leadership. Weissmandl was not a member of the Jewish Center, but, as an Orthodox leader, was a frequent visitor. Unbeknownst to most, he was using his visits to help facilitate an Orthodox-led smuggling operation involving his father-in-law, Rabbi Shmuel Dovid Ungar, whose compound in Nitra had been nicknamed "the Jewish Vatican."[23] By summer, nearly seven thousand Jews had made their way over the Hungarian border, while fifty thousand others had been deported to Poland. It's unclear when members of the UZ first became aware of the fate of the deportees, but an ad hoc group began to form in response to the growing rumors. Although it had no formal structure, a small disparate underground cell began to coalesce under the leadership of Gisi Fleischmann. Because of Weissmandl's connection to the Hungarian smuggling operation, he quickly became a central force in the network that called itself the Bratislava Working Group. In later years, Weissmandl would refer to the group by its Hebrew name, Hava'ad Hamistater—the Hidden Committee.[24]

Meanwhile, sometime in June or July of 1942 a report had reached the rabbi that Dieter Wisliceny had released a Jew destined for deportation in exchange for ransom. The news inspired Weissmandl to approach the Working Group with a plan. Wislicleny had tasked the Jewish Center with ensuring the deportations proceeded smoothly. While Fleischmann and other members did everything they could to sabotage or slow the operation, the Germans knew they could count on the cooperation of a Jewish engineer named Karel Hochberg, a member of the Judenrat who had functioned as Wisliceny's assistant in coordinating the deportations, designated the head of the "department for special tasks." Weissmandl proposed using Hochberg to offer Wisliceny a significant bribe to stop the deportations.[25] The rest of the Working Group immediately rejected the idea of using the "traitor" for such a task—worried that he would turn them in. But Weissmandl was convinced that Hochberg would welcome the opportunity to assuage his guilt for helping to facilitate the deportation of his people.[26]

· To add to the cloak-and-dagger nature of the scheme, the rabbi forged a number of letters. He invented a fictitious representative of World Jewry based in Switzerland: Ferdinand Roth,[27] who had allegedly visited Bratislava to explore the possibility of ransoming the remaining Jews. Hochberg agreed to relay the offer. Ondrej (Andrew)

Steiner, a founding member of the Working Group, later recalled the key to these negotiations. "Slovak Jews were not strong enough . . . but if we told him world Jewry was behind it, then he would have to believe it. That is exactly what happened. This was the old idea of the secret power of the Jews, the Protocols of the Elder of Zion."[28]

Soon afterwards, Hochberg returned with the news that Wisliceny had agreed to delay the next three transports to Poland—scheduled for the coming Tuesday and Friday and the next Tuesday—at no charge. But on the following Friday, he would expect a first installment of $25,000. That would postpone the deportations for an additional seven weeks. At the end of the seven weeks, an additional $25,000 would be due. He warned, however, that the Jews would also have to persuade the Slovakian leaders to withdraw their demands for deportations.[29]

Buoyed by the unexpected success of the gambit, the Working Group set to work raising the funds for Wisliceny's bribe. The first installment of $25,000 was obtained from a wealthy Slovakian Orthodox businessman.[30] At the same time, Steiner approached Julius Pecuch, the Slovak Interior Ministry official in charge of forced labor camps and offered him 10,000 Czech crowns to stop the deportations.[31] As the Nazi had promised, there were no additional deportations for seven weeks. Funds for a second installment, however, did not come so easily. Furiously mining wealthy contacts in Slovakia, they still came up short. That's when Gisi decided to write to Saly Mayer in Switzerland to ask him for the $21,000 still needed to fulfill the second ransom payment. She also asked for $100,000 in bribe money, suggesting the group considered bribes to Slovak officials every bit as important as the ransom payments to Wisliceny.

Since August 1940, Mayer had served as the Swiss representative of the American Jewish Joint Distribution Committee (JDC)—the New York–based relief organization tasked with providing funds to Jews in need throughout the world. And while the JDC could at one time receive direct funding from the United States, America's entry into the war had severely restricted such transfers. Now, Mayer was often forced to use funds raised through the Swiss Jewish community—much of which were already committed to financing relief for Jewish refugees confined to Swiss internment camps. Nevertheless, he was so moved by the opportunity to rescue Slovakian Jewry that he committed to send $5000 immediately with an additional $5000 installment promised for the following month.[32] The rest of the money, according to Steiner, was obtained from funds that Orthodox Jews kept "hidden in the ground."[33]

Once the second installment had been paid, Wisliceny—whom the Working Group referred to as "Willy"—worked out a suspension of the deportations with the Slovak leadership and arranged exemptions for the remaining Slovakian Jews. And, although four additional transports would leave for Poland—including two after the second installment was paid to Wisliceny in September—the October 20 transport would be the last deportation of Slovakian Jews for nearly two years. Weissmandl would claim until his dying day that it was the Working Group and its $50,000 bribe that was responsible for this two-year reprieve. Some historians have expressed skepticism, postulating that it was in fact pressure on the Tiso regime by the Vatican that brought about the moratorium, especially considering the relatively paltry sum involved in the bribe.

Whether or not the Working Group was responsible for halting the deportations of the remaining twenty-four thousand Slovakian Jews, there is no question that the group members believed it. Emboldened by their apparent success, they soon came up with a far bolder scheme. The Europa Plan, according to Rabbi Weissmandl, was born in September 1942, when he was arrested by the Slovakian authorities on suspicion of circulating information about the fate of the deported Jews in Poland.[34] He claims that he first conceived the idea during the week he spent in prison. Ondrej Steiner later recalled how he became involved: "Rabbi Weissmandl came to one of the meetings and said, 'If we succeeded in stopping the deportations from Slovakia, why don't we now try to stop deportations or the killing in Europe?'"[35] Some members of the group initially balked at the audacious scheme, fearing its failure might trigger renewed deportations. "Rabbi Weissmandl was someone who always worked with large sums, and he wanted to dazzle with large amounts," Group member Ernst Abeles testified at Eichmann's trial in 1961. "I cannot say that I myself had any great hopes for this plan."[36]

But when Gisi Fleischmann endorsed the idea, the others soon followed. Using Wisliceny's assistant, Hochberg, once again as a go-between, Weissmandl forged another letter from the fictitious "Ferdinand Roth." Playing on the widespread Nazi belief of an all-powerful Jewish conspiracy, Roth implied that the previous ransom had originated from a "world rabbinical authority" who were now ready to bargain for the rest of the Jews held captive by the Germans.

The group had to wait some time for an answer. Wisliceny had been called to Berlin and didn't return to Slovakia until late November. To their amazement, Wisliceny appeared receptive to the proposal. The Germans, he suggested, would be open to the "cessation of the European deportation except for Old Germany, Austria, and the Bohemian-Moravia Protectorate."[37] No monetary figure was mentioned. Instead, he left it open for the Jews to suggest a sum. Each of the group members could still remember the daunting struggle just to raise the second installment—a mere $25,000—for Wisliceny's original bribe. But for an opportunity to rescue the vast majority of European Jewry, surely the Jews of the world would pay whatever it took. Still, the group wanted to put out feelers before they made any concrete monetary offer.

With her extensive European contacts and formal affiliation with the Joint Distribution Committee, Fleischmann took the lead in securing funds for what they all agreed would have to be a major ransom effort. Recalling that Saly Mayer had come through with funds for the original bribe, she had high hopes that he would secure significant funds from the Joint to finance the operation. She still assumed that Mayer had unlimited funds at his disposal or could secure the required amounts from the Joint's offices in Lisbon or New York. Fleischmann also traveled to Hungary shortly before Christmas to raise funds from Jewish leaders in the neighboring country. After that trip proved largely fruitless, however, she complained to the committee, "Hungary's Jews have neither feeling of Jewish solidarity nor any sense of social responsibility; nor do they know how to give."[38] Failing to receive a response from Mayer, she wrote him another letter, revealing her mounting frustration. From his continued silence, she wrote, she "must therefore conclude that the will to help is not present."

Unbeknownst to the Working Group, Mayer was in fact very interested in Fleischmann's proposal. Hampered by rigid currency restrictions and a lack of funds, however, he simply did not have the resources to provide the large sums needed to satisfy the Nazi extortionists. Although skeptical of the plan, Mayer believed the group's claim that it had successfully put a halt to the deportations through the much smaller bribery scheme that he had abetted months earlier. He made dozens of copies of Gisi's plea and circulated her request widely. He also met with Swiss Jewish leaders, including Gerhart Riegner, to rally support. Most either refused to believe the scheme possible or immediately condemned the idea of ransom. Richard Lichtheim of the Jewish Agency in Geneva, dismissed it out of hand, stating that "this proposal is a lie and deception."[39] At the same time,

Herbert Katzki of the JDC's Lisbon office ordered Mayer not to cooperate.[40] Despite those instructions, he secretly began to dip into his limited budget. Breaking his silence, he finally wrote to Gisi Fleischmann and promised a monthly payment of 20,000 Swiss francs. In addition, he was willing to commit to an additional 100,000 francs "in après."[41] This would involve a formal commitment to pro-vide payments from JDC funds after the war that could be used to secure a bank loan with Mayer's promise of payment.

In March 1943, Wisliceny finally relayed his offer to the Working Group. For U.S. $2 million, he would arrange to stop the deporta-tions. He required $200,000 as a down payment. When Mayer heard the terms, he stepped up his original offer. Instead of an après commitment of 100,000 francs (approximately $23,000), he would formally commit to $100,000 après. Fleischmann was so moved by his apparent willingness to support the plan that she responded effu-sively after he committed to sending funds: "Dear good Uncle, many many thanks for your goodness and helpfulness, may God preserve your health for all of us."[42] In subsequent correspondence with Mayer, she always addressed her letters to "Onkel Saly." In this correspon-dence, Mayer employed his own unique code used to describe certain individuals and events. His code word for Heinrich Himmler was particularly apt: *Deviller.*

Although the tone of Fleischmann's future letters expressed her extreme frustration with his inability to supply the requested funds, they continued to correspond throughout the spring of 1943. And, although she appeared to retain a genuine affection for Mayer, Fleischmann often could barely disguise her anger at his failure to deliver concrete funds. "The unique event in history will have taken place, that there was a possibility to save the lives of doomed people and that this chance was passed by,"[43] she wrote after more disappointing news. Israeli historian Yehuda Bauer sounds an ironic note about the Working Group's attitude during these negotiations. "They thought, in Slovakia, that the free Jewish world would and should be capable of producing millions of dollars with ease," he writes. "In a way, they had fallen prey, unconsciously, to anti-Semitic arguments about infinitely rich World Jewry and its power to persuade warring nations to transfer funds whenever they were needed."[44]

Meanwhile, Mayer was working furiously behind the scenes to convince Jewish leaders to come up with the necessary funds. Weissmandl had already reached out to delegates of the Zionist Jewish Agency in Istanbul hoping that money could be secured from Palestine.[45] Jewish Agency leader David Ben Gurion—who would later become the first prime minister of Israel—became aware of the plan in February 1943. At the time, the Zionist leader was immersed in negotiations with the British for the admission to Palestine of thousands of Polish Jewish orphans and apparently believed that this operation took precedence. Later, it emerged that he had confused the Europa Plan with the original bribe to prevent the deportation of Slovakian Jewry.[46] When the Istanbul delegation briefed him in March 1943, he had a change of attitude and immediately expressed support for the Europa Plan.

While the Working Group was struggling to come up with at least the $200,000 down payment, Wisliceny had temporarily been reassigned by Eichmann to Salonika to "solve the Jewish problem" there. From January until the spring of 1943, he participated in rounding up the entire Jewish population of Greece: fifty-six thousand people were herded onto cattle trains to their deaths at Auschwitz, adding to the ever-mounting toll of the Final Solution.[47]

By the time Wisliceny returned to Slovakia, the group had still not come close to raising the down payment.[48] In May, Willy met with

Fleischmann and her Working Group colleague Ondrej Steiner. He informed them that Hitler was now intent on the total destruction of European Jewry. Appearing to increase his demand, he assured them that it was within his power to stop the deportations, provided they come up with "$2–3 million." At this meeting, they promised him $100,000 if the deportations were suspended immediately. He informed them that he would have to travel to Prague to consult with his "superior." Until this point, Eichmann's name had not entered into the negotiations with the Bratislava Working Group, although he must have known of the previous bribe. It's inconceivable that Wisliceny could have suspended the deportations on his own. For the first time there was an indication that the negotiations were being overseen from a higher level. Indeed, even Eichmann couldn't have sanctioned such an operation. There was only one member of the Nazi hierarchy—other than the Führer himself—who had the authority to put a halt to the mechanics of the Final Solution if he so chose.

A hint is provided in a note to himself that Himmler jotted down on December 10, 1942. "I have asked the Führer with regard to letting Jews go abroad for ransom," he wrote in an aide-mémoire captured by the Allies after the war. "He gave me full powers to approve cases like that, if they really bring in foreign currency in appreciable quantities from abroad."[49] He makes no mention of the Slovak negotiations, but the note comes not long after the group first made overtures to Willy about the Europa Plan, and there can be little doubt that it is to this that he is referring. The reference to hard currency came at a time when the Reich was desperately scrambling to acquire the material necessary to fight a war that had already gone on longer than Germany had anticipated and when the fortunes of the Axis were beginning to turn.

On May 10, 1943, Wisliceny met with the group again and stuck to his original demand for $200,000. In the meantime, he promised a one-month moratorium on further deportations. If they came up with the payment by June 10, he assured the group, it would buy the Jews of Europe a reprieve of two more months.[50]

Mayer had secured 180,000 Swiss francs and an additional $10,000 from the Zionist youth movement, HeHalutz. But the group was still well short of the required down payment. On June 18, eight days after the initial deadline had passed, Fleischmann informed "Onkel Saly" that the Nazis had pushed back the deadline until July 1. The money could be paid in eleven installments, Willy had informed them.

Meanwhile, the Jewish Agency had committed to $50,000, bringing the total of funding from Zionist groups in Istanbul and Switzerland to more than $130,000.[51] With this and an additional $50,000 promised by Mayer, the group was close to its goal. By this point, however, they knew that it would be virtually impossible to get their hands on the entire $2 million. At best, they could hope for a temporary reprieve, assuming the Nazis kept their word. Many members of the Working Group, in fact, were skeptical that Wisliceny even had the authority to stop all deportations. Nor did most of the groups they approached for funds believe the scheme possible. On September 3, 1943, Wisliceny met again with members of the group to tell them that he no longer had any interest in continuing negotiations. The Europa Plan was dead. Nine days later, Gisi Fleischmann handed the SS-Hauptsturmführer $10,000, but Willy merely told her he considered this money a "down payment."[52]

Weissmandl would later spend much of his life bitterly denouncing the Zionists and members of the Jewish establishment who he believed had allowed the Holocaust to continue by refusing to come up with the ransom. Considering that Zionists had supplied the majority of the funds raised by the Working Group during the short life span of the Europa Plan, these accusations were largely unfounded. "The European Jews must accede to suffering and death greater in measure than the other nations, in order that the victorious allies agree to a Jewish State at the end of the war," the rabbi wrote in a 1948 tract he titled *Ten Questions to the Zionists*. These types of accusations would later take hold among various circles and help perpetuate a number of myths about the failure of Zionists to stop the Holocaust. Gisi Fleischmann was also bitter, but, as a committed Zionist herself, she blamed the establishment in general for failing to support the plan she believed could have been the salvation of the Jewish people.

ELEVEN

THE SPY CHIEF AND THE DEVIL'S DOCTOR

B y the end of 1943, there were two men who exerted considerable influence over Himmler. One was an ardent Nazi, the other something of a puzzle. Both appeared to believe that a separate peace with the Western Allies was still possible; both saw Himmler as the only logical vehicle for such an approach. Neither Walter Schellenberg nor Felix Kersten would ever cross paths with Isaac or Recha Sternbuch. Yet each would soon find himself inadvertently conspiring to find common cause in a massive deception that would affect the fate of the remaining Jews of Europe.

The war was not going well for Germany. In February 1943, its military suffered a catastrophic defeat at Stalingrad after an epic five-month battle that saw the Soviet Red Army surround three hundred thousand besieged Axis forces and deal a crushing blow to Hitler's plans. Weeks earlier, German troops had also been pushed back from Moscow, thwarting the plan to occupy the Russian capital that was a cornerstone of the Führer's political and military objectives when he launched Operation Barbarossa in the summer of 1941. The two defeats—resulting in hundreds of thousands of Axis casualties—proved devastating and almost certainly marked the beginning of the end of Hitler's dream of a thousand-year Reich.

After a string of German military victories in 1941 and 1942, the war in Europe had begun to turn in the Allies' favor with a crucial desert victory at the second battle of El Alamein in November 1942, followed by the German defeats on the Russian front. America's entry into the war after the attack on Pearl Harbor meant that the Axis now faced a formidable enemy with unlimited military and financial resources. When Allied forces invaded Sicily in July 1943, it appeared to be only a matter of time before the inevitable invasion of Europe and a swift defeat of the Reich. Even Goebbels's propaganda machine couldn't soften the devastating effect on German morale after Stalingrad. In fact, it was Goebbels who in January 1943 was tasked with delivering the speech to mark the tenth anniversary of the Nazis' rise to power. It was the first time Hitler—clearly dispirited by the direction of the war—didn't deliver the speech himself.

By the autumn of 1943, none but the most optimistic members of the Nazi high command could have still believed a German victory was possible. But although the war was not proceeding as planned, the Final Solution was rapidly moving toward its goal of *Judenrein*. Between April and November 1942 alone, the Nazis had murdered more than two and a half million Jews,[1] and that figure had reached more than four million by the end of 1943.

At the beginning of October, Himmler gathered his most senior SS officers in the town of Posen (Poznań), Poland, and delivered two speeches in which he candidly talked of the ongoing Holocaust without any of the usual euphemisms to disguise the brutal reality of the Nazi killing program. Himmler no longer spoke about "evacuation to the East." There was no need to be coy since each of the men gathered had played an active role in the genocide. On October 4, at the Posen town hall, he delivered a rambling address to ninety-two men—a speech preserved for posterity in a phonographic recording. In it, he commends his men for remaining "decent" while they brought about the "extermination of the Jewish people."

Although the October 4 address is better known, the Reichsführer delivered a second speech two days later that is arguably more chilling: "We were faced with the question: what about the women and children? I decided to find a clear solution to this problem too. I did not consider myself justified to exterminate the men—in other words, to kill them or have them killed and allow the avengers of our sons and grandsons in the form of their children to grow up. . . . The Jewish question in the countries that we occupy will be solved by the end of this year."[2]

Days later, Himmler met privately with Prince Max Egon Hohenlohe-Langenburg, an Austrian-born member of the old European aristocracy who had acted as a go-between between the Nazis and the West during the Sudeten Crisis of 1938 and was said to be a confidant of Hermann Göring. Hohenlohe envisioned Himmler as a potential "moderate" replacement for Hitler.[3] The prince had long believed England and Germany should ally and had made numerous overtures to the British along those lines, acting as a confidential informant. By 1943, he had hinted that certain elements within the Nazi hierarchy were open to a separate peace.

Following a "lengthy conversation" with Himmler in Prague on October 28, Hohenlohe reported the substance of the meeting to Allen Dulles, who, as head of the Office of Strategic Services' (OSS) mission in Bern, Switzerland, was the Americans' leading European spy chief. The prince reported that, although Himmler denied any plans to overthrow the Führer, he foresaw the Reichsführer-SS as the most logical successor in the event of the death of Hitler, who was rumored to be in ill health. In his dispatch of November 9, he reported his firm belief that Himmler was the Nazi official most likely to deal with the West.[4] A year earlier, Italy's foreign minister, Count Ciano, son-in-law to Mussolini, had expressed similar sentiments. "Himmler himself, who was an extremist in the past but who now feels the pulse of the country, wants a compromise peace," he wrote in his private diary on April 9, 1942.[5]

The Allied leaders, however, appeared to permanently rule out the possibility of any such compromise when Franklin Roosevelt met Winston Churchill at the Casablanca Conference in January 1943. Both leaders agreed that they would settle only for the "unconditional surrender" of the Axis.[6] In the months since, the Western powers had shown no signs of wavering. If anything, the defeat of the Nazis at Stalingrad and other military setbacks had only weakened any potential German negotiating position.

It was at this point that Felix Kersten and Walter Schellenberg came together to hatch their plan.

Julius Caesar famously observed that history, especially in war, can turn on very slight forces. In this light, it is possible to speculate that the total extinction of the Jews of Europe may have been averted by a stomach ailment.

Since his days at agricultural college in the early 1920s, Himmler had suffered from crippling abdominal pains. Although the pain may well have been psychosomatic, it would plague him throughout his career. None of the myriad drugs or treatments he tried had succeeded in alleviating the agony until he met Felix Kersten, the man he would describe as his "magic Buddha."

Kersten was born in Estonia in 1898, but he usually described himself as a "Baltic German" because of his ancestors' resettlement in the German town of Göttingen. When the First World War broke out,

Kersten was drafted to fight for the Kaiser shortly after graduating from university with a degree in agricultural engineering. Instead, he volunteered to join a unit of expatriate Finns who were enlisted to fight in the Finnish war of liberation against Russia. In gratitude for his service, the Finnish government granted Kersten citizenship in 1920.

During the war, the young infantryman had developed a case of debilitating rheumatism and was treated at a military hospital in Helsinki. As part of his treatment, he was prescribed a course of massage that greatly relieved his symptoms. It was then, he recalled, that he made the decision to become a physical therapist.[7] His mother, Olga, had been a masseuse, which may have played a role in Felix's affinity for the unlikely discipline. In 1921, he moved to Berlin to pursue further training in what was called manual therapy. A year later, he encountered a Chinese practitioner known as Dr. Ko, who claimed to have studied in a Tibetan monastery with monks who were masters of the eastern techniques of healing through massage. Ko took on the young Kersten as his apprentice, sharing his "secret" technique, which Kersten would label "physio-neural therapy."[8] He described the technique as "therapy of the nerves," which involved penetrating beneath the skin to relax the "sub-cutaneous and muscular tissues and vessels." Kersten would later attribute his "special gift" to his "very highly developed sense of touch" that took advantage of the close connection between blood circulation and the central nervous system.[9]

When Dr. Ko decided to return to Tibet in 1925, Kersten opened a Berlin practice of his own. Whether his pseudo-scientific techniques had any merit or he was simply a very artful salesman, Kersten's reputation grew. Soon, he was being driven from appointment to appointment in a limousine as he acquired a stable of wealthy clients, including many aristocrats. As word of his talents reached beyond Germany, patients from all over Europe flocked to his practice.

In the case of a select few, Kersten would go to them. In 1928, Queen Wilhelmina of the Netherlands summoned him to treat her consort, Prince Hendrik, who was suffering from a heart condition and had been given less than six months to live. (Hendrik was the brother of Kersten's aristocratic patient Duke Adolf Friederich of Mecklenburg, who recommended him to the queen.) When Hendrik made a "miraculous" recovery, the queen appointed Kersten as a physician to the royal court.

Establishing a second home in The Hague, Kersten commuted back and forth between the Netherlands and Germany to attend to his growing and very lucrative practice. He would use a part of his fortune to purchase a lavish three-hundred-acre estate east of Berlin, which he christened Gut Hartzwalde. Soon after, he met and married a Silesian woman named Irma Neuschaffer, with whom he had a son.[10]

In March 1939, Kersten received an unusual call from one of his clients, Dr. August Diehn of the German Potash Syndicate. "Herr Kersten," he asked. "I have never asked a favour from you before; now I have one to ask. Will you examine Heinrich Himmler? I think you would find him an interesting patient." Diehn admitted that he had an ulterior motive for his request. The Nazis were considering nationalizing a number of private industries in anticipation of the imminent war. Diehn believed that Kersten if successful, might persuade his patient to "do us a great service" and spare the potash industry.[11]

Reichsführer Himmler was suffering from painful "intestinal spasms," sometimes to the point of unconsciousness. Kersten claimed that it took only five minutes of manual therapy to relieve his patient's pain. Himmler was so delighted, Kersten later recalled, that the Nazi begged him to remain in "personal attendance."[12] Kersten didn't know at first what to make of his new patient, whom he described as "a narrow-chested, weak-chinned, spectacled man with an ingratiating smile." He was surprised to discover that Himmler was reading a book on the Prophet Muhammad and the Muslim faith, along with the Koran, translated into German. He would later discover that Himmler also devoured books about Hinduism, leading him to describe his patient as "a pedant and mystic."

But although Kersten agreed to provide regular treatments whenever he found himself in Germany, he was reluctant to leave the Netherlands, where he was attending to the royal court. That arrangement continued for the next year, until the spring of 1940, when Germany invaded, forcing the Dutch royal family to take refuge in England. Soon after, Himmler repeated his offer of employment to Kersten, letting it be known through an emissary that the Gestapo would not be responsible for his family's safety unless he agreed to move to Berlin. Kersten later claimed it was this threat that prompted his reluctant move, although it's entirely possible that this was an excuse after the fact to justify having gone to work for one of history's most notorious villains.

Many of Kersten's recollections have to be taken with a grain of salt. Although he would later publish his memoirs in the form of wartime diaries, numerous entries were only added after the war, often based on his notes, but occasionally only on his questionable memory. However, there is no indication that he fabricated stories or lied to cover up any Nazi collaboration. Yet, Kersten was something of a self-aggrandizing blowhard who tended to exaggerate his role in historical events. Consequently, it is necessary to rely on contemporary accounts to verify or disprove many of his claims, along with documentation such as Himmler's appointment calendar. Unfortunately, many historians have tended to repeat Kersten's diary entries as gospel, resulting in considerable misinformation and a distortion of the historical record. Despite these difficulties, there is no doubt that he played an extraordinarily important role in rescue. And although history has inextricably linked Felix Kersten with Heinrich Himmler, he would also cross paths with a Nazi figure with whom he would become just as closely aligned.

The first time Walter Schellenberg saw the black uniform of the Führer's elite guard unit, he decided that he had found his life's calling. Although he claims to have been drawn to the "dashing and elegant" apparel of the SS, he would later admit the true appeal. The SS, he recalls, is where one found the "better type of people." Membership brought considerable social advantages. The brown-shirted thugs of the SA, in contrast, represented the most extreme and violent tendencies of the Nazi movement.

Born in Germany in 1910, Schellenberg spent his childhood years in Luxembourg before returning to attend medical school in Marburg. Quickly deciding that medicine wasn't for him, he turned to the law, attending the University of Bonn as a nineteen-year-old. The ambitious young student had calculated that a law degree would serve him better in the SS, where he was already making a name for himself. In law school, he recalled, he found his powers of persuasion were more suitable for the indoctrination of his fellow students than for the courtroom. It was while he was delivering an impromptu lecture on campus against the influence of the Catholic Church that he caught the attention of Reinhard Heydrich, who was visiting the campus that day. Not long after the Nazis took power, Heydrich extended an invitation to the eloquent young Nazi to join the foreign security section of the SD, the intelligence service of the Third Reich.

On the eve of assuming his new post, however, the twenty-four-year-old would carry out one last task as a member of the SS guard unit to which he had been assigned. On June 30, 1934, his unit was assigned to accompany Hitler as the Führer moved against Ernst Röhm during the Night of the Long Knives. The brutality he witnessed that day does not appear to have dissuaded him from his allegiance to the party. Quite the opposite. Soon afterwards, he went to work for Heydrich in the counter-intelligence division of the SD, becoming one of his most trusted deputies. It was here that his quick mind and attention to detail would attract the attention of Heydrich's superior, the Reichsführer-SS.

Only days after the invasion of Poland, Schellenberg was tasked with drawing up the organizational plan for the new security service—the RSHA—which would consolidate Himmler's control over the entire state security apparatus under Heydrich's command. The new organization would be responsible for combating "enemies of the Reich." Schellenberg was promoted from deputy to chief of counter-intelligence in the powerful new security apparatus. It was in this post that he would engage in the clandestine operations for which he would become best known, many of which sound as if they were drawn from the pages of a bad spy novel.

The first such escapade took place only weeks after Schellenberg assumed his new post. On November 8, 1939, a German laborer named Johann Esler tried to assassinate Adolf Hitler in the Munich beer hall where Hitler had staged his infamous *putsch* sixteen years earlier. Esler had planted a time bomb near the platform where the Führer was scheduled to speak. When Hitler finished his speech earlier than anticipated, he famously evaded the explosion that killed eight people. The Nazi press immediately blamed the British secret service and Neville Chamberlain for the assassination attempt.[13] The truth was somewhat more convoluted. In the days before the incident, it emerged, Schellenberg had been orchestrating an elaborate masquerade in the Netherlands, where he personally posed as a "Major Schaemmel"—a disaffected Nazi officer allegedly involved in a plot to kill Hitler. Under this guise, he had been meeting secretly with two British intelligence agents. He had let it be known that the plotters were looking for an assurance from the British that a newly installed anti-Nazi regime would be treated fairly after they did away with Hitler. On November 7, Schellenberg arranged to meet the two officers in the town of Venlo, where he had promised to bring a German general to begin negotiations. At the last minute, he postponed the meeting until the 9th. Meanwhile, Esler—who had been interned at Dachau as a suspected Communist—was enlisted in a purported scheme to assassinate Hitler. The hapless laborer was presented with blueprints of the beer hall, along with detailed instructions on how to carry out his mission.

The day after the bombing, on November 9, Schellenberg arrived for his meeting as scheduled at the Venlo meeting place, the Café Backus. Instead of bringing a general as promised, his operatives kidnapped the two British officers and spirited them back to Germany. Under torture, they were soon induced to reveal details of British intelligence operations and provide the supposed proof that the British were responsible for the assassination attempt a day earlier. It was the kind of cloak-and-dagger operation that Schellenberg loved. Indeed, the success of the operation gained him a reputation of almost mythic proportions within the SS and helped give rise to the portrayal of sinister and ruthlessly efficient Nazi intelligence operations that would soon become a regular feature of Hollywood films. The truth is that German intelligence operations were often a shambles of almost comic proportions. A year later, in fact, Schellenberg would become immersed in another operation that more closely illustrated the true bungling depths of the Nazi intelligence apparatus.

Schellenberg later revealed that in July 1940, he was approached by German foreign minister Joachim von Ribbentrop with a plan to kidnap the Duke of Windsor—formerly King Edward VIII, who had abdicated his throne in 1936 to marry the American divorcée Wallis Simpson. The disgraced monarch—who, like much of the British aristocracy, was known to have harbored German sympathies before the war—had recently been named by the British government as the governor of Bermuda. His exile was likely as much due to the embarrassment of the abdication crisis as to any Nazi sympathies he may have still harbored. But Ribbentrop claimed he had information that the duke—living with Simpson in Portugal at the time—was being kept a virtual prisoner by the British secret service. He wanted Schellenberg to establish contact with the former monarch during a forthcoming hunting trip in Spain to which the duke had been invited. The intelligence chief was instructed to make Edward a "material offer" to deposit 50 million Swiss francs into a special account. "Hitler attaches great importance to this operation," Ribbentrop told him. If the duke should prove reluctant, Schellenberg should "help him make the right decision by coercion."

Two months earlier, Schellenberg had been tasked with another high-priority mission involving English dignitaries. As Germany was drawing up plans for an imminent British invasion—code-named Operation Sea Lion—the intelligence chief was assigned by Heydrich to compile a "Special Search List" containing the names of 2300 prominent British residents who would be immediately arrested in the hours and days after German forces occupied the island. Apart from Churchill and members of the cabinet, the list included such names as H.G. Wells, Aldous Huxley, Bertrand Russell, Sigmund Freud and many other prominent writers, scientists and politicians.

Now, as Schellenberg launched his intelligence enquiries, he quickly discovered that stories of the duke's Nazi sympathies had been vastly overblown, that he didn't consider himself a prisoner and that he had no desire to come to Germany. Upon being appointed governor, Edward had remarked that he would rather have lived anywhere in Europe than in Bermuda, but that is as far as his dissatisfaction apparently ever went. Nevertheless, an order by the Führer could not be ignored. Schellenberg immediately dispatched operatives to watch the duke's residence in Estoril, Portugal. German agents even managed to infiltrate the royal household staff. In the end, however, the duke failed to accept the Spanish hunting invitation, the planned abduction was thwarted and Edward sailed to Bermuda without incident.[14]

Although Schellenberg would later recall espionage operations such as these with great relish, he downplayed his involvement in other tasks that were undoubtedly less savory. Tried at Nuremberg after the war, he would be indicted by the Allied authorities for his alleged participation in the creation of the Einsatzgruppen—responsible "for the extermination of all opposition in the territories of the Soviet Union." In the end, however, no evidence was presented that he had direct participation in the war crimes of the mobile killing units and he was acquitted of the charge. But his close involvement with Heydrich does raise questions about the role he may have played in other activities. It is difficult to imagine that the intelligence chief could have risen so rapidly in the SS without direct knowledge of and participation in its crimes. Schellenberg, however, would always maintain that he was strictly involved in "overseeing information matters."[15]

Shortly before Heydrich was assassinated in June 1942, he had appointed Schellenberg to the post of German head of foreign intelligence—Department VI, described as the "political secret service."[16] After Heydrich was gunned down in Prague, Himmler failed to replace the head of the security services for almost seven months, taking control of the RSHA himself before appointing Ernst Kaltenbrunner to assume the post in January 1943. It was during this void that Schellenberg consolidated his considerable influence with the Reichsführer-SS. Kaltenbrunner would later describe him as "Himmler's most intimate friend."[17]

It was also during those months after his appointment as intelligence chief that Schellenberg claims he came to a life-changing realization. By August 1942, it was evident that the campaign in the Soviet Union was flailing. German forces had failed to take Moscow and were encountering ferocious and unexpected resistance from Stalin's armies. The intelligence chief believed that Hitler had blundered badly by turning his armies to the east, forcing Germany to fight a war on two fronts. He thought the military high command had also underestimated Britain's resolve to defend itself, evidenced by Hitler's decision in September 1940 to postpone the invasion of England indefinitely after the German defeat at the Battle of Britain. Before Germany could defeat Bolshevism, Schellenberg now believed, it would first be necessary to forge a separate peace with Britain and the Western Allies. As the natural successor to Hitler, he theorized, Himmler would be in an ideal position to become Führer and lead the Reich to glory.

"For these reasons I determined at the first opportunity to exploit the possibilities of my position with him and make an attempt to launch plans for negotiations [with the Allies]," Schellenberg later wrote.[18] He intended to press this point when he met up with Himmler at his eastern headquarters at Zhitomir, deep in the heart of the Western Ukraine, in August 1942. It was at this meeting that Schellenberg bonded with Felix Kersten for the first time, though the two had first met some months before. When his intelligence chief complained of chronic intestinal pains over dinner, Himmler recommended his own personal healer who had done wonders. Kersten, who happened to be at Zhitomir that weekend, would be happy to treat him, Himmler offered. Schellenberg, however, appeared to believe that Himmler's recommendation was based on more than simple concern about his well-being. "So great was Himmler's faith in Kersten's ability that he submitted everyone in the Third Reich whom he regarded as important to a sort of test, which consisted of a physical examination by Kersten," he recalled. They met later the same evening.

Although it appears clear that the two men shared a common goal—the glue that would cement their relationship for the next two years—they clearly had very different motivations. Schellenberg was undeniably still very committed to Nazi ideology even if he didn't approve of some of its "excesses." There is no evidence that he harbored extreme anti-Semitic tendencies or approved of the Final Solution, though he had to have known early on that the SS apparatus he served was committing mass genocide. Likewise, there is no evidence that he ever wavered in his loyalty to the Third Reich. Like many Nazis, he feared the Bolshevization of Europe above all, and his later advocacy of a separate peace merely reflected a strategic change of heart. He had come to believe that Hitler was the greatest obstacle to the aims of the Reich rather than their embodiment. It was an attitude shared by an increasing number of Nazi Party officials as German military prospects soured.

In contrast, there is evidence that Kersten had a strong distaste for Nazi policy early on, even as he remained personally fond of Himmler.[19] Kersten claimed that Himmler frequently talked to him about the Jews but bizarrely noted that his patient wasn't a "rabid Jew-hater." Instead, he was merely following the "dicta" of the Führer. Still, Kersten found his patient's obsession extremely unsettling as he was forced to listen to "hour-long diatribes" on the Jewish question. In his diary entry of March 3, 1940, Kersten describes telling Himmler that he had never understood anti-Semitism. After all, he argued, the

Jews had been a "great stimulus in all departments of life." This prompted a lecture, with Himmler asserting that wherever Jews appear, they "try to do business. . . . they weave a network of connections with their fellow Jews in every country. . . . The Jewish empire comes before all others, draining them of their materials, their strength, their riches, their influence."[20] He proceeded to weave for his therapist an elaborate conspiracy beginning in the Middle Ages and culminating in the modern day "Elders of Zion."[21]

In a later diary entry from November 1942, Kersten records Himmler explaining that the extermination of Jews only began when Goebbels gained the "upper hand." Goebbels's attitude, he explained, was that "the Jewish Question could only be solved by the total extermination of the Jews. While a Jew remained alive, he would always be an enemy to National Socialist Germany." In this conversation, Himmler told his therapist that he believed early on it "would be enough to expel the Jews" and that he had advocated giving Jews a large piece of territory to set up an independent state as early as 1934. Did he have in mind Palestine for such a state? Kersten asked. "No, Madagascar. It's an island which has good soil and a climate which suits the Jews." When the war came, it "brought with it circumstances which sealed the fate of the Jews."[22]

Despite his apparent distaste for his patient's central role in the Final Solution, however, Kersten appeared more concerned with the fate of those from the various countries to which he had a direct allegiance, especially Sweden, Finland and the Netherlands. He cites the German invasions of the Netherlands, Denmark and Norway in 1940 as the pivotal moment when he began to use his influence on behalf of the "underground." That same year, Kersten claims to have visited the Finnish envoy to Germany, Toivo Kivimäki, in Berlin and volunteered his services.[23]

Later, he intervened on behalf of Finland's consul to Oslo, Johannes Bødtker, who was interned by the Nazis, and the former commander of the Dutch army, General Jonkheer Röell, when he was sentenced to death following the invasion. Most notably, he claims to have intervened to free the former Dutch prime minister Hendrikus Colijn, who was released from prison and allowed to stay in a comfortable villa. "Almost at once, I became the secret Ambassador for Dutch patriots in distress," he writes.[24] In his memoirs, Kersten includes a letter from SS-Brigadeführer Erich Naumann discussing a list of prisoners that Kersten has enquired about, including a Dutchman, Frederick Deinum, who had been imprisoned for hiding Jews, and others who had been accused of aiding the resistance.[25] He also cites the case of the Aascher family, rich Jewish diamond merchants whom he claims to have freed. Occasionally, he recalls, Himmler would protest his continuing appeals. "You are sympathizing with swine. You are defending traitors," he once blared. Echoing these accounts, Himmler's biographers Roger Manvell and Heinrich Fraenkel quote Himmler as complaining, "Kersten massages a life out of me with every rub."

By 1944, Kersten claims his reputation for freeing persecuted prisoners from the clutches of the Nazis had spread. "In that year I was inundated by letters of appeal from people abroad who despaired as to the fate of some Jewish relatives in Germany," he writes in one diary entry. "To the very last, I did not hesitate to approach Himmler with my pleas for the victims of the Nazi terror." He writes that it gave him great joy whenever he was able to use his influence to free a prisoner, more often than not a Jewish prisoner.[26]

Like many in the circle around Himmler, Schellenberg didn't entirely trust Kersten at first. He was, after all, a foreigner, and appeared to exert considerable influence over the Reichsführer. Moreover, he had refused to don the SS uniform or even join the Nazi Party. But a combination of the doctor's physique and temperament appears to have caused the naturally suspicious spymaster to let down his guard. "In appearance he was a fat, jovial man, weighing almost 250 pounds," Schellenberg later wrote. "His massive hands would never have led one to suspect the extreme sensitivity of his finger tips. . . . On the whole, he was good-natured and kindly . . . some people even suspected him of being a British agent. Once I asked Himmler about this. 'Good God!' he replied. 'That fat fellow?'"[27]

Schellenberg had observed that Kersten always knew how best to exploit Himmler to his own advantage. Now, as they talked far into the night, he made the fateful decision to take the Finn into his confidence. "After a long conversation, I was quite sure that Kersten not only agreed with my ideas regarding a compromise peace, but was enthusiastic about them," Schellenberg later recalled. "He had completely fallen in with my plans and agreed to use his influence with Himmler to prepare the way for me. . . . Here at last was the first active supporter of my plans." Kersten pledged to enlist others who he knew exerted influence on Himmler and who might support efforts toward a separate peace.

In return, Schellenberg promised to support Kersten against his many perceived enemies who he believed envied his close relationship with the Reichsführer. Number one on this list was Gestapo chief Heinrich Müller, a formidable and dangerous opponent who did indeed maintain a dossier on the Finn. Still, he pledged to protect his new ally. "When I went to bed early in the morning, I could not sleep," Schellenberg writes. "Again and again my thoughts returned to the question of how to convince Himmler of my ideas." The next day, he asked to meet Himmler in private. After relating a lengthy anecdote—a parable of sorts—about a piece of advice that he had received early in his law school career, he steeled himself to broach the subject at hand: "Well, you see Herr Reichsführer, I have never been able to forget this advice given to me by a very wise man. May I be so bold as to ask you this question: 'In which drawer of your desk have you got your alternative solution for ending this war?'"

Himmler, he writes, sat before him staring for a full minute "quite aghast." At last he spoke. "Have you gone mad? You've been working too hard. Shall I give you five weeks' leave right away? Are you losing your nerve? And anyhow, how dare you talk to me in this way?" Holding his ground, Schellenberg reminded his superior that even Bismarck at the height of his powers always kept an alternative solution. "Today Germany still stands at the zenith of her power. Today we are still in a position to bargain—our strength makes it worthwhile for our opponents to seek a compromise with us."[28] He argued that America's entry into the war had been a turning point and there was "no longer hope of eventual success."[29]

After a lengthy discussion, Himmler suddenly changed his defensive tone. "As long as that idiot Ribbentrop advises the Führer, this can not possibly be done," he said. Still, Schellenberg took note that the man he considered the most powerful in the Reich no longer dismissed out of hand the idea of a separate peace with Britain and the Western Allies. Softening his tone, Himmler acknowledged that the plan might be workable as long as Hitler's private secretary, Martin Bormann, didn't get wind of the idea. "He'd wreck the whole scheme or he'd twist it round to a compromise with Stalin. And we must never let that happen," insisted the man who had always believed the Bolsheviks were as much a threat as the Jews. Then he allegedly gave what Schellenberg took as tacit approval to proceed. "Would you be able to start the whole thing moving right away—without our enemies interpreting it as a sign of weakness on our part?" he asked.[30]

Over the next hours, the two men turned to the practicalities of such a plan, envisioning what a separate peace would look like. Schellenberg believed that the British would insist on a German evacuation of the northern coast of France. The fate of the Netherlands and Belgium could provide some basis for negotiations. Schellenberg suggested returning the Alsace region to the French and retaining the Sudeten territories for the Reich, along with southeastern Europe, including Greece and the Balkans. The men parted at 3 a.m., with Himmler's tentative approval for his subordinate to pursue such a plan. "Of course it remains to be seen whether I shall be able to convince Hitler by Christmas," he said before retiring.

Schellenberg's account of this extraordinary encounter, described in his postwar memoirs, reads more like a description of an elaborate game of Risk than the alleged turning point in Himmler's attitude toward the war. It also comes off as treason. From that evening on, Schellenberg recalls, he determined that all his waking efforts were to be directed toward "extricating Germany from her present situation." And although, like Kersten, Schellenberg often had an inflated sense of his own importance, the events that followed suggest that the encounter at Zhitomir was consequential.

Keeping his promise to bring Schellenberg together with influential like-minded individuals, Kersten arranged a meeting with a prominent Berlin lawyer, Carl Langbehn, who had known the Reichsführer-SS for more than a decade through the friendship of their respective daughters who were schoolmates.[31] Langbehn harbored anti-Nazi views but pragmatically had kept them mostly to himself. He was known to have been particularly incensed when one of his Jewish law professors, Fritz Pringsheim, was sent to a concentration camp in 1938. Drawing on his powerful contacts, Langbehn secured from Himmler the professor's release and permission to leave the country.[32] As a leading lawyer, he had many Nazi clients, but he had also represented several leftists and had once offered to represent the Communist leader Ernst Torgler when he was implicated in the 1933 Reichstag fire. Langbehn had been in discussions with Johannes Popitz—a deeply conservative monarchist who had served as the Prussian finance minister since shortly after Hitler took power but who had never officially joined the Nazi Party. In the days following Kristallnacht, Popitz vigorously protested the pogrom to Hermann Göring and demanded action be taken against the perpetrators. The Nazi interior minister is said to have replied, "My dear Popitz, do you want to punish the Führer?"

Popitz had begun to question Germany's military prospects as early as the fall of 1942 and told Langbehn that he believed "peace feelers" were in order.[33] Langbehn indicated that he had a "Swiss friend" who believed peace negotiations with the West were "not out of the question." They both agreed that if such negotiations were to occur, there would have to be a change of government. The Führer was "an obstacle to peace." Ribbentrop, they agreed, was "utterly incapable." There was only one man who could take power without the Fatherland sinking into "internal chaos." These talks would eventually bring both men into the circle of plotters who would attempt to assassinate Hitler in July 1944. It is in this context that Kersten brought Langbehn together with Schellenberg, who confided his belief that Himmler was open to a separate peace. On August 26, 1943, Popitz and Langbehn—already plotting against Hitler—were summoned to a meeting with Himmler at the Reich Ministry of the Interior, recently taken over by the SS.

During the course of this conversation, Popitz would later recall, the two men broached the possibility that the war could still end in a "stalemate" but only if the Führer was replaced by a prominent figure—"someone with a name, a person of decision and courage." The Führer is a genius, they argued, but he is someone who follows his own laws. There was reason to believe that Great Britain and the United States recognized the "great danger in Bolshevism." For this and other reasons, there was a genuine possibility for peace negotiations. But the Allies would never negotiate "as matters now stand."[34]

If Popitz's account is accurate, Himmler could have had both men shot on the spot for this treasonous talk. Instead, he appears to have asked Langbehn to travel to Switzerland to make discreet inquiries, or at least to have implied that such a trip would be desirable. Would the Allies actually be prepared to negotiate directly with Himmler if Hitler were deposed? In September, Langbehn traveled to Switzerland to gauge Allied interest. There, he would eventually make contact with Allen Dulles. The OSS European intelligence chief, however, was unequivocal. He made clear the Allies would accept nothing less than unconditional surrender. Shortly afterwards, it appears word of Langbehn's overtures had reached the Gestapo. Langbehn was arrested and eventually executed, though Himmler himself would not be implicated in his activities. Nor would he ever be tied directly to the conspirators of the July 20 plot—the group around Claus von Stauffenberg who conspired to assassinate Hitler in 1944. Many historians believe Himmler must have had knowledge of the plot, yet the case for his involvement is largely circumstantial. Indeed, even as he saw the wisdom of a separate peace, there is no evidence at this point that Heinrich Himmler was willing to commit treason against his Führer.

Dulles, who would later become the first director of the Central Intelligence Agency, appeared to believe that, if Himmler had so chosen, he could have successfully overthrown Hitler during this period and still kept the Reich alive. "Himmler's power was greatest during the year 1943," Dulles later wrote. "The SS would have obeyed him unconditionally. But within the clique of tyrants he had enemies, of whom Martin Bormann became increasingly powerful and dangerous because he had the unqualified confidence of the Führer."[35] If anything, this power would continue to grow, especially as Hermann Göring's own influence with the Führer began to erode.

In September 1943, just weeks after Himmler entertained the plotters, Felix Kersten suddenly requested permission from his patient to move to Sweden. The pretext for such a move, as he would tell it, was a desire to treat Finnish soldiers who were convalescing in Sweden. The move would still allow him to return frequently to treat Himmler wherever he might be. Curiously, Kersten claimed that the Reichsführer consented to this move because he wanted to "avoid any sort of friction" with Finland, with whom relations were growing "tense."[36] Given Himmler's dependence on the magic fingers of his longtime healer, this explanation makes little sense. In the context of his supposed new quest for a separate peace, however, it appears possible that he may have been using Kersten as an emissary of sorts in his apparent new desire to reach out to the West.

Kersten's previous experiences with Swedes had involved a 1942 meeting with the director general of the Swedish Match Company, who was seeking the freedom of seven Swedish men arrested in Warsaw for espionage. That connection led Kersten to the famed Swedish banker Jakob Wallenberg, who had deep ties to both the German resistance and to U.S. intelligence. One of Wallenberg's American contacts was Abram Stevens Hewitt, an OSS officer who had recently been sent to Sweden on economic warfare matters under the cover of a businessman working for the United States Commercial Company.

Wallenberg had recently contacted Hewitt explaining that he was "in touch with a cross-section of the high-ranking German financial and manufacturing interests." He informed his American contact that resistance "cells were forming in Germany for the purpose of overthrowing Hitler." He asked Hewitt if he "would be willing to meet with representatives of such cells."[37]

Kersten had arrived in Sweden on September 30, 1943. Only days later, he claims, he was visiting a friend, a man named J. Holger Graffman, when Hewitt just happened to come over for coffee.[38] Feigning a back problem, Hewitt asked if Kersten could provide a diagnosis. Thus began a series of daily massage treatments in which Kersten was very forthcoming about his most notorious patient. For his part, Hewitt revealed enough about his high-level contacts that Kersten was left with the impression that he was a friend of President Roosevelt and that he had the ability to act as a crucial go-between with the West.

Apparently sensing an extraordinary opening to realize the plans he and Schellenberg had been discussing for months, Kersten wrote to Himmler on October 24, informing him of the opportunity to strike a deal with Hewitt that could lead to a compromise peace: "I have an American patient here in Stockholm; his name is Abram Stevens Hewitt (he is not a Jew) and he is in close contact with the American government. We have worked out proposals for peace talks. . . . It is not easy for me, a Finn, to conduct peace negotiations with Germany. I ask you, therefore to send somebody to me here in Stockholm who enjoys your entire confidence so that I can introduce him to Mr. Hewitt. Please don't hesitate, but decide at once, Herr Reichsführer—the fate of Europe hangs on it."

More remarkable than this overture are the seven points that Kersten claims to have worked out with Hewitt, including "Abolition of the Nazi party" and "Removal of the leading Nazis and their appearance before a court charged with war crimes." "These points are all acceptable to all parties," he concludes, "and I beg of you to seize the favorable opportunity, Herr Reichsführer. Fate and history itself have placed it in your hands to bring an end to this terrible war."[39] It is hard to imagine that Kersten would have dared put such inflammatory demands in writing. Indeed, there's no record of Himmler receiving this correspondence, which Kersten claims was sent via the Finnish diplomatic pouch. There is only Kersten's diary entry of October 24 to back up his account. What is known is that Schellenberg arrived in Stockholm in early November and it appears that he did travel there at the behest of Himmler to pursue further talks.

On November 2, 1943, Kersten arranged for Schellenberg to meet Hewitt at the American's suite in Stockholm's Plaza Hotel. Reverting to spymaster mode, the German chose on these occasions not to reveal his true identity. Instead, he introduced himself as an army colonel with contacts in the Nazi high command who had been wounded in North Africa.

Hewitt's written account essentially corroborates the other two men's versions of their clandestine negotiations. Taking over the negotiations from Kersten, Schellenberg informed the American that the German military situation was dire. Hewitt then suggested that they work toward negotiations for ending the war on the Western Front. They both agreed the ultimate aim was preventing the Bolsheviks from taking over Western Europe. "In this connection, no elaborate views were expressed," Hewitt later reported. "We were both in the same position, neither of us knew what would be said about these matters in our respective countries." Much of what they discussed over the two days was familiar ground to Hewitt since it echoed his earlier conversations with Kersten.

When Hewitt stressed that the U.S. would not negotiate with Hitler, Schellenberg immediately assured him that there would be no need to involve the Führer, implying that Hitler could be deposed.

He invited the American to travel to Germany to meet Himmler as soon as possible.[40] Hewitt believed such a trip would be futile, at least until he had received clearance from Washington to embark on such a mission. Schellenberg urged him not to delay since Allied bombing of Germany would soon make such a trip perilous. They agreed that when the time was right, Hewitt would travel to Germany via Portugal. They worked out a prearranged coded signal that would indicate Washington's willingness to pursue further negotiations. If Hewitt could interest his superiors, an ad would be placed in a Stockholm daily for eight consecutive days: "For Sale Valuable Goldfish Aquarium at 1524 Kr."[41]

Returning to Germany, Schellenberg reported the results of his conversations to Himmler, who reportedly believed his intelligence chief had gone too far and put a halt to such negotiations, at least for the time being. "I was lucky not to be arrested by Himmler," he later wrote. "Nothing can break the spell which Hitler still exercised upon those around him."[42]

Both Schellenberg and Kersten were apparently frustrated by Himmler's indecision, especially in light of the golden opportunity they believed had just presented itself in the guise of Hewitt. In his diary entry of December 4, Kersten notes that he had that morning at Hochwald tried to make Himmler realize that it was time to decide about whether to negotiate with Hewitt. "No country in Europe is getting anything out of this war," he claims to have told the Reichsführer. "It's time it was stopped."[43] Himmler's reply was not what he was hoping for. "Ach, don't torment me, give me time," came the purported reply. "I can't get rid of the Führer, to whom I owe everything. It was he who gave me the position I now hold—and am I now to use my position as Reichsführer to overthrow the Führer? It's quite beyond me, Herr Kersten. Try to understand. Read the pledge of loyalty which I have taken as my motto. Am I to ignore all that and become a traitor? For heaven's sake, don't ask that of me, Herr Kersten."[44]

Responding to the list of seven items that Kersten sent from Stockholm, Himmler described the demands as "hair-raising." He would be willing to discuss such conditions only if the situation became truly "grave." Everything done in Hitler's Germany, he insisted, has been carried out with a due regard for the law. When Kersten asked if that included the annihilation of the Poles and the Jews, Himmler was unequivocal. "Certainly, that also assumed a legal form," he replied. "Because the Führer ordered the annihilation of the Jews in Breslau in 1941. And the Führer's orders are the supreme law of Germany."[45] He proceeded to respond to the list point by point, arguing forcefully against some of the conditions, such as the demand that top Nazis be tried for war crimes, which he called a "piece of nonsense." Others, he agreed, he might be willing to live with, such as giving up Germany's territories. But on one point he was still unwilling to budge, protesting that he had no power to remove the Führer. The conversation concluded on an ambiguous note, with Himmler pleading for more time to "think it over." The war is a "disaster" for everybody, he conceded, but America must also show some signs of "goodwill."[46]

Meanwhile, Hewitt had compiled a report on his talks with Kersten and Schellenberg for America's ambassador to Sweden, Herschel V. Johnson, who would summarize them in a telegram to Secretary of State Cordell Hull on January 10, 1944. "Such ideas as those advanced by Kersten are those of men in desperation," Johnson wrote. "Germans have in past made many attempts to sow distrust in Allied camp and it is difficult to find reason to put faith in statements of a Finn who is obviously a Gestapo agent himself."[47]

Hull agreed that Kersten's proposal was a nonstarter. But when

Hewitt returned to Washington in late January, he had a meeting with the intelligence branch chief of the OSS, William Maddox, where he presented a different assessment than the one he had submitted to the Stockholm embassy. In this report, Hewitt appears to be much more optimistic about the prospect of the negotiations and believes that a trip to Germany might be worth pursuing, though he acknowledges that such a mission would be "potential dynamite."[48] Undertaking a trip to Germany might allow him to explore the Nazis' frame of mind "and the relations of the important Germans with each other." It might also provide an opportunity to provoke a "putsch," or a civil war.[49] He also recognizes the potential disadvantages, including the possibility that the Nazis could use such a trip for propaganda purposes to discredit the Allies.

On a matter of such importance, only one American was in the position to make the decision. Or so, apparently, thought OSS director William Donovan, who personally forwarded a copy of Hewitt's report to President Roosevelt on March 20, 1944. In his cover letter to FDR, Donovan wrote, "Here is a statement made by Abram Hewitt, who I think you know." Donovan, however, included a disclaimer, informing the president that he had warned Hewitt not to embark on such a trip "as I assumed you would not care to have Americans in Germany on such a basis."[50] In the end, Hewitt was instructed to drop the overtures to the Germans. His involvement in the episode, in fact, appears to have damaged his career in the OSS, and he left the intelligence service soon afterwards. In his postwar memoir, the head of the OSS Scandinavian espionage division, Calvin Hoover, reflected on the impact of Hewitt's negotiations. "I felt sure that if Himmler tried to arrest Hitler, he would fail; the effect on the morale of the Nazi Party and the German Army would be shattering," he claimed. But in retrospect, Hoover believed that

Hewitt should have been allowed to travel to Germany to meet Himmler and pursue the Kersten/Schellenberg plan. "If a split between Hitler and Himmler could have been achieved," he wrote, "the resulting disorganization might have resulted in the collapse of Germany before it did, in fact, occur. The lives of at least a million people would have been saved."[51]

Himmler's fear of the Führer appears to have been responsible for his vacillation regarding the plan at this stage of the war. But the fact that neither Kersten nor Schellenberg lost their influence with the Reichsführer, despite their involvement in these treasonous negotiations, is undoubtedly the reason for their fateful decision to continue to pursue their plan. It would soon find them tangled in a scheme with a group of Swiss Jews that would lead directly to the gates of Auschwitz.

TWELVE

BLOOD FOR TRUCKS

By the beginning of 1944, there was only one country under the Nazi sphere of influence where Jews had not yet been rounded up to fulfill the Führer's edict. Hitler's decision to finally turn his attention to Hungary would galvanize the Sternbuchs and other rescuers to thwart his dream of a *Judenrein* Europe. It would also mark the moment the world finally stopped burying its head in the sand.

On the grisly list of European nations enumerated by Heydrich at the Wannsee Conference in January 1942 and its Jews targeted for extermination, Hungary is mentioned prominently. Its Jewish population was listed as 742,800, though a 1941 census had set the figure at 825,000—a little less than 6 percent of the total population.[1] That figure, however, included approximately 100,000 Christian converts who were classified as Jews under Hungarian race legislation, passed in 1941, that was closely modeled on Germany's own Nuremberg racial laws.[2]

The country had been ruled since 1919 by Admiral Miklos Horthy, a conservative nationalist who, upon taking power, moved quickly to undo the democratic reforms won after the First World War. Authoritarian and doctrinaire, Horthy ruled the country with an iron fist yet had mostly left Hungarian Jews alone during his first two decades in office. But as Hitler rose to power in Germany, Horthy gradually came under severe pressure from nationalist Hungarian forces to embrace fascism and ally with the National Socialist regime. It was in this context that the country began to adopt anti-Semitic laws between 1938 and 1941, curtailing the participation of Jews in most spheres of economic life.[3] The alliance was cemented when Hitler helped Hungary regain some of the territory it had lost with the collapse of the Austro-Hungarian Empire, including areas of Czechoslovakia, Romania and Yugoslavia. In November 1940, Hungary formally joined the Axis. Its forces would participate alongside Germany in the invasions of Yugoslavia and the Soviet Union.

Even before Hungary allied with Nazi Germany, Jews had been forbidden to serve in the country's armed forces. Instead, more than twenty thousand were conscripted into forced-labor battalions. In 1941, Horthy deported more than twenty thousand Jews—ineligible for Hungarian citizenship—from its new territories to Ukraine, where most were slaughtered by the Einsatzgruppen. Despite the growing anti-Semitic persecution, however, Horthy's prime minister, Miklós Kállay, resisted increasing pressure from Germany and calls from his own country's radical elements to deport its Jewish population.[4] With Horthy's backing, Kállay's refusal spared the overwhelming majority of the country's Jewish population during the first years of the war.

The turning point came in early 1944. Hungarian troops had fought alongside the Germans at Stalingrad and had suffered significant casualties. By then, it was obvious to both Kállay and Horthy that they had backed the wrong horse. As early as the summer of 1943, Kállay had already been pursuing peace with the West, secretly sending an envoy to Istanbul to establish contact with the Allies. In

September, contact was made with the British ambassador who relayed to his government Hungary's offer of unconditional surrender. Negotiations ensued, but Hungarian forces were reluctant to collaborate with the Russians. They vowed to join only an Anglo-American alliance. Consequently, Hungary would have to wait for the approach of the Western armies to formalize the country's surrender. Meanwhile, Kállay proved increasingly uncooperative with his Axis allies, who were still unaware of the secret peace deal. The last straw for Germany was his refusal to supply additional military reinforcements to defend against the approaching Red Army.[5]

Finally, receiving reports of Kállay's betrayal, Hitler lost his patience. Summoning Horthy to a conference in Austria, the Führer took advantage of the regent's absence to move his troops in from three directions. On March 19, Hitler completed the occupation of Hungary—code-named Operation Margarethe—without a shot being fired. Kállay fled to sanctuary inside the Turkish embassy, but Horthy was permitted to remain as regent. To replace Kállay, the Germans arranged for the installation of the pro-Nazi and rabidly anti-Semitic General Döme Sztójay, who was installed as prime minister.

A day later, Jewish leaders were summoned to a meeting with the occupying authorities and informed that the affairs of Hungarian Jewry were now under the auspices of the SS. The Germans had already begun to round up hundreds of anti-Nazi politicians, Communists, Social Democrats and other figures considered a threat to the regime, including Jewish political activists. Among those arrested was Shmuel Freudiger, the brother of Pinchas (Philip) Freudiger, one of the leaders of the Orthodox community. When he discovered that Shmuel was being held at the rabbinical seminary—converted into a temporary jail—Philip Freudiger made his way there the next morning to plead for his brother's freedom.

Word had already spread through Budapest that the occupying army had been accompanied by a man already well known to Freudiger—Dieter Wisliceny, otherwise known as "Willy." As one of those who had met with Gisi Fleischmann during her fund-raising trips to Hungary two years earlier, Freudiger was very familiar with the Europa Plan and Willy's role in the attempted ransom of European Jewry. Freudiger's wife was from Bratislava, and he had been friendly with most of the Working Group members. Now, discovering that the notorious SS officer was in Hungary, he was filled with a sense of foreboding. Wisliceny was also working with another SS officer named Hermann Krumey, who had been instrumental in the logistics of the liquidation of Polish Jewry during Operation Heydrich, though few in Hungary had ever heard of him.

Freudiger sensed that Wisliceny's presence did not bode well for Hungary's Jews. "They had not sent him for a sightseeing tour of Budapest," he later recalled thinking. A portion of the money that had been used to bribe Willy to stop the Slovakian deportations had been raised by Freudiger and his circle. He decided to seek out the Nazi to plead his case. Willy promptly assured him that nothing would happen to his brother. He instructed Freudiger to attend a meeting that afternoon at the rabbinical center. Here, the Jews of Budapest were ordered to set up a eleven-man Zentralrat—essentially the same as the Judenrat that functioned in other Nazi-occupied territories. Freudiger was designated as one of two members representing the Orthodox community.

After the meeting, he was asked by Wisliceny to remain behind, along with the Zionist leader Nison Kahan.[6] Willy took out a letter and handed it to the two Hungarian Jews. The letter, written in Hebrew, was from Rabbi Weissmandl in Slovakia. "Fate has ultimately overtaken the Jews of Hungary," the rabbi wrote. He advised that the Jewish leadership should resume the Europa Plan, begun with Wisliceny in Slovakia two years earlier. Weissmandl assured the Hungarians that further negotiations would bear fruit and that Willy could be trusted to keep his word—little knowing that in just a few short months the remainder of Slovakia's Jews would be deported. "From today onwards, we need the funds that are reaching you from abroad," Wisliceny informed Freudiger at this meeting.

As an Orthodox leader, Philip von Freudiger was closely involved in the Agudath Israel. As was Rabbi Weissmandl in Slovakia and the Sternbuchs in Switzerland. It would be their common Agudah ties that would soon bring these players together in an underground rescue network. But for now, Freudiger calculated that he and his small religious community were not well suited for the monumental task demanded by the Nazi leader. He would never be able to raise sufficient funds to meet the extortionist's demands. Instead, his thoughts turned to a secular Jewish group that stood against almost everything he believed but with whom he shared a common enemy.

On the night before the Germans rolled into Hungary, three agents arrived at the Majestic Hotel to warn Joel Brand that the occupation would begin the next morning and that he was on the Nazis' "arrest list." The thirty-seven-year-old Brand was a Romanian Jew raised and educated in Germany. As a youth, he had joined the Communist Party and briefly worked as a party functionary during the Weimar Republic. When Hitler came to power, he was arrested for subversive activities. After a brief stint in jail, he was released on a promise to leave the country. With his wife, Hansi, Brand returned to Transylvania, the region of his birth, before resettling in Budapest, where the couple ran a small factory manufacturing knitted goods.[7] He abandoned radical leftist politics and joined a labor Zionist group.

Like Brand, Rezső (Rudolf) Yisrael Kasztner was born in Romania in 1906, though the town where he was born, Cluj, frequently shifted back and forth between Romanian and Hungarian jurisdiction. His father was a devout Jew, but as a youth, Rezső had rejected the Orthodox beliefs of his parents and embraced Zionism, which for most but not all Jews were still mutually exclusive. Graduating from law school, he worked for a time for a Hungarian Zionist newspaper, *Új Kelet*, in Cluj. He had returned to his hometown in 1928 to take care of his mother after his father died while reading the Torah in synagogue. When anti-Semitic legislation closed all Hungarian Jewish newspapers in 1941, he was forced to move to Budapest to look for another job. He soon became involved in the labor Zionist movement, where he encountered Joel Brand and other like-minded activists at a time when much of the country's Jewish population considered themselves patriotic Hungarians first, Jews second. As in Germany, Zionists made up only a small percentage of the country's population. As early as 1941, Kasztner and a fellow Zionist named Otto Komoly had founded an aid and rescue committee commonly known as the Vaa'da. At first, they worked to aid refugees, helping smuggle hundreds of Polish and Romanian Jews over the border. When Hansi's sister was threatened with deportation to Ukraine in July 1941—unable to prove Hungarian citizenship—Joel bribed a government official to save her.[8] It is this incident that he later credited with his involvement. Because most of their activities were forbidden by Hungarian authorities, the committee functioned as an illegal underground cell. It was the Vaa'da, in fact, to which both Freudiger and Gisi Fleischmann had turned when the latter arrived in Hungary in 1942 to raise funds to prevent the deportation of the Slovakian Jews.

It is still unclear what the exact sequence of events was that saw Brand and Kasztner take over the negotiations from Freudiger, who had originally been approached by Wisliceny with Weissmandl's letter. However, on April 5, the two young Zionist leaders were invited to meet with Willy, whom they described as so fat that he could not sit in a chair. Because Brand spoke what he called "purer" German than Kasztner, he was designated as the Vaa'da's negotiator.

Familiar with the terms of the Europa Plan, the group informed Eichmann's deputy that they were prepared to offer $2 million—payable in ten installments of $200,000 each—if the Germans would promise to end the deportations and the ghettoization of Hungarian Jews. In addition, they sought permission for the Jews to emigrate to Palestine. Brand believed the war would be over long before most of the installments were due. Wisliceny's response gave the two Vaa'da representatives cause for hope, promising no ghettoization of the Jews and no deportations if they came up with sufficient funds. On the final point—emigration to Palestine—Willy was less encouraging. The Nazis had come to an agreement with the Mufti of Jerusalem, promising not to send Jews there, he revealed. They should instead seek out other havens such as North Africa. If the Jews subsequently made their way to Palestine, that would no longer be of any concern to the German authorities.

Kasztner argued that it would be easier for the community to raise the required funds if they could show concrete results. A ship was due soon to leave for Turkey. The group had acquired from the Istanbul-based Jewish Agency a number of certificates for emigration to Palestine—between six hundred and seven hundred—and safe passage to Turkey would help facilitate their departure. If the Germans would approve this, it would go a long way toward ensuring "goodwill." Willy was noncommittal, though he did ask for a list of names. As for the $2 million, Willy thought the offer was low, but he would seek instructions from his superiors.

An appeal for funds soon went out through Freudiger and other members of the Zentralrat to raise the first $200,000 installment. Willy had apparently assumed such funds could be raised with ease. The Hungarian Jewish community, after all, was much larger and more affluent than the one he had dealt with during his time in Slovakia. The first installment was due on April 9. By early April, the group had come up with the equivalent of $169,000 in Hungarian pengő.[9] Despite the payment of this enormous sum, the Nazis had granted only limited concessions, including the release of a number of arrested comrades. Members of the committee were also issued "immunity certificates" guaranteeing them free passage through Budapest, and were excused from wearing the yellow star.

Willy was said to be "furious" when the group only managed to pay the first installment in portions. When they failed to come up with the full amount by April 9, the group was informed by their German intelligence liaison, Josef Schmidt, that deportations would soon begin. They redoubled their efforts to raise funds. "It became absolutely clear to us that an acute competition was taking place between the Hungarians and Germans for plundering Jewish wealth," Brand recalled.[10]

Meanwhile, by mid-April, Hungarian authorities had ordered Jews living in small towns to concentrate in larger cities, the apparent beginning of the ghettoization that the group had been working furiously to avoid. All Hungarian Jews were also now required to wear the yellow star.[11] Gendarmes were dispatched to the countryside to herd the Jewish population to urban centers. Within weeks, nearly five hundred thousand were living in primitive enclosed areas, their perimeters guarded by Hungarian police. As in the Polish ghettos, food and medicine became scarce, though it soon became clear that these Hungarian ghettos were only temporary.

On April 25, more than a week after reports reached the group about the formation of the ghettos, Joel Brand was instructed to show up at 9 a.m. in front of a Budapest coffeehouse.[12] There, a car would pick him up to take him to meet Adolf Eichmann. Informing his fellow committee members of the meeting, he received instructions to stick with the original demands presented to Willy weeks earlier. At the appointed time, he was brought to the Majestic Hotel, where Eichmann maintained an office on the ground floor. As he entered, he noticed the sign on the door:

Sondereinsatzkommando – IVB – Jewish Department

Years later, when Eichmann sat in the glass booth at his 1961 war crimes trial, Brand identified him as the same man he met that day at the Majestic Hotel: "There was a table between the anteroom and the room, by the door. I approached the table. . . . Eichmann stood in front of it, legs astride, with his hands on his hips . . . and shouted, I would say, bellowed at me. You . . . do you know who I am? I am in charge of the Aktion [operation]! In Europe, Poland, Czechoslovakia, Austria it has been completed; now it is Hungary's turn . . ."[13]

Eichmann told Brand that he chose him for this negotiation because he had had him "tested" as a representative of the JDC and the Jewish Agency and determined that he would be able to "perform." That's when he delivered the chilling proposal. At Eichmann's trial, Brand testified about this first encounter: "He had summoned me in order to propose a deal. He was prepared to sell me a million Jews— 'goods for blood,' that was his way of speech at that time."[14] When Brand protested that he would need to consult his closest friends to arrange the payments, Eichmann gave permission with the caveat that he would "pay with your head" if the Hungarians found out. When he reported the conversation to the committee hours later, they were skeptical but hopeful. "We clung to the belief, as to a straw, that perhaps it would be the salvation of the Jewish people," Brand recalled.[15]

Brand met with Eichmann again on May 8. The Nazi enquired whether he had given thought to the kind of goods Jews would be willing to offer in exchange for a deal. Revealing that he had received authorization for the negotiations from Berlin, he informed Brand that the Germans desperately needed military vehicles. He needed newer, better trucks for front-line regiments. Brand later described the terms of the deal Eichmann offered that day: "'And so you want to have a million Jews?' And I replied that I would like to have all of them. He said: 'One million, that's what we're discussing now—ten thousand trucks, one hundred Jews equals one truck. You're getting a bargain.' But the trucks must be new from the factory, with accessories, with trailers, and equipped for winter operation."[16]

Brand claims that he was "dumbfounded, desperate and happy" at the prospect of freeing a million Jews, but he knew that it would be nearly impossible to fulfill the Nazis' demand. He would be permitted to travel to Turkey to relay the offer to whatever authorities he believed could make it happen. It was at this point that Eichmann delivered a sweetener: "He said that he could give his word of honour to my allies—my 'allies' was the term he used—that these trucks would not be used along the [Western front] but solely on the Eastern Front."[17] It is this element of Eichmann's offer that is the most significant. By promising that the trucks would not be used against the Western Allies but only against Stalin's forces, he was clearly signaling the Germans' desire for a separate peace. Of course, it's inconceivable that Eichmann could have entered into such negotiations without authorization from his SS superior, Heinrich Himmler. Less notice has been taken of Eichmann's other offers to Brand: He was prepared to release 10 percent of the promised Jews to any designated border. And he was also prepared to "blow up the installations in Auschwitz."[18]

On April 7, 1944[19]—three weeks after the occupation of Hungary— two Slovakian Jews managed a feat that had been accomplished only a handful times before. Rudolf Vrba and Alfred Wetzler had been part of the original deportations of Slovakian Jews in 1942 before the Working Group's bribe to Willy or other factors succeeded in halting the deportations. Vrba—born Walter Rosenberg—had been apprehended by Slovak authorities in March 1942 as he made his way to Hungary to escape the roundup already under way. After two months in a transition camp, he was sent first to the Majdanek concentration camp and then transported to Auschwitz. Upon arrival, he had the number 44070 tattooed on his arm. During his first year, Vrba was assigned to the extermination camp Birkeneau (Auschwitz 2), where he worked for ten months sorting out the valuables and property of prisoners at the "Canada" warehouse for shipment back to Germany. For a time, he was also tasked with removing the dead bodies from arriving trains. He would later claim that he was struck by the naïveté of the new arrivals, whose choice of clothing and personal goods revealed that they had no idea what was in store.[20]

In June 1943, Vrba was given administrative work in the quarantine section of Birkenau. Here, he encountered a fellow Slovakian, Alfred Wetzler, working in the camp mortuary. The two became involved in the Auschwitz resistance movement, though Vrba would claim he became disillusioned with the resistance in March 1944 when it became obvious that they had no interest in a mass uprising. Instead, they appeared only interested in "the survival of members of the resistance," he recalled.[21]

He now believed that the best way he could help his fellow prisoners would be to escape and inform the world of the horrors he had witnessed. On Friday, April 7, the eve of Passover, with help from fellow resistance members, the two inmates hid themselves under a woodpile outside the camp's barbed-wire inner perimeter. There, they spread Russian tobacco soaked in gasoline to mask their scent against guard dogs used to patrol the grounds—a technique they had learned from a Russian POW. For three days, the two prisoners remained hidden until they sensed an opportunity and managed to get by an external perimeter. It was not until April 10 that the camp commandant received word that two prisoners had escaped, setting off an alarm and a massive manhunt. By then, the pair had long since embarked by foot on the journey that would eventually take them to the Slovak border eleven days later. From there, they reached the town of Tczaza on April 24, where they located a Jewish military doctor and asked for medical help. Both men were suffering from exhaustion and malnutrition. While being treated by Dr. Pollak, they told their story. Of the sixty thousand Slovak Jews deported in 1942, they revealed, only about sixty men and four hundred women were still alive.

They asked to be put in touch with representatives of Jewish organizations to whom they could relay their account. The doctor arranged for both men to board a train the next day bound for the town of Zilina, where they would be met by a trusted contact named Ondrej Steiner, a member of the Judenrat. To him, they conveyed the chilling news.[22] When they mentioned the gassings, Vrba notes that Steiner merely listened. "He didn't say whether he believed it or didn't believe it," he later recalled. Steiner and his colleagues summoned two Jewish lawyers from Bratislava who they claimed were experts in "criminal investigations." The lawyers separated the men into different rooms, supplied them with paper and asked them to write down their stories. Vrba got the impression that the men didn't believe their accounts. For two days, he recalled, twelve men checked their "data"

Heinrich Himmler reviews an SS regiment with Hitler at Nuremberg in 1937. Although Himmler had carried out with ruthless efficiency the Führer's edict to liquidate European Jewry, Hitler ordered his "Loyal Heinrich" expelled from the Nazi Party after he discovered Himmler was negotiating a peace with the West behind his back in the final days of the war. (US Holocaust Memorial Museum, courtesy of Richard Freimark)

Finnish osteopath Felix Kersten stands with his long-time patient Heinrich Himmler who believed that only Kersten's "magic fingers" could cure his severe stomach pains. The Finn used his influence over the SS chief to save countless Jews in the final months of the war. (Courtesy of the Kersten family)

The gentile Swiss police captain Paul Grüninger helped Recha Sternbuch smuggle in hundreds of Jews fleeing from the Third Reich. When anti-Semitic Swiss authorities learned of their underground network in May 1939, Grüninger was dismissed from his post and Recha was arrested.
(Courtesy of the Paul Grüninger Foundation, St. Gallen)

Julius Kühl used his position at the embassy of the Polish government-in-exile to facilitate the Sternbuchs' rescue efforts and to make the embassy's cipher codes available to the Rescue Committee to communicate news of the Holocaust to America.
(Courtesy of the Kühl family)

While most of the Jewish establishment placed their faith in the Roosevelt administration and Allied forces to stop the Holocaust, ultra-Orthodox leaders collaborated with the Revisionist Zionist Peter Bergson to publicly demand rescue. Here, 400 rabbis march to the Capitol from Washington's Union Station on October 6, 1943, in an action that helped lead to the creation of the War Refugee Board. (Courtesy of the David S. Wyman Institute for Holocaust Studies, www.WymanInstitute.org)

Slipping out a back entrance of the White House, President Roosevelt deliberately avoided meeting with the rabbi marchers. Instead, they took their protest to the Capitol building. Here, they recite "Kel Maleh Rachamim," a memorial prayer for the Jews murdered by the Nazis. (Courtesy of the David S. Wyman Institute for Holocaust Studies, www.WymanInstitute.org)

As a devout Catholic, former Swiss president Jean-Marie Musy was sympathetic to the Nazis' anti-communist ideology before the war, but was revulsed when he learned of the Final Solution. The Sternbuchs enlisted Musy on a remarkable rescue mission to save European Jewry during the final months of the war. (Courtesy of Edouard Musy)

Accompanying his father on a number of dangerous journeys inside Germany, Benoit Musy was given permission by Himmler to enter the concentration camps. He played a vital role in preventing thousands of Buchenwald inmates from death marches. (Courtesy of Edouard Musy)

Auschwitz-Birkenau's notorious Crematorium ll lies in rubble after being destroyed on the orders of Himmler in November 1944, effectively ending the Final Solution. The Sternbuchs and others conspired to deceive Himmler into believing the Allies would be open to a separate peace. (US Holocaust Memorial Museum Archives, courtesy of Instytut Pamięci Narodowej)

Roswell McClelland of the War Refugee Board was a frequent obstacle to the Sternbuchs' rescue efforts. Here, he stands outside a quarry at a Mauthausen sub-camp after the concentration camp was liberated by Allied forces before the Nazis could carry out a plan to dynamite 60,000 inmates. (US Holocaust Memorial Museum Archives)

Heinrich Himmler, the architect of genocide, lies dead after swallowing a cyanide capsule in Allied custody on May 23, 1945. (US Holocaust Memorial Museum Archives)

When British and Canadian forces liberated Bergen-Belsen in April 1945, they found thousands of corpses of inmates who had recently succumbed to starvation and disease. Allied authorities had refused to authorize gasoline for the Red Cross to deliver relief supplies to the camp. Anne Frank had been one of the inmates. (US Holocaust Memorial Museum)

Wearing her trademark turban, Recha Sternbuch hosts a postwar meeting of the Vaad ha-Hatzalah in Montreux. Her husband, Isaac, who was equally devoted to rescue, stands behind her while Rescue Committee secretary Hermann Landau takes minutes at Recha's right. (Courtesy of the Amud Aish Memorial Museum)

After the war, Recha (center) traveled throughout Europe to rescue countless orphans being raised Catholic and bring them "back into the Jewish fold." These children had been placed in convents by their parents who were then deported to death camps. (Courtesy of the Amud Aish Memorial Museum)

Sternbuch Rescue Committee secretary
Hermann Landau, back right in fedora,
greets a train carrying 1210 Jewish inmates
liberated to Switzerland from the
Theresienstadt concentration camp
in February 1945, in a deal brokered
by former Swiss president Jean-Marie
Musy on behalf of the committee.
(Courtesy of Hermann Landau)

Shortly after their liberation from Theresienstadt, passengers from the Musy train read
on beds of straw at a schoolhouse in St. Gallen, Switzerland. (US Holocaust Memorial
Museum Archives, courtesy of Stadtarchiv, St. Gallen)

in a state of great excitement, attempting to verify the claims made in the thirty pages of detailed information that Vrba and Wetzler had supplied. Their report also included a detailed map of Auschwitz and its various annexes and sub-camps drawn by Vrba from memory.

Time was of the essence, the two escapees stressed. Before they made their escape, they had heard a report from a Polish kapo that "a million Hungarians" were soon expected. Vrba also overheard SS guards discussing the imminent arrival of "Hungarian salami."[23] The coded slang of Auschwitz used foodstuffs to differentiate the nationalities of new arrivals, based on the food that they would pack for their journey, immediately confiscated upon arrival and eaten by the camp personnel. When transports of Dutch prisoners arrived, the guards talked of "cheese." With the French, it was "sardines." The Greeks sparked talk of "halvah and olives." Hungarian Jewry needed to be warned. It is this account that would later come under some dispute. Vrba insists that he warned the Slovaks of the imminent Hungarian deportations immediately upon arrival but that he was dissuaded from including this in his report. Although the report was being translated into both German and Hungarian for dissemination, he was told that the warnings about the extermination of Hungarian Jewry should be omitted.

"[The warnings were] reiterated again and again, by both of us, Wetzler and myself," Vrba later insisted. "And we were told, if I remember well, that it is good for the veracity of the report that we do not prophesize the future, but say only what we know. In other words, we should limit ourselves to things which happened, not which will happen. We of course explained exactly that the machinery of murder in Auschwitz is based on the principle of resistance and tricking of the victims into gas chambers. And that we consider it as of utter importance that the content of that report should be spread

among those . . . this part of the Hungarian population which immediately being threatened by execution, the Hungarian Jews."²⁴ The committee was still reluctant to include the warnings, but they assured the pair that their report would be sent to a Hungarian resistance leader named Rudolf Kasztner. Neither Vrba nor Wetzler had ever heard of him.

Even as Adolf Eichmann was proposing his "blood for goods" deal in April, he was already making plans.²⁵ In her 1963 book *Eichmann in Jerusalem*, Hannah Arendt portrayed Eichmann as a small-minded functionary eager to please his superiors. Watching him answer for his crimes at his 1961 war crimes trial, she failed to detect "any particularity of wickedness, pathology, or ideological conviction of the doer." It was a phenomenon she labeled the "banality of evil"—an oft-quoted phrase that has since become something of a cultural cliché. But as he arrived in 1944 to carry out his last major task in service to the Reich, there was a sense among those he commanded that Eichmann was doing more than simply following orders. Dieter Wisliceny would later testify to a conversation he once had with his SS superior. "He said he would leap laughing into the grave because the feeling that he had five million people on his conscience would be for him a source of extraordinary satisfaction," Willy told his Nuremberg inquisitors not long before he himself was sentenced to hang.²⁶ It was clear that by the spring of 1944 Eichmann's particular form of evil was anything but banal.

Rudolf Höss had been the commandant of Auschwitz from before its birth as an extermination camp in 1942 until November 1943, when he was reassigned by Himmler to become the deputy inspector of the concentration camp system. During his initial tenure, he had turned Auschwitz into the most efficient killing machine the world had ever

known. It was Höss who replaced the old method of suffocation by carbon monoxide with a far more efficient technique, introducing prussic acid (Zyklon-B). With this technique, he could exterminate at least 7000 to 8000 prisoners a day. He would later estimate that a total of 2.5 million people were transported to Auschwitz for extermination, though historians have estimated the number murdered at the camp as closer to 1.1 million.[27] Now, with the fate of Hungary's 800,000 Jews waiting to be sealed, Höss was reassigned back to his old post on May 9, apparently at Eichmann's request.

His first order was to accelerate preparations for the new arrivals, expected the following day. The liquidation process had slowed considerably in the last several months, a circumstance blamed on the "inefficiency" of the former commandant, Arthur Liebehenschel, who many considered "soft." The furnaces of Crematorium V were in a state of disrepair. In the first four months of 1944, only 25,000 prisoners had arrived—most from France and the Netherlands. Before arriving at Auschwitz to resume his post, Höss later revealed that he had traveled to Budapest three times to meet with Eichmann and obtain an estimate of the number of "able-bodied Jews" that might be expected. It was on these trips that Eichmann revealed his timetable. He planned to send four trainloads of Jews daily, carrying between 3000 and 3500 persons, most of whom would be gassed upon arrival. Höss protested that the camp and its extermination apparatus could not handle that schedule. Consequently, the plan was revised so that the camp would receive five trains every two days instead. "Eichmann was absolutely convinced that if he could succeed in destroying the biological basis for Jewry in the east by complete extermination, then Jewry as a whole would never recover from that blow," Höss wrote in his diary. "[28] In preparation for the upcoming task, Höss had ordered a long-abandoned rail spur extended inside the Birkenau camp—enabling the trains to deliver the new arrivals only a short distance from the gas chambers for maximum speed and efficiency.

On May 27, two more Auschwitz inmates, Czesław (Zeslov) Mordowicz, a Pole, and Arnost (Ernst) Rosin, a Slovak, managed another daring escape. Members of the camp's resistance, they were apparently inspired by the success of Vrba and Wetzler's feat a month earlier. Like their predecessors, they also found their way to Slovakia— swimming the Sola River to freedom—where they arrived on June 6, the same day the Allies landed in Normandy. They too made contact with the Jewish Council and gave their own eyewitness account, which backed up that of the two Slovaks. But whereas Vrba and Wetzler escaped before the deportation of Hungarian Jewry commenced, the two new arrivals witnessed the unfolding catastrophe. Hungarian arrivals, they reported, were being murdered at "an unprecedented rate." Their account would later be circulated by the War Refugee Board in a memo that described what happened from the first day Hungarian deportees arrived at the death camp: "On May 15 mass transports from Hungary began to arrive in Birkenau. Some 14,000 to 15,000 Jews arrived daily. The spur railroad track which ran into the camp to the crematoria was completed in great haste, the crews work-ing night and day, so that the transports could be brought directly to the crematoria. Three crematoria worked day and night. . . . Thus the 'exterminating capacity' became almost unlimited."[29]

Together, the separate accounts of the four escapees would become known as the *Auschwitz Protocols*. As with the previous report a month earlier, the Slovaks circulated the document to a number of sources, including the Vatican and members of the Hungarian under-ground. Among the Hungarian recipients were both Rezső Kasztner and Philip Freudiger. Both chose not to broadcast the report widely, apparently so as not to jeopardize the ongoing ransom negotiations with Eichmann. Kasztner in particular would later be accused of complicity in the liquidation of the Hungarian victims due to his failure to warn the Jews of their fate.

As always, Eichmann—aided by the Hungarian gendarmerie—had relied on a campaign of deception. His men assured the deportees that they were simply being "resettled." To support the charade, Hungarians in Budapest began to receive postcards in May from friends and loved ones assuring them that all was well. Freudiger would later testify that he had received Vrba and Wetzler's alarming Auschwitz report at the end of May or the beginning of June: "Before receiving this report we may have been aware that they were sending the Jews to Auschwitz. But we did not know what Auschwitz meant. When I spoke to Krumey, as I have said, he always maintained that they were being sent to work."[30]

Rudolf Vrba had grown up in Nitra, on the same street where Michael Weissmandl's father-in-law, Rabbi Ungar, resided. "This Rabbi Ungar was of course considered a wonder Rabbi," he later recalled, "and I remember as a child being sometimes with an errand in his kitchen. . . . so I knew of course that Weissmandl was his sort of legitimate heir, his recognized heir, very respected in the [religious] community."[31] Vrba had no reason to seek out Weissmandl, who he assumed had died along with the majority of Slovakian Jewry. But in June,[32] a representative of the Jewish Council informed him that Weissmandl wished to see him at the yeshiva in Bratislava over which he presided. The Jewish Council had received word that warrants had been issued by Slovakian authorities for the arrest of the Auschwitz escapees. It was, therefore, risky to venture into the Bratislava Jewish quarter. Nevertheless, it was an honor to be summoned by a figure such as Weissmandl even though neither Vrba nor Wetzler were particularly observant.

Ushered into the rabbi's office by a yeshiva student, they were struck by the "penetrating look" on Weissmandl's "benevolent face." "He was dressed like a great Talmudic scholar," Vrba later recalled. "This means extremely sloppy, but relatively clean." It was immediately clear to both men that Weissmandl had studied their reports very carefully and "knew every word." He was struck by the difference in tone between this deeply religious Jew and the ones he had first encountered on the Slovak Jewish Council. "He showed first an enormous amount of compassion," recalled Vrba. "He spoke in a very moving style about the catastrophe. . . . don't forget that we were coming from Auschwitz where compassion, display of compassion, was dangerous, and the ethics develop in such a way that what was dangerous in Auschwitz finally becomes repugnant. That's how the human mind works."[33]

Consequently, as the rabbi spoke, the two visitors remained "cool . . . not too friendly." The turning point was the words Weissmandl spoke an hour into the encounter as they sat drinking coffee: "He said, 'Now you are from there, it is my duty to treat you like the ambassadors of those people who died there. Because you came back and you are the only ones who can speak for them.'" Weissmandl asked the pair what he could do. "We explained to him that from all that we know and what we had seen, the principle consists in the ignorance of the people who are going to be slaughtered. That those people board trains, that the trains are not even guarded, that they come voluntarily to the trains, and the trains come then to Auschwitz . . . so the only thing is that when they come up the ramp then the only thing they can do is to choose between being butchered on the spot or being driven to the gas chambers." They should be warned, the men explained, "that they should not obey orders, that they should run away wherever they can. They should be hunted like deer, not slaughtered like pigs."[34]

Weissmandl immediately offered his assistance. "He gave me to understand that he has connections abroad, and that he can muster help from abroad to Auschwitz, say from the side of the Allies, militarily," Vrba remembered. If he could summon military help, the rabbi asked, what was the most effective way to stop the slaughter? Vrba had spent every waking moment for months thinking of this very question. He knew exactly what needed to be done. The logistics of the Auschwitz mass-killing machine rested on the railway transports. If the Nazis planned to liquidate eight hundred thousand Hungarian Jews, it would require the railways operating smoothly. "So if the train . . . the railway tracks around Auschwitz, forty, fifty miles would be bombed and the people wouldn't come but would have to be transported forty or fifty miles on foot, already this would slow the murderous machinery," Vrba informed him. It would be no good to destroy the camp itself or its installations. The salvation of Hungarian Jewry would require the bombing of the railways.

Weissmandl immediately embraced the plan. To the surprise of his visitors, this deeply religious figure—"a very holy Man," they described him—even endorsed the idea of dropping weapons into the camp by air so that the resistance could fend off the guards and defend themselves against their tormentors. "Once it came to this sort of discussion, I had nothing but very warm feelings for him, because it was the first time we spoke with a man who wasn't just curious or investigating the dates. But he was discussing with me seriously the maps and the plans and the possibilities of what could be done."[35]

When Weissmandl had promised "military assistance" from abroad, Vrba was initially skeptical that this sloppily dressed, bearded rabbi—however compassionate he may have seemed—could possess the kind of connections to stop the slaughter that had gone on unopposed for more than two years. During the weeks since achieving his freedom, he had heard Weissmandl's name mentioned in connection with the efforts of Gisi Fleischmann and her committee to stop the deportation of the remaining Jewish community of Slovakia. This, he was told, was why more than twenty thousand Jews survived and were permitted to live relatively unharassed for more than two years after he and the others had been deported. In the years since, however, Weissmandl had largely ceased working with Fleischmann and the other members whose religious and political beliefs often collided with his own. Instead, he had become immersed in a new rescue effort—the underground network guided by his father-in-law, Rabbi Ungar of Nitra, whose ties to the Agudah had brought him into contact with the Vaad ha-Hatzalah. The Vaad had connected him with a Swiss group of Orthodox Jews dedicated to rescue. And so began a collaboration between the Slovakian underground and the Sternbuch rescue committee.

The newly created War Refugee Board had at first appeared to be a godsend to the committee—until they encountered the man who had been sent to head up the Swiss office. Roswell Dunlop McClelland was a thirty-year-old Quaker who was studying for a doctorate in history at the University of Geneva at the time that he received the call to head up the War Refugee Board's division in Bern.[36] Announcing his appointment in February 1944, a Treasury Department memo described him as a "very capable, aggressive person." Before taking up his post, McClelland had spent many years working at the relief arm of the Quakers' American Friends Service Committee in Rome, France and Geneva. His qualifications for the new post appear to have been based on the extensive relationships he had built on behalf of the Quakers with Swiss relief organizations.[37] A few weeks before he took up his assignment, Isaac Sternbuch also assumed a new post, having been designated the Swiss representative of the Union of Orthodox

Rabbis—the organization under whose auspices the Vaad operated. During the latter months of 1943, the Vaad had decided to abandon its previous policy, which, since its creation in 1939, had seen the organization focusing its rescue activities on saving Orthodox Jews.

At its annual conference on January 5–6, 1944, the Vaad had finally endorsed the decision to devote its efforts to save as many Jews as possible, regardless of their religious affiliation.[38] The Sternbuchs, though deeply devout, didn't require a special resolution to come to the conclusion that the Torah commanded them to save all Jews. "Recha always said a Jew is a Jew," recalls her cousin Renée Landau.[39] "When we sent out the passports, we didn't ask if the people were Orthodox or not," Hermann Landau recalled.[40] And while the Vaad had previously worked with the Sternbuchs on relief for the Shanghai Torah scholars, they had been reluctant to appoint HIJEFS as its representative in Switzerland. That appears to have changed around the same time as their resolution to save all Jews. The Sternbuchs were now seen as the most effective conduit for the rescue of European Jewry.

Having designated Isaac Sternbuch as its new Swiss representative, the union was granted a U.S. Treasury Department license to transmit $100,000 to the Sternbuchs for use in enemy territory for "the purpose of arranging the evacuation of persons in such territory whose lives may be in imminent danger."[41] Such a license was in fact required for any transfer of funds from the United States to Switzerland during the war, and every transaction had to be strictly scrutinized by U.S. government authorities, including the State Department. Now, as McClelland took up his War Refugee Board post, he would be the conduit for all such future payments. Apart from facilitating payments under the Treasury license, McClelland also allowed the Sternbuchs to transmit and receive messages from the Vaad and other foreign contacts. The committtee was no longer exclusively dependent on the Polish embassy's telegraph room, though Alexander Lados still made the diplomatic code available to transmit any cables they wanted to keep from the eyes of Allied authorities.

Although Recha Sternbuch was still the guiding force behind the committee's rescue efforts, it was almost always Isaac who dealt with McClelland and other government officials. Likewise, it was Isaac's name that appeared on most correspondence with the Vaad, leaving the impression that it was he who was solely in charge of the committee. Given the times, Recha understandably believed that the rabbis would not have taken a woman seriously. The archives, in fact, reveal hundreds of letters and telegrams simply signed "Sternbuch" or "Sternbuch, HIJEFS," which the recipients and later historians assumed had been written by Isaac but had in fact often been written or dictated by Recha.[42] Aside from the fact that he believed Isaac headed the committee, McClelland also falsely believed that he was a rabbi.[43] He described Isaac as "A little busy man with a wild little beard and one eye that went off to the right, who was always in a hurry, who was always harassed, who was always under terrible pressure, who was taking things terribly hard and to use an inadequate term—representative of what one thinks of as the stereotype of eastern Jewry, Galicia, Poland . . . you know, emotional, devoted."[44]

As the rabbis' new representative in Switzerland, Isaac also came into frequent contact with Leland Harrison, the U.S. minister (ambassador) in Bern. As the first American official to gain knowledge of the Holocaust—transmitting Gerhart Riegner's cable about the Final Solution in 1942—Harrison appeared more tolerant than McClelland if the Sternbuchs' activities weren't always by the book. They rarely were. McClelland later explained that he worked one floor below the U.S. commercial attaché, Daniel Regan, who "had instructions to put anybody who used American money to buy parcels for their relatives in Germany on the blacklist for trading with the enemy."[45] And, although McClelland later described such regulations as "silly," he apparently believed that it was his job to enforce them. Harrison had to have known that the $100,000 transmitted to the Sternbuchs by the Vaad in early 1944 would be used for bribes and ransom. On February 19, he informed the State Department that Sternbuch had turned over the funds to "three persons in Hungary who are prepared to undertake rescue work."

Harrison noted that Sternbuch was also endeavoring to "make available a large amount of funds for rescue work in Slovakia." The $100,000 would in fact be split between the Hungarian and Slovakian underground to be used for smuggling of refugees. Early on, Isaac Sternbuch made no attempt to hide his activities from the Americans, though bribery was never explicitly mentioned. This he only revealed to the Vaad leadership. In one dispatch to the Vaad sent through the Polish embassy, he confided, "We need part of the money for bribes to save people. But we can not tell [McClelland] about it."[46]

HIJEFS secretary Hermann Landau later recalled that Weissmandl's initial financial requests had escalated significantly throughout 1943 and 1944. At first, he recalls, the Slovaks were asking only $100 or $200 per person. "But when we got the other letters where he writes that he needs millions and millions of dollars, we began to get a little skeptical about whether it would be possible to raise the money. He was acting in the old Talmudic way, that you have to bribe the Gentiles if you want to save Jewish lives. You have to buy them, and you have to bribe them. This was, in the middle ages and the olden times, always the case."[47] In early March 1944, in fact, Rabbi Ungar, Weissmandl and the Slovakian Orthodox committee had successfully smuggled twenty-two refugees into Hungary little knowing that only two weeks later, the Germans would occupy the country and Hungary would no longer be considered a safe haven for Jewish refugees.

By May, ties between the Slovakian underground and the Sternbuch committee had grown increasingly strong. Now, Weissmandl discovered the horrifying truth about the destination of the Hungarian Jews whose deportations to Auschwitz were already under way. There was no time to waste. With their newly established credentials and official channels to the American authorities, the Sternbuchs were considered the ideal conduit to get the message out. It's still unclear to whom else Weissmandl may have communicated his clarion call. The Vrba report had reached various circles in Istanbul and Hungary and a number of other contacts, verified by copies dispatched by the Slovakian Jewish council in late April. Hermann Landau—who had been appointed secretary of HIJEFS shortly after Recha secured his release from a Swiss refugee prison—recalled that the committee received Weissmandl's message on a Friday sometime in late May.

Because it had been written in a rudimentary Hebrew code devised by Weissmandl—like all communications between the Swiss and Slovakian rescue committees—it took some time to decipher the message.[48] The letter contained details of the Hungarian deportations taking place as well as a plea for Allied forces to bomb the Polish railway tracks and bridges being used to deport the Jews to Auschwitz. It also instructed the committee to galvanize influential figures and alert the world. "Furthermore, one has to warn the heads of the countries in the hand of the evil, and their people, about the punishment they deserve," Weissmandl wrote. "One has to reach the Pope, that he will scream loudly to heaven and earth about this murder."[49] It is interesting to note another passage of Weissmandl's letter, written a full year before the end of the war and long before a full six million had perished. "On the other hand it is necessary that the heads of the countries and the radio will say what they did with us, that they killed in murder houses in Bełżec, Sobibór and Auschwitz up till now, six times a thousand thousand Jews of Europe and Russia."[50]

It was already Shabbat by the time the committee discovered that the fate of Hungarian Jewry was at stake. Without delay, Isaac Sternbuch boarded the train to Bern. The mission was so urgent it couldn't wait until Monday. Before he left, he got in touch with Julius Kühl to determine the home addresses of the military attachés of the three Allied countries—Britain, the United States and the Soviet Union. Hoping his diplomatic ties would help smooth the way, Kühl offered to accompany Isaac on these house calls. Landau would later recall being told that one of the attachés greeted the two Jews in his underwear. The response from the Allied officials was not what the men had hoped. "The English replied, 'We are leading the war from a strategic and not a humanitarian point of view.'" The American representative cabled the United States for a response. "And New York replied they were sorry they couldn't help because it was not in their 'range of operation.'" The Russians were silent, Landau recalls.[51]

On May 25, Sternbuch asked McClelland to pass along a message to the Union of Orthodox Rabbis, informing them that "we received news from Slovakia" and asking for air raids over the town of Kaschau, which served as a transit point for deportations. "Do the necessary that bombing should be repeated at short intervals to prevent rebuilding," he writes. Because of its "military nature," however, McClelland chose to pass along the message to a military attaché. It appears this message never reached its intended recipient.[52]

The Sternbuchs must have learned their dispatch had not reached New York. A week later, on June 2, they sent another letter to the rabbis. This time, they buried the plea in the middle of a letter about other matters. Instead of explicitly discussing the bombing of targets, they resorted to coded language to get the message across: "Concerning the increasingly terrible situation in Hungary, we are quite desperate. There are already on the deportation lists 300,000 Jews. It is urgently asked by the Rabbi of Neutra [Nitra] and others that 'airmail' be sent to the towns of Munkacs, Kascahau and Presov. 15,000 Jews daily are deported over this route to Poland since May 15th. The people are in despair that nothing has been done up to the present. Do not miss another hour in this matter. This is one means of rescue. Do intervene! All this is strictly confidential."[53] The reference to "airmail" being sent to the three towns was a coded plea for Allied planes to bomb three key points along the deportation route. Two years earlier, the Sternbuchs had been primarily responsible for alerting the world to the Final Solution. Now, they transmitted the cable that is usually credited with being the first to convey the Auschwitz bombing plea to the West. Seven decades later, one of the most controversial debates surrounding the Holocaust focuses on why this plea was never heeded.

When Joel Brand left for Istanbul on May 17 to pursue the "blood for goods" proposal, he was aware that the deportations were imminent. It made his mission all the more urgent. Eichmann had originally promised that he would delay the evacuations for a "fortnight" to give Brand time to secure the ransom. But only hours before Brand was to leave for the airport, Eichmann informed him that he was about to commence the deportations. He promised, however, to delay the transports for two weeks in Czechoslovakia or Vienna while he awaited an answer to the ransom proposal. He did not keep this promise.

Eichmann told Brand that he would be accompanied on his trip by a man named Bandi Grosz—a Hungarian smuggler turned German intelligence agent tasked with ensuring that the Jewish emissary didn't let too much "out of the bag" during his journey. Brand's journey turned out to be ill-fated. Arriving in Istanbul, he succeeded in making contact with the Zionist leadership, including the Jewish Agency chief David Ben Gurion, who was highly skeptical of the Nazis' offer but eventually endorsed the idea of ransom if it meant a chance to save a large number of Jews from Hitler's clutches. It was in fact the future Israeli prime minister who first alerted the British government to Eichmann's proposed ransom when he informed the U.K. high commissioner of it on May 26.[54] Two weeks later, an official of the Foreign Office cabled Chaim Weizmann, president of the World Zionist Organization: "The Nazis propose that instead of annihilating the remaining Jews in Romania, Hungary, Poland and Czechoslovakia, they will make it possible to evacuate the latter to Spain or Portugal, but not to Palestine, in exchange for ten thousand lorries and certain quantities of tea, coffee, cocoa and soap."[55]

The Jewish Agency believed it paramount to take advantage of the Nazis' apparent willingness to ransom Jewish lives. Convinced that Brand needed to return to Budapest with something to offer Eichmann, or at least with the appearance that Jews were ready to negotiate, an "interim agreement" was drafted by Jewish Agency official Menachem Bader, dated May 29, and informing the Nazis that the agency accepted in principle that negotiations should go ahead. The Jewish Agency "empowered" Brand to transmit in their name four points. Among these: The deportations were to "cease immediately everywhere" in exchange for a monthly payment of 10,000 Swiss francs. Moreover, overseas emigration to neutral countries such as Spain would be permitted for a sum of 1 million francs for every thousand persons.[56] Until the conclusion of a final agreement, Brand was given the authority to negotiate and enter into "binding obligations" of the protocol. Conspicuously absent from the offer were the goods that Eichmann had demanded. Clearly, anything that could be used to aid the Nazi war effort was a nonstarter. On May 27, Brand had cabled his wife, Hansi, that "in principle positive answer to our proposals just received." Receiving no answer from her, he reiterated the same message four days later. On June 3, he cabled that the interim agreement was essential to negotiations: "Interim agreement executed. Travelling in accordance with your instructions first to Palestine for purpose of further negotiation of technicalities and fixing early meeting place."[57]

Four days later, Brand was arrested and imprisoned in Aleppo, Syria, by British intelligence forces on his way to Palestine—likely because England feared he was being used as a pawn by Himmler to divide the Eastern and Western Allies. Failing to hear from her husband, it was Hansi Brand who first suggested that Kasztner make contact with Eichmann to take up the negotiations where Joel had left off. And that is how Rezső Kasztner became the face of the ransom negotiations between Jews and Nazis that would forever taint history's view of him. An arrogant, overbearing and deeply flawed individual who lacked Brand's evenhanded judgment, Kasztner shared one important characteristic with his jailed comrade. He was resolute in his determination to rescue his people.

Eichmann still had no idea that Joel Brand had failed in his mission. He knew only that his Jewish emissary had claimed to have secured an interim agreement. These words were meaningless to the Nazi, whose superiors were expecting concrete results. "An interim agreement is not a reply," he told Hansi and Kasztner when they arrived to resume negotiations. He issued a bleak warning: "If I do not receive a positive reply within three days, I shall operate the mill at Auschwitz."[58]

On May 22, Rezső Kasztner took up negotiations with Eichmann once again. With the interim agreement not yet arrived, he was determined to pursue the apparent commitment made by Hermann Krumey on April 21—the date the Vaada delivered a portion of the first $200,000 installment—to allow six hundred Jews holding Palestinian certificates to emigrate. While Palestine was out of the question because of the Nazis' promise to the Mufti, Eichmann's man had intimated that they would be permitted to embark for any other neutral country as a gesture of goodwill. It was at that point that Kurt Becher entered into the negotiations as Eichmann's personal liaison to the committee.

Unlike Krumey, Wisliceny and others the committee had dealt with to this point, Becher was not part of the Sonderkommando attached to Eichmann. Instead, he reported directly to Himmler's office. Becher, who had an affinity for horses dating back to his childhood, had spent much of his career in the elite cavalry unit, the Reiter-SS. After the invasion of Germany by the Soviet Union, horses had become invaluable to navigate muddy or snowy stretches impassable by vehicles. His cavalry unit was part of an SS contingent—the Kommandostab Reichsführer—that followed the army performing "special security tasks" under Himmler's personal command. Between July and September 1941, the unit was known to have killed at least fifteen thousand Jewish men, women and children, though Becher would absurdly claim he had no participation in such activities because he was merely an "administrative officer."[59] For his services in this campaign, he would eventually be awarded Germany's highest military decoration, the Iron Cross first class, in 1941. By the time Becher arrived in Hungary in March 1944 with the German occupation forces, he no longer rode a horse. He had been given a new assignment: procuring the animals for the SS.

He was also in charge of "obtaining equipment." It was in this capacity that Kurt Becher attracted Himmler's attention when he negotiated the takeover for the Nazis of the Weiss Metalworks—one of the largest defense contractors in Europe, controlled by four families descended from the nineteenth-century industrialist Baron Manfred Weiss. Among the shareholders, nearly half were Jews. In the complicated maneuvering that allowed the Nazis to take control of the valuable company, Becher had arranged for forty-five family members to emigrate to Portugal and Switzerland while still retaining a good portion of their wealth and valuables. Becher's prowess in the takeover evidently made him the ideal candidate to negotiate with Kasztner and his committee. Becher would later testify that before entering into the negotiations, he had been personally authorized by the Reichsführer-SS to allow a certain number of Jews to emigrate for a price. "Get out of the Jews everything that can be got out of them. Promise them what they are asking for. As to what [promises] we will keep, we'll just have to see," he claimed Himmler told him.[60]

Before long, Becher had agreed to facilitate the evacuation of the 600 Jews Kasztner had been granted, though the exact terms are still murky. These Jews would be brought from the "provinces"—ghettoized Jews awaiting deportation to Auschwitz, where transports had begun a week earlier at the rate of 12,000 per day. Of the hundreds of ghettos to choose from, it was decided that 388 would be taken from Cluj (Kolozsvar), which just happened to be the hometown of Rezső Kasztner. Of this total, an unusually large number would turn out be Kasztner's friends and family members, including his brother, mother and grandfather. This naked favoritism would be just one of a number of accusations that would be leveled at him during a decades-long vilification.

On June 10, the contingent of 388 Jews arrived from Cluj, where they were placed in a "privileged camp" in Budapest consisting of a specially built barracks constructed in the courtyard of the Wechselmann Institute for the Deaf. By then, however, the agreed-to group of 600 Jewish emigrants had swelled to more than 1000. Wisliceny had received permission from Himmler to extract as much money from the Jews as he could. He proceeded to do just that. Soon, the numbers authorized to depart had been inflated to 1200, then 1600. Their exit, however, would not come cheap. According to Kasztner, Eichmann had originally suggested a rate of $200 to $500 per head, but when Becher took over, he raised the price to $2000, before finally settling on $1000 per passenger.[61] "It was a real jungle," Hansi Brand later recalled. "Everyone set an amount, both Eichmann and Becher."[62]

Among the travelers whose wealthy families had purchased passage was the future Barrick Gold tycoon Peter Munk, sixteen years old at the time. After reserving fourteen places on the train, Peter's grandfather delivered most of the family fortune in a suitcase to Kasztner's office.[63] Those suitcases filled with riches, and many more like them, would later become known as the "Becher Deposit," although Becher would dubiously claim he was keeping them until after the war to turn over to Jewish relief organizations. Becher had himself reserved at least 50 seats for individuals who had paid him up to $25,000 for their freedom.

Meanwhile, members of the Zentralrat, including Freudiger, had conceived of a plan that would see 150 places reserved for wealthy Jews whose payment would help subsidize those who couldn't afford the hefty price tag. On this list were included many prominent Orthodox figures, including the revered Satmar Rebbe, Joel Teitelbaum, and more than three dozen other Orthodox rabbis whose presence on the train would unwittingly prove fortuitous. By June 30, the total of those who were lucky enough to earn a spot on the transport to Switzerland had swelled to 1684 individuals, for what Kasztner would later describe as his own "Noah's Ark."[64]

The trains left Budapest shortly after midnight. The group had been promised they were headed to a neutral country. "We did not know where the train was going," Olga Munk later recalled. Nor did they know whether they would survive the journey or if they had been victims of an elaborate trick. "But we were absolutely certain we would not live to see the end of the war if we stayed in Budapest."[65] When they discovered they had arrived not in a neutral country but in Nazi Germany itself, the passengers were convinced they had been swindled. To their horror, the destination turned out to be a concentration camp. The reasons are still unclear, but Becher would later testify that it was Eichmann who had ordered the last-minute diversion. The transport that ended up in Bergen-Belsen in July 1944 would later become known as Kasztner's Train, named for the man who had negotiated the freedom of 1684 Hungarian Jews, most of whom would almost certainly have otherwise ended up in the ovens of Auschwitz.

But while Kasztner is best known for organizing the transport for which his name would go down in history, little attention has been paid to his apparent role in the movement of a far larger contingent of Jews—six trainloads in all—who had departed for Austria days earlier. Kasztner would claim that for a mere $100 per head, he had convinced Eichmann to allow thousands of Jews to be sent to labor camps in Austria where they would be kept "on ice" rather than be deported to Auschwitz.[66] At some point, according to their agreement, they would be allowed to leave for Spain. Between June 25 and 28, 1944, approximately 17,000-18,000 Jews arrived at the Strasshof labour camp, just outside Vienna where Ernst Kaltenbrunner had requested able-bodied Hungarian Jews to rebuild the city, which had suffered heavy Allied bombing.[67] Eichmann was frank about his attitude at this stage of the war, explaining that he intended "to pump out the necessary labour from Hungarian Jewry and sell the balance of valueless human material against valuable goods."[68]

THIRTEEN

AN UNLIKELY ALLY

The front page of *The New York Times* on July 3, 1944, contained a number of articles detailing the progress of the war. Prominently displayed above the fold was an item revealing that Americans would soon have to pay more for underwear because of an increase in the price of cotton. Farther down, the president of the U.S. Chamber of Commerce was quoted about his recent trip to Siberia, which he predicted had a "brilliant future." On page 3, a small item in the middle of the page reported on a development that *Times* editors apparently considered less newsworthy:

INQUIRY CONFIRMS NAZI DEATH CAMPS
1,715,000 Jews Said to Have Been Put to Death by
the Germans Up to April 15

GENEVA, Switzerland, July 2 - Information reaching two European relief committees with headquarters in Switzerland has confirmed reports of the existence in Auschwitz and Birkenau in Upper Silesia of two "extermination camps" where more than 1,715,000 Jewish refugees were put to death between April 15, 1942 and April 15, 1944.[1]

It had been a full two years since the Sternbuch cable had helped alert the West to the nightmare of the Final Solution. The Allies could not claim that they were unaware of Hitler's chilling plan. And yet it appeared once again that they were indifferent. The Sternbuchs' frustration was palpable. "Some Jews would convince themselves that such things were the will of [God]," recalled Hermann Landau, "But not Recha. She had no patience for that kind of talk." It was this impatience that would finally result in her improbable alliance with the Swiss fascist to whom she would entrust the fate of her people. From the moment that Jacob Rosenheim had received the Sternbuchs' report about the Hungarian deportations in early June, the Vaad had been sounding the alarms. He and the Orthodox leadership went to work on two fronts: exerting intense pressure on the Roosevelt administration to take action to stop the Hungarian slaughter and vigorously lobbying for the bombing of the Auschwitz railways demanded by the Sternbuchs on behalf of Rabbi Weissmandl. On June 18, Rosenheim wrote Morgenthau to press for the bombing: "Every day of delay means a very heavy delay for the human lives at stake."

Within days of the Hungarian occupation in March, the Vaad had issued an urgent dispatch to John W. Pehle in Washington: "A cold horror and fear has gripped the approximately one million Jews of Hungary," it began. In the name of Orthodox Jewry, the rabbis "respectfully suggest" that the government of the United States "give immediate and special warning" to the people and government of Hungary that they would be held responsible for the safety of the Jewish population and should resist any attempt to carry out the mass murders.[2]

Coincidentally or not, Roosevelt issued an uncharacteristically strong public warning the same day in which he, for the first time, explicitly mentioned the Jews rather than "persecuted peoples" in connection to the Holocaust: "In one of the blackest crimes in all history, the wholesale, systematic murder of the Jews of Europe goes on unabated every hour. None who participate in these acts of savagery shall go unpunished."[3] The Sternbuchs had also been working tirelessly to save Hungarian Jewry since receiving Weissmandl's cable in late May. Hundreds of pleas were dispatched to world leaders and to American government officials, imploring them to save the Hungarians. Recha's cousin Renée Landau remembers that Isaac's once thriving clothing business, Helco AG, had come to a standstill. "Instead of sewing, Isaac had every one of his employees writing letters all day long to anybody he thought could intervene," she recalled.[4]

The Sternbuchs had already been collaborating for months with the papal nuncio, Archbishop Bernardini. Now, they urged the influential cleric to lobby the Vatican to intercede. At the same time, they communicated daily with Roswell McClelland, demanding that the War Refugee Board and the U.S. government intervene to stop the slaughter and press for the bombing of the railways. On June 17, McClelland cabled Washington that there was "no doubt" the majority of the Jewish population east of the Hungarian Danube had been "deported to Poland." He drew the department's attention to four sections of railway that were being used to transport Jews to the "extermination camps of Auschwitz and Birkenau" and then recommended action: "It is urged by all sources of this information in Slovakia and Hungary that vital sections of these lines, especially bridges, be bombed as the only possible means of slowing down or stopping further deportations." At least 335,000 Jews had already been deported, he noted, recommending broadcasts and pamphlets strongly warning the Germans against further deportations. "If it is possible, the Vatican should be prevailed upon to associate itself with such protest."[5] His appeal was forwarded by J.W. Pehle to the assistant secretary of war, John McCloy. McClelland would later claim he forwarded the same recommendation to McCloy "on three or four occasions" but to no avail. The powerful war department official was unmoved by these appeals, informing the WRB that such a bombing could "only be executed by diversion of considerable air support essential to the success of our forces now engaged in decisive operations."[6] Not for the last time, Allied authorities argued that the war effort took priority over saving Jews.

McClelland later claimed that McCloy also told him that even if the bombings had been practical, they might have provoked even more vindictive action on the part of the Germans. "Well, this, of course, was absolute nonsense," he recalled. "I mean, how can you treat people even more vindictively than gassing and burning them up afterwards."[7] These exchanges would later play a significant role in the debate over whether bombing Auschwitz would have saved Jews—a debate that carries on among historians to this day. In 1968, McCloy would tell Henry Morgenthau's son that the decision not to bomb had in fact been made by Roosevelt himself. "The President had the idea that [bombing] would be more provocative and ineffective and he took a very strong stand, took it right out of our hands," he told Henry Morgenthau III.[8] McCloy, however, confessed that he too was very much against the idea: "I didn't want to bomb Auschwitz. . . . It seemed to be a bunch of fanatic Jews who seemed to think that if you didn't bomb, it was an indication of lack of venom against Hitler."[9]

Although by mid-June a wide variety of groups were calling for action, the most important wake-up call appears to have been a June 15 report on the BBC—drawn largely from the Vrba-Wetzler report—revealing that seven hundred thousand Jews had already been murdered by the Nazis at a camp called Auschwitz.[10]

On June 30, King Gustav V of Sweden issued a personal appeal to Horthy to stop the deportations, begging him "in the name of

humanity to take measures to save those who still remain to be rescued of this unfortunate appeal." Horthy wrote back, assuring the
king that he was "doing everything that under the present circumstances is in my power in order that the principles of humanity and
rightness be respected." After members of the Vaad and others
appealed to Henry Morgenthau to intervene, Roosevelt's Treasury secretary wrote his former deputy Pehle demanding to know what was
being done. Pehle informed him that the WRB had appealed to the
pope to intervene with Hungarian authorities, to warn the Hungarian
people and to enlist the assistance of the Catholic hierarchy. "The
Pope appealed to Admiral Horthy and gave appropriate instructions
to Catholic clergy in Hungary," he revealed.[11] In addition, tens of
thousands of copies of Roosevelt's strongly worded warning of March
24—translated into Hungarian—were dropped by Allied aircraft
throughout the country. Finally, Roosevelt himself issued a new
threat. "Hungary's fate will not be like any other civilized nation . . .
unless the deportations are stopped," he warned. .

On June 26, a senior representative of the Jewish Agency in
Geneva, Richard Lichtheim, sent a telegram to the British Foreign
Office detailing the mass exterminations in Hungary—though it
was hardly new information to them. However, Lichtheim's dispatch was unique in that he provided the names of seventy
Hungarians and Germans who were most directly involved in the
deportations. Deliberately failing to encipher the telegram before he
sent it, Lichtheim made sure it would be read by Hungarian or German
intelligence agents. At the end of June, the telegram was brought to
the attention of Horthy.[12] In the early days of July, American bombers
rained their deadly cargo on Budapest—destroying a number of oil
refineries and military installations. As if to leave no doubt in the
mind of Horthy why his city was being targeted, they also dropped

thousands of leaflets promising to "punish" those responsible for the Auschwitz deportations.

In England, meanwhile, the proposal to bomb Auschwitz had received a more sympathetic ear than it had in the United States. Receiving from Zionist leader Chaim Weizmann a request to bomb the railways, Foreign Secretary Anthony Eden wrote Churchill on July 6 recommending the bombing. A day later, the prime minister wrote back: "Get anything out of the Air Force you can, and invoke me if necessary." Eden then wrote the Ministry of State for Air to enquire about the feasibility: "I very much hope that it will be possible to do something. I have the authority of the Prime Minister to say that he agrees."[13]

The same day that Churchill endorsed bombing the Auschwitz railway line, Admiral Horthy made a fateful decision that would make such a bombing unnecessary, although nobody could have known this at the time. Many historians credit the forceful intervention of Pope Pius as the most important factor in Horthy's decision, which would contradict the present-day criticism that Pius stood idly by during the Holocaust. Whether the decision was a result of Vatican pressure, U.S. diplomatic intervention or international condemnation, Horthy issued the order to stop the deportations on July 7. The very last transport of Hungarian Jews to Auschwitz left two days later. In the ensuing period, Heinrich Himmler himself authorized a halt to the deportations. His reasons for doing so, like many of his subsequent actions, remain in dispute more than seventy years later.

Over a period of less than two months, some 424,000 Hungarian Jews had been deported to Auschwitz. Of these, 320,000 were liquidated almost immediately, while an additional 110,000 were assigned to forced labor or sent to other camps. The decision to halt the deportations left just under 200,000 Jews remaining in the capital and

80,000 "labour service conscripts" assigned to the Hungarian army.[14] These were what the Vaad would describe as the "pitiful remnants" of Hungary's prewar Jewish population of nearly 800,000.

While the Sternbuchs worked for the rescue of Hungarians Jews, Recha and the committee were also preoccupied with a crisis arising from one of their earliest operations. By July 1942, the Sternbuchs had dispatched hundreds of documents obtained from the embassies of Paraguay, El Salvador and Honduras, as well as more than two hundred entry certificates for Palestine. The recipients of those foreign papers had been rounded up by the Germans on July 17 and brought to Pawiak Prison, the Gestapo headquarters that also served as a political prison. From there, the majority of the so-called passport Jews had been sent to two internment camps—one in Vittel, France, the other Bergen-Belsen in northern Germany. They enjoyed special privileges at first—likely because the Germans were keeping them for bargaining purposes.

The Sternbuchs continued to send forged passports to the ghetto, but for weeks they did not realize that most of the documents had not reached their intended recipients, many of whom had already succumbed to starvation or disease. Instead, as it turned out, the passports had been intercepted by two corrupt Jewish ghetto dwellers. In the weeks after the beginning of the liquidation of the ghetto in July 1942, Jews who had been hiding on the Aryan side received word about a Warsaw hotel—the Hotel Polski—where foreign passports could be purchased, guaranteeing freedom from deportation. Hundreds, possibly thousands, converged on the hotel. Those who managed to secure the documents were sent to Pawiak Prison and, like Gutta, deported to the "privileged" camps. Most of those holding South American papers were sent to Vittel, while the Palestinian certificate holders were sent to Bergen-Belsen.

In September 1943 the Swiss government discovered that Julius Kühl had conspired with the Paraguayan honorary consul, Rudolphe Hügli, to supply hundreds of forged passports to Jews. Both men were immediately stripped of their diplomatic credentials because of their role in falsifying documents "in favour of foreign Jews," though Kühl would retain his post at the Polish Embassy.[15] Less than three months later, the Germans discovered through an informant that the papers of the Vittel and Bergen-Belsen internees were suspect. The status of the passport Jews changed overnight. "The *Vaad* got word that unless El Salvador or some other Latin American government would recognize the papers, these inmates would be sent to Auschwitz," recalled Irving Bunim.[16] The Vaad had learned in April 1944 that the Germans were preparing to move almost 250 Vittel inmates to Drancy—a notorious French internment camp outside Paris from which thousands of French Jews had already been deported for extermination. News that the holders of Latin American passports were now in imminent danger hit particularly close to home for members of the Vaad. Thanks to the Sternbuchs' efforts, a number of relatives of prominent Agudath Israel figures had received foreign passports and were interned at Vittel. Among those were family members of Jacob Rosenheim, Michael Tress and Shabse Frankel, three of the organization's leading figures. Moreover, Recha's parents, her two brothers and their wives had also received Paraguayan passports—almost certainly saving their lives after the Nazi invasion of Belgium four years earlier. Thus, the latest crisis hit very close to home in both Switzerland and New York. Now began a frantic effort to save the passport Jews.

A day after the Vaad heard about the planned deportations, a delegation led by Rabbis Kalmanowitz and Frankel—accompanied by longtime Bergson associate Rabbi Baruch Korff—traveled to Washington to urge Morgenthau to intercede with the State Department on behalf of the Vittel internees. In the course of their meeting, Kalmanowitz became so agitated that he collapsed on the floor of the treasury secretary's office. (It was later revealed that the group had staged this dramatic episode to gain the treasury secretary's sympathy.)[17] Morgenenthau, who had already protested that he was powerless to help, was so moved that he canceled his appointments. He then spent the next four hours convincing the State Department to press South American countries for acceptance of the papers.[18] Discussing these efforts with Treasury staff the next day, Morgenthau lamented the obstructionist tactics of State Department official Paul Culbertson who had recently complained "that damned Jew in the Treasury must have gotten to the President" when he was overruled about a decision involving refugees. Culbertson had apparently also tried to interefere with Morgenthau's efforts to aid the Vittel internees.

"He said it once before," Morgenthau fumed to his staff. "And now most likely he will say, 'God-damned Jew.' It is a badge of honor."[19]

His intervention appears to have succeeded. On May 25, Sternbuch advised the Vaad that the U.S. embassy had "taken the necessary steps to bring the internees back to Vittel." He added that the situation was "not clear" and nobody knew how many of the Vittel internees remained at the Drancy camp.[20]

Even as the forged papers from two years earlier were being called into question, the Sternbuchs were vigorously attempting to secure more passports for their rescue operations. In May, they cabled the Vaad to intercede in the "name of humanity" with the governments of Uruguay, Paraguay, Bolivia and Chile to place new passports at the disposal of their committee who "would utilize such documents to

save those in greatest danger." They further emphasized, "We unconditionally guarantee these passports will be used to save lives and will
be returned to the countries of issue when such purpose is utilized."[21]

The situation was precarious and remained so for months—
especially after the inmates were transferred to Germany after the
liberation of France. Unconfirmed reports indicated that all but
twenty had already been transported to Auschwitz.[22] Meanwhile, the
Sternbuchs also pressed McClelland and Harrison to intervene with
Swiss authorities to open their borders to refugees. "The influx formerly feared by Switzerland, the influx of Jews from France, Poland,
and Holland will not happen anymore," Isaac wrote McClelland on
June 29, "since these people have been deported and killed by our
enemies in a beastly way. Only a small number of such people is left,
hidden somewhere in those various countries."[23]

Since nearly the beginning of the Nazi reign of terror, Recha
Sternbuch had taken great risks with little regard for her personal
safety while helping thousands of Jews in peril. But when her beloved
parents faced the same fate as had already claimed millions, she was
determined to save them. In her past rescue operations, she had
always been assisted by Christian allies. Paul Grüninger and Alexander
Lados were just two such gentiles whose assistance had proved invaluable. Nonetheless, the man Recha enlisted for the most important
rescue mission of all was a surprising choice.

Jean-Marie Musy was born in 1876 in the tiny village of Albeuve in
Fribourg, one of the seven Catholic *Sonderbund* cantons defeated in
a civil war against the Protestant-dominated central authority three
decades earlier. The Catholic character of the picturesque area—
located at the foot of the Bernese Alps—had survived the Reformation,
which saw much of the country turn to Protestantism. Today, the

region is dotted with churches and monasteries that attest to its long Catholic heritage. Having made their fortune in land development, Musy's relatives were prominent members of the Fribourgeois elite—a distinguished family whose aristocratic roots could be traced back to the pre-Napoleonic Ancien Régime. While his father was a simple innkeeper in Albeuve, it was his grandfather, Pierre-Joseph Musy—a prominent local politician—who would have the strongest influence on the young boy. Musy attended law school in Munich and Berlin and returned to Switzerland to practice law for nearly a decade. In 1912, he was persuaded to run for a seat in the cantonal government under the banner of the Conservative People's Party (PDC). Formerly called the Catholic People's Party, the PDC had removed the reference to religion from its name but not its platform, which was dedicated to preserving a "Christian world view."

In 1919, Musy was elected to the Federal Council, which became a launching pad for his long career in Swiss politics as the standard-bearer of the conservative Catholic right. As a councillor, Musy quickly demonstrated a particular proficiency for economic matters and was eventually appointed chairman of the federal finance department. He imposed austerity measures that helped stabilize the country's finances while ingratiating himself with the powerful banking industry by blocking legislation that would have regulated Swiss banks.[24] This helped vault him to the presidency of the Federal Council for the first time in 1925. Briefly toppled by the council four years later, he regained the post in 1930, before stepping down for the last time in 1934.

As president, Musy often described himself as a centrist. Toward the end of his tenure, however, he became increasingly more preoccupied with the perceived threat of Bolshevism posed by the Soviet Union. Although he had been raised Catholic, it was his wife's family who were considerably more devout. The father of Marie-Thérèse had served many years in the pope's Swiss Guard and was eventually named a papal count—a connection that gave Jean-Marie direct access to the Vatican.[25] Growing increasingly devout himself, he had watched as Stalin cracked down on the Russian Orthodox Church. Declaring war on most religious groups, the Soviet dictator was particularly determined to wipe out any traces of the once powerful Russian Orthodox religion, along with Roman Catholicism. Thousands of clergy were killed or sent to labor camps. By 1926, only a year into Musy's presidency, not a single Roman Catholic bishop remained in the Soviet Union.[26]

As the Church became increasingly vitriolic in its attacks on Communism, so too did Musy perceive Bolshevism to be the greatest threat facing Europe. During most of his political career, the Swiss Social Democratic Party (SP)—whose members were considered moderate socialists—was among the most powerful in Swiss politics. Although the SP was never pro-Communist, Musy worked hard to keep its members out of government, apparently believing that the party was secretly aligned with the Soviets. When Musy helped usher in a social insurance system in 1925, he went to great lengths to stress that it was "social insurance, not socialist." To the left-wing press, he represented the most reactionary forces of Swiss society, and he would become their frequent target long after he stepped down from political office.

When he resigned the presidency in April 1934 to return to practicing law, the Nazis had been in power for just over a year. Although he had never shown any extreme tendencies during his years in federal politics, Musy's increasing use of anti-Communist rhetoric in the latter years of his presidency had drawn the attention of forces on the Christian right who sought a spokesperson for a "popular front" against Bolshevism. Among these were a number of figures strongly aligned with fascism, including Arthur Fonjallaz, the founder of the Swiss Fascist Federation. Fonjallaz had met Benito Mussolini in 1932 and become an ardent proponent of an Italian-style fascist system for Switzerland. Before that, he had headed a group called the Helvetic Action Against Secret Societies, which railed against the dangers of Freemasonry. Although Musy was never aligned with his movement, Fonjallaz invoked his name during a conference organized by the Swiss fascists in March 1934, a month before he stepped down as president. "The Federal Councillor Musy speaks the truth," Fonjallaz declared. "He is a brave man. He has predicted that if we continue to follow the same political course as we are today, it will lead us to catastrophe." In the same speech, Fonjallaz described Musy as a "prophet."[27]

Although Musy rebuffed calls to lead such extremist elements, his own words and actions betrayed a growing sympathy for radical anti-Communist ideas. And like many conservative Catholics at the time, he watched approvingly as Hitler and the Nazis publicly denounced the grave threat posed by Bolshevism.

Growing up in Fribourg, Musy would have frequently been exposed to a traditional religious form of anti-Semitism common in Catholic circles at the time, according to professor Daniel Sebastiani, whose 2004 doctoral thesis analyzed Musy's life and political career. But the attitudes common in the conservative Catholic environs at the time never embraced Hitler's racially based hatred of the Jewish people. Still, unlike most Swiss, Musy refused to reject Nazi ideals outright. "He didn't agree with all their ideas but the ardent anti-Semitism of the Nazis didn't pose an insurmountable problem for Musy," writes Sebastiani.[28]

The only evidence of anti-Semitism found in his numerous political papers and speeches is contained in a private letter to a friend Musy wrote in March 1934, in which he reveals that he has recently read the "famous" "Protocols of the Elders of Zion." "The world needs to be aware of the great dangers revealed by this book before it's too late," he warns.[29] Musy's papers also reveal that he was "sensitive" to the idea of a Freemason plot at a time when the Catholic Church was warning that the Freemasons, like the Communists, posed a significant threat to Christianity. Many of his prejudices, in fact, echo the Church's own during this period.

In 1933, Musy's son Pierre had married a woman with Jewish roots named Erna Mende, but it appears that her family had long since converted to Christianity and it's uncertain whether any members retained their ties to Judaism. Nevertheless, Germany's ambassador to Switzerland, Otto Kocher, would note Musy's Jewish family connection in an unfavorable report to Berlin in February 1941.[30] Musy had appeared on the Nazis' radar for the first time in 1934, when the socialist newspaper *Le Travail* described the Swiss politician as a "fascist." The Geneva-based German consul Wolfgang Krauel forwarded the clipping to Berlin.[31]

After leaving office, Musy returned to private practice, where he built up a sizable personal fortune. By the late 1930s, as his anti-Communist views became more pronounced, he appears to have become increasingly enamored of the National Socialist regime. His first direct link with the Nazis came in April 1937, when he encountered Heinrich Himmler for the first time. It was a meeting arranged by von Ribbentrop's Foreign Ministry, which had established a department to convert anti-Communist sentiments into pro-Nazi sympathies in a number of European countries, including Switzerland. Under these auspices, Musy had been invited to Germany as a guest of von Ribbentrop. There, he was introduced to the Reichsführer-SS, whose fierce anti-Communist principles he had long admired. As it turned out, the feeling was not at first mutual, according to a note written after the visit that was discovered in the archives of Emil Schumburg—the Reichsführer's Foreign Ministry liaison. It observed that Himmler didn't believe that Musy, as a former politician, could be of much use to Germany except as a "vehicle for anti-Communist propaganda."[32]

To this end, he was soon introduced to a Swiss medical student named Franz Riedweg—a fanatically pro-Nazi figure who, like Musy, considered Communism to be the greatest threat facing civilization. As a sixteen-year-old, he had joined the pan-European movement that called for a united, federal Europe under Christian leadership to combat the Communist threat. Hiring Riedweg as his personal secretary, Musy appears to have found a kindred spirit. Together, they founded an organization called Swiss National Action against Communism and organized a number of high profile Swiss rallies to combat the Boshevik menace.[33]

In 1938, Riedweg secured funding—likely from Nazi sources—to produce an anti-Communist propaganda film with Musy called *La Peste Rouge* (The Red Plague). Most of the production took place in Munich, bringing Musy to Germany several times that year to oversee the production. On one of these trips, he sought an audience with Hitler. Though no such meeting ever took place, Musy was invited in 1938 to hear Hitler speak at the Nazi Party Congress in Nuremberg, where he encountered a number of National Socialist dignitaries.

That same year, as he was being courted by the German regime, Musy hosted an Austrian woman well known in anti-Nazi circles. Following the Anschluss in March, Alwine Dollfuss had fled her country to Switzerland, where she was given refuge by Musy at his Fribourg estate. Alwine was the widow of Engelbert Dollfuss, the former Austrian chancellor who had been assassinated in 1934 during a failed coup by Austrian Nazis hoping to implement National Socialism in the country. Alwine would remain a guest at the estate until September, when a scandal erupted in Switzerland surrounding the Nazi affiliations of Musy's former secretary and political collaborator Riedweg, who had stayed behind in Germany and joined the SS. Madame Dollfuss quickly changed residence, later telling the French ambassador that she had no idea Musy was associated with such extreme elements. The Riedweg affair would help discredit the former president in the eyes of the Swiss public. "Are these individuals on the far right any better than the Moscow agents that Musy constantly denounces?" asked one editorial in the socialist press.[34]

Unlike Riedweg, however, Musy had never embraced Nazi ideology except insofar as it aligned with his own anti-Communist views. Not long after Hitler's troops marched into Poland, in fact, he appears to have soured somewhat in his admiration. According to the Swiss historian Georges André Chevallaz, Musy returned from one trip to Germany in 1940, reporting "unfavorable impressions" about the regime.[35]

While he may have changed his mind about the Nazis, his fears about the threat of a Bolshevik Europe had grown stronger than ever. In 1942, he purchased a magazine called Le Jeune Suisse—formerly the organ of the young Swiss Conservatives—and turned it into a fiercely anti-Communist mouthpiece. Its content never explicitly supported the Nazis or vilified Jews, but it frequently wrote of the "Asian Peril" (a term frequently used at the time to describe Soviet communism). "In Musy's Jeune Suisse, the Germans have a zealous ally," writes Sebastiani. "In the Jeune Suisse, German domination is never called into question."[36]

By early 1944, Musy had folded the magazine and returned to working full time at his law practice and as a director of the La Genevoise insurance company in Geneva. As early as the fall of 1942, a group of Genevan Jews had approached the former president to enlist his help in saving Dutch Jewry after mass deportations from the Netherlands began in July that year. At the time, he did not reject the appeal out of hand. In October, he traveled to Geneva to meet a man named D. April, who presented him with a list of Amsterdam Jews in imminent danger. Musy's wife, Marie-Thérèse, strongly urged him to get involved in the mission, but he declined. In his notes, he wrote that he didn't see the need to "take great risks" in order to save Jews.[37]

Eighteen months later, he appears to have reconsidered his stance. At the beginning of March 1944, a Swiss Jewish couple, the Loebs, came to see the former president at his Geneva office. They had recently learned that Mr. Loeb's sister, Rosalie, and her husband, René Bloch, had been interned in a French concentration camp. Loeb had been a longtime law client and his son had served in the same Swiss army cavalry regiment as Musy's son Pierre. Now, drawing on the personal relationship, the Loebs pleaded for the well-connected former politician to intercede on behalf of their family members. This time, Musy agreed to help.

In mid-March, he dispatched a letter to SS general Karl Oberg in Paris, requesting permission to visit. Oberg had been appointed by Himmler in 1942 as the SS leader responsible for Nazi-occupied France in preparation for the imminent deportation of French Jewry.[38] Since assuming the post, he had been responsible for the deportation and ultimate extermination of at least forty thousand Jews.

On April 12, Musy drove to Paris to see Oberg. When word spread in Switzerland that he had entered France using a diplomatic passport—accorded to him as a former president—one socialist newspaper complained that it was an "abuse" of the privilege. Had they known the purpose of his visit, the strongly anti-fascist journal would undoubtedly have approved. But Musy had told no one except his wife the reason for his journey. The mission was a success. Oberg's adjutant informed the Swiss emissary that his request had been approved and the Blochs would soon be released, but the process would take several days. Musy had to be back in Switzerland for a wedding, but he made plans to return, telling his son Luigi that he was determined to bring the couple out of the country personally to "make sure they were out of danger." Sure enough, on April 29, Musy crossed the Swiss border safely with the Blochs in his backseat. He later claimed that when plans were finalized, Karl Oberg told him, "Never before has an Israelite who entered a concentration camp come out again."[39]

When Daisy Thorel heard in July that Musy had accomplished the impossible feat of freeing Jews from a Nazi concentration camp, she wasted no time. It was her friend, the daughter of the Swiss tobacco magnate Maurice Burrus—a longtime acquaintance of Musy in Swiss social circles—who had heard the story of the Bloch intervention. Daisy's son Alain, a French Catholic, had been arrested by the Germans in October 1942, allegedly for political activities, and held in a number of concentration camps. Despite his mother's repeated pleas, the Germans had refused to release him. Now, Daisy became convinced that Musy was her last hope.[40]

In July, Musy once again wrote Karl Oberg asking for a meeting. It's uncertain whether he received a reply, but the Allies had landed in Normandy weeks earlier. The liberation of France was now at hand. Paris would be free on August 25, but the same couldn't be said for Alain Thorel, who, like many French prisoners, had already been transferred to a concentration camp inside Germany. Musy refused to give up. It has never been clear why Musy was so motivated to free the young Thorel. It's possible that the tobacco heiress who had brought him together with Daisy was paying him for his services, but the only record of payment was a transfer of 10,000 Swiss francs— approximately U.S. $2300—apparently to cover expenses. This appears an insignificant sum for a man as wealthy as Musy.

Daisy Thorel wasn't alone in hearing of Musy's accomplishment. Word had traveled quickly throughout Switzerland following the liberation of the Blochs. Among those who heard the story was Louise Bolomey, the widow of a distinguished Swiss colonel. A devout Catholic, Bolomey knew Musy well from Church circles. Mrs. Bolomey had been introduced to Recha Sternbuch a year earlier by the papal nuncio, Filippo Bernardini, who had been working closely with the Sternbuch Rescue Committee.

On the evening of October 10, 1944, the widow called on her old acquaintance. "This lady told me she was in touch with a woman who was very much concerned about the fate of the Jews in camps in Germany," Musy later recalled, "and knowing that I had effected the release of people begged me to meet her friend, Mrs. Sternbuch. I finally agreed and Mr. and Mrs. Sternbuch came."[41] Interrogated by U.S. military authorities after the war, Musy gave the date of this meeting as the middle of October. The Swiss authorities were still tapping the Sternbuchs' phone, and their records show that Recha and Musy talked for the first time on October 15. Meanwhile, Alain Thorel had been transferred to Germany and Karl Oberg could no longer be of any assistance. Musy had instead decided to contact the only man he knew with the power to release an inmate of a concentration camp inside Germany. As it happened, he had already written to Heinrich Himmler requesting a meeting to discuss the Thorel case. He was still awaiting a reply.

Time was running out for the Jews of Europe. The Sternbuchs knew from Mrs. Bolomey of Musy's devout Catholic beliefs. Now, as they met at his Fribourg estate, they implored the Swiss fascist to summon his faith on behalf of their people. "We are both servants of God," Recha told him. "The Nazis are an affront to every one of your religious beliefs. You must help us." Her plea evidently achieved its desired effect. Musy agreed that he would take up the cause of the

Jewish people when he met with Himmler. Reuben Hecht had joined HIJEFS only a few months earlier after being introduced to the Sternbuchs by Sam Woods, the American consul general in Geneva who had developed a close relationship with the rescue committee. Hecht, a revisionist Zionist, was the only member of the Sternbuch committee who wasn't an Orthodox Jew. Like Recha, he was originally from Antwerp and the two had developed a close bond. He claims that the group was initially skeptical when Recha announced that Musy had agreed to the improbable mission, but it didn't take her long to convince them.

"The committee came to the realization that a person had to be obtained who could acquire Himmler's confidence and needed not fear retribution," Hecht later recalled. "It was impossible to find any Christian international personality who was ready to intervene for the benefit of the Jews with the National Socialist regime. This had to be a man who would intervene, who could influence, who would take it upon himself the risk of life in the many journeys involved. Musy was considered towards the end of the war as a very conservative politician, reactionary and Catholic. He was also a strong opponent of Communism in Europe. Therefore, we were convinced he was the suitable man who could be received by Himmler and gain his confidence."[42]

Musy later described his first meeting with Recha: "This Mrs. Sternbuch had her father and mother, and brothers and sister. She was particularly interested in seeing her father and mother again. The parents had been at Drancy and later at Vittel."[43] When Musy mentioned that he had already written Himmler requesting a meeting about the Thorel matter, Recha could not contain her excitement. Through the German legation in Bern, Musy soon received word that the Reichsführer-SS was prepared to receive him. When the committee learned that the former Swiss president was preparing to meet the man reputedly in charge of the extermination of their people, they thought immediately of the fate of the Vittel passport Jews. The U.S. Army had liberated Vittel on September 10, but the Germans had already transferred the important inmates to Germany ahead of the Allied arrival—presumably to be used in a future exchange. More than 2300 passport Jews had once resided at Vittel, but there was no way of knowing their identities or how many had already been sent from Drancy to Auschwitz.

For now, the committee's goals were modest. They implored Musy to intervene to free 216 members of the Vittel contingent who reportedly had been deported from Drancy to "an unknown site in Germany or in a German-occupied region." On October 18, Recha offered, on behalf of HIJEFS, 1 million francs to be put at Musy's disposal to rescue "216 Israelites." A cheque was supplied on the committee's bank account for 500,000 francs, representing half the amount. Some believe that this agreement proves that Musy embarked on his mission for monetary gain, but it is clear that the funds were to be used for bribes if needed, an assertion confirmed by HIJEFS's secretary, Hermann Landau, after the war.[44] The agreement did contain a provision for Musy to be paid if he succeeded in his mission, but it was a modest amount—a mere 30,000 francs, and would be paid only when the Jews were safely over the border in Switzerland. The committee also agreed to supply 60,000 Swiss francs for expenses.

With this amount, Musy purchased a new Mercedes for the journey. By the autumn of 1944, Allied bombers were unleashing their deadly cargoes over Germany almost unchallenged. Particularly hard hit was Berlin, where Musy had been scheduled to meet Himmler. Well aware of the risks, he made one last purchase before embarking on the trip. With the expenses supplied by the Sternbuchs, he acquired a sizable life insurance policy for himself and his twenty-six-year-old son, Benoît, who was to accompany him.

On October 23, Musy crossed the Swiss–German border at Konstanz with Benoît at the wheel. Days earlier, HIJEFS had informed the Vaad that there was an important opportunity for rescue and let them know that they had used Vaad funds for the operation. After a brief stop-off in Munich, the pair arrived in Berlin on November 1—All Saints Day—where they had been instructed to report to a building next to the offices of the German Red Cross. It was here that Musy met SS brigadier general Walter Schellenberg for the first time and detailed the purpose of his trip. The intelligence chief immediately pledged his complete support. He informed the pair that Himmler would be ready to meet them within a few days.

In a written report to the Sternbuch committee, Musy described in detail what happened next. On November 3, a knock came on the door of their hotel room. A messenger escorted them outside, where Schellenberg waited in an SS staff car. They were to drive to Breslau, where they would meet up with the Reichsführer's train. Recalling the Swiss statesman's visit in his postwar memoirs, Schellenberg wrote that he was "an utterly selfless man." He had hoped that Musy "might exercise a beneficial influence on Himmler."[45]

Shortly past midnight, they reached their destination: Himmler's mobile headquarters, a nine-car train known as Sonderzug *Steiermark*—code-named "Heinrich" by the Germans—which came equipped with sophisticated communication facilities. When they arrived, the train was stationed in a tunnel to evade Allied aircraft. After they boarded, Schellenberg left the father and son in a lounge compartment and told them to wait. The train started up again, bound for Vienna. At 4 a.m., Schellenberg reemerged and the two Swiss emissaries were brought to a private car, where Himmler sat behind a desk drinking tea. Warmly, he greeted his old comrade, whom he hadn't seen in more than three years.[46] Musy introduced his son, and a steward brought glasses and poured from a bottle of fine French cognac.

Schellenberg finally broke the ice: "President Musy has a very interesting proposal, Reichsführer." He and Benoît then left the two men alone to talk. The Swiss emissary outlined his mission. He had come at the request of "Chief Rabbi Sternbuch." Recha had sent him on this mission to press for the release of the Vittel Jews, including her family. But at some point Musy had apparently made the decision to ask for more, reporting later, "I asked Himmler to liberate Thorel and all the Jews who were confined in concentration camps for religious reasons. Not just Mrs. Sternbuch's relatives."[47] He told the Reichsführer that he was offering Germany the chance to make a great "humanitarian gesture" and turn world opinion in its favor. He asked Himmler what it would take to free all the Jews. There was a note of bemusement in Himmler's reply: "You have quite the task, Herr Musy. Do you think the Jews will ever thank you for this?"[48]

There are any number of theories as to why Musy had decided to expand beyond the scope of his original mission. Some have claimed he was attempting to "redeem" his reputation or gain a "political alibi" now that it was obvious that the Nazis had lost the war. "Those who knew him well in this period assert that, despite his anti-Semitism, Musy was truly appalled at the German extermination of the Jews and also was troubled as a devout Catholic by fear of hell," writes historian Paul Lawrence Rose. "It seems psychologically plausible, however, that Musy was moved by all these motives simultaneously."[49]

Himmler was not at first inclined to grant the request, but the skilled lawyer and veteran politician patiently explained the reasons why such a move was in the best interests of Germany. "You will not win the war," Musy told him bluntly. And the killing of Jews was not in fact in the National Socialist platform. Germany should, therefore, have no objections to getting rid of them. "I told him that there was an American organization which would be willing to assist in the transportation," he later testified.[50] To his surprise, after a two-hour conversation, Himmler claimed that he was ready to accede to Musy's request and liberate the Jews, even to transport and feed them as far as the border. In exchange, however, the Germans would require "material compensation." He explained the Reich's desperate shortage of trucks, machinery and tractors. Himmler would be willing to free the remaining Jews "without need of Hitler's approval" if these materials could be supplied in return.

"Unfortunately," Himmler added, almost as an afterthought, "many of the Jews have been working too hard in the labour camps and there are only 600,000–800,000 left."[51] Musy was by then all too aware of the Final Solution and understood that Himmler's cryptic reference meant that hundreds of thousands of Jews had been murdered in only a few short months. The imperative of his mission was driven home. He knew too from the Sternbuchs of the failed results the last time Himmler had proposed such a ransom and was anxious not to go down this futile road again. In his report, Musy writes, "After he proposed the ransom, I told him, 'You know the Allies have strictly forbidden any such deal. Let's not waste our time discussing fantasy. Don't be a meat peddler, Heinrich.'"

Himmler was not easily dissuaded. He insisted that the Jews controlled Roosevelt and had only to whisper in his ear to make the deal happen. Musy countered by arguing that any such deal would have to be approved by Stalin, and he would never agree. "I pointed out to him . . . that it would probably be easier to secure money as Sternbuch had mentioned the possibility of obtaining large sums. Himmler did not wish to entirely abandon the idea of compensation in goods and asked me to try for that, but if I was not successful, that a compromise might be effected on the subject of foreign exchange. He said they would start immediately with the liberation of Jews."[52]

As Musy left Himmler's private railway car to rejoin Schellenberg and Benoît for the remainder of the journey to Vienna, one distinct impression of the Reichsführer remained. "His tone was that he had had enough of the entire Jewish question and that they can have them all," he recalled.[53]

FOURTEEN

FALL OF THE KILLING MACHINE

On the morning of November 25, 1944—only twenty-two days after Musy's meeting with Himmler—Auschwitz-Birkenau prisoners in close proximity to the building known as Crematorium II heard a deafening explosion as the gas chambers and furnace came crashing down. Not long afterwards, Crematorium III suffered the same fate.[1] Most prisoners in the vicinity of the blasts assumed the notorious murder machinery had been felled by the camp resistance movement. Each silently cheered. Only six weeks earlier, Crematorium IV had been burned down by female members of the Sonderkommando—inmates forced to work in the crematoria who had recently learned that their own liquidation was imminent.[2] The resistance had become increasingly emboldened since the escape of Vrba and Wetzler in April. After the rapid extermination of more than three hundred thousand Hungarian Jews, prisoners no longer held out even the faintest hope of survival. There was nothing left to lose.

The deadliest killing apparatus in history, however, had not been brought down by sabotage, but rather by the decree of the architect of genocide who had ordered its construction three years earlier. It was, in fact, Heinrich Himmler who had issued the order to dismantle the machinery in Birkenau that had snuffed the life of more than a million helpless victims since 1942. More than seventy years later, his motive remained an unsolved historical mystery.

Now, new evidence has emerged that may help historians map a clearer picture of events. The trail leads directly back to the Sternbuchs' dining room table in Montreux, where a small group of pious Jews led by a thirty-nine-year-old woman heeded the Old Testament passage, "Who will rise up for me against the evildoers?"

The long-overlooked clue leading to Himmler's Auschwitz decree begins shortly after Rezső Kasztner's train departed from Hungary, with its 1684 passengers on board believing they were on a journey to freedom from Nazi tyranny. The train reached Bergen-Belsen on July 8, only a day after Admiral Horthy had ordered a halt to any further death camp deportations. Soon, an array of factions emerged among the Jewish leadership inside and outside Hungary. Relieved that the transports had been halted, nobody yet knew whether the reprieve was merely temporary. The fate of nearly two hundred thousand Jews remaining in Budapest was still uncertain.

Ten days after he ordered a halt to the deportations, Horthy showed that he had apparently received the recent Allied message loud and clear when Roosevelt warned that the regime would be considered complicit in the extermination of the Hungarian Jews. It was likely this pressure that prompted an unexpected proposal since dubbed the "Horthy offer."[3] In mid-July, the regent offered to allow certain categories of Jews to emigrate to Palestine. A thousand orphans and 8243 families holding Palestinian emigration certificates would be permitted to leave. The inclusion of families swelled the total numbers to 40,000 potential emigrants. After much hand-wringing, Britain finally agreed to relax its restrictions on Jewish emigration to Palestine while Sweden and Switzerland also agreed to take in a number of Hungarian Jews.[4] Horthy indicated at the time that he had received permission from the Germans to allow the emigrations. But this was misleading. Eichmann argued forcefully with the regime against the emigration plan. Aware that he was constrained by so-called Hungarian sovereignty, he none-theless succeeded in delaying the transit visas. Mindful of Germany's commitment to the Mufti, Eichmann—the man who had once claimed to sympathize with Zionism—argued against allowing any of the Jews to emigrate to Palestine.

Finally, Ribbentrop made Germany's position clear. The emigra-tions would be permitted to proceed, but only if deportations were allowed to resume at the same time.[5] When Horthy resisted, Hitler himself intervened, making clear his displeasure in a letter to the regent on July 17: "The Führer expects that the measures against the Budapest Jews will now be carried out without any further delay by the Hungarian government." Nonetheless, Hitler gave permission for the "exceptions" conceded by Germany, presumably the emigration terms of the Horthy offer.

Kasztner was likely unaware of the standoff between the Germans and the Hungarians, but he was acutely conscious of the precarious situation of the remaining Jews of Budapest. He was anxious to resume the ransom negotiations that had at first appeared to have great promise with the departure of his train on July 1. He had so far received no satisfactory explanation as to why its passengers were stranded in Bergen-Belsen. On August 12, he reached out to the Germans once again and let it be known that he was ready to resume negotiations. His chief goal, it would appear, was to preserve the safety of Budapest Jewry even above the onward journey of his train.

When Kasztner asked Kurt Becher for an assurance that same day that the capital's Jews would not be deported, the wily SS officer's reply was worrisome: "Until we finish our talks, there will be peace in the city. If the talks have a negative outcome, the situation in the city could turn critical."[6] The threat was ominous, but it also held out some promise. It meant that ransom was still on the table. Aware that he had few bargaining chips, Kasztner turned to the one man who he believed had the means and ability to strike a deal: Saly Mayer.

For Kasztner, Saly Mayer was the ideal candidate to carry on the talks that he and Brand had initiated in May. For one thing, he knew that the Nazis regarded the Joint Distribution Committee as an embodiment of the world Jewish conspiracy. And just as importantly, the JDC had an unlimited pipeline of funds from America—or so Kasztner believed—which was essential to meeting German ransom demands. There is no question that Mayer had significantly more funds at his disposal than he had two years earlier when Gisi Fleischmann and her Bratislava Working Group had issued a desperate plea for bribe money to halt the Slovakian deportations.

News about the fate of Hungarian Jewry had finally woken people up to the horrors of the Nazi inferno, though most still had not grasped the severity of the situation. Despite thousands of articles in American newspapers about the liquidation of European Jewry over the preceding two years—including reports after the Vrba-Wetzler escape that more than one million Jews had died at Auschwitz—a Gallup poll in November 1944 showed that most Americans had failed to grasp the extent of Nazi atrocities. Seventy-six percent of those surveyed now believed that the Germans had murdered "many people in concentration camps." But according to Gallup, a plurality of these respondents—36 percent—believed that the number of those killed totaled only 100,000.[7] Still, millions of dollars poured into the JDC coffers—mostly from American Jews desperate to help their European brethren. In 1944 alone, Mayer was allocated

$6,467,000 for his work—more than he had received in the previous war years combined.[8] Yet despite the increased funds at his disposal, his hands were still tied by frustrating currency restrictions that imposed strict quotas on the conversion of Swiss francs.

As the WRB representative in Switzerland, Roswell McClelland had been designated to oversee Mayer's activities. This, too, presented a number of obstacles. The American's instructions from Washington had been clear. While the State Department was now committed to relieving the desperate plight of Hungarian Jewry, McClelland was forbidden to authorize "ransom transactions of the nature indicated by the German authorities."[9] Moreover, the Americans had no problem with Mayer negotiating with Nazi officials, provided that he participated as a "Swiss citizen and leader of the Jewish community, and not as a representative of any American organization."[10] The goal of his negotiations, it was made clear, should be "gaining time" and nothing more. These restrictions represented a significant about-face from a memo forwarded to the State Department from McClelland in early July. Discussing the "trucks for blood" proposal, he wrote, "It is difficult to predict whether such ransom proposition will produce practical results. It can only be hoped that something will come of it."[11]

Since then, the Allied governments' attitude toward ransom negotiations had abruptly changed. On July 20, 1944, the British press had got wind of the Brand negotiations and the "cold-blooded" German offer to "spare lives of remaining Jews in Hungary in exchange for war materials, including 10,000 trucks not to be used on the western front." A slew of articles condemned the "fantastically macabre" proposal, calling it "monstrous" and describing it as "blackmail." The diplomatic correspondent for *The Times* (London) described the offer as one of "the most loathsome stories of the war." Only the defeat of Germany would provide security for Jews and other oppressed peoples, he wrote, noting that the offer seemed to be "simply a fantastic attempt to sow suspicion among the Allies."[12]

Not surprisingly, the Russians had been shocked at the Germans' naked attempt to divide the Allied nations, and they immediately demanded assurance that England and the United States would not betray the alliance. Both Roosevelt and Churchill were acutely aware that Russia's formidable military machine was indispensable to the war effort. Neither leader had any intention of betraying Stalin. The media revelations about the Brand negotiations had likely killed any hope for such a ransom. The Russians would never abide such negotiations.

In response to the Brand proposal, the British Foreign Office issued strict instructions to its diplomatic personnel. "It is essential, especially in the interests of our relations with Moscow, that no suspicions should be aroused that Allied persons are negotiating with the enemy."[13] Now, every step of the way, the State Department would go to great lengths to keep the Russians apprised of the negotiations while assuring them that no ransom would ever be paid to the Nazis.[14]

On August 29, 1944, Slovakian partisans and resistance organizations—emboldened by approaching Soviet troops—staged a national uprising against the Tiso government. Unwilling to give up Slovakia just yet, German troops moved in to quell the rebellion. Among their first orders of business was finishing the roundup of Jews that had been halted two years earlier after the "Willy bribe." This time, the Working Group was helpless to prevent the swift deportations of most of the country's remaining Jewish population. As Einsatzgruppe A swept in, 12,600 Jews were deported to Auschwitz and other camps in the space of a few days. Among those deported were most members of the original Working Group, including Rabbi Weissmandl, whose entire family was rounded up. On the train to Auschwitz,

Weissmandl used a wire hidden in a loaf of bread to saw through a lock.[15] Jumping to the tracks, and leaving his family behind, he managed to find his way back to Bratislava, where he hid in a bunker until he could eventually be smuggled safely to Switzerland, reportedly with the help of Rezső Kasztner.

Arrested in October by the SS, Gisi Fleischmann was taken to the Sered labor camp, where she was offered the opportunity of freedom in exchange for the names and locations of Slovakian Jews, including Weissmandl, who had gone into hiding. When she refused to cooperate, the formidable underground leader was sent on the very last transport from Slovakia to Auschwitz with a notation beside her name, "*Rückerr unerwünscht*" ("Return Undesirable"). In the files of Saly Mayer's archive at the JDC offices in New York, there remains a poignant letter he sent to Gisi in February 1945 filling her in on the latest developments.[16] Unbeknownst to him, she had become one of the last Jews exterminated at Auschwitz four months earlier.

On Sunday, August 20, Saly Mayer met up with three SS representatives and Kasztner at the Swiss–Austrian border town of St. Margarethen.[17] Mayer would later name this group "Arba"—the Hebrew word for the number four. They were originally to have met in Switzerland, but the Swiss refused to allow border passes for the Germans to enter.[18] For his part, Mayer couldn't bring himself to enter the Reich. As a compromise, the men literally met halfway, on the bridge spanning the two countries. Kasztner was present, as was his SS negotiator, Kurt Becher. Eichmann's man, Hermann Krumey, and Hauptsturmbannführer Max Grüson also participated. There, the SS men took up where the "blood for trucks" proposal had left off months earlier, demanding 10,000 trucks. In exchange, the Germans promised to release not just the Hungarian Jews but all Jews still held in German camps, a number they estimated at one million. The Jews would be permitted to leave for America or any other country with the exception of Palestine. The Germans suggested they could leave on the same ships that delivered the 10,000 trucks.

As a "goodwill gesture," the SS negotiators had arranged for 318 of Kasztner's original 1684 passengers to be brought from Bergen-Belsen to the Swiss border, where they would be permitted to leave Germany. This group ranged in age from two to eighty-two and included several rabbis. The Germans also promised that two hundred more passengers would be delivered within forty-eight hours, but those people never arrived.[19]

Hearing the Arba offer, Mayer was unequivocal. Such a ransom proposal, he declared, would almost certainly be met with a categorical refusal by the United States, which would never consent to the delivery of war material to be used against an Allied country. Another "formula" would have to be found, he informed the negotiators. Mayer requested ten days' "breathing space" before the group met again. Kasztner remained behind to brief him about the latest developments from inside Hungary.

From there, he painted a complex picture of three competing circles. One extreme faction of the Gestapo (dubbed Group C) was impatient to continue extermination and had wanted to resume deportations as early as August 19. This group, which he said represented "Hitler's attitude," wanted to liquidate the Jews even if Germany lost the war. The Hungarian regime was either powerless to act or indifferent to the plight of the Jews, he explained. This group would permit no emigration whatsoever. Himmler's faction (Group B), whose attitude toward the Jewish Question was "indifferent," represented a middle course, he explained. This group didn't oppose the release of Jews, especially if they could be used to obtain goods of value to the Reich in exchange. Meanwhile, a third faction (Group A) believed extermination as a policy was undesirable. However, it was unclear to Kasztner how large or influential this last group was.[20]

Additional meetings took place in early September, but Mayer knew his hands were tied. He had been explicitly forbidden to offer anything to the Germans. By September 16, McClelland reported, the negotiations were "exceedingly difficult and trying" because Mayer could do nothing more than tell the Germans that he needed to refer their demands to "higher quarters" and await an answer. "My personal opinion, and that of SM also, is that all time possible has now been gained and that in all probability the Gestapo has lost patience," he cabled.[21] Meanwhile, Mayer was instructed to "stall and bluff" as long as possible.

On October 15, while Russian troops massed at the Hungarian border, Admiral Horthy publicly declared that Hungary was withdrawing from the Axis. Days earlier, he had dispatched a delegation to Moscow to negotiate a surrender. As in Slovakia two months earlier, however, the Germans had unfinished business. Hitler refused to allow Hungary to fall into the hands of the enemy just yet. Horthy's son was taken hostage and spirited to Germany, leaving the regent little choice but to accede to the Führer's demands and offer his resignation.

This set the stage for a takeover by the ultra-nationalist Arrow Cross Party, led by Ferenc Szálasi, who had strongly embraced the Nazis' ideology of racial purity and anti-Semitism. Within hours, Szálasi's forces embarked on a murderous rampage against its political enemies. Roving death squads roamed the streets wreaking havoc, killing and torturing thousands. Arrow Cross thugs immediately targeted the Jews of Budapest, even storming Jewish hospitals and shooting patients in their beds. Less than seventy-two hours after Szálasi assumed power, the capital witnessed the return of a familiar figure. Adolf Eichmann's entrance into the city on October 18 sent an ominous signal to the Jews of Budapest, who feared their time had finally come. Members of the Arrow Cross were loudly urging Szálasi to resume the deportations.

As it turned out, Eichmann hadn't in fact arrived to complete the job he had been reluctantly forced to abandon three months earlier. Instead, he had orders to round up a significant number of Jews to be used as slave labor for the German war effort, especially in the construction of underground facilities producing fighters and V-2 rockets. Also desperately needed were workers to construct a southeastern wall—fortifications designed to stop the advance of the Red Army.[22] Szálasi agreed to hand over only fifty thousand workers. Meanwhile, the new regime ordered the establishment of a Jewish ghetto, though its boundaries and restrictions were much less severe than the ghettos established by the Nazis in Poland before the Final Solution.

In early November, thousands of Jews were gathered for the long trek to the Austrian border, where they would be handed over to the SS for transportation to various labor camps. As the Jews were being marched out of the city, recalled Hansi Brand, many Hungarians looked on "dully." She described those as the "better ones." Many others, she claimed, were pleased, especially those who had been driven out of their homes by Allied bombing, because they were now going to have "nice Jewish flats."[23]

It was the Hungarian forced marches of November 1944 that would soon vault to prominence a Swedish businessman turned diplomat named Raoul Wallenberg. Recruited by the War Refugee Board and assigned to Hungary by the Swedish Foreign Ministry, the thirty-two-year-old Wallenberg had arrived in the capital shortly after the deportations were halted in July, with 650 passports designated for rescue. In the months that followed, he would issue thousands of protective letters in the name of the Swedish government. These exempted their holders from forced labor and excused them from wearing the yellow star after the Budapest ghettos were established. When the forced marches began in November, the balding diplomat could often be seen driving alongside the road delivering food and medicine to the exhausted Jews. After he discovered that the Arrow Cross authorities were willing to recognize Swedish protective papers, he used the documents to extract hundreds from the marches and return them to the capital under Swedish protection. With funding from the WRB, he also ran a network of safe houses to shelter Jews. Those actions created his reputation as one of the heroes of the Holocaust. It's a story made all the more poignant by his mysterious arrest and lifelong imprisonment by Soviet forces following liberation. Less known to history but arguably as important in saving Hungarian Jews is the role of Carl Lutz, the Swiss vice-consul in Budapest who issued protective papers to thousands of Hungarian Jewish children and families.

Budapest would not fall to the Red Army until February 13, but the forced marches were brought to a sudden and unexplained halt at the end of November, only hours after the Auschwitz gas chambers were felled. The timing likely wasn't coincidental.

FIFTEEN

FORTY TRACTORS

History books have recorded November 25 as the date Himmler ordered the destruction of the Auschwitz murder apparatus, shortly after he decreed an end to the mass exterminations.[1] Most claim the decision was prompted by the Nazis' desire to destroy evidence of the Final Solution before the arrival of the advancing Red Army. This is certainly a logical conclusion. New evidence, however, points to a different explanation, tracing the order directly back to a massive deception formulated months earlier and successfully designed and executed to set Himmler against the agenda of his beloved Führer.

The Nazis unquestionably had a long history of attempting to cover up their crimes. In the hours before Soviet forces liberated the Majdanek death camp in July 1944, SS guards dismantled and burned down the crematorium.[2] Similarly, the Germans dismantled the Treblinka, Bełżec and Sobibór killing centers in 1943 after liquidating most of Polish Jewry at these camps.[3] As early as 1942, Reinhard Heydrich had initiated Aktion 1005—an operation designed to hide and destroy evidence of the mass killings perpetrated by the Einsatzgruppen in the Soviet Union along with the earliest death camp exterminations.[4] It's hardly surprising, then, that the Germans would be anxious to conceal the largest killing operation of them all. But on November 25, the Red Army was still at least two months away. When the Soviets liberated Auschwitz on January 27, 1945, the majority of the inmates—almost 60,000 mostly Jewish prisoners—had already been evacuated from the complex and forced to march to Wodsislaw in upper Silesia, from there to be taken to Germany by train. Yet some 7650 inmates—those who were too sick to march—were left behind to greet the liberators and furnish eyewitness accounts of the unprecedented evil that had taken place inside the facility since 1942.[5]

At a 1974 Yad Vashem Institute symposium focusing on Holocaust rescue attempts, the respected Israeli historian Yehuda Bauer took issue with the conventional narrative that Himmler halted the exterminations and destroyed the killing apparatus merely to cover up his monstrous crimes. "There are those who claim that the order was the result of the advance of the Soviets and Americans, etc., but it can also be assumed that the advance of these forces might have led to exactly the opposite result, i.e., it could have hastened the extermination process," Bauer told the gathering.[6] Indeed, the Nazis could have easily murdered all the remaining survivors if the intention was simply to hide the evidence of their crimes. But the decision to destroy the extermination machinery wasn't the only order Himmler had given that month. Less attention is paid to another directive.

Kurt Becher, the SS officer who had played a key role in the Kasztner negotiations, successfully evaded prosecution for war crimes after the war. Instead, the prosecution called Becher as a witness in its case against Himmler's notorious security chief, Ernst Kaltenbrunner. Before the trial got under way, he issued an affidavit with historic implications, declaring, "Between the middle of September and the middle of October 1944, I caused the Reichsführer SS Himmler to issue the following order, which I received in two originals, one each for SS Obergruppenfuehrer Kaltenbrunner and Pohl, and a copy for myself: 'By this order, which becomes immediately effective, I forbid any extermination of Jews and order that, on the contrary, care should be given to weak and sick persons. I hold you'—and here Kaltenbrunner and Pohl were meant—'personally responsible even if this order should not be strictly adhered to by subordinate officers.'"[7]

Becher claims he personally took the order to both Kaltenbrunner in Berlin and to Oswald Pohl, who had administered the concentration camp bureaucracy since 1935. In a sworn statement he gave during Eichmann's war crimes trial in 1961, Becher also described a conversation that he claims took place between Himmler and Eichmann at which he was present. Before this meeting, Becher had suggested to Himmler that Eichmann was attempting to circumvent the previous order to halt the killing of Jews. Becher testified, "I remember one thing that Himmler said to Eichmann in this connection. He shouted at him something like: 'If until now you have exterminated Jews, from now on, if I order you, as I do now, you must now be a fosterer of Jews. I would remind you that in 1933 it was I who set up the Head Office for Reich Security, and not Gruppenfuehrer Mueller or yourself, and that I am in command. If you are not able to do that, you must tell me so!'"[8]

The existence of that directive was corroborated by Dieter Wisliceny, who was convicted of war crimes in Czechoslovakia and hanged in 1948. Two years earlier, he had served as a key witness at the Nuremberg trials of major Nazi war criminals, testifying in detail about the evolution of the Final Solution. In an affidavit sworn in November 1946, he also confirmed the existence of a directive from the Reichsführer-SS: "Late in 1944, Himmler directed that all executions of Jews were to cease, but Eichmann did not carry out this order until he received a written directive signed by Himmler."[9] Finally, at his own Nuremberg trial in 1946, Kaltenbrunner himself confirmed the existence of such an order: "It is clear to me that Himmler gave such an order to Pohl as the person responsible for those concentration camps in which Jews were kept."[10] Of course, we must always be skeptical about the postwar testimony of Nazis, but there was another witness to this alleged decree. According to Rezső Kasztner, Becher showed him a written order from Himmler on November 27, dated two days earlier, prohibiting the "further killing of Jews."[11]

Sigmund Sobolewski—known as Prisoner 88—had arrived in Auschwitz on the very first transport in June 1940 and was the eighty-eighth inmate to enter the camp. A Polish Catholic, Sobolewski remained in the camp until early 1945 and was assigned for much of this time to the Auschwitz Fire Brigade, a unit made up of approximately twenty-five inmates. Having witnessed the destruction of Crematorium IV by female inmates of the Sonderkommando in October 1944, he and the brigade were tasked with putting out the ensuing fire. Six weeks later, they were called on again to clean up the rubble from Crematorium II— the largest of the Birkenau murder apparatus—after the Nazis ordered it destroyed. Sobolewski—who lives in Alberta and was ninety-three years old in 2016—did not witness the complex come down but believes that the Nazis dismantled the underground gas chambers by hand and then used dynamite to bring down the ovens and chimney of the crematorium. Crematorium III suffered a similar fate soon afterwards. "After they destroyed the two buildings, there was still one crematorium operating that the Germans used to dispose of prisoners who died of disease, but it often didn't work so they would bury the bodies in a field a kilometer away," he recalls.[12]

Doctor Igor Bartosik, senior curator of the Auschwitz-Birkenau Museum and Memorial, confirms that the apparatuses of the two buildings were destroyed in November when the exterminations came to a halt. He believes they were dismantled at night by Wehrmacht "sappers" (military engineers). "It is true they dismantled ovens, engines for ventilation and other equipment. Even roofs and chimneys," he explains. The mass exterminations, he confirms, ended, but Bartosik cites evidence that a number of inmates were shot by the German guards after this date in Block 11—the complex at the main camp of Auschwitz 1 where prisoners were punished or tortured for suspected sabotage or escape attempts.[13] Many histories have inaccurately claimed that the Germans destroyed Crematoria II and III as they were fleeing the camp in January, but Bartosik notes that the fleeing Nazis only destroyed Crematorium V—the building used to burn prisoners who died or were shot after the exterminations ceased November 1944. He explains that Wehrmacht "sappers" destroyed this complex on the night of January 25–26, 1945.[14]

There can be little doubt that Himmler halted the exterminations and ordered the destruction of the murder apparatuses late in 1944. The question that remains is, why? Historian Paul Lawrence Rose believes Himmler's decision may have been connected to his recent talks with Jean-Marie Musy, with whom he had met three weeks earlier and to whom he had reportedly promised to begin the liberation of the Jews. At the 1974 Yad Vashem symposium on rescue, Yehuda Bauer notes that Himmler's order to stop the Hungarian death marches came at the same time as the "cessation of the extermination." He believes this order was "in some way connected with the negotiations which were being conducted."[15] At the time, this was merely speculation. Now, evidence has emerged that suggests that the termination of the Final Solution in November 1944 was almost certainly linked to those negotiations.

———

The momentous sequence of events leading to the end of the Auschwitz extermination operation begins during the mass confusion following the departure of the Kasztner train on July 1, 1944. Even before the transport had reached its destination, a rumor had begun to spread through the Hungarian and Slovakian Jewish communities that a train carrying 1200 rabbis was on its way to a German death camp in Poland.

The train had passed through Bratislava on July 6, where a source had talked to Rabbi Teitelbaum of Satmar, a member of the convoy. The Rabbi "wept a great deal and asked that people in Switzerland be informed." He revealed that the passengers had been en route for six days and that it was rumored they were on their way to Vienna where they would stay fourteen days before being taken to Spain in an exchange for war prisoners. For some, the news that the eminent Satmar Rebbe was endangered would have been enough on its own to warrant a major rescue operation.

The news caused immediate panic in Orthodox circles, not least in Montreux, where the Sternbuchs and their committee wasted no time. They had few details other than the presence of 1200 rabbis and other religious leaders. Could this contingent be the last surviving remnants of the leadership of European Orthodox Jewry?

There followed two weeks of frantic cables between Switzerland and New York. On July 7, a day after the Satmar Rebbe was spotted on the train, Philip Freudiger had cabled the Sternbuchs complete details about a proposed ransom deal to save Teitelbaum and the other rabbis. A Swiss manufacturer was willing to sell forty tractors at a price of 17,300 francs per unit, he revealed. To the dismay of the rescue committee, however, they didn't have nearly enough money on hand to undertake such a purchase.

The tractors were to be used by Hungarian "agricultural

cooperatives" for the benefit of Germany whose population and military forces faced increasingly severe food shortages.[16]

On July 15, Isaac Sternbuch visited McClelland and presented what he called the "Freudiger plan." He showed the American two telegrams from Orthodox contacts in Bratislava and Budapest suggesting that the Nazis were no longer interested in "sheepskins" (the Orthodox code word for money), only tractors. The telegrams—which McClelland would later describe as "couched in the usual Hebraic commercial jargon used by these gentlemen"—indicated the possibility of "prompt delivery" of forty tractors upon Sternbuch's agreement to issue a credit for payment. The cable goes on to state that "Negotiations for the remaining Hungarian Jews are still possible." In a second (undated) telegram, the contacts indicated that if the credit is not "forthcoming within 2 days, remaining 400,000 Jews in Hungary will be irrevocably deported to Poland."[17]

In order "not to break off negotiations," Sternbuch had already cabled his contacts that he was "ready in principle to go ahead." When he approached McClelland, he revealed that he would need 700,000 Swiss francs to purchase the tractors, which he characterized as a "special plan of the Orthodox community in Budapest."[18]

On the following Monday, July 17, Sternbuch contacted McClelland again but no longer believed the tractor ransom was necessary to prevent the deportation of the remaining Hungarian Jews. Now, he merely warned that if the credit for the tractors was not issued, the train carrying 1200 Orthodox pasengers would be sent to Poland. "In order not to miss the 48 hour [deadline], we have agreed to the credit," Sternbuch informed him.[19]

Over the next several days, as Isaac recovered from an illness, Recha repeatedly contacted McClelland urging him to support the tractor purchase. But the WRB official insisted that he would first need more details about the "genesis of the plan, the names of the contracting parties . . . and an indication of what guarantees they had that the terms of the deal would be followed."[20]

On July 26, McClelland cabled Washington to inform his superiors for the first time about the scheme: "The following proposition has recently been submitted by Sternbuch; he declares it to be the 'Freudiger Plan.'"[21] He reported that the Budapest Orthodox leaders Philip Freudiger and Gyula Link had asked Sternbuch to open a credit account of 700,000 Swiss francs through the Intercommerz bank "in order to prevent the deportation to Poland of a convoy of 1200 prominent Orthodox Jews, among them Rabbis" who had been reported to have departed Hungary on their way to Spain. "The group has recommended the purchase of forty agricultural tractors in Zurich to be shipped for final delivery to Budapest. This payment was to be made to the Willy Tractor Company in Lucerne, owned by Thomas Willy," he cabled.[22] The scheme, McClelland informed his superiors, was "an independent endeavor of Orthodox Jews." He next explained the origin of the rumor, and from his description it is clear that the purported transport containing 1200 rabbis and Orthodox figures was in fact the Kasztner train, which, in reality, had only about forty rabbis on board and a relatively small number of Orthodox Jews.

Amid the panic and confusion, apparently no price was too high to save 1200 Orthodox leaders potentially headed for imminent liquidation. But only one man had access to the funds to do so. The Sternbuchs had turned to their longtime nemesis Saly Mayer, of the Joint Distribution Committee, whom Recha had never forgiven for failing to support her underground rescue network before the war. McClelland informed Washington that Sternbuch had approached Mayer for 500,000 Swiss francs to support the tractor purchase—representing the balance of the 700,000 francs needed to complete the transaction. The Sternbuchs' rescue committee would supply the remainder of the funds, he noted.[23] Mayer, however, had immediately rejected the proposal because there was "no satisfactory guarantee that fulfillment of the tractor purchasing conditions" would lead to the release of the 1200 passengers.[24]

The news that Mayer had refused outright to free what was still believed to be 1200 prominent Orthodox Jews sent shock waves through the community. This outrage could not be tolerated, declared the Orthodox leadership. The Vaad immediately set about lobbying Mayer's superiors in New York. On July 25, Rabbi Israel Rosenberg cabled an urgent telegram to the JDC: "It becomes clear that Sally Meyer [sic] refused to cooperate in urgent matter of rescue. I am told by authoritative persons who know Mayer personally that not only is he always a staunch antagonist to the Orthodox, but also stubborn by nature."[25]

Four days later, JDC chief Moses Leavitt cabled Mayer informing him that "Orthodox groups here are greatly disturbed by this situation and exerting great pressure on us."[26] Leavitt urged his Swiss representative to ensure "every possible measure is utilized by you to effect their rescue."[27] Informed soon afterwards that Isaac Sternbuch was accusing him of failing to cooperate because of a bias against Orthodox Jews, Mayer told JDC official Robert Pilpel, "For all I care, Sternbuch can go to hell."[28] Clearly, the mutual loathing of these Swiss Jews had not abated.

On the same day that Mayer was being urged by his JDC superior to spare no effort in rescuing the group, McClelland cabled his own boss at the WRB in Washington along with the State Department. Describing Sternbuch's tractor proposal, he referred to it as a "ransom scheme" that would provide direct aid to "the enemy war effort." He also noted that Willy, the firm from which Sternbuch proposed to purchase the tractors, was on the blacklist of companies with ties to the enemy. "Willy is notorious for his disregard of the interests of the Allies and [the bank] is a German concern," he declared.[29]

In the same cable of July 29, McClelland noted that Sternbuch had proposed cash ransom payments as an alternative to the tractor deal. Such payments, he argued, would also violate American policy prohibiting payment of ransom to the enemy. In his communications with Washington, McClelland made very clear his bias against Orthodox Jews, whom he disparagingly referred to as the "Holy men" and the "tractor crowd." He also indicated that he was skeptical about the veracity of the scheme because he had recently received an [erroneous] report that Philip Freudiger—the main advocate of the plan—had been killed in an aerial bombardment of Budapest on July 3. "This again casts doubt on this whole proposition coming through Sternbuch," he wrote in one memo.[30]

On August 2, he received a cable back from the State Department validating his position. "It is not feasible to undertake the transaction at this time," wrote acting secretary of state Edward Stettinius Jr.[31] As always in his communications with the American official, Isaac Sternbuch was exceedingly polite when he responded to McClelland's letter informing him that the tractor deal could not proceed. Acknowledging receipt of the American's "esteemed letter," Sternbuch assured him that he was "the last person who would want to see those scoundrels get a single cent, but it is an urgent necessity."[32]

Mayer's hands had long since been tied by his instructions from New York and Washington, which obligated him to adhere to the U.S. government policy prohibiting ransom. The Orthodox rescue groups, however, had never considered themselves bound to these regulations. Rabbi Eliezer Silver, the head of the Union of Orthodox

Rabbis, had already made clear that the Vaad's position on such matters was governed by the religious obligation known as *Pidyon Shvuyim* (the ransoming of captive Jews): "By command of the Holy Torah, we are prepared to violate many laws vis à vis the authorities in order to save lives. We are ready to pay ransom for Jews and deliver them from concentration camps with the help of forged passports. . . . We are ready to smuggle money illegally into enemy territories in order to bribe as many as necessary of the killers of the Jewish people, those dregs of humanity. We are even ready to send special emissaries to plead with the chief murderers, those ruthless criminals, and try to appease them at any cost."[33] By August, the worst fears of the Orthodox groups were allayed somewhat by the news that the train had been diverted to Bergen-Belsen. It wasn't one of the notorious death camps in Poland as they had feared, but it was still a German concentration camp. On August 20, Saly Mayer met with Kasztner and the SS agents on the bridge at St. Margarethen. On that very same day, 318 passengers from the original Kasztner transport were allowed to leave Bergen-Belsen for Switzerland. Four days later, on August 25, Sternbuch cabled the Vaad again via the Polish diplomatic cable: "320 persons arrived by train to Basel. Among them many personalities and Rabbis. Other transports are said to be on the way, with them probably also [the Satmar Rebbe] will come."[34]

The release of 318 Jews on August 20—the same day as Saly Mayer's meeting on the bridge—has always been portrayed as a German gesture of "goodwill." But the Sternbuchs would maintain that it was in fact their credit for the first ten tractors that was responsible for the release. On September 26, the Vaad received a cable from Isaac Sternbuch: "Recently we deposited 260,000 Swiss fr in the Swiss Bank for the Gestapo trustees in Budapest. It's a great pity we were not allowed to do it two months ago for we deposited on our own 170,000, saving in this way 320 persons."[35] Historian Paul Lawrence Rose also believes that this credit was the deciding factor in the release of the 318 Bergen-Belsen Jews.[36]

Meanwhile, unbeknownst to both Kasztner and Mayer, the Hungarian minister of the interior was already preparing to resume deportations of most of the remaining Jews of Budapest.[37] The Jews were scheduled to be herded into three camps beginning on August 25, with daily trains to Auschwitz set to begin rolling on August 27. On August 24, however, Himmler cabled Hungary's SS security chief, Otto Winkelman, ordering all deportations stopped. Yehuda Bauer argues that it had been the start of the Saly Mayer negotiations three days earlier that prompted the Reichsführer's change of heart.[38] Indeed, they almost certainly played a significant role. But Mayer had offered nothing in his first meeting beyond stalling tactics. Could the Sternbuchs' credit for ten tractors and the implication that the Nazis would finally receive the ransom they sought have influenced Himmler's decision? Again, it's possible that the two factors combined to play a role.

The expected 400,000 francs promised by Rosenheim of the Vaad had never materialized because of strict U.S. currency restrictions that prevented him from obtaining the francs necessary for sending the funds to Switzerland. In a joint meeting between the JDC and the Vaad on July 25, Rosenheim asked for help in converting the funds—approximately U.S. $100,000—but the JDC informed him that they had only enough francs to cover their own expenses.[39] It appeared that the committee would not have sufficient funds to purchase the additional tractors and complete the ransom. More than 1300 Jews from the original convoy remained in limbo at Bergen-Belsen.

By September, Saly Mayer was getting frustrated and so were the Nazi negotiators. His stalling tactics were wearing thin. The German emissaries with whom he was negotiating were growing increasingly impatient. Under orders from the Americans, Mayer had rebuffed the Germans' demands for merchandise time and time again. Instead, he had hinted at vast quantities of foreign cash but offered nothing concrete. The cat-and-mouse game was no longer working. In Budapest, the remaining Jews were still safe, but no one knew for how long. The deportations could start up again at any time. It appears to have been at this point that Mayer thought again of the tractor scheme. He had already met personally in Montreux on August 25 with a group that included Isaac Sternbuch, Nathan Schwalb of the Jewish Agency and others who pressed him hard to finance the deal.[40]

The Sternbuchs had been dealing with a man named Carl Trümpy, who had acted as the original go-between to facilitate the tractor deal. Trümpy was the private secretary of Emil Georg Bührle, the German-born CEO of the Swiss manufacturer Oerlikon,[41] one of Europe's largest arms manufacturers and a major supplier of armaments to Nazi Germany.[42] It's unclear what his motives were, but Trümpy appears to have offered himself up as an intermediary to save Jews on more than one occasion, including an earlier unsuccessful attempt to facilitate the flight of twenty thousand Hungarian Jews to Romania.[43] In late summer, Trümpy had attempted to determine what the Nazis were after in exchange for releasing Jews. He met with a high-ranking Vienna-based SS officer named Haster, who told him the Germans were prepared to release the Kasztner train passengers from Bergen-Belsen in exchange for undetermined further payments.[44] It was at that point that Trümpy approached Saly Mayer for the first time.

After meeting Trümpy in August, Mayer appeared to believe that the middleman's primary motive was money, presumably in the form of the commission he would get brokering the tractor sale. His suspicions appeared to be confirmed when Trümpy repeatedly demanded "expense" money to buy an automobile, among other dubious purchases. Mayer was also very wary of Trümpy's boss, Bührle, whose company, Oerlikon, was on the Allied blacklist. Mayer notes that he had learned the executive was "Strictly anti-Semite, but that he would be willing to make a great sacrifice if he could therefore be taken off the Black List."[45] It's possible, then, that Bührle dispatched Trümpy to help with the negotiations in order to create a favorable impression. At first, Mayer made it clear that he wanted nothing to do with the man or the tractor scheme. However, something appears to have happened during the next six weeks that convinced him to change his mind.

In a handwritten note to himself found in Mayer's files dated October 11, the JDC official has jotted down the price of the tractors, noting that forty would cost 692,000 francs at a price of 17,300 francs apiece. It's unclear at this point whether Mayer is aware that the Sternbuchs had already established a credit to purchase ten of the tractors with their own funds. What is clear is that Saly Mayer—the conservative Swiss official long vilified by Orthodox Jews for his refusal to pay ransom to save his people—would spend the next month negotiating the logistics of a sale that had already been officially designated as trading with the enemy. And yet his participation is not altogether unsurprising, considering the sums he had funneled to the Bratislava Working Group two years earlier to fund the ill-fated Europa Plan, also without the authorization of his superiors.

By late November, according to receipts and memos in his office files, Mayer had navigated the complex bureaucracy involved in purchasing thirty-six tractors and also secured the export permission required to ship the agricultural equipment to Hungary. Presumably to cover himself against charges of trading with the enemy, he later assured his superiors that he had not "contracted" the deal.[46]

To order such a quantity of equipment, a bank credit for the full amount was required. The money would be paid upon delivery. Before the tractors could be packed and shipped, however, an export permit was required from the Swiss government. Processing of this document began on November 16.[47] With the final bureaucratic hurdle out of the way, the company, Willytraktor of Lucerne, sent Mayer an invoice for the required down payment of 31,400 francs, which he kept for his files along with the export permit. The date on the document is November 20.[48] Five days later, Himmler ordered the Auschwitz gas chambers and crematoria destroyed. At first glance, the episodes have nothing to do with each other. Indeed, they have never been linked—until now.

Two Holocaust historians have, more than any others, specialized in studying ransom negotiations between the Germans and Jews during this period: Professor Yehuda Bauer of the Hebrew University in Jerusalem and the late professor Paul Lawrence Rose of Pennsylvania State University. Each has added significant new historical scholarship around these negotiations. Bauer and Rose have both written about Mayer's unexpected role in funding the tractor ransom, though each attaches a different significance to its impact. Neither historian, however, appears to have taken note of two startling documents that may shed new perspective on the importance of the tractor ransom and place Himmler's Auschwitz decree in an entirely different light.

In the archives of the War Refugee Board—in a folder marked "Records Formerly Classified as Secret"—sits a cable that was dispatched to Washington by Roswell McClelland on August 11, 1944. In this document, McClelland begins by informing his WRB superiors of the "desperate efforts" of Budapest Jewish circles to keep negotiations with the Gestapo going after the failure of the Joel Brand mission. He cites the "affair of 40 tractors," which Sternbuch brought to his attention as part of a larger deal that saw Jewish negotiators promise the Germans a credit of 2 million francs in Switzerland to cover tractors and "sheepskins."[49] On the basis of these offers, he writes, the Gestapo refrained from sending to Auschwitz a total of 17,290 Jews, including the Kasztner transport and the 15,000 Jews "on ice" in Austria.

That's when he reveals that, according to Rezső Kasztner, Jewish groups had met with a Gestapo official on July 21 and assured the Nazi that three hundred tractors were available in Switzerland: "A very favorable impression was created by this news with the Gestapo chief in Budapest, since as is reported by Kasztner, tractors are what are most desired and used here. Before Joel Brand's departure, the Gestapo in Budapest had declared that they were willing to trade 1000 Jews for every 10 tractors and even went as far as to give assurance that if the delivery of the tractors was begun seriously, 'they would destroy the plants at Auschwitz.'"[50]

We know that Adolf Eichmann—the "Gestapo chief" referred to in the cable—had made a similar promise to Brand before he left for Istanbul in May. If the Hungarian emissary came back with a confirmation that the Allies had agreed to the proposed ransom of ten thousand trucks, the Germans were prepared to release 10 percent of the Jews and "blow up the facilities at Auschwitz." But this, of course, never happened, nor did the Allies ever consider acceding to the ransom demand. Thus, when the buildings at Auschwitz were blown up six months later, it was never linked to the ransom negotiations.

If McClelland's August 11 cable was the only evidence, we might conclude that he confused tractors with the original promise Eichmann made to Brand to release Jews and destroy Auschwitz in exchange for trucks.

But a second crucial piece of documentation has surfaced in the archives of the War Refugee Board to fill in the gaps. More importantly, it originates from a source directly involved in these ransom negotiations. On July 28, 1944, Rezső Kasztner dispatched a letter to Nathan Schwalb at the Geneva offices of the Zionist organization, Hechalutz.[51] In this communication, Kasztner briefs Schwalb on the status of his negotiations with the Nazis since Joel Brand left for Istanbul in May.

He reveals that [Dieter Wisliceny] had been informed on July 21 that 300 tractors were available for the Germans in Switzerland (a fabrication concocted by Rabbi Weissmandl to prolong the negotiations) as part of the ransom that the Nazis had been demanding. This, he explains, was exciting news to the Germans because there was an enormous demand for such machinery.[52]

Kasztner then informs Schwalb that the Nazis had promised to "deliver" 1000 Jews for every 10 tractors. During the past two months, he explains, he met with Eichmann several times during which time the Nazi repeatedly refused to reconsider the deportation of Hungarian Jewry. Instead, Eichmann's primary stated goal was to sell "worthless human material" for goods of high value. During these talks, however, Kasztner had grown increasingly pessimistic about the ransom negotiations after he learned that the Americans had forbidden the payment of ransom to Nazis. When he subsequently informed Eichmann that the delivery of tractors might not be possible after all, the Gestapo functionary told him that if the deliveries were made, he would be willing to "strike a deal that would include the destruction of the facilities at Auschwitz."[53]

The significance of these two documents cannot be overstated. It is the first time that the tractor bribe has been linked to a full-scale release of Jews or a promise to halt the exterminations rather than simply the release of the Kasztner train passengers. The promise of three hundred tractors may be small compared to the Germans' initial demand for ten thousand trucks but it would represent the first time during these extraordinary negotiations that any ransom had ever been paid in high-value goods rather than in cash—goods that the Nazis had long been demanding but had never received because the Allies had explicitly forbidden such transactions.

Thus, when evidence emerged in November 1944 that the Sternbuch/Mayer tractor shipments had "begun seriously," it may have been just what Himmler needed as cover with Hitler to halt the exterminations while at the same time providing the Western Allies what he believed they required to consider his goal of a separate peace.

At the very least, these cables confirm that just the promise of the tractors had already "caused a very favorable impression" with Eichmann and that it may have prevented more than fifteen thousand Jews from being deported.[54] At that point, the negotiators certainly believed that it would merely take the start of the delivery of the tractors—what the Nazis "most desired"—to bring to a halt the Auschwitz exterminations.

Yehuda Bauer has always downplayed the significance of the tractor ransom. In *Jews for Sale?*, he notes that the "tractors were shipped, without any noticeable effect on Nazi policy."[55] This assertion is based on the fact that the first tractors were not shipped to Hungary until early December, almost two weeks after the Auschwitz crematoria were felled. However, another crucial document discovered in Saly Mayer's archives suggests that the process of delivering the tractors had in fact begun much earlier.

By the time Jean-Marie Musy met with Himmler on November 3, 1944, the Reichsführer had still been demanding trucks, tractors and autos as a condition for the release of the Jews. Two weeks later, on November 18, Musy wrote Himmler falsely informing him that the American authorities had approved funds for the "liberation of Jews detained in Germany and occupied territories." He claimed that the U.S. authorities had also put up to 20 million francs at the disposal of the Union of Orthodox Rabbis and that "goods" would be available for Germany to purchase with these funds. More importantly, he noted that the rabbis had obtained "the authorization to export merchandise."[56]

That cable was dispatched only two days after the Swiss government had indeed begun to process the export permit for the shipment of the Willy tractors as part of the illegal Sternbuch/Mayer ransom— the permit discovered in Mayer's JDC files along with receipts and other documentation surrounding the transaction.[57] This leaves no doubt that Musy used the Sternbuch tractors as leverage in his negotiations. Documents discovered at the archives of the Vaad ha-Hatzalah— which the Vaad kept in a file marked "Incoming, Illegal Sternbuch" and "Outgoing, Illegal Cables"—reveal that Himmler appears to have responded to this news with an extraordinary concession.

On November 20, 1944, the same day that the first tractors were confirmed ready for shipment and only two days after Musy cabled Himmler, Sternbuch cabled the Vaad a piece of electrifying news through the Polish diplomatic code: "Our delegate brought from Berlin the proposal to deposit larger amount for a gradual evacuation of Jews from Germany. The negotiations are continuing. . . . In interim secured promise to cease extermination in concentration camps . . ." Two days later, on November 22 (the day the tractor export permit was officially approved), Sternbuch cabled the Vaad again confirming that the papal nuncio in Bern—Recha's friend Archbishop Bernardini—"received promise slaughters will cease."[58] Three days later, the Auschwitz crematoria and gas chambers were destroyed.

This series of historic dispatches, combined with confirmation of the tractor ransom the same week that Himmler issued the destruction order, is powerful evidence that the negotiations almost certainly played a role and that the tractors may have been the deciding factor. But like most unresolved questions surrounding the Holocaust, it is impossible to be certain about the motives of madmen. Whatever the reason, Himmler's order to terminate the exterminations in November 1944 marked the end of the Final Solution, which had already claimed well over five million lives. Yehuda Bauer accepts that Himmler's November decree brought to a halt the "planned, systematic and total extermination" of the Jews.[59]

To this day, conventional wisdom and many historians maintain that it was the Allied liberation of the camps that halted the exterminations. This is a convenient argument. But it is difficult to ignore the evidence that suggests the Nazis' wholesale liquidation of European Jewry ended almost six months before VE Day. The same evidence may well explain why there were any survivors of the camps at all.

Despite this incredible turn of events, the remaining Jews of Europe were not safe yet. Far from it. The Final Solution had come to an end, but the Holocaust continued.

SIXTEEN

DEAL WITH THE DEVIL

T he Sternbuchs were anxious not to jeopardize Musy's negotiations in any way—so anxious that they would not reveal his
name at first, even to their American sponsors. Censorship wasn't
the problem because they were using the Polish diplomatic code facili-
tated by Julius Kühl. But they couldn't take any chances. When Musy
had left on his first trip in late October, they had alerted the Vaad that
"the person who we gave 60,000 in expenses left Sunday for Berlin."[1]
Almost a month later, they were describing him as "our delegate."

On November 21, the Vaad leadership received a cable with electrifying news: "After finishing negotiations with H, our delegate
informed us about the possibility to evacuate 300,000 Jews for the
amount of 20,000,000 Swiss Francs to neutral states. Such evacuations could be accomplished in groups of 15,000 persons monthly, the
money to be deposited in a Swiss bank in proportionate rates of one
million Swiss francs after arranging the evacuation of each group."[2]

On December 7, the Kasztner transport arrived in Switzerland
with the balance of its original 1684 passengers. There is still no
consensus about what caused the Germans to release the convoy
from Bergen-Belsen, although Paul Lawrence Rose is convinced

that the release was prompted by the shipment of the first four tractors days earlier.[3]

That same week, the Sternbuchs finally let McClelland know about Musy's efforts—apparently hoping that the American would help facilitate the ransom Himmler had demanded in November to free the Jews. On December 9, McClelland informed Washington of the latest development, but dismissed the Sternbuchs' "scheme" as "vague" and unreliable because of Musy's "extremely questionable reputation here." Noting that the former president is spoken of as the "potential Swiss Quisling," he recommended that the War Refugee Board refrain from supporting the idea.[4]

What the Sternbuchs didn't know was that McClelland was immersed at the time in a different set of negotiations. After Saly Mayer had complained in October that his stalling tactics were no longer working, the American WRB official had conceived a new strategy. On November 5, McClelland met personally with the SS emissary Kurt Becher in Zürich to demonstrate—disingenuously—that the Americans were fully behind Mayer's negotiations. As a signal that they were serious, he even produced a cable from Secretary of State Cordell Hull authorizing a transfer of 20 million francs in Mayer's name to be used for bargaining purposes. Of course, Mayer was not authorized to release the funds without McClelland's approval, and Washington had no intention of authorizing ransom of any sort. Once again, the agreement had been designed merely as a bluff. And yet the Germans hadn't asked for money, only goods, so it's impossible to say whether Mayer's stalling tactics had achieved the desired result.

If McClelland had known that Saly Mayer had recently helped negotiate and finance the Sternbuchs' brazen ransom scheme, it is unlikely he would have embraced the JDC official the way he did. It is clear from his files and correspondence, in fact, that he was much more comfortable dealing with Mayer than with Isaac Sternbuch. Mayer was his kind of Jew. In contrast, he always kept Isaac Sternbuch at arm's length. "He was a solid citizen, almost a ponderous man in some ways, always dressed in severe black suits," McClelland said of Sternbuch after the war. "Inevitably because I am a rational white Protestant American brought up in total other traditions, my reaction was that Saly was the more congenial person to deal with. He was more rational and business-like. . . . I had confidence in a more practical approach to the problem rather than an emotional approach to the problem."[5]

Knowing that Himmler was not willing to accept the "large sums of money" that he had offered on November 3, Musy returned to Switzerland seeking something he could offer as an alternative. As the director of a giant insurance company and a well-established corporate lawyer, the former president had extensive business contacts with one of the country's largest pharmaceutical concerns, Ciba AG. In mid-November, he visited the company's Basel headquarters to enquire about securing a large quantity of their most important drug, the antibiotic Cibazol. Knowing that Germany was desperately short of medicine for both its civilian population and its military forces, he believed he could convince Himmler to accept the drugs in fulfillment of the ransom as a condition for freeing the Jews.

Securing a commitment from the company to release a significant quantity of the drug, Musy then returned to Berlin in mid-December, where he met with Schellenberg to sound him out on the Cibazol gambit. Himmler, however, wasn't available to receive the offer. Like most of the high command, he was preoccupied at the time with preparations for the upcoming Battle of the Bulge. The Germans were about to launch a surprise attack against Allied forces in the

Ardennes, designed as a last ditch attempt to buy time for the Axis by seizing the Antwerp harbor and regaining a critical foothold.

Now, with Himmler away, Schellenberg for the first time confided his peace plan to his apparently like-minded guest. Musy had long shared the intelligence chief's fear that the end of the war would bring Bolshevism to Europe. Unlike Schellenberg, however, the veteran statesman knew the Allies would never enter into an alliance with a regime that had committed crimes on the unprecedented scale of the Nazis. Still, as he heard Schellenberg discuss his plans to bring about a separate peace, the Swiss emissary didn't contradict him. Instead, he calculated how he might use Himmler's delusion to his advantage.[6]

When Musy reported these developments to the Sternbuchs and the rescue committee in Montreux, they too believed that deceiving Himmler was the key to success. Reuben Hecht later recalled how the strategy was formulated. "We received the information through Musy that a struggle for power had developed between Himmler and Hitler. Hitler wanted to fight to the end and annihilate all the Jews, and Himmler wanted to approach the West. Our hope was to make clear to him that he had no hopes because of his atrocities towards the Jews but if he ceases those atrocities now and releases the remnant of the 600 or 800 thousand Jews, this terrible impression would be somewhat reduced." Only when he met this condition would the Allies likely be willing to negotiate a separate peace. "We knew from the Americans that this was out of the question, but they agreed we should give him this answer," Hecht explained.[7]

By January, the German Ardennes offensive had been turned back after Patton's forces broke the siege at Bastogne. The defeat meant an Allied victory was at most months away. Few except Hitler still clung to any hope for the survival of the Third Reich. Musy used the opportunity to request another meeting with Himmler. In the first week of

January, he received word from the German legation in Bern that the Reichsführer-SS wished to see him. On January 10, Musy embarked on the journey once again by car with his son Benoît at the wheel. Arriving in Berlin two days later, he first met with Schellenberg, who explained that Himmler was holed up near Stuttgart "commanding his troops." Hitler had recently given the Reichsführer sole command of an army unit tasked with defending the Upper Rhine, but Himmler had proven to be an inept military tactician and would soon be relieved of the command. Two days later, after a journey of more than seven hundred kilometers, the two men arrived at the town of Bad Wildbad in the Black Forest. On the evening of January 15, Musy was ushered into a hotel room where the Reichsführer-SS was waiting for him.[8] This time Schellenberg was permitted to stay.

No sooner had Musy sat down to resume negotiations than Himmler confronted him. He informed the Swiss emissary that a JDC representative named Saly Mayer and an American named McClelland had recently met with an SS-Obersturmbannführer, Kurt Becher, on a mission claiming to have the power to negotiate. "Who is really the one with whom the American government actually maintains contact?" he demanded to know. "Is it a Rabbi Jew or is it the Joint?"[9] At their last meeting, Musy had told him that he represented a "Grand Rabbi" named Sternbuch. Now he poured it on. He had been sent on his mission as an agent of the Union of Orthodox Rabbis of the United States. Musy knew well that the Nazis believed Roosevelt was controlled by powerful Jews. This was who had sent him, he implied. It was as if he had been anointed by the Learned Elders of Zion themselves.

The JDC was merely a philanthropic organization, Musy insisted. The rabbis, on the other hand, were a political group with great influence in America. As a former president of Switzerland and an erstwhile ally in the battle against Bolshevism, Musy likely cut a more impressive figure than McClelland had when he was "stalling and bluffing" Becher weeks earlier. Musy promised to provide definitive proof of the rabbis' influence as soon as he returned to Switzerland.

Now, he attempted a new approach. With the present food shortages, he argued, it would be in Germany's best interests to free thousands of Jews, especially women, children and old people. Himmler conceded that Musy was right, but he was also uncomfortably reminded of Hitler's December 1942 decree that Jewish lives could only be negotiated for money and goods. He needed something to appease the Führer. He wasn't particularly interested in having Jews "crowd" the country as they did after the First World War, Himmler told the Swiss emissary. If America or England wanted the Jews, they were welcome to them. Of course, just as the United States charged an immigration tax of $1000,[10] Germany should also receive $1000 per head for every emigrant. The veteran Swiss politician had engaged in enough delicate negotiations to know he was making progress. He realized that the Nazi was more interested in goodwill than money. Musy made a counter offer. To prove that the American rabbis who sent him were serious, he would have them deposit 5 million francs in Musy's name— funds that would be turned over to the International Committee of the Red Cross (ICRC) for German relief efforts after the war. He added that this was the only form of ransom the Allies would accept. Musy recorded Himmler's response: "Money is not enough. We would need to be guaranteed credit for freeing the Jews. The world press attacks us every day. This must stop."[11]

Himmler presented another obstacle. "The Jews could not stay in the Reich. Who would take them? The last time we offered to let the Jews go before the war, nobody would accept them," he said. Musy knew he was on firmer ground here. He assured Himmler that Switzerland and the United States would welcome as many Jews as

Germany agreed to release and would pay the full costs of their care and transportation. The Reichsführer appeared amenable to this arrangement. Of course, he would need a guarantee that none of those released would be permitted to go to Palestine. He couldn't do that to those "poor people martyred by the Jews."[12]

By the end of the meeting, Himmler agreed to engage in further negotiations if Musy could secure an agreement in principle by the United States. As a token of good faith, Himmler agreed to improve the treatment of the Jews in the interim and allow the ICRC to deliver relief packages to the inmates. Himmler still wanted to know which Jews he should be dealing with. If he was satisfied with the answer, arrangements could begin immediately for the evacuation of the camps. Musy had brought with him a complete list of those he wished freed, including Recha's relatives and a number of other figures whom he had pledged to free independent of the Sternbuch mission, such as Alain Thorel. Himmler assigned Schellenberg to see to the liberation of the individuals on the list—at least those who could be located. Before leaving, according to an aide-mémoire Himmler wrote about the meeting, the former Swiss president stressed that the Jewish question was just an "ancillary matter." Their negotiations, he stressed, had a much broader significance.[13]

The sixty-eight-year-old statesman was eager to return to Switzerland to report on these promising new developments. On January 17, he briefed the Sternbuchs about his meeting and Himmler's request for proof of the group's influence. They quickly cabled New York for the proof that Himmler was seeking—in the form of a letter stressing the strong links between the Union of Orthodox Rabbis and the U.S. government—which Musy then forwarded on to Berlin.[14]

In New York, the Vaad leadership had not known at first who the Sternbuchs' "delegate" was, but they did know that he had come back from meeting Himmler with a chance to save at least three hundred thousand Jews. When the Sternbuchs finally identified Musy as their representative—a former president of Switzerland with close ties to Himmler—the news was greeted with tremendous enthusiasm. For more than four years, there had been at first a trickle and then a deluge of catastrophic news about the plight of their European brethren. The Orthodox leadership had stopped believing in Roosevelt's commitment that America would do all it could to save the Jews. The creation of the War Refugee Board had been a hopeful sign, but so far not a lot had been accomplished. Now here was a chance to save lives, and for only "$17 a head." Irving Bunim was put in charge of raising the funds to pay the 1 million francs (approximately U.S. $230,000) indicated in the Sternbuchs' first cable of November 21 as the amount required to liberate the first fifteen thousand Jews.

In the synagogues of New York and Chicago, the response to the fund-raising drive was overwhelming, although occasionally someone would question the propriety of paying ransom to the Nazis—especially if they had a son in the army. "This money might buy the gun that kills my child," one man told Bunim. Still, most of those he approached were eager for any opportunity to save lives. Herman Hollander of the religious Zionist organization Mizrachi, later recalled the day he heard about the ransom: "That Friday afternoon I proposed to my wife that we sell our very comfortable three-story home and give the difference between the mortgage and the selling price to the *Vaad ha-Hatzalah* for the release of the ransomed Jews."[15] Unfortunately, not everybody welcomed the Vaad's fund-raising success, as illustrated by an inter-office memo circulated at the headquarters of the United Jewish Appeal (UJA) in December 1944.

On December 22, a UJA official, H. Peretz, informed his colleagues that he had received a call from the president of a Brooklyn synagogue. The caller noted that the Vaad ha-Hatzalah had been receiving enormous contributions from members of its congregation to support the efforts of a "Swiss fascist named Muzzi" to save fifteen thousand Jews. One congregant, he revealed, gave $10,000, another $6000. Altogether, $45,000 was raised from just one congregation to be sent to the Sternbuchs in Switzerland. This was happening all over New York, he noted. Consequently, he informed his colleagues, a member of the UJA executive was proposing to "cooperate with a group to counteract the *Vaad ha-Hatzalah* activities, which he is convinced will do great harm to our 1945 [fund-raising] campaign."[16] Predictably, the UJA ignored these petty complaints and refused to interfere with the promising rescue mission.

Meanwhile, Musy had heard back from Berlin that Himmler had accepted Sternbuch's credentials from America and had decided to deal with the rabbis instead of Saly Mayer. Better still, the Reichsführer was also willing to entertain Musy's proposal to deposit 5 million francs for the Red Cross to use for German relief work after the war. Schellenberg had assigned his aide, Franz Göring, to locate Recha Sternbuch's relatives along with the other names on Musy's list. Some of them had now been found. Musy was invited to return to Berlin to retrieve them and to work out the details about releasing more Jews. For the third time, Musy embarked on the arduous journey to Berlin. Before he departed, he was forced to share some bittersweet news with Recha. Her two brothers, Jakob and Joseph, had been located by the Germans in a labor camp and would soon be released. Her parents, however, could not be located. She knew immediately the meaning of these words. (In April, Benoît Musy was told that the Rottenbergs had been deported to Auschwitz months earlier.)

Arriving in Berlin, Musy met again with Schellenberg, who informed him that Himmler was preoccupied with the war. The

Reichsführer, however, had now authorized his intelligence chief to finalize the details of an agreement. Over two days, they worked out three key points:

1. Every fourteen days, a first-class train would bring approximately 1200 Jews to Switzerland.

2. The Jewish organization with whom Musy was collaborating would give "active support" in solving the Jewish problem. They would have to bring about a change in the "world-wide propaganda" against Germany.

3. Finally, 5 million francs would be deposited by the Americans in an account naming Musy as a trustee. Proof of such a deposit would have to be furnished before any Jews were permitted to leave Germany.[17]

If all conditions were met, Schellenberg pledged, the first trainload of Jews would arrive in Switzerland via Konstanz in a little over a week. Bidding father and son farewell, Schellenberg informed them that he had a "gift" for them. Outside, Recha's brothers were waiting. They would accompany the rescue committee's delegate back to Switzerland on February 2, the first two Jews liberated through the Musy mission.[18]

When Musy returned to Switzerland during the first week of February to report to the committee, the news that the Germans planned to start releasing Jews elicited some surprising reactions from the key players. Informing McClelland of the latest developments on February 3, Isaac Sternbuch admitted to the American that he was "skeptical." He would only believe in Musy's "efficacy" when the trains actually began to arrive in Switzerland. For his part,

McClelland, in his cable to Washington informing the WRB of the latest developments, was considerably more circumspect than in some of his previous dispatches. While once he had been openly contemptuous of Musy and suspicious of his motives, he now wrote that he "personally reserve[d] judgment."[19]

It was McClelland's job to approach the Swiss authorities to secure permission for a trainload of Jews to enter the country from the Reich. His liaison in the matter happened to be the notorious Heinrich Rothmund, the anti-Semitic government official largely responsible for his country's restrictive refugee policies. Yet Rothmund did not hesitate to grant permission for the entry. Characteristically, he did wonder aloud how soon the Americans would arrange for the Jews to be "evacuated to another territory."[20]

On February 6, the day the first transport of Jews was due to leave Germany, Isaac Sternbuch arrived with Musy at the American legation shortly after 6 p.m. to introduce him for the first time to Roswell McClelland. Although Recha was fluent in French, Isaac was not proficient in the language and so he didn't participate in the conversation between the former Swiss president and the American. Still, Musy waited until Sternbuch was out of the room to share what McClelland later described as a confession. He did not care much for the Jews, Musy admitted, but "they had suffered greatly." It was why he had agreed to the mission, he explained. He proceeded to fill McClelland in on his numerous trips to Berlin during the last three months, revealing that he and his son had traveled nine thousand kilometers by car, enduring "machine gunning and bombing, refugees" and other "hardships."[21]

Meanwhile, Schellenberg had put his aide, Franz Göring, in charge of selecting 1200 Jews to be part of the first transport to Switzerland.

Himmler had made it clear that the initial evacuations should refrain from bringing out able-bodied workers whom the Reich still desperately needed for armaments production. With this in mind, Göring made his way to Theresienstadt in German-occupied Czechoslovakia. Originally established as a ghetto for the Jews of Bohemia and Moravia, Theresienstadt had eventually been converted to a transit camp for those en route to the death camps. In its early days, the ghetto had been largely reserved for middle-class German Jews and "persons of merit," including distinguished musical and theatrical figures. Until recently, the camp had been known for its cultural activities and relatively civilized treatment of its internees—so much so that the Germans invited the ICRC to visit in June 1944 when the Danish government enquired about the fate of more than four hundred Jews deported from Denmark in 1943.[22] In advance of the visit, camp authorities deported a number of inmates to avoid the appearance of overcrowding and "beautified" the camp, transforming it into a "model village."[23] Following the carefully stage-managed visit, the ICRC delegate, Maurice Rossel, issued a glowing report, noting, "The SS police gives the Jews the freedom to administer themselves as they see fit. . . . We were convinced that its population did not suffer undernourishment."[24] The positive ICRC report made for effective Nazi propaganda and later tarnished the reputation of the Red Cross. Starvation and disease, in fact, would claim at least a quarter of the camp's inhabitants, while another eighty-eight thousand would be deported for extermination.

Before Göring arrived at the camp in early February—accompanied by Benoît Musy—to seek volunteers for the transport, he had assumed that he would have no problem filling the seven cars designated for the journey to Switzerland. Testifying at Nuremberg after the war, however, Schellenberg's aide described an unexpected obstacle that he had encountered upon his arrival. When it was announced that a train of 1200 Jews would be going to Switzerland, he recalled, only a few hundred inmates stepped forward to volunteer for the journey. When he enquired why there was so little interest, he soon found out the reason for their recalcitrance: "It finally appeared that all the Jews were firmly convinced that this transport was one of the notorious death trips to Auschwitz. Even when the train was already underway, there was a large number of elderly people in particular who were unwilling to really believe they were journeying toward their freedom."[25]

Indeed, when inmate Walter Lode heard about the transport, he didn't believe it at first. "I was working in the shoe repair shop when the production manager came in and told us, 'Men, you're all going to get out of here—straight to Switzerland,'" Lode later recalled. "You should have heard us guffaw, all twenty of us we simply roared. Nobody believed it." When he discovered the opportunity was genuine, the forty-three-year-old Dutchman eventually reported to the assigned area to seek approval. "I heard the commandant ask a girl from Berlin, 'Where's your father?' 'Shot.' She got no permit. Slowly, we wised up and told people if they start asking questions, just say 'dead.' They were afraid of what we'd tell abroad—as if we'd keep silent once we were rescued from their fangs."[26]

Gertrude Narev remembered it was a Sunday afternoon, February 3, when she heard the news. "Excitement soared in the factory. All Danes and Dutch were to be transported to Switzerland. Not so, the next rumor said, quite the contrary. That midnight, on returning bone-tired to my room, I was handed a summons for transport by the house elder—ostensibly to Switzerland, immediate decision required. Now what?" Her son Bob begged her to go. He wanted to ride a train. "Are we really going to Switzerland?" she recalled thinking as the train left. "Goodbye, Theresienstadt. Goodbye to two and a half years of fear, hunger, sorrow, grief and vermin. Three of my beloved are gone: Husband, mother, grandma. My child, my only child, the only one still left is with me."[27] Bob Narev was nine years old when he and his mother secured their spot on the train—though, as of 2016, neither he nor his mother had ever heard of Jean-Marie Musy or his role in securing their freedom. He remembered arriving in Theresienstadt as a six-year-old child from Frankfurt, where his father had worked as a teacher before he lost his job under the Nuremberg laws. He recalled little about his time in the camp, where his father and two grandmothers died. Placed in the camp "children's home," he remembered hearing that the Germans used the camp as a supply depot because its status as a concentration camp meant it was unlikely to be bombed by Allied aircraft. "I remember trucks coming in filled with potatoes and all the kids chasing after them hoping one or two would fall off," he recalled.

Living in New Zealand in 2016, the eighty-year-old Narev remembered little about the train ride to Switzerland.[28] However, Bertha de Vries, fifty-two years old when she left, later remembered the passage vividly. "It was a passenger train with real passenger cars, not the usual cattle car train," she told researcher Joan Fredericks in 1969. "The Nazis sent along on our train much food, so much that it was shown and photographed in Switzerland—supposedly proof that we had never suffered from hunger. Just one of their usual propaganda lies. We never had a chance to clean ourselves in Theresienstadt, but just before the frontier we were ordered to comb our hair and fix ourselves up as best as possible. That's how their minds work, everything for show."[29]

The train reached the border on the evening of February 6, a full day before the Swiss authorities had been expecting it. It took most of the night for border police to clear up the confusion. Ida Stahl recalled the passengers' dread while waiting at the border. "Still, the danger was not over. Would the Germans let the train go through? The Swiss accept us? Yes, we thought whenever the train moved forward, No when it was shunted back and forth, No when we spent that long night in Konstanz, waiting and waiting and waiting forever—surely, we thought, they've been ordered to get us back. We could see the lights and the Swiss emblem and that, somehow, made it worse. To be near and still so far. . . ."

In the end, Musy personally intervened with the Swiss president, Eduard von Steiger, imploring him to allow the Jews over the border. Finally, just before noon on February 7, passengers noticed the train slowly moving. When it stopped minutes later, Greta Stanley remembers an officer boarding to announce, "On behalf of the Swiss population, I am bidding you welcome." Outside, there were people waving and smiling. Hearing about the imminent arrival, dozens of locals had emptied the shelves of a nearby shop to purchase gifts for the refugees. The people had wanted to present them personally but were told the passengers had to first spend time in quarantine. The Swiss officers offered to distribute the gifts. "I found myself suddenly with four bars of chocolate in my hands," Stanley recalled.[30]

Among those on the platform on hand to greet the new arrivals was Jean-Marie Musy. Marianne Keyser, seven years old at the time, remembered peeking out through the curtain as the train arrived at the station. "When we arrived at the frontier, a gentleman was pointed out as having achieved all this. I don't remember how he looked—only that he wore a beautiful brown jacket—we watched all apparel so closely then."

In all, 1210 inmates had made the journey, representing three nationalities: 450 were Dutch, 120 had originated in the Czech protectorate and 640 were German.[31] Among them were 58 children under the age of 12, including a number who were born in Theresienstadt. As the passengers disembarked, many wept with joy while several kissed the ground. Overwhelmed by the sight, Hermann Landau—representing the rescue committee along with Recha and Isaac—remembers thanking God for letting him play a part in their liberation. The Sternbuchs were also jubilant, but had little time to celebrate their achievement. They knew they had to work quickly to engineer the positive media reaction that Himmler had demanded as a condition for further transports. The first results were encouraging. The next day, *The New York Times* ran a small item under the headline "First Jewish convoy reaches Swiss Haven":

> BERN, Switzerland, Feb. 7—A convoy of 1,200 Jewish refugees
> from the Theresienstadt concentration camp in Austria [*sic*] arrived
> at Kreuslingen today following negotiations by Jean Marie Musy,
> former Swiss Federal Councilor, with Heinrich Himmler.

A day later, another item appeared in the *Times* noting a gathering in New York of "somberly clad Rabbis" at the headquarters of the Vaad ha-Hatzalah to celebrate the release of the Theresienstadt Jews, which the paper credited to the efforts of seventeen committee members.[32] The Jewish Telegraphic Agency reported that a group of twenty Orthodox Jews had achieved "one of the most fantastic feats of rescue."[33] The Swiss press also took note of the achievement, but many American newspapers ignored the story altogether. It was hardly the positive reaction that Musy had promised. He had been scheduled to return to Berlin the following week to make arrangements for future convoys.

Before his planned February 16 departure, however, he reported to the Sternbuchs that Berlin was furious at the lack of discernible press reaction. Isaac phoned McClelland to let him know that he had just been upbraided by the former Swiss president for the silence of the Western media. Obviously the government of the United States didn't care whether Germany released the Jews, Musy had charged. The Sternbuchs immediately cabled the Vaad to inform the American leadership that future transports were in jeopardy: "Musy will not depart before receiving the clippings. Other transports have ceased. Cable immediately the clippings. . . . The action is depending on the publication of these articles."[34] A trickle of press reports followed.

Meanwhile, the committee designated Reuben Hecht to convince his Swiss press contacts to act. Hecht later described the intense pressure: "I had the very unpleasant task to go to the Swiss President of the confederation and to the journalists, especially to the socialist journalists, who hindered our saving work by saying, 'Look now these Nazi beasts are letting out a few hundred or a few thousand Jews, and for this they want to be praised? And I had to explain to them that, in order not to destroy the rest of the Jews, but to save them, we are ready to work with the devil and we are also ready in a certain way to fulfill their demand."[35]

In the United States, the Vaad was equally persistent in pressing for positive coverage of Musy's successful operation. The rabbis sent to Switzerland a summary of the media reports, which included extracts from three New York papers noting the "excellent condition" of the Theresienstadt Jews when they arrived in Switzerland. In all, more than a thousand American papers had written about the episode. They promised that more such clippings would follow.[36]

If there were still any doubts at the State Department regarding Musy's motives, they were dispelled on February 19 when a French exile named André Enfière visited the U.S. Consulate in Geneva asking whether Musy might be induced to intervene on behalf of Edouard Herriot, the former mayor of Lyon who was interned in Germany.

Having heard of Musy's role in liberating the Theresienstadt Jews, he was offering up to 1 million Swiss francs if Musy could help free Herriot. When U.S. consul general Paul Squire approached the former Swiss president about the offer, however, Musy "declined remuneration." Instead, reported Squire, he was only interested in obtaining cooperation in getting the U.S. government to issue a statement that "they would be happy to see the deported Jews return to their homes."[37]

Nevertheless, McClelland found the clamor from Berlin for favorable press "highly suspect." It strengthened his belief that there was more behind the Musy affair than just the release of Jews. He cabled Washington that it was likely just the "curtain raiser" to proposals of far greater importance to the Nazis. Indeed, on February 9, the American legation in Bern took note of intelligence they had received from an informant. Musy had recently confided to a journalist, M. Naef, that he had been "charged by Himmler to get in contact with the American government to learn the conditions of peace."[38]

Meanwhile, the committee was scrambling to come up with the 5 million francs—nearly U.S. $1 million—that was needed to fulfill another key promise. Musy refused to return to Germany without proof that the funds had been deposited.[39] The Vaad had raised a considerable sum for what they thought was the initial installment required to save the first fifteen thousand Jews. But it wasn't nearly enough. It appeared that once again they would have to turn to the JDC for help. Despite Saly Mayer's crucial role in funding the tractor bribe, however, it would appear the hostilities were as intense as ever. As McClelland informed Washington when he apprised them of the situation, Sternbuch "would rather die in his tracks" than ask Mayer for funds.[40]

The Vaad leadership had no such qualms. They had sent a significant sum to Switzerland already but needed an additional $937,000 to fund the Musy deposit. Tasked with making the request, Irving Bunim noted that the JDC leadership initially recoiled when they heard what the funds would be used for. "I called up Joint President Moe Leavitt," he later recalled, "and I told him the story. 'What?' he shouted. 'Ransom! You want to give ransom to these Germans, to these Nazis! England wouldn't like it. And it will *never* go through Washington.'"[41] But faced with the prospect that the organization would be blamed for a failure to save the remaining Jews of Europe, the JDC finally agreed to a loan. However, they still needed a Treasury Department license to transmit the funds, and Washington was in no mood to facilitate ransom of any kind.

The transcript of a February 27 meeting called to discuss the license reveals that most Treasury Department officials believed the million-dollar deposit sounded like a "personal pay off" to Musy, who was "obviously a scoundrel." Only Josiah E. DuBois Jr.—whose report was instrumental in creating the WRB a year earlier—argued that saving lives was worth the risk.[42] Advised that the rabbis had been conducting most of their communications through the uncensored Polish diplomatic pouch, Henry Morgenthau showed considerable displeasure. "It looks to me like one of the reasons we are in this trouble is because these rabbis have completely gone around us," he complained to his staff.[43]

Unaware of these behind-the-scenes discussions, the Vaad leadership requested an emergency meeting with Morgenthau to plead for the license. But the treasury secretary was still reticent. On March 13, he told the rabbis that American Jews "could bring great harm to themselves and dangerous anti-Semitic publicity" if it emerged that Jews were dealing directly with Himmler.[44] Acknowledging his concern, the Vaad's Irving Bunim adopted a tactic that the Sternbuchs had used several times in their own dealings with Roswell McClelland whenever the same subject came up. The Vaad would never pay ransom to Nazis, he assured the secretary, but the money could be useful for transportation costs and necessary "gratuities" to German and Swiss authorities. "Even Nazis are entitled to be reimbursed for feeding and transporting thousands of people," he told Morgenthau.[45]

In the end, John W. Pehle—who had recently stepped down as head of the WRB to return to the Treasury Department— recommended that the license be granted. If the money doesn't go, he cautioned his colleagues, "The rabbis are going to tear the town loose." The department granted the license and even allowed the money to be deposited in Musy's name. But unbeknownst to the Swiss statesman—though with the full knowledge and approval of the Sternbuchs—the funds had been carefully restricted so that they could never leave Switzerland.[46] With the last obstacles removed, it appeared that the regular convoys promised by Himmler would soon resume. The Sternbuchs eagerly awaited the second train. It never arrived.

SEVENTEEN

WAITING IN VAIN

A s it turned out, Reuben Hecht's efforts at convincing the Swiss press to comment favorably about Musy's mission had not been entirely successful. In a political career spanning twenty-five years, Jean-Marie Musy had made some powerful enemies on the left. His apparent 'embrace of fascism after leaving office was especially abhorrent to the left-wing press, who were deeply suspicious of his motives and refused to believe that Musy was engaged in humanitarian pursuits. It had been widely reported in Switzerland that the February 7 train from Theresienstadt was just the first of many promised by the Nazis. When no further transports had arrived by February 25, the country's largest socialist newspaper, the *Arbeiter Zeitung*, described Musy as the author of the "hoax": "Monsieur, well-known friend of the Nazis, negotiated with Hitler about the release in order to make the public believe that the Nazi atrocities against the Jews are exaggerated. . . . Hitler gets a good price for every Jew he releases."[1]

A number of similar articles appeared, disparaging the deal with headlines such as "We Don't Need Any Favours from Germany." The Germans were accustomed to such attacks from the socialist press, so that kind of negative publicity would hardly have been a disqualifying factor. But just as Musy had many opponents in Switzerland, Himmler had accumulated a number of powerful enemies of his own. The imminent defeat of the Reich sharpened the internecine rivalries among those surrounding the Führer. Ernst Kaltenbrunner—appointed by Himmler to replace Reinhard Heydrich as RSHA chief in 1943—had been suspicious of Schellenberg's maneuverings as well as his cozy relationship with Felix Kersten. Indeed, the Finnish masseur was warned that Kaltenbrunner had accused him of being an agent of British intelligence. Only Himmler's patronage had apparently saved him from the fate of the many whose lives had been snuffed on the whim of the man whose reputation was every bit as ruthless as his predecessor's. Schellenberg described Kaltenbrunner's features as "gorilla like—huge and tough, with small, penetrating eyes set in a wooden, expressionless face, they looked at one fixedly, like the eyes of a viper seeking to petrify its prey." According to Kersten, Himmler issued an ominous warning to his security chief when informed that he planned to eliminate the Finnish masseur. "My dear Kaltenbrunner, if anything were to happen to Kersten . . . your own health might suffer to an appreciable degree. I fear you would only survive Kersten by a few hours."[2] Although Kaltenbrunner outranked him in the Nazi hierarchy, Schellenberg reported directly to Himmler, which gave the intelligence chief considerable influence within the SS. It also made him a formidable threat. The two were fierce rivals. Schellenberg would later tell his Allied interrogators that after the July 20 assassination attempt against the Führer, Kaltenbrunner did his "utmost to undermine Himmler's position with Hitler."[3]

Although it is unclear how much Hitler knew of the Musy negotiations, there is no evidence that Himmler was negotiating behind his back, at least not in the early stages. His demand for what turned out to be a symbolic ransom was almost certainly meant to cover him with the Führer, who had in December 1942 given Himmler full powers to release Jews in exchange for "foreign currency from abroad." The Reichsführer's demand for positive media coverage would further suggest that he wasn't trying to hide the Musy negotiations. Nor, apparently, had the Führer expressed any displeasure with the departure of the Kasztner train from Bergen-Belsen in December or the Musy convoy on February 7. At least not yet.

The details are still murky, but in late February, a member of his inner circle brought Hitler decoded messages from "one of DeGaulle's centers in Spain." They suggested that Himmler had negotiated with Musy through his representative Schellenberg for the release of Jews in exchange for a "right of asylum" in Switzerland for "200 leading Nazis."[4] Enraged, Hitler summoned the Reichsführer-SS to his Berlin headquarters. No Jews would be allowed to leave the Reich under any circumstances, he bellowed. The consequences for any German helping a Jew escape—and that went for Allied POWs as well—would be death.

Neither Musy nor the Sternbuchs knew anything yet about these developments. All they knew was that no second convoy had arrived. With proof of the promised 5-million-franc deposit, Musy had been planning to travel once again to Berlin to seek answers. For two weeks, Recha had been agonizing along with the rest of the committee, waiting for news of further transports. Now, she summoned Musy to Montreux and informed him that she planned to personally accompany him to see Himmler. "That's quite impossible, Madame Sternbuch," the Swiss statesman told her. But Recha Sternbuch was not accustomed to taking no for an answer. Musy agreed to enquire about a visa at the German embassy in Bern.

The idea of an Orthodox Jewish woman making the journey into the mouth of the lion should have been inconceivable, but it came as no surprise to committee member Reuben Hecht, who accompanied Recha and Musy to the German legation that week. "Recha was the strongest personality in the whole community," he later recalled. "Unbelievable. And there is no doubt that she had a tremendous driving force and courage and she did things which people thought were not unbelievable but impossible."⁵ Predictably, the visa request was turned down, but Recha remained undeterred. She insisted that Musy write to Himmler personally to request permission. Before he could do so, however, Isaac intervened. Such a trip was far too dangerous, he argued. He forbade his wife to make the journey. Renée Landau remembers her cousin's fury when Isaac finally put his foot down. "She didn't speak to him for a week, she was so upset."⁶

At the end of February, Musy returned to Berlin once again and sought out Himmler's intelligence chief. It was here that he learned that Hitler had forbidden the release of any further Jews. Schellenberg later recorded the Swiss emissary's reaction upon hearing the news: "Musy was desperate and shed tears of rage and bitter disappointment."⁷ On March 3, Musy returned to Switzerland. When he phoned the Sternbuchs, HIJEFS secretary Hermann Landau answered the phone. "If there are no more trains, you can blame Saly Mayer," Musy declared.⁸ According to Schellenberg, it was Mayer who had scuttled the operation by supplying Kurt Becher with a dossier about the negotiations, which Kaltenbrunner in turn brought to Hitler.

Schellenberg later told his Nuremberg interrogators that the report about two hundred leading Nazis being granted asylum in Switzerland had been passed "by Saly Mayer via Becher to Kaltenbrunner. . . . Hitler abruptly ordered that the operation be stopped immediately and forbade the release of any Jew."[9] This serious accusation against Mayer reverberates to this day, but it is almost certainly untrue. It was no secret in New York that Mayer had opposed lending the Vaad the money used to finance Musy's mission. He was so upset, in fact, that when he heard the JDC leadership had approved the loan, he tendered his resignation. He only changed his mind after the JDC leadership in New York successfully convinced him that his work was too important to give it up.[10]

The minutes of a February 26 meeting at the JDC office in St. Gallen reveal that Mayer was undeniably bemused by Musy's success and perhaps even a little jealous. His own negotiations with Kurt Becher and Arba had been handcuffed from the beginning by his marching orders from Washington. Still, Mayer's bluffing game was effective and may have played a key role in gaining time for the remaining Jews of Budapest. At the February 26 meeting, Mayer stressed that he "[did] not take notice of Mr. Musy's deals." The recorded minutes, however, indicate otherwise: "S.M. states that there may be a certain amount of disappointment in the JOINT that certain things have been done under the name of Mr. M. and the Orthodox Rabbis of USA which he, as the JOINT's representative, could not do. S.M. notes that work is sometimes made difficult because certain people mainly think of their own interests."[11]

Mayer was one of the few people who knew about his own role in facilitating the illegal tractor bribe that likely played a role in Himmler's change of policy. Unlike Musy, however, he could not trumpet his actions in the press. Instead, he was forced to sit back and watch Sternbuch and the rabbis get the credit. It is instructive to take note of another JDC meeting involving Mayer the same month. The minutes again record Mayer discussing the Musy mission: "S.M: It was said that Mr. Musy, former federal Councillor, has dealt with the

Germans on philanthropic grounds, there was nothing said of tractors."[12] Here again is further evidence that Mayer at least believed that
the tractor bribe had played a central role in the latest developments.
Still, despite his obvious resentment, he makes one thing clear: "I am
very happy that through the intervention of Mr. Musy that things
have been brought on a humanitarian basis."[13]

Like Yehuda Bauer, historian Paul Lawrence Rose dismisses the
accusations against Mayer as unfounded. "What temporarily derailed
Musy's operation was not really internal Jewish feuding but rather
infighting among the Germans," he writes. "Schellenberg had run the
Musy line since its beginning in October 1944 but Becher with his
Kasztner/Saly Mayer connection was determined not to be left out."[14]

When the Vaad contacted the JDC to inform them that Mayer
had allegedly "sabotaged" the Musy negotiations, McClelland was
asked to look into the allegations. A letter he sent to Mayer on
February 28 reveals the lack of seriousness with which he took the
accusation. "I understand that Musy returned in somewhat of a
dither claiming that Becher-Mayer coalition were attempting to
sabotage his humanitarian efforts," McClelland wrote. "I hope to
have more on this subject and will keep you posted, you saboteur!"[15]

Although the facts behind the stalled negotiations remained
foggy through the rest of the war, the true story eventually emerged
when Kaltenbrunner was tried for war crimes at Nuremberg in 1946.
Asked by his inquisitors whether he had in fact intervened to stop the
concentration camp evacuations, the Nazi was unequivocal. Although
he had vigorously denied responsibility for many of the crimes of
which he had been accused, he had no hesitation about confirming
the incident: "I heard about this through the intelligence service and
immediately attempted to stop this, not through Himmler because I
would have failed but through Hitler. At that moment any personal

credit of Himmler with Hitler was undermined, for this action might have changed the reputation of the Reich abroad in the most serious manner."[16] Kaltenbrunner apparently believed that it was his patriotic duty to halt the release of Jews.

EIGHTEEN

DITHERING

T he failure of the second convoy to arrive weighed heavily on both the Sternbuchs and Musy. But neither was willing to accept the apparent breakdown of the plan.

When the Swiss statesman had last met with Himmler in January, both men knew that Germany's defeat was imminent. Allied troops were racing toward Germany from two directions. In late March, the British crossed the Rhine into northern Germany under the command of Field Marshal Bernard Montgomery while Soviet forces moved toward Berlin from the east. The Soviets had earlier discovered evidence of the Nazis' ghastly legacy, but the West had yet to witness the full extent of Hitler's crimes.

When British and Canadian troops entered the gates of the Bergen-Belsen concentration camp on April 15, 1945, they discovered a scene of unimaginable horror. Accompanying the liberators, BBC war correspondent Richard Dimbleby was the first to report what they found: "I passed through the barrier and found myself in the world of a nightmare. Dead bodies, some of them in decay, lay strewn along the road. . . . 25,600 people, 3/4 of them women, are ill from lack of food or actually dying from starvation. . . . Two youth and two girls who found a morsel of food were sitting on the grass picnic fashion sharing it. They were not six feet from a pile of decomposing bodies. . . . Inside the huts it was even worse. I've seen many terrible sights in the last five years but nothing, nothing approaching the dreadful interior of this hut in Belsen. The dead and the dying lay close together. I picked my way over corpse after corpse in the gloom."[1]

A newsreel film crew captured the gruesome scene, and the graphic images would be seen by millions of cinemagoers around the world. The Belsen images—particularly stacks of corpses piled on top of each other—would become indelibly imprinted onto the conscience of humanity and finally wake the world up to the magnitude of the Nazi barbarity. They would become the defining images of the Holocaust. And yet the corpses encountered by the liberators that day were not in fact a product of the Final Solution—Hitler's edict to systematically exterminate European Jewry. At least not directly.

By April, Soviet forces had already liberated a number of German death camps in Poland, where millions of Jews, Slavs, Gypsies, homosexuals and other enemies of the Reich had been exterminated and incinerated since late 1941. Yet for some reason, the Soviets had chosen not to broadcast the evidence that they had uncovered at Auschwitz, Majdanek, Sobibór and other killing centers months earlier. That's not to say they were kept a secret, however. On August 29, 1944, journalist Raymond Davies sent a telegram to Montreal's Yiddish newspaper, the *Keneder Adler*, describing his visit to the recently liberated Majdanek death camp: "There is no doubt that Majdanek will go down in history as one [of the] most horrible experiences in mankind. . . . Men, women and children taken to Majdanek into bathhouses were immediately gassed . . . Things fill huge warehouses in Lublin and I saw with my own eyes piles of shoes numbering at least eight or nine hundred thousand, boxes of eyeglasses . . . whole shelves of [Jewish prayer shawls]. . . . I saw mountains of children's toys. . . . I saw partly burned bodies their arms and legs chopped off to make it easier pushing into ovens and I saw great mountains of grey urns Germans used to collect ashes. . . ."[2] But there were no images to accompany those scenes of horror. Belsen, then, became the embodiment of the Nazis' evil for a world to see.

In his 2005 book about the liberation of Bergen-Belsen, British historian Ben Shephard suggests that the repugnant sights that greeted the liberating troops in April 1945 came as a complete surprise. "There is no trace in the surviving military files of any awareness of the humanitarian disaster" unfolding there, he writes.[3] He does note that a Jewish prisoner named Rudolph Levy, released from Belsen in early March, had been interviewed by Liverpool port security on March 19. There, he furnished an account of recent developments, including overcrowding in the camp caused by "evacuating the camps in the east" and a recent typhus outbreak. Levy's report, however, had only reached the POW division of the British Foreign Office on April 2. In a hand-written notation accompanying the report, an official wrote, "Unfortunately, they do not appear to have got the exact location of the camp."[4] The Allies, of course, also knew that the passengers recently arrived on the Kasztner train had spent months in Bergen-Belsen before their onward journey to Switzerland. Still, the British claimed, they had only a "vague" idea of the camp's whereabouts. Moreover, there was allegedly no indication that the inmates were in imminent danger, especially after the Allied governments learned that the Nazi extermination policy had been rescinded in late 1944.

For decades, this version of history has been widely parroted and accepted. The conventional narrative is that Allied forces were completely unprepared for the scope of the humanitarian catastrophe they encountered when they liberated Belsen and subsequent concentration camps during the final weeks of the Second World War. Heroic Allied liberators supposedly arrived just in time to avert an even greater catastrophe. Moreover, the Allies didn't even know the location of some camps because the Germans had kept them such a well-guarded secret. It is a myth that began to unravel when historians exposed the Auschwitz bombing controversy. But as Shephard's account suggests, it is still widely accepted that the scope of the Bergen-Belsen tragedy could not have been anticipated.

In recent years, a different historical controversy has erupted over claims that the liberators bungled the medical treatment and feeding of the inmates, despite decades of claims that the British had performed the "most gallant action" ever fought against disease in the history of medicine, as one doctor wrote in 1947.[5] Yet few have ever challenged the conventional narrative, which holds that the Western Allies had no idea of the unfolding humanitarian catastrophe in the German concentration camps during the spring of 1945.

A series of declassified files uncovered in the archives of the Franklin D. Roosevelt Presidential Library tells a very different and troubling story.

The stated mission of the International Committee of the Red Cross is to protect the lives and dignity of victims of conflict. For most of the Holocaust, it dramatically failed in this mission. By the eve of the Second World War, the ICRC—founded in Geneva in 1863—had achieved a reputation as the world's preeminent humanitarian organization. During the First World War, it distinguished itself on a number of fronts but was most notable for its willingness to intervene on behalf of civilians. It had even established a special section to advocate for deportees, hostages and people living in occupied territories. In recognition of that work, the ICRC was awarded its first Nobel Peace Prize in 1917.[6]

By the time the Second World War broke out, it became evident that the organization's once stellar commitment to interned civilians didn't extend to the Jews in Nazi concentration camps. Officially, the organization claimed that the Nazis' treatment of their Jewish internees was an "internal matter" and it could not jeopardize its neutrality by interfering. It did not help that the German Red Cross had become thoroughly Nazified after the chief medical officer of the SS, Ernst-Robert Grawitz, took over as president in 1937.

At the outbreak of war, Swiss diplomat Carl Burckhardt—who had served a stint in Turkey for the ICRC in the early 1920s—returned to the organization as vice-president. When Gerhart Riegner first heard about the Final Solution, he reached out to Burckhardt, whom he had come to know well when he studied at the Institute of International and Development Studies, where the respected professor taught history from 1932 to 1937. Burckhardt immediately confirmed to the WJC that he had learned of the Nazi plan to exterminate world Jewry from two German government officials—a revelation that was instrumental in convincing Riegner to cable the alarming news to America.[7] Burckhardt also confirmed the information to U.S. consul general Paul Squire, but stressed that his information was "private and not for publication." In his memoirs, Riegner wrote that he found it strange that Burckhardt apparently had never spoken to his ICRC colleagues about the information he had received from his German sources, or attempted to use the organization's hallowed position to alert the world.[8]

It's unlikely that Musy knew much about the internal dynamics of the ICRC, but he certainly knew about its glaring failure to intervene on behalf of the Jews during the first five years of the war. (He also knew Burckhardt well from diplomatic circles and as a passionate anti-Communist.) As early as his first meeting with Himmler on November 3, Musy had already discussed a role for the Red Cross in the Nazi concentration camps of "upper Silesia"—almost certainly a reference to Auschwitz-Birkenau. Weeks later, Carl Burckhardt was named acting president of the ICRC, replacing the organization's longtime leader Max Huber. The new president had barely assumed his post when Musy met for the second time with Himmler on January 15, 1945. In his written report to the Sternbuch committee about this meeting, Musy suggested a role for the Red Cross in saving the remaining Jews. "Considering the immense job to be done, I thought the International Red Cross could be useful," he wrote. "Up until that point, the Red Cross had barely been concerned with the liberation of people who were deported or interned. I've discussed the role of the Red Cross at length, especially the new president Mr. Burckhardt, who is very capable. I insisted on the value of a meeting between Mr. Burckhardt and the German authorities. . . . He said an invitation would be extended."⁹

Arriving back in Switzerland, the Swiss statesman met with Burckhardt and implored his old friend to help "secure the liberation of those deported and detained in German concentration camps."¹⁰ Musy returned to Berlin at the end of January to finalize the arrangements for the first Theresienstadt train, scheduled to depart the first week of February. It was during this trip that Himmler agreed, through Schellenberg, to the idea of a deposit of 5 million francs in Musy's name for ICRC relief efforts on behalf of German civilians after the war. This was not the Reichsführer's only significant concession.

Among their myriad rescue activities during this period, the Sternbuchs had never stopped advocating for the "passport Jews"— the hundreds of Warsaw Ghetto deportees who had received forged passports from Recha and the rescue committee, entitling them to special privileges. Most of those who had received Latin American passports, including Recha's parents, had been sent to Vittel—the resort in France where they were given special privileges until the Nazis discovered that the documents were forged. But the couple had also provided more than a hundred Palestinian certificates, purchased from corrupt British officials. The holders of those papers were sent to another camp, where they were interned along with hundreds of other "exchange Jews who had important connections abroad"—in anticipation of a possible prisoner swap between the Germans and the Allies. The name of this camp was Bergen-Belsen.

As a result, the Sternbuchs had for some time paid special attention to the camp, located near Hanover in northern Germany. With Passover only two months away, the rescue committee had received funding from the Vaad in February to obtain ten thousand kilograms of the special *shmurah* flour required to make unleavened bread—matzoh—that Jews traditionally consume during the eight days of Passover.[11] The committee had previously sent packages of food and religious articles to a number of concentration camps, including Belsen. But Passover was special. They wanted to ensure that the flour reached its destination before the holiday and that it was distributed in time to bake matzoh. Roswell McClelland was eager to cooperate with this effort, even if his knowledge of Judaism was lacking, as evidenced from his correspondence in which he always referred to the matzoh as "Easter bread."

Before Musy departed for Berlin in late January, the Sternbuchs had asked him to request permission for the ICRC to be allowed into the concentration camps to distribute the matzoh along with relief supplies. On February 6, hours before the arrival of the Theresienstadt train, McClelland cabled Washington about the progress of the mission. Among his revelations was the response Musy had received from the Germans about his Red Cross request: "Regarding the question of packages for the camps in Germany, [Sternbuch] stated that Himmler would allow no one to visit them with one exception—Musy's son. M's son could do this in collaboration with the ICRC. Tomorrow M's son will talk to Burckhardt of the ICRC about this whole question. Looks as though the Musy family wishes to play a very beau and humanitarian role!"[12]

Musy wasn't the only figure who believed the ICRC might finally be convinced to intervene on behalf of the remaining Jews. In December 1944—a month after Musy first proposed a Red Cross role to Himmler—Saly Mayer had shifted his strategy. Abandoning the ruse of preventing deportations by dangling ransom in front of the Nazis, he had become convinced of the necessity of keeping the Jews safe in the camps until the end of the war, under Red Cross supervision.

The Roosevelt administration had also finally shown the first signs of deviating from its policy, which held that the best way to save Jews was to win the war as quickly as possible. The shift in direction was likely influenced by the new secretary of state, Edwin Stettinius Jr. On January 17, 1945—only six weeks after he succeeded Cordell Hull in the post—Stettinius approached McClelland about a potential new role for the ICRC. "In view of the large number of relief parcels recently reaching camp Bergen Belsen, please urge upon Intercross the desirability of an Intercross delegate being stationed in or sent on an extended visit to that camp to assist in the distribution of such parcels," he wrote.[13]

Five days later, McClelland informed Washington of another camp, Landsberg am Lech, in Eastern Bavaria, where the German commander had signaled his willingness to distribute Red Cross parcels to Jewish inmates, who comprised 80 percent of the camp population. In this January 22 communiqué, McClelland describes an imminent crisis: "The German concentration camps are crammed with acutely undernourished people and when the German food supply organization breaks down, it will be but a matter of days, at most ten, before hundreds if not thousands of people will simply die or reach a stage at which they cannot be saved."[14] In this same dispatch, he reveals that the camp commandant was "unusually accommodating." If the Red Cross had any means of transportation or parcels to send, the SS commander indicated that "there would have been no difficulty about delivering them personally directly to this camp."[15]

In the year since he had arrived to head the Swiss office of the WRB, McClelland had never particularly distinguished himself in the post. The Sternbuchs were frustrated by his lack of concrete support, and his obstructionst tactics, while even Saly Mayer appeared to sour on the American's handling of the Arba negotiations. However, as he sounded the alarm about an impending humanitarian disaster in January 1945, it appeared that Roswell McClelland had finally risen to the occasion of his monumental task.

On January 22, noting the rapid deterioration of German rail networks available to distribute Red Cross parcels, McClelland lobbied Washington for five to seven trucks that he could turn over to the ICRC for delivering food parcels to "accessible camps."[16] If army trucks were unavailable, he suggested the WRB could rent or buy vehicles in Switzerland. On February 12, McClelland cabled Washington that he had just spoken with Raoul Nordling, Swedish consul general in Paris, who was confident that one man held the key to a major ICRC relief operation in Germany: "A large number of things point to the way being open for the ICRC to enter Germany with foodstuffs and probably sanitary teams, since Nordling says he has every reason to believe that if Burckhardt took the matter up personally with the Nazis, they would permit sending of medical missions. No difficulty will be made from the German side for the entry of trucks of food parcels with ICRC drivers and representatives."

In his dispatches since January, McClelland had repeatedly advised Washington about an imminent humanitarian catastrophe. He had warned that if relief was not sent soon, thousands would almost certainly starve to death. By mid-February, there were indications that his superiors were beginning to take notice. On February 20, 1945, several of the most powerful members of the Roosevelt administration convened at a meeting of the War Refugee Board at the offices of Secretary of War Henry Stimson. Treasury Secretary Henry Morgenthau chaired the meeting. Among the other attendees were acting secretary of state Joseph Grew and leading WRB officials.[17]

There was only one item on the agenda. For almost two hours, the men were apprised of McClelland's dire warnings about the deteriorating situation inside Germany and the need to acquire supplies and transportation equipment for the Red Cross to deliver concentration camp relief. It had been left to the recently appointed WRB executive director, General William O'Dwyer, to sum up the grim news. He informed the gathering that while the Germans had abandoned the wholesale extermination of Jews as a general policy, "large numbers of physically unfit detainees face imminent death from starvation, exposure, or deliberate neglect." The only thing that could save them, he warned, was the delivery of food and medicine.[18]

Seven weeks after that meeting of the War Refugee Board, the British would liberate Bergen-Belsen and claim that they had no advance notice about its whereabouts or the unfolding humanitarian crisis that had been taking place there for weeks. However, the minutes of the February 20 WRB meeting provide definitive proof that the high-powered Allied participants were informed of a February 2 cable sent from Bern reporting that more than twenty-five thousand Jewish deportees had recently arrived at Bergen-Belsen from Auschwitz and were in a state of "acute undernourishment." According to the report, the inmates were housed in "primitive conditions" and receiving insufficient supplies. There is no evidence, however, that these reports were ever passed on to the British. The Germans had been permitting the delivery of Red Cross packages, according to the "best information available," but the supply was "pitifully inadequate" due to the deterioration in land transport.[19] Before adjourning, the board unanimously approved the immediate acquisition of trucks for the delivery of WRB food parcels and medical supplies to the camps by the Red Cross. Ominously, Secretary Stimson designated his assistant, John J. McCloy, to make the arrangements—the same War Department official who had blocked the bombing of the Auschwitz railway tracks months earlier because he believed the war effort took priority over saving Jews.

Anticipating that he now had the full support of Washington to arrange for the delivery of relief supplies, McClelland went to work. Only ten days after the WRB meeting, he reported that 60,000 parcels, each containing 2.5 kilos of food, had arrived in Geneva from Toulon, France. He had 150 tons' worth of relief parcels ready for delivery.[20] What he lacked were the trucks to deliver them. The Swiss army was willing to supply the vehicles, he reported, but it faced an acute shortage of tires, which rendered 357 of its fleet inoperable. The good news was that the ICRC had expressed a willingness to deliver supplies to *Schutzhaeftlinge*—the German word for Jews in "protective custody."

Six days later, it appeared that the transportation problem had finally been solved. On March 8, the ICRC reported from Geneva that a fleet of trucks had been put at its disposal by "United States authorities." They had also received 120 tons of food, medicine and a "very large quantity of gasoline."[21] This report, however, makes no mention of relief for concentration camps. Instead, it notes there will be a "flying column" of twenty-five trucks dispatched to meet Allied POWs who have been transferred from camps in eastern Germany. A second column will be sent northwards to distribute the supplies to POW camps in the neighboring regions.

Also on March 8, McClelland cabled Washington that Carl Burckhardt had heard back from Himmler and planned to meet the Reichsführer during the next week. The ICRC had also been informed that the Germans were now willing to allow the exit from Germany of elderly persons, as well as women and children of "Nordic" extraction or French nationality who were unsuited for labor. In this cable, he noted that the Supreme Headquarters Allied Expeditionary Force (SHAEF)—the central Allied command headed by General Dwight Eisenhower—had agreed to supply fuel "but only for transport relief to POWS and not for unassimilated groups." This was the term used for Jews and other concentration camp inmates. Thus, two weeks after the secretary of war heard that concentration camps were facing a colossal humanitarian disaster of starvation and disease, the U.S. Army refused to release the relatively small amount of fuel required to provide relief to the suffering inmates. Undeterred by this setback, McClelland cabled Washington that he was working on obtaining five to eight wood-burning trucks to deliver sixty thousand WRB parcels to the concentration camps.

It becomes clear from his increasingly exasperated correspondence that the well-meaning Quaker was frustrated by the misplaced priorities of the higher-ups. As early as February 24, in an attempt to focus Washington's attention on the plight of the Jews, McClelland had informed Washington that "POWs are less likely to starve and are in better physical condition" than the concentration camp inmates. In Washington, O'Dwyer appeared to be receptive to his pleas. On March 10, he assured McClelland that he was taking measures to alleviate the situation: "The War Department today has cabled General Eisenhower recommending the release of 50 tons of trucking capacity with 1,500 to 2,000 gallons of gasoline per week."[22] As supreme Allied commander in charge of SHAEF, Eisenhower oversaw military operations for British, American and other Allied forces in Europe.

But the future U.S. president was not quick to cooperate, even after McCloy cabled him personally on March 8, recommending the release of transport vehicles and fuel. By March 27, almost three weeks later, SHAEF had still not authorized the request. During the interval, McClelland had traveled to SHAEF headquarters outside Paris to personally plead the case for the victims of concentration camps. He met twice with the SHAEF supply officer, Brigadier General Morris Gilland, who first refused to release any trucks or gasoline on the grounds that there were "mounting army transportation requirements."[23] His refusal hardly rings true, considering that the Allies had by this point enjoyed months of unimpeded supply lines and a ready supply of fuel.

Meanwhile, at Bergen-Belsen the shortage of food was growing so acute that the inmates reportedly resorted to cannibalism. British medical officers accompanying the liberating forces would tell Reuters that they had discovered bodies devoid of flesh, with the liver, kidneys and heart removed.[24] And while Allied leaders later claimed they had no warning of the unfolding humanitarian crisis before early

April, news of the deteriorating situation had even reached New York much earlier, as evidenced by a March 24 cable from the Vaad leadership to the Sternbuchs: "Send more food parcels to Bergenbelsen and other camps through International Red Cross and other means. Internees starving for hunger in all camps."[25]

The World Jewish Congress was also anxiously looking to the Red Cross for a last-ditch effort to stave off catastrophe. While McClelland sought help from his own government, Gerhart Riegner had turned to the British, pleading for intervention. On March 3, he received a similar response: "For sending relief to camps in Germany, Anglo Saxon authorities have agreed to make available trucks to ICRC, but they had insisted that they had to be used for prisoners of war only, civil detainees being excluded."[26]

Until early March, most of these pleas had centered on the imminent likelihood of starvation. With American troops heading toward the Rhine, German supply lines had been cut off, Allied bombings had destroyed hundreds of bakeries, and Germany's own civilian population faced desperate food shortages. But now a new crisis was about to unfold. On March 11, Felix Kersten noted in his diary "an outbreak of typhus in the Bergen Belsen camp, for whose occupants the World Jewish Congress was so concerned."[27] A day later, Carl Burckhardt crossed the Swiss border into Austria for the meeting that, according to Schellenberg, was brought about by Musy's efforts.[28] Only weeks earlier, Burckhardt had been offered the post of Swiss minister to Paris, but in light of his expected meeting with Himmler, McClelland had asked him to postpone the appointment because his efforts on the part of internees "appeared of greater urgency than his going immediately to Paris."[29]

Due to "pressing military duties," Himmler was unable to meet the ICRC president personally. Instead, he sent a letter delegating full powers to Ernst Kaltenbrunner to negotiate in his place. Burckhardt had arrived with a long shopping list of requests he had hoped to take up with Himmler. Only six weeks earlier, he had asked that the ICRC be allowed to visit all concentration camps, but the request had been refused at the time on grounds of "national defense." Instead, he had been informed, each request had to be personally approved by Himmler. Although he had no idea of Kaltenbrunner's role in sabotaging the Musy negotiations, Burckhardt was not optimistic when the Reichsführer sent a subordinate to negotiate. Still, he presented his case. The first meeting broke up without any resolution. They agreed to meet again in Switzerland the next day. In Kreuzlingen on March 13, the negotiations continued with Kaltenbrunner present, along with two members of Ribbentrop's Foreign Ministry.

On March 14, Burckhardt emerged from the negotiations with news of a significant breakthrough and an astonishing concession. The Germans had given permission for the ICRC to station delegates in all major camps for both POWs and *Schutzhaeftlinge* in order to personally supervise the distribution of relief supplies. The only condition, he reported, is that the ICRC personnel must agree to remain in the camps "until the end of the war and not, repeat not, circulate particularly back and forth to Switzerland." The SS, he revealed, would "permit relief deliveries of all kinds to [internees] by truck or other means of transport, irrespective of race or nationality."[30] It was a critical development, but there was still one hitch, as evidenced by Burckhardt's February 22 cable to the WRB: "Our delegates can only get into camps if they bring something with them, and if they have gasoline and can still manage to travel on the roads."[31]

While starvation and typhoid ravaged Belsen and other camps, McClelland spent most of March desperately pleading for action. Finally, after further pressure from Washington, General Gilland in

Paris agreed on March 28 to release two thousand gallons of gasoline a week to the WRB effort—a relatively small amount considering the distances and the number of trips required, but still a potential godsend for the starving and disease-ravaged inmates. Gilland, however, still refused to release any vehicles for the WRB effort "because of the military necessity for using them elsewhere."[32]

Nevertheless, the news that he would finally have access to gasoline came as "beautiful news" to McClelland. However, just when it appeared that one major obstacle had been removed, another arose in its place. By early April, the WRB's supply of food parcels had been nearly exhausted after most of it was dispatched to Allied POWs the month before. Fortunately, he had located an additional 206,000 POW parcels currently stored in a Swiss warehouse. With starvation already taking a severe toll in the concentration camps, he knew this food could potentially save thousands of lives. As he was preparing to ship the parcels on a number of newly obtained trucks, however, McClelland received devastating news. General O'Dwyer informed him that the War Department had inexplicably "exacted a condition of repackaging before these parcels are forwarded to war refugees in concentration camps."[33] For reasons still unknown, Washington wanted all traces removed linking the packages to the U.S. Army—possibly because of the potential political fallout should it be revealed that food meant for POWs had been diverted to concentration camp inmates. Such a repackaging would require a laborious effort.

It took two more weeks to coordinate the relief operation. None of McClelland's remaining Red Cross packages destined for the camps left Switzerland until the second week of April. For one camp, they arrived too late.

When British and Canadian troops entered Bergen-Belsen on April 15, they discovered that more than twenty thousand inmates had died of starvation and disease since mid-February when Roswell McClelland had first sounded the alarm and tried to compel the Allies to come to the aid of the inmates of Belsen and other camps.[34] Among those who perished during this period were two teenage Dutch sisters who had arrived on a transport from Auschwitz in November. Their names were Margot and Anne Frank. Their barracks leader, Irma Sonnenberg Menkel, later recalled the toll that hunger had taken on the famous diarist during the last weeks of her life. "There was so little to eat. In my early days there, we were each given one roll of bread for eight days, and we tore it up, piece by piece. One cup of black coffee a day and one cup of soup. And water. That was all. Later there was even less. When I asked the commandant for a little bit of gruel for the children's diet, he would sometimes give me some extra cereal. Anne Frank was among those who asked for cereal, but how could I find cereal for her?"[35]

Both sisters eventually succumbed to the typhus epidemic that swept the camp in the late winter of 1945. Anne's date of death is officially listed as March 31—only two weeks before the camp's liberation. Some accounts suggest that she may have died earlier. One thing is for certain. If Red Cross relief efforts for the concentration camps had not been blocked by Allied authorities, the Frank sisters and thousands of others might well have survived.

The blame for every concentration camp death, of course, ultimately rests with the Nazis whose despicable policies placed people there. But the tragedy of Bergen-Belsen illustrates that even at this late stage in the war, the fate of the European Jews had still hardly pierced the consciences of the Allied leaders.

NINETEEN

AGREEMENT "IN THE NAME OF HUMANITY"

While Allied authorities were still dithering in March over relief supplies for the camps, an extraordinary series of events was unfolding that would have a far greater impact on the fate of the remaining Jews.

Neither Felix Kersten nor Walter Schellenberg had given up on their efforts to move Himmler to usurp Hitler and seek a separate peace with the Western Allies. And, although each had different motivations, both men forcefully argued that the key to such a settlement was an improvement in the treatment of the Jews. Kersten claims he never missed an opportunity to work on the conscience of his powerful patient each time he had Himmler under the spell of his magic fingers.

The Finnish masseur had moved to Sweden with his family in September 1943, but he frequently returned to Germany to attend to Himmler's bouts of abdominal agony. On those occasions, he purports to have succeeded in freeing a number of people—both Jews and non-Jews—from concentration camps. Kersten claims that he was even instrumental in convincing the Reichsführer—"after many

335

difficulties"—to bring about a meeting with Jean-Marie Musy, even though Himmler "knew in advance that Hitler would refuse such a wholesale release of Jewish prisoners."[1]

Many biographers and some historians have accepted his myriad claims at face value, even though a number of these claims have since proven demonstrably false or highly exaggerated. Like Schellenberg, Kersten appeared to believe that he deserved credit for every idea that he may have discussed in passing with Himmler. After the war, Schellenberg would claim to have prevented a German occupation of Switzerland, and Kersten would write that he had singlehandedly prevented the deportation of three million Dutch citizens to the east. Both claims have since been thoroughly discredited. Despite both men's penchant for hyperbole and self-aggrandizing, however, there can be no doubt that they played an extraordinarily important role in the events of spring 1945, when the lives of the remaining Jews of Europe hung in the balance.

Whether or not Kersten exaggerated his own importance, news of his close association with and influence over Himmler had indeed spread widely in Sweden after he successfully intervened to commute the sentences of the seven Warsaw Swedes arrested for espionage in 1942. Since that time, he had established frequent contact with the Swedish foreign minister, Christian Günther, who had apparently used Kersten a number of times as an advocate for Denmark and Norway— the two Scandinavian countries living under German occupation.

Although the majority of Danish Jews had successfully escaped, thousands of other Danes—including five hundred Jews—had been deported to German concentration camps since 1940, along with more than eight thousand Norwegians. In a series of meetings beginning in April 1944, Kersten and Günther discussed making an overture to Himmler whereby the Scandinavians might be released to Sweden.

To ensure they didn't pose a threat to the Germans, they could be kept there in an internment camp for the remainder of the war.

Meanwhile, Kersten had convinced his patient to release fifty Norwegian students and fifty Danish police officers, thereby bolstering his credibility with the Swedes. In early December, he reported to Günther that he had secured Himmler's permission to release an additional one thousand Dutch women, along with thousands of Scandinavian women and children interned in Germany, provided that Sweden would agree to intern the group for the remainder of the war. The transportation details would have to be worked out by the Red Cross if Sweden approved the arrangement.

While most of the Western world had long ago abandoned the Jews of Europe, Sweden was one of the few nations whose record could be described as laudable. Sweden had, in fact, played a major role in one of the most important episodes of Holocaust rescue when it came to the aid of Denmark's Jewish community after Hitler ordered the Scandinavian country's Jews deported in October 1943. In the decades since the war, millions have heard the inspirational story of Denmark's King Christian, who allegedly donned a yellow star after the Nazis ordered his Jewish subjects to wear the symbol. Inspired by their monarch's gesture, the people of Denmark all donned the star and thus saved the Jews from deportation. Alas, the story is merely an urban legend—concocted by a PR agency after the war and reported in the New York *Daily News* and later repeated in Leon Uris's 1958 novel *Exodus*.[2]

Nevertheless, many Danes, including both the king and the state church, did play an important role in standing up to the German occupiers and saving most of the country's Jewish population. In reality, it was the country's mostly Communist resistance movement that organized a daring rescue in the fall of 1943 to thwart the deportations

scheduled for the night of Rosh Hashanah—the Jewish New Year—
when Jews were expected to be in their homes and therefore easily
captured. When the Nazis arrived to begin the roundups, all but a few
had already disappeared to fishing villages along the coast. From there,
they were spirited to neutral Sweden in the dead of night in a variety
of vessels. The operation could never have succeeded if Sweden had not
agreed to give refuge to the more than 7200 Danish Jews—90 percent
of the country's overall Jewish population—who made their escape
that week. It was a marked contrast to the majority of Western countries, whose doors remained closed to Jewish refugees even after the
Final Solution became widely known to their governments. When
Raoul Wallenberg intervened to save thousands of Hungarian Jews in
the autumn of 1944, he was also acting on behalf of Sweden.

By mid-February, Himmler had not yet agreed to the full-scale
evacuation of Scandinavians to Sweden. But he had consented to the
establishment of a special camp in Neuengamme, near Hamburg,
where the Danish and Norwegian inmates could be interned for the
duration of the war under the supervision of the Red Cross. The
man chosen to carry out the task was a Swedish nobleman named
Count Folke Bernadotte, the nephew of King Gustav. It appeared
that Bernadotte was well suited to carry out the complicated logistics of such an operation. As director of the Boy Scouts before the
war, he was best known for organizing and training the Scouts into
a defense unit of the Swedish armed forces that could be quickly
mobilized should the Germans invade their country. In recognition
of this effort, he had been named vice-chairman of the Red Cross in
1943. Now, Bernadotte was prepared to fly to Germany to work out
the complicated arrangements for transporting thousands of
Scandinavians to relative safety. His first trip to the Reich took place

on February 16—the same week that Hitler terminated Musy's operation to evacuate Jews to Switzerland. "It was against this background that I began my work in Germany," Bernadotte later recalled.
"Hitler raging because of the concession made, and Himmler not
being able, not daring, or not caring to oppose his master."[3] The
Swede had been given instructions to press for more than internment inside Germany. The real goal was to evacuate all Scandinavians
to Sweden. His efforts would take some time to produce results.

By the end of February, word of the count's negotiations had
leaked in Sweden, as had the role that Felix Kersten had played in
initiating the talks. Although Stephen Wise has been vilified for his
supposed inaction during the Holocaust, the organization he had
led since its founding in 1936—the World Jewish Congress (WJC)—
had played a critically important role. While Wise undeniably placed
too much faith in the Roosevelt administration, a number of World
Jewish Congress figures in Europe were effective advocates. Two WJC
officials in particular stand out for their tireless advocacy of rescue.
Both worked in close contact with Wise. The first was Gerhart
Riegner in Geneva, who believed no avenue should be spared to stop
the genocide. The second was a man named Hillel Storch—a Latvian
Zionist who had taken refuge in Stockholm after the Soviets invaded
his country in 1940. Since arriving in Sweden, Storch had come to
represent both the Jewish Agency and the WJC, and he soon became
a well-respected figure in Swedish political and social circles, where
his list of acquaintances included King Gustav V. Storch was, in fact,
instrumental in the Swedish government's benevolent refugee policy
and had reportedly convinced the king to forcefully intervene with
Admiral Horthy on behalf of the endangered Hungarian Jews in the
spring of 1944. That gesture may well have played an important role
in ending the deportations.[4]

It becomes clear that, although men like Hillel Storch, Gerhart Riegner and other Jewish leaders were involved in important rescue work during this period, there was very little cooperation between these figures and the equally urgent efforts of the Sternbuchs and other Orthodox rescuers. A combination of mutual suspicion and traditional deep divisions between the secular and religious Jewish communities appears to account for the unfortunate and counterproductive rift.

During the last months of the war, Storch redoubled his efforts. On February 25, 1945, he asked a banking acquaintance, Ottokar von Knieriem, to introduce him to the man rumored to enjoy unparalleled influence over Himmler. It was over drinks at a Stockholm hotel that Storch first implored Felix Kersten to save his people. Although Kersten claims to have previously intervened with Himmler to save many Jews before this date, there is little documentation to back up these claims. Nor is there any suggestion that Kersten was an anti-Semite or that he shared his patient's animosity toward the Jewish people. But even if he hadn't previously given much thought to the plight of the Jews, Kersten listened to Storch's panicked pleas that day and assumed the role for which he would be remembered by history.

Storch had recently learned from his usually reliable European intelligence network that Hitler had vowed to blow up the remaining Jews in captivity upon the approach of the Allies. So far, this was merely a rumor. But even if it should prove to be false, there were incontrovertible reports of a new phenomenon almost as alarming. Ahead of the approaching Soviet liberation forces, the Germans had evacuated the eastern camps and transported the surviving Jewish prisoners to Germany, where they would be interned in concentration camps and used for forced labor or as hostages. In areas where railways had been bombed, many of those evacuations had taken place on foot. Thousands were forced to march under terrible conditions. Most notoriously, sixty thousand inmates had been evacuated from Auschwitz and its sub-camps in mid-January and forced to march through the bitterly cold Polish winter toward the nearest intact railway depot, Wodzisław Śląski, fifty kilometers away. From there, they were to be placed on trains to Germany. Thousands died before they could reach the town, many from exposure and exhaustion, others shot by SS guards for failing to keep up.[5] Survivor Lily Appelbaum Malnik, sixteen years old at the time, remembered being told that she and her fellow inmates were being evacuated from Auschwitz "because the Russians were coming." They walked for days, she recalled, before being herded into cattle cars. "And then we walked again. And as we walked we heard gun shots and they told us to keep on marching. And they were shooting people in the back who couldn't keep up. It ended up being called the death march because the ravines and the gutters, they were all red from blood."[6]

Brutality at the hands of the SS was not the only hardship the death marchers were forced to endure. Gisela Teumann, who survived a forced march from Neusalz to Bergen-Belsen, later recalled that German civilians were also unspeakably cruel: "We passed through some German town. We asked for food. At first the people thought we were German refugees. The SS man who accompanied us shouted: 'Don't give them anything to eat, it's Jews they are.' And so I got no food. German children began to throw stones at us."[7]

No precise figures exist for the numbers of fatalities, but these gruesome scenes would be repeated in many other camps, and tens of thousands are known to have perished in the Nazi death marches of the winter and spring of 1945.

Kersten hadn't yet heard of this phenomenon, though he had been privy to far worse during his years of ministering to the patient who he well knew was responsible for crimes unparalleled in human history. Hearing Storch's desperate plea, he now pledged to intervene with the Reichsführer-SS. For two days, he and the Swedish WJC official worked out a set of proposals that he agreed to take to Germany on his next trip in early March. Among these was a promise to ask for the dispatch of food and medicine to Jewish prisoners. In addition, he would propose that all Jews be assembled in special camps where they would come under the care and control of the Red Cross. He would also ask for the evacuation of Jewish prisoners to Sweden and Switzerland.

In his March 2 diary entry, Kersten outlines the proposals in detail and indicates that he or Storch had already broached them with Swedish government officials, who, he writes, shared the WJC's opinion "that the blowing up of the concentration camps will be carried out as a gesture of desperation."[8] Three days later, the Finn had returned to Germany, where he found his patient in a "very nervous condition." Kersten's diary account of what happened next appears at first the stuff of fairy tales, or of his highly charged imagination. He writes that when he raised Storch's concerns, he found Himmler at first ready and willing to carry out Hitler's sinister edict. If the Reich is fated to be destroyed, Himmler reportedly argued, "then her enemies and the criminals in concentration camps shall not have the satisfaction of emerging from our ruin as triumphant conquerors. They shall share in the downfall. Those are the Führer's direct orders."[9]

After "exhausting" discussions replete with "dramatic moments," Kersten allegedly convinced his patient that this "final burst of large-scale slaughter was quite senseless." Finally, after stormy and difficult negotiations, Himmler agreed not to carry out the order. It was at this point that it would appear Kersten revived the delusion that he and Schellenberg had worked so hard to cultivate, but so far to no avail. The Allies would likely still be willing to negotiate a separate peace with Germany, he argued, but would only negotiate such a truce with a German who had intervened to save "humanity."[10]

On March 12, 1945, the two men sat down at a desk at Kersten's German estate and drafted an agreement that, if it is authentic, would stand as one of the most significant documents of the war:

1. Himmler will not pass on Hitler's order to blow up concentration camps on the Allies' approach; none is to be blown up and no prisoners killed.

2. On the Allies' approach, concentration camps are to show a white flag and be handed over in an orderly manner.

3. Further killing of Jews is suspended and prohibited. Jews are to receive the same treatment as other prisoners.

4. Concentration camps will not be evacuated. Prisoners are to be left where they are at present and may receive food parcels.[11]

When two copies of the draft were completed, Kersten claims, Himmler affixed his signature, *"Heinrich Himmler, Reichsführer SS."* Underneath, the doctor countersigned, *"In the name of humanity, Felix Kersten."* He then handed Himmler one copy, and pocketed the second. Neither document has ever been found. It's quite likely, in fact, that no such written agreement ever existed. It is difficult to believe that Kersten could lose a document of such significance. Subsequent events, however, suggest that Himmler did agree to many of these conditions—at least orally—and that Felix Kersten may very well have achieved the impossible.

Only two days after the purported "Contract in the Name of Humanity" was written, the ICRC head, Carl Burckhardt, came to an agreement with Himmler's subordinate, Ernst Kaltenbrunner, that certainly resembles Kersten's pact in spirit, if not of the same scope. Henceforth, Red Cross personnel would be permitted to station themselves inside the concentration camps and deliver relief supplies for the remainder of the war.

Because many of the entries were only added after the war, Kersten's diary itself is practically worthless in authenticating his assertions. But three decades after the war ended, the American government declassified a top-secret wartime communiqué that lends enormous credibility to Kersten's claims and may be equally as significant.

On March 28, the American minister to Sweden, Herschel Johnson, cabled Secretary of State Edwin Stettinius Jr. that Himmler's masseur, Felix Kersten, had recently returned from Germany and presented "a rather incredible account" of his discussions with Himmler. Kersten reported that there were 350,000 Jews left in Germany. Himmler had expressed a "most sympathetic interest in the Jewish problem" and was especially interested to know that the 2700 Jews from the Kasztner and Musy transports had arrived safely in Switzerland.

He was also now receptive to the idea of placing Jews in special camps under the jurisdiction of the Red Cross. On March 24, Kersten reported, Himmler had called a special meeting of all "Jewish camp" administrators in order to "give strict orders for the improved treatment of Jews hereafter. This will reportedly include instructions that each camp leader hereafter will be held strictly accountable for the death of any Jews in his camp."[12]

If those disclosures sounded unlikely to Washington, Kersten's next revelation must have appeared a fantasy. Himmler had "expressed a willingness to receive at once a special emissary" from Sweden to personally discuss the "Jewish problem." This emissary, revealed Johnson, would be Hillel Storch, "a stateless Jew of Latvian origin" who had acted as the American legation's intermediary on several occasions. In view of the "delicate nature" of such a trip, he added, and "rather well-known mixed feelings in Germany with respect to Jews, the entire matter must be handled with the greatest discretion."[13]

With time running out for the Jews of Europe, the stage was set for one of history's unlikeliest encounters.

TWENTY

AT DAGGERS DRAWN

T he events that led to Himmler's bewildering decision to meet with a representative of the hated race had been set in motion five days after he allegedly signed his name to Felix Kersten's "Contract in the Name of Humanity." In his diary entry of March 17, 1945, Kersten describes the evolution of the plan. Given subsequent well verified events, there is no reason to disbelieve this account:

> *The idea came to me of arranging a meeting between Himmler and the representative of the World Jewish Congress. It was an attractive proposition. If it succeeded, Himmler would have accepted an atmosphere of agreement in which he might be ready to make great concessions; it would also serve as a test for the sincerity of all his promises. It would moreover be a great historic event, the day when Himmler and the representative of the WJC sat down at the same table with each other. I was curious to see Himmler's reaction to the proposal. At first he promptly refused. "I can never receive a Jew. If the Führer were to hear of it, he would have me shot dead on the spot." I had expected that—always this fear of the Führer; yet it was an*

encouraging sign, for he said nothing about refusing on his own account.[1]

The Finn claims he used his considerable powers of persuasion to gradually bring Himmler around to the idea. He even offered the use of his own Harzwalde estate for the meeting, reasoning that its remote location would ensure that neither Goebbels, Bormann nor Hitler would hear anything about it.

For a man who believed in the mythical power of world Jewry, the idea of meeting a representative of the World Jewish Congress at this stage must have seemed the ideal opportunity to present himself not as the enemy of the Jews but as their savior—especially after Jean-Marie Musy convinced him that a powerful cabal of Jews was ready to advocate on his behalf. If Himmler could do this, it would surely be an opportunity to redeem him in the eyes of the Allied powers whose strings they pulled. The idea defied all logic. But Kersten knew well how his patient's mind worked and he was determined to cultivate his delusion. By March 22, Himmler had agreed not only to meet with Storch but to release thousands of Scandinavians and Jews.

Christian Günther had been dumbfounded when Kersten informed him that Himmler was willing to meet a representative of the WJC. He found it impossible to believe that the Nazi would agree to meet a Jew inside Germany. But when the masseur produced the letter from Himmler, the Swiss Foreign Minister's doubts were somewhat allayed. At the same time, Kersten produced a second letter, also on SS stationery, from Himmler's adjutant, Rudolf Brandt, assuring the Finn that "the Reichsführer SS intends to fulfill the requests which you expressed a few days ago."[2]

Günther was frank. He was eager to take advantage of the opportunity but said Himmler was wasting his time—that the Allies would never deal behind Stalin's back. "Even if Himmler were to free all the Jews now, he would still hang," the Swede told him. Kersten departed, having secured a promise that Sweden would bear all expenses incurred to fetch any prisoners freed from German camps. He went immediately to the offices of the WJC to share the news with Hillel Storch, who was even more surprised than Günther at Himmler's purported willingness to meet a Jew. To him, the thought of a face-to-face meeting with the butcher of his people was incomprehensible. "How would I refrain from grabbing Himmler by the throat and extracting vengeance for the blood of six million, including eighteen members of my own family?" Storch later wrote, recalling his conflicting emotions.

But events in Washington were conspiring to spare him the dilemma. Immediately after his encounter with Kersten, Günther had informed the U.S. embassy of Himmler's proposed meeting. The Americans evidently regarded Hillel Storch as something of a trouble-maker. As a representative of the Jewish Agency's rescue committee in 1943, he had been the ransom negotiator for the removal of twenty thousand Jewish children from Reich territories to Sweden. But when the attempt failed because of apparent obstacles from British and American authorities, Storch had publicly blasted the "inert and indifferent bureaucracy" of the Allies. The Americans were thus not keen on having him placed in charge of such delicate negotiations. Ambassador Johnson expressed his reservations in his March 28 cable to Secretary of State Edwin Stettinius Jr: "In the past the principal merit of these discussions has been the time-gaining factor but the tempo of the war as well as the level to which this approach has reached suggest strongly that a basic policy and appropriate instructions are now most urgent. There is also the question of whether Storch should be permitted to go to Berlin. We are of the opinion based on our personal knowledge of Storch's capabilities that it would be most unwise for him to go unless accompanied by a top-flight neutral thoroughly conversant with these problems who could dominate the discussions. This is apart from the overall question of whether any such discussions should be held at all."[3]

On April 7, Stettinius cabled his reply: "Department and Board approve the continuation of discussions designed solely to save the lives of Jews and other victims of enemy oppression by means of relief supplies or evacuation to safety. However, such discussions should be severed immediately if, in the opinion of Minister Johnson, they become political in nature. Board and Department leave entirely to discretion of Minister Johnson the question of continuing the indiscreet contacts already made and the question of Storch's going to Berlin."[4]

Storch was devastated when Günther asked him to cede his place at the Himmler negotiations. His initial reluctance at meeting the notorious SS chief had given way to excitement over the potentially lifesaving results of such a meeting. As a stateless Latvian granted refuge in Sweden, he needed permission and a temporary passport from the Swedes for such a trip. Now, the foreign minister made it clear that, because of American political pressure, no such permission would be granted. In desperation, Storch approached the British government through its embassy in Stockholm and asked England to support his visit to Berlin. He proposed that, upon his return, the list of Jews to be released from Germany would be handed over to the British legation, which would make arrangements for their release.

In a letter to Winston Churchill dated April 1, 1945, British foreign secretary Anthony Eden described the situation: "A naturalized Finn named Kersten, who has been in Germany for some years as a masseur to Himmler and others, with frequent visits to Sweden, has just come back to Stockholm with a letter from

Himmler, representing the fruits of a negotiation carried on by Kersten with the knowledge of Storch, the Swedish representative of the World Jewish Congress, for the release of Jews. Himmler has apparently agreed to let 10,000 Jews go to Sweden or Switzerland and wishes Storch to go to Berlin to arrange the matter."[5]

In the letter, Eden weighs the consequences of refusing to support the plan, fearing "an accusation by the Jews that we were blocking a proposal which might result in the saving of Jewish lives." Nevertheless, he recommends that England stay out of the matter, fearing the wrath of Stalin. "Do you agree?" he asks. On April 5, Churchill sent his reply: "I agree. No truck with Himmler." A cover letter from the prime minister's office accompanying Churchill's response notes that the London "Jewish societies" should not be allowed to learn of these negotiations, because they were likely to insist on "the rescue of Jews at any price." It recommends against "[horse-trading] for the release of Jews."[6]

The British minister to Stockholm, Sir Victor Mallet, was immediately wary of the proposed trip, especially when he discovered that it had been brokered by Kersten. A month earlier, he had cabled an assessment of the Finn to the Foreign Office in London: "Kersten is known to me as a Nazi and a thoroughly bad man."[7] It's not clear what he bases this assessment on other than Kersten's association with Himmler.

Mallet also had serious misgivings about Storch, apparently believing that he had links to Soviet intelligence. With questions swirling about Storch's motivations, the Swedes were not inclined to grant the necessary permission. Politics had conspired to deprive him of his chance to make history. Disappointed, he had Günther agree to one concession. He wanted to tell colleagues that his wife had vetoed the trip because of the potential danger. The minister agreed not to reveal the real reason. In Storch's place, the WJC appointed Norbert Masur, a German Jew who had acquired Swedish citizenship in 1921.[8] Masur was a veteran WJC official who, like Storch, had long been active in efforts to rescue European Jews.

No date had yet been set for Masur's meeting. During the first two weeks of April, he met a number of times with Kersten and Günther to formulate a strategy for the coming negotiations. The priority, they agreed, would be to hold Himmler to his recent promise to prevent the dynamiting of the camps and to surrender the remaining concentration camps to the Allies intact. Masur was given a list of names of prominent women confined in the Ravensbrück camp, including Gemma La Guardia Gluck, sister of the half Jewish New York mayor Fiorello La Guardia, a close friend of President Roosevelt. The Americans had been exerting particular pressure for her release. Finally, on the morning of Thursday, April 19, Masur got word that he would be received by Himmler later that day or Friday at the latest. A plane was waiting at the airport to take him and Kersten from Stockholm to Berlin. When they took off shortly after 2 p.m., they were the only passengers on the aircraft, which sported a large swastika on its fuselage.

Kersten slept during most of the flight while Masur contemplated the unbelievable turn of events. Only a few days before, he had been a mid-level official safe from the inferno raging through Europe. All day, he had sat in an office reading reports about the desperate plight of his people and crimes so horrific that he could barely breathe, never dreaming that he would one day have a chance to confront the perpetrator. He would later describe what went through his mind as he embarked on the journey: "For me as a Jew, it was a deeply moving thought that in a few hours, I would be face to face with the man who was primarily responsible for the destruction of several million people."[9]

As the plane neared Berlin, he thought of one of the reports he had read earlier that week. It was a detailed account by the Soviet army of what they had found when they liberated Auschwitz three months earlier. Though most of the inmates had been evacuated before the Soviets arrived, the Germans had left behind thousands of prisoners too sick to be moved. They told a story so frightening, so ghastly, that many of their liberators at first thought them delusional. Like Storch, Masur wondered how he could remain gracious when confronting the purveyor of this nightmare. It was a question that occupied him throughout the four-hour flight.

The plane landed at Berlin's Tempelhof Airport shortly after 6 p.m and a group of police officers were waiting on the airfield. As Kersten and Masur disembarked, the police greeted them with words long familiar to the masseur: "Heil Hitler." Masur swallowed nervously, then took off his hat and curtly responded, "Good evening."[10] He had passed his first test of diplomacy. One of the officers handed Kersten a safe conduct pass for Masur, which had been signed by General Schellenberg.

The staff car Himmler had promised to send had not yet arrived. As the pair sat impatiently in the waiting room of the terminal building, they heard a crackle from the loudspeaker. Suddenly a voice boomed. It was Joseph Goebbels, Germany's propaganda minister, whose fanatical celebration of Nazism was familiar to all Germans: "Rejoice, people of Germany," the voice said. "Tomorrow, April 20, is the birthday of the beloved Führer."[11]

A chill went through Masur. He knew the German people had no reason to rejoice for the madman who had led them to such misery. Finally, an SS car arrived to take them to Kersten's Harzwalde estate eighty kilometers away. As they passed through Berlin, they witnessed a scene of utter devastation. Night had fallen and blackout conditions were in effect. Through the darkness, their eyes were drawn to row upon row of blackened shells—buildings that had been destroyed by relentless bombings by the Allied squadrons. "The ruins of the houses were like ghosts," Masur recalled.[12]

Within a few hours, the skies overhead would fill with planes ready to resume their deadly night missions. The two men were anxious to reach the safety of Kersten's estate. Normally, the journey would have taken just over an hour, but their path was constantly impeded by rubble and bomb craters. Twice they had to disembark to push aside huge concrete slabs that blocked their path. When they finally exited the city two hours later, they heard the ominous wail of an air raid siren signaling the imminent arrival of the bombers. Twenty minutes outside Berlin, the car was stopped by an army patrol. Despite his safe conduct pass, Masur was terrified. What if they were to recognize his distinct Jewish features? His fears proved unfounded. The patrol simply ordered them to put out their headlights to avoid attracting the attention of enemy aircraft. Behind them, they could see the sky above the city alight with the explosions of falling bombs. Masur did not know whether to cheer on the Allied bombers or fear for his own safety.

As they passed through the town of Oranienburg, Masur was again reminded "of the terror of the concentration camps." Here, in one of the first SS camps, a number of his relatives had been interned for their political affiliations in the months after Hitler took power, before Masur negotiated for their emigration to Sweden.

Finally, close to midnight, the car arrived at Harzwalde— Kersten's lavish estate and hobby farm. They were met by Kersten's sister Elizabeth, who showed the exhausted Masur to his room. After their guest retired, the Kerstens discussed arrangements for closing up the estate. Kersten planned to return to Stockholm immediately following the talks with Himmler. With the Soviets closing in, he knew they would not be safe in Germany. The Russian army would be anxious to exact retribution on anybody associated with the Nazi leadership and, despite his work "on behalf of humanity," the doctor feared he would be stained by Himmler's crimes. In addition, he had carried arms against Russia as a Finnish officer in 1919. The Soviets, he knew, had long memories.

Meanwhile, despite the exhausting journey, Masur tossed and turned upstairs. "That night I was not able to sleep," he recalled, "not because of the constant noise from the planes but tension at the thought of meeting with Himmler, the feeling that possibly the destiny of thousands of Jews were dependent on my words."[13]

Knowing he would likely never return, Kersten thought sadly of how much he would miss the estate where he had spent so many happy times. He gazed into the woods where he loved to hunt deer and remembered an outing with Himmler years before. Himmler never could understand Kersten's passion for deer stalking, and the doctor would never forget Himmler's ironic words that day: "How could you find any pleasure, Herr Kersten, in shooting from behind cover at poor creatures browsing on the edge of a wood. . . . Properly considered, it's pure murder."[14]

Just after 2 a.m., Walter Schellenberg arrived to brief Kersten on recent events. He brought mixed news. The week before, Allied troops had liberated Bergen-Belsen and Buchenwald, two of Germany's largest concentration camps. Himmler, defying Hitler's order, had kept his promise to surrender the camps intact, although Schellenberg had to intervene at the last minute to stop a planned evacuation of Buchenwald ordered by Kaltenbrunner. When the Allies arrived, they found a white flag flying from the water tower. As a result, Schellenberg reported, the party leadership was furious. Hitler's top lieutenant,

Martin Bormann, was demanding that Himmler obey the Führer's instructions. If the regime fell, the reasoning went, as many of its enemies as possible should be liquidated in the process.

Kersten realized that his written agreement with Himmler the month before was worthless when put up against the Reichsführer's fear of Hitler. Kersten knew that Himmler's spinelessness before the Führer could jeopardize all his efforts. Late into the morning, Kersten and Schellenberg discussed strategy. Schellenberg proposed an idea he thought might work if Himmler's nerve failed. "The essential thing," he said, "is to get Himmler to confirm the promises he made you in my presence. In that case, even if he goes back on his word after you have left and gives orders for the extermination, Brandt and I will take the necessary steps to see the orders are not passed on."[15]

At 9 a.m., while the two were still talking, Masur came downstairs, where Kersten introduced him to Schellenberg. As Elizabeth served breakfast, the intelligence chief explained that Himmler had been detained in Berlin over plans for the celebration of Hitler's birthday that evening. After the planned birthday dinner, he would get to Harzwalde as quickly as possible. Masur couldn't help but be struck by the almost comical irony. "Hitler should have only known that Himmler, after the birthday party, would be negotiating with a Jew!" he thought.

Masur outlined his proposals to Schellenberg, who promised his full support. "He seemed to have complete understanding of my wishes with attempts to rescue Jews and promised energetic support," Masur later wrote. Schellenberg cautioned the Jewish representative that Himmler, due back later that night, might not be as receptive as they had originally hoped. "There's no telling what his mood will be after meeting the Führer," said the intelligence chief.

Masur spent the afternoon inspecting Kersten's farm and talking to the workers, many of whom were Jehovah's Witnesses whose release from concentration camps Kersten had secured in 1941. "It was an odd assemblage of people," he recalled. "They belonged to a sect which refused military service on religious grounds. Also they would not say, 'Heil Hitler,' as 'Heil' (salvation) can only come from God." The prisoners, most of whom had been interned in Buchenwald, told him that they had been the victims of savage abuse until the Jews arrived in 1938 "and the guards were able to pursue their sadism towards them."[16]

By midnight, Himmler had still failed to appear. Masur's anxiety increased. He had been promised a meeting that evening. Had something gone wrong? Had Himmler changed his mind? Would his presence be discovered by those opposed to these negotiations? Kersten was worried as well. He had feared that the Reichsführer's invitation to Hitler's birthday celebration was merely a pretext concocted by the party leadership as an excuse to arrest him for defying orders about the destruction of the camps. Before Schellenberg returned to Berlin, he took Kersten aside and confided the real reason for the delay. Himmler had only stayed a short time at the Führer's party, but before he could travel to Harzwalde, he was waiting for the departure of Kaltenbrunner, who was scheduled that evening to return to his headquarters in Austria. He didn't want the talks to come to the attention of his rival, who would undoubtedly regard the meeting as treason and report them immediately to Hitler.

Reassured, Kersten returned to packing his belongings. As he did so, he thought back to his first conversation with Himmler about the Jews in 1941. The Final Solution was not yet officially underway, but the Reichsführer had already declared that the destruction of the Jewish people was imminent. Kersten had stated it was fearful cruelty to want to destroy men simply because of their religion. "It's a blood guilt of the Jews which has swallowed up countless millions of victims and will consume more," Himmler retorted. "It's the destructive Jewish spirit which has caused the lack of unity in Europe. You can only meet the Jews with their own methods and their own words: an eye for an eye and a tooth for a tooth."

Four years later, these words remained with Kersten as he awaited the fateful meeting. After hours of waiting, Kersten too had almost given up hoping Himmler would come. He was just thinking of retiring for the night when, at precisely 2:30 a.m., the Finn heard the sound of a car coming down his driveway. He stepped outside to see Himmler getting out with his adjutant, Rudolf Brandt. Anxious to gauge the Reichsführer's mood, Kersten asked his sister to show Brandt inside so he could have a private talk with his patient.

It was a warm spring night. In the moonlight, as they stood on the porch outside, Kersten could see that Himmler was wearing his full military uniform, covered with military decorations. Each one, he reflected, represented some act of brutality in the name of the Reich. Kersten recorded this talk in his diary: "I asked Himmler to be not only amiable but magnanimous towards Masur. Not the least important factor in considering Masur's requests was the chance to show the world, which had been so disgusted by the harsh treatment accorded to the Third Reich's political enemies, that this had been reversed and humanitarian measures undertaken. It was of the first importance to produce such evidence, otherwise history would make a one-sided judgment on the German people. Various earlier talks had shown me how receptive Himmler was to this type of argument. Himmler promised to do all he could towards granting Masur's requests. His actual words were: 'I want to bury the hatchet between us and the Jews. If I had had my own way, many things would have been done differently. . . .'"[17] When they finished conversing, Kersten showed Himmler into the house where Masur waited with Schellenberg. Kersten made the introductions.

"Reichsführer Heinrich Himmler . . . Herr Norbert Masur, delegate of the World Jewish Congress." The two men sized each other up. Once predator and prey, they were now in the refuge of Kersten's neutral estate. There was an uncomfortable silence, the only sound the crackling of the flames in the giant fireplace. Finally, Himmler said, "Good day. I'm glad you've come."

"Thank you," Masur responded coolly.

Kersten described the encounter in his diary: "Here around the table of my Harzwalde house were peacefully seated the representatives of two races who had been at daggers drawn, each regarding the other as its mortal enemy. And this attitude had demanded the sacrifice of millions; the shades of these dead hovered in the background. It was a shattering reflection."[18]

Masur thought Himmler looked better in person than in photographs. "Perhaps his errant and piercing gaze was an expression of sadism and harshness," he reflected in his report, "however, had I not known his past, I would never have believed that this man was singularly responsible for the most extensive mass murders in history."[19]

After finishing his coffee and several pieces of cake, Himmler wiped his mouth with a napkin and launched into a long, somewhat pedantic speech about how his generation had never known any peace and how it had been a victim of the unjust terms of the Versailles treaty after the First World War. Masur listened patiently to this part tirade, part revisionist history lesson, occasionally exchanging bemused glances with Kersten, who also remained silent. Finally, Himmler came to the subject of the Jews, who he claimed had played a leading role in the German civil war immediately following the First World War, particularly during the Spartacist (communist) uprisings.

"The Jews," he said, "were an alien element in Germany; earlier ages had failed to drive them out of the country. When we took power, we wanted to solve the Jewish question once and for all. With this in view, I set up an emigration organization which would have been very advantageous to the Jews. But not one of the countries which had been so friendly towards your people would accept them."[20]

Masur interrupted for the first time, pointing out that international law had never found it acceptable to drive people from a country in which they and their ancestors had lived for generations. Himmler ignored his interjection. He went on to speak of the ferocity of Germany's war with Russia. "The Russians are no ordinary enemies. Their mentality is impossible to understand. We must conquer or perish. The war in the East is subjecting our soldiers to the most brutal test. If the Jewish people have suffered from the ferocity of war, it must not be forgotten that the German people have not been spared anything either.

"These Eastern Jews aid the partisans," he continued, "and help the underground movements; they also fire upon us from our ghettos and are the carriers of epidemics such as typhus. It was in order to control these epidemics that crematorium ovens were built for the countless corpses of the victims. And now they threaten to hang us for that."[21]

Masur's expression changed to a contemptuous glare. Himmler's argument would become familiar in some circles after the war, and would form the eventual basis for the poisonous claims of the Holocaust denial movement. Himmler continued to defend the concentration camps. "They should have been called education camps, for criminal elements were lodged there besides Jews and political prisoners," he said. "Thanks to their erection, Germany, in 1941, had the lowest crime rate for many years. The prisoners had to perform heavy labour, but that was true of the German people too. The treatment was always just."[22]

Masur could not allow this lie to go unchallenged. "Surely you cannot deny that crimes were committed against the prisoners in those camps," he said.

"Oh, I concede these things have happened occasionally," Himmler replied, "but I have also punished those responsible."[23]

Kersten did not like the direction of the discussion and proceeded to interrupt. "We are not here to argue about the past. Our real interest is in seeing what can still be saved."

"This is true," Masur said. "The least that must be done is that all the Jews still in Germany must have their lives guaranteed. Even better would be for them all to be freed."[24]

Himmler ignored Masur's plea. Instead, his voice rising in anger, he reminded the assembled men of recent events. "It was my intention to turn over the concentration camps without defending them, as I had promised. I turned over Bergen-Belsen and Buchenwald, but I got no thanks for this."[25] He cited a photo that had already been circulated in the world press, printed under headlines such as "Nazi Monsters!" The photo showed an SS guard tied up alongside a pile of corpses discovered by the British troops upon their arrival at the camp.

He reminded Masur about the consequences of the recent Musy mission: "When I let the Jews go to Switzerland, it was made the subject of a personal campaign against me in the press, asserting that I had only released these prisoners in order to construct an alibi for myself. But I have no need of an alibi!" he shouted. "I have always done what I considered just, what was essential for my people. I will answer for that. Nobody has had so much mud slung at him in the last ten years as I have. I have never bothered myself about that. Even in Germany any man can say about me what he pleases. Newspapers abroad have started a campaign against me, which is no encouragement for me to continue handing over the camps."[26]

Masur interrupted this outburst. It was impossible to tell news-papers throughout the world what they should write, he protested. The Jews had not been responsible for the articles. He cited all the positive articles about the release of the Theresienstadt Jews in February. He pointed out that most of the coverage stressed that the Jews had arrived healthy. Masur pressed his point, having been briefed about Himmler's desperate desire for an alliance with the West. "The Allies will look very favorably upon the release of more Jews," he pleaded. "Perhaps," he added, referring to the Ravensbrück inmates, "you will agree to at least release the women." This approach seemed to calm the Reichsführer. He asked Schellenberg to take Masur out of the room so he could discuss the situation with Kersten and Brandt. Once they had left, Himmler expressed his greatest fear: that Hitler would find out about the negotiations. He was willing to release a number of women from Ravensbrück, but the Führer had issued explicit orders forbidding the release of any more Jews.

Kersten had an idea. He suggested that the Jewish women be listed as Poles to disguise their true identity. That way, Hitler would never discover that his order had been defied. He mentioned the list of prominent women Masur had brought with him, which included Jews and non-Jews. It was the insurance Himmler was looking for. He agreed to release one thousand Jewish women from Ravensbrück to the Red Cross along with all the prominent Scandinavians named on Masur's list. To Kersten, he pledged this was only the beginning: "There will be more." At the same time, he issued a number of other formal pledges, some reiterating commit-ments he had previously made:

1. No Jews would be shot.

2. No further forcible movements would take place, even if the fronts approached the camps.

3. Foodstuffs and medicines were permitted to be sent through the Red Cross to all internment camps.

4. Commanders of camps would receive orders for the good treatment of the Jews and for turning over the camps to the Allies if the fronts should approach any camps.

Masur was summoned and, to his immense relief, informed by Kersten that his mission was a success. After the tantrum he had witnessed earlier, he had assumed he was destined to return home empty-handed. Watching Himmler put his signature to a document authorizing the release of the Ravensbrück women and thanking him for the concession, he asked the Nazi to spare a thought for the hundreds of thousands of Jews still held captive. "I give you my word they shall be protected," Himmler replied. "It is very necessary that not only your visit here must remain secret, but also the arrival of the Jews in Sweden must remain that way."[27]

It was 5 a.m. Himmler could not resist one last lecture, a warning about the consequences of a German defeat. He likely knew his words would get back to the Western Allies, whom he still hoped to persuade of the wisdom of a truce. "The Americans will agree that we were the last bulwark against Bolshevism," he thundered, "Hitler will be remembered in history as a great man, because he gave the world the National Socialist solution, the only one which is able to stand up against Bolshevism." This, Masur recalled, was the only time Himmler had mentioned Hitler by name. Himmler concluded by predicting that American and British soldiers would be infected by the "spirit of Bolshevism" and would cause great social problems when they returned to their countries. He stated emphatically that he would never surrender unconditionally. "That will never happen," he insisted. "I am not afraid to die."[28]

The historic meeting had come to an end. Masur proffered his hand graciously, anxious not to offend Himmler at the last minute and jeopardize the agreement. Relieved to be done with the chilling encounter, the Swede reflected on what had just happened, surprised that Himmler hadn't requested anything in exchange for what he had just agreed to. "He did not ask for any concessions from us," he wrote in his report to the WJC upon his return. "For sure he did not think that he could buy his own life at this late hour. He was too clever to assume this, he knew very well that his list of sins was too large. . . . The shallowness of his argument was unbelievable. He used nothing but lies in his defense. No logic in building of thoughts, no deep thoughts, which even a criminal might have had . . . only lies and excuses."[29]

After the farewells were dispensed with, Himmler went outside with his longtime confidant and healer for some parting words. Kersten expressed his gratitude for the meeting's success. Suddenly, the Reichsführer asked him, "Have you any access to General Eisenhower?" Surprised, the Finn said he had none. Himmler continued. Would Kersten agree to act as his personal emissary to the Americans? Could he approach Eisenhower with the suggestion that hostilities against Germany be stopped so that a single front's war against Russia might be waged? "I am ready to concede victory to the Western Allies," Himmler revealed. "They have only to give me time to throw back the Russians. If they would let me have the equipment, I could still do it."[30] Kersten knew such a plan was impossible, but he didn't dare say so. Instead, he suggested that Himmler put the proposal to Count Bernadotte of the Red Cross, with whom he was scheduled to meet again later the same morning.

The two walked to the car, where a chauffeur was waiting. Himmler got in, then stretched out his hand to the man he called his "Magic Buddha." "Thank you for everything, Kersten," he said. "I don't know how much longer I shall live. Whatever happens, please don't think ill of me. No doubt I've committed great faults. But

Hitler wanted me to follow the road of severity. Without discipline, without obedience, nothing is possible. Have pity on me. I'm thinking of my poor family. Farewell."[31] Kersten wrote that Himmler had tears in his eyes. He shut the door. Kersten knew they would never see each other again.

TWENTY-ONE

RACE AGAINST TIME

I f the Third Reich had once been known as a model of unparalleled efficiency and order, by the spring of 1945 it had degenerated into a state of near total chaos. As the Reich began to taste defeat, conflicting loyalties and individual rebellions, hidden throughout the war years, reared their heads and compounded the anarchy. In Berlin, a small inner circle of disciples began to close around Hitler—men like Goebbels, Bormann and Speer—while Himmler and Göring increasingly appeared to be pursuing their own agendas. Meanwhile, as Walter Schellenberg set his course firmly with Himmler, Ernst Kaltenbrunner chose to honor to the end his blood oath to the Führer.

As RSHA security chief in charge of the Gestapo and the police, Kaltenbrunner was a Nazi figure with immense powers but still very much subordinate to the Reichsführer-SS. As the end drew nearer, however, he became increasingly bold, willing to defy Himmler's authority. When Count Bernadotte arrived to organize the transportation of the Scandinavians in February, it was Kaltenbrunner who had been assigned to accommodate him. Yet, according to the Count's postwar memoir, Kaltenbrunner was not at all cooperative in acting on Himmler's orders regarding the evacuation of the Scandinavians.

"I do not intend to assist you in this matter you have brought up," he told the Swede on March 5. Bernadotte stood his ground. "And I am not going to stand one of Himmler's subordinates trying to sabotage an arrangement agreed upon between him and myself," he replied.[1]

Tried at Nuremberg, Kaltenbrunner later made it clear that he had stood firmly opposed to the maneuverings of Himmler and Schellenberg and their efforts to free "opponents of the Reich" during the last months of the war. "I have criticized Himmler for these tricks and complained and discredited them with Hitler, stating that it was demeaning to the cause and the Reich that in so important a matter these methods should be used by Himmler and Schellenberg," he told his inquisitor in 1946.[2] Schellenberg clearly sensed that his master's position was weakening, especially after Hitler removed Himmler as commander of the Army Group Vistula on March 20. In his postwar memoir, he described what he called an "almost daily struggle between Himmler and me in which I wrestled for his soul."[3]

For nearly two years, Schellenberg had attempted to steer the Reichsführer away from what he considered the disastrous course set by Hitler, to no avail. He attempted one final gambit. In a "stormy conversation" in late March, he argued that it was Hitler's advisers who had "succeeded in removing him from the Führer's side." He urged Himmler to return immediately to Berlin to "arrange preparations for peace." If need be, the Reichsführer "must use force." But the idea of usurping the Führer was anathema to Himmler, he recalled. "What should he do? He could not shoot Hitler; he could not give him poison; he could not arrest him in the Reich chancellery, for then the whole military machine would come to a standstill. I told him that all this did not matter; only two possibilities existed for him; either he should go to Hitler and tell him frankly all that had happened during the last years and force him to resign; or else he should remove him by force."[4]

Himmler protested that if he were to take such a course, Hitler would fall into a violent rage and have him shot. But Schellenberg was adamant that the Reichsführer had enough support among the SS that he was in a strong enough position to arrest Hitler and take command of the Reich. In the end, however, Himmler's pathological fear or loyalty to his Führer prevailed.

Meanwhile, it would appear that Kaltenbrunner's attempts to discredit his superior were bearing fruit. On April 3 or 4, Hitler summoned Himmler, Schellenberg and Franz Göring to a meeting. He had heard that negotiations were underway to release Jews from the concentration camps. Any such releases were forbidden, Hitler had made clear. Nor could the camps be permitted to fall into the hands of the Allies. To that end, he ordered the evacuation of fifteen major camps on foot toward a *réduit*—central zone—inside Southern Germany. The evacuations were to begin immediately.

Despite the devastating setback to his efforts in February when the second train failed to arrive, Jean-Marie Musy had not given up on his mission. Nor had the Sternbuchs. On April 3, Musy embarked on his sixth journey to Berlin, hoping yet again to press for the resumption of the transports. Upon his arrival, Schellenberg informed him of Hitler's new orders. Panicked, Musy pleaded for the intelligence chief to arrange a meeting with the Führer. He had to be persuaded to rescind this barbaric order. Such a meeting was out of the question, Schellenberg told him. One does not argue with Adolf Hitler. By this point, Musy knew about the deadly toll that had been exacted during the forced marches from Auschwitz and elsewhere. "I realized that this would undoubtedly occasion the deaths of hundreds of thousands of people," he later testified. "It would have been more humane to simply shoot the prisoners."[5]

Frantically, the Swiss emissary implored Schellenberg to intervene with Himmler.

The next day, Musy was summoned for another meeting. Schellenberg had spoken to Himmler about the evacuations. The Reichsführer had agreed to disregard Hitler's order and "preserve the status quo" in the camps on one condition. The Allies would have to promise not to shoot the camp guards upon their arrival. All SS guards and administrative personnel found in such camps when American and British forces arrived must be treated as soldiers and prisoners of war. Reports had circulated about atrocities committed after the liberation of the Polish camps by Soviet troops against German officers and guards who had not yet fled. Himmler had a fierce attachment to his men, and they to him. It was the Reichsführer in fact who had designed the inscription every SS officer wore on his belt: *Meine Ehre heißt Treue* (My Honor Is My Loyalty). Schellenberg told Musy that he had very little time before the evacuations were set to begin. Himmler required an answer before 7 p.m. on April 11. Musy promised to quickly secure a pledge of restraint.

Meanwhile, in Stockholm, Hillel Storch had received an alarming report from two of his German contacts. The Germans were planning to blow up Bergen-Belsen on the orders of Ernst Kaltenbrunner. Storch immediately made his way to Felix Kersten's residence and relayed the news. In his presence, Kersten immediately telephoned Himmler's adjutant, Rudolf Brandt, who confirmed the Reichsführer's promise to hand over the camps intact. Storch contacted Count Bernadotte, who was in regular communication with Himmler's office. Two days later, Bernadotte received Brandt's assurance that the demolition of Belsen had been halted. When British and Canadian troops liberated the camp five days later, they found a scene of utter devastation, but they also found a white flag flying from the water tower and the camp intact. Storch later credited Kersten and Bernadotte with saving the inmates. Israeli historian Dov Dinur cites Kersten's intervention on April 8 for preventing the camp's destruction. He claims that he saw depositions from eight Belsen survivors attesting to dynamite being laid out under the barracks that night. Were it not for Himmler's countermanding order, he suggests, the liberators would have been greeted with a sight far more gruesome than the horror they encountered a week later, which shocked the world to its core.[6]

Jean-Marie Musy had no idea of those machinations as he raced back to Switzerland to report on the pending evacuations and Himmler's plea for the safety of the SS guards. For the first time during his mission, the aging Swiss statesman had taken the wheel of the battered Mercedes for the long journey back. On April 8, the same day Kersten phoned Brandt to save Bergen-Belsen, Musy arrived in Montreux, where the Sternbuchs were anxiously awaiting his report. He detailed his recent discussions with Schellenberg and emphasized the importance of a formal pledge by the Americans. The next day, Isaac accompanied Musy to see McClelland in Bern, where they related the dramatic developments. Would the Americans be willing to give such an assurance? "To the best of my knowledge, it is not the practice of the American or British armies to shoot anyone in uniform who properly surrendered without resisting," McClelland told him. But Musy insisted on a formal guarantee that he could bring back to the Germans.[7] Cabling the request to Washington, McClelland noted that he found it difficult to understand the Nazis' proposal since it was "apparently of such small advantage to them."[8] Still, he furnished Musy with an oral guarantee that the guards would not be mistreated.

Meanwhile, Benoît Musy had remained behind in Berlin. Himmler had given him the authorization in January to travel to any concentration camp in the company of Schellenberg's aide, Franz Göring, and

Benoît had come to regard the mission as a moral imperative. He had never shared his father's pro-German views and so perhaps saw this as a chance to exorcise the demons of his legacy. During their many meetings, he had also gained great respect for the Sternbuchs and the courage they demonstrated on behalf of their people.

The first evacuations had been scheduled to take place at Buchenwald, outside Weimar, where the Americans were within striking distance. On April 8, Benoît set off with Göring to check on the camp. When the pair arrived the next morning, they beheld a sight that Musy would later describe as "a convoy of the doomed." SS guards were in the full stages of preparation for an evacuation. Emaciated prisoners who could barely stand were already being lined up to be marched to Dachau. Göring later described the scene in an affidavit: "The prisoners were struck over their heads in order to drive them more quickly into the marching formations. It was a picture of horror to witness people whose faces were marked by death being chased toward the road."[9]

Schellenberg's aide immediately asked to see the camp commandant, who informed him that Ernst Kaltenbrunner had personally ordered the evacuation on the instructions of the Führer. Musy demanded that Göring intervene, but the Haupsturmführer (equivalent in rank to a captain) was powerless to countermand a directive from the powerful Kaltenbrunner. Only Himmler himself could issue such an order. Frantically, the pair raced back to Berlin to report the news, their return trip slowed significantly by the thousands of refugees and army deserters clogging the roads. The desperate mass of humanity was attempting to reach American lines, preferring capture by Western forces to the specter of occupation by the Soviets, who were then within weeks of taking Berlin. Only three hours from their destination, the SS staff car Musy and Göring were driving was caught in a strafing attack by Allied aircraft that lacerated two tires and destroyed the gas tank. Their driver went to seek help, and finally a Polish mechanic was located who agreed to repair the car in exchange for three hundred cigarettes. The delay cost them half a day. When they eventually reached SS headquarters the next morning, the junior Musy angrily told Schellenberg about the Buchenwald evacuation and demanded that Himmler keep to his agreement.[10] The intelligence chief assured him something would be done.

When Himmler discovered his order had been disregarded, he was reportedly livid. He reportedly ordered that the evacuation be halted immediately and that the camp be turned over to the Allies intact. Failure to obey would result in execution. The order came too late for the thousands of prisoners who had already been evacuated, but when the American army arrived two days later, on April 11, they found a white flag flying from the water tower and twenty-one thousand inmates still in the camp. Perhaps emboldened by the halt to the forced march and by news of the Americans' imminent arrival, members of the camp's resistance had stormed the watchtowers earlier that day and seized control of the camp. The first test of Himmler's "Contract in the Name of Humanity" had passed with mixed results.

Two days later, Himmler's pledge would again be severely tested. Alois Dörr was the commandant of Helmbrechts, a women's concentration camp near Hof in Bavaria. On April 13, he had ordered the evacuation of more than 1100 prisoners, 580 of them Jewish. Their destination was Dachau, outside Munich. The marchers were accompanied by 47 guards, split almost equally between men and women. The male guards carried rifles while the women carried rods. On the first day of the march, ten of the women were beaten to death by the female guards for walking too slowly.

Late on the second day, an SS lieutenant located the column of prisoners walking along a road. He was a courier who had been sent from Himmler's headquarters with an order from the Reichsführer expressly forbidding the killing of any prisoners. According to a guard's postwar testimony at Dörr's war crimes trial, "We, the guards, had to assemble, and this lieutenant announced to us that he was an adjutant of Himmler's. He further said that negotiations were being conducted with the American troops and that the prisoners must be treated humanely." The women guards were then instructed to dispose of the wooden rods they regularly used to beat the prisoners.[11] Upon the approach of the Allies, the guards were ordered to release the women into the woods.

This testimony demonstrates once again that Himmler appeared to be going out of his way to keep his promises to Musy and defy Hitler's edict even as Kaltenbrunner did his best to carry out the murderous decree. Still, those promises had merely focused on keeping the Jewish inmates safe inside the camps. Masur's dramatic encounter with Himmler on April 21 once again raised the possibility of liberating them.

Himmler had not yet slept. After leaving the Führer's birthday celebration, he had journeyed to Kersten's Harzwalde estate, where his discussion with the Jewish delegate, Norbert Masur, lasted until 5 a.m. An hour later, he was eating breakfast with Count Bernadotte at Hohenlychen—the converted nursing home where Himmler had resided since January. Bernadotte had been pressing the Reichsführer for some time to allow the remaining Scandinavian prisoners— many already en route to Denmark—to journey to Sweden. It's unclear whether or not the count had been informed of Himmler's concession to Masur only ninety minutes earlier, agreeing to the release of a thousand Jewish women. Before the meal was over, however, he had apparently also consented to the release of every Ravensbrück inmate, "regardless of nationality."[12]

Bernadotte cabled the camp's commandant with the news that Himmler had given permission to release the women. A little over twenty-four hours later, in the late morning of April 22, Benoît Musy arrived with Franz Göring to oversee the evacuation of the Jewish women prisoners promised to Masur. Göring reported to the camp commandant, Fritz Suhren, to arrange for the release of the Jewish women, as per Himmler's order. A convoy of Swedish Red Cross buses and ambulances were expected imminently but had not yet arrived. A Red Cross delegate, Albert de Cocatrix, had already been stationed in the camp for some time under the agreement with Himmler, and had been overseeing distribution of relief supplies, but he had little influence over the commandant.

Commandant Suhren was not at first inclined to cooperate with the new arrivals. He had already received a set of conflicting orders. Ernst Kaltenbrunner, he reported, had relayed an order from the Führer himself. The prisoners were to be kept in the camp and liquidated before the arrival of Soviet forces. Suhren further confided that among the inmates were seventy or so women—fifty-four Poles and seventeen French—who had been subjected to medical experiments. "When I asked him what kinds of experiments he meant," recalled Göring, "he explained to me that the persons in question had been injected with bacilli, which had developed into a disease, which then had been healed through operations." Suhren revealed that he had been expressly ordered that under no circumstances was he to release these women—known among the inmates as *kaninchen* (experimental rabbits).[13] It would also later emerge that, upon Kaltenbrunner's orders, Suhren had exterminated a number of inmates in specially constructed gas chambers long after Himmler's cessation decree of November 1944, even though Ravensbrück was not officially a death camp. Moreover, he had recently evacuated thousands of Russian women on a death march toward Mecklenberg. For these crimes, he would be tried and executed by a French court in 1950.

Benoît Musy immediately telephoned SS headquarters, where he reached Rudolf Brandt. Himmler's adjutant ordered Suhren to release all the prisoners, including the *kaninchen*. They would be turned over to the Swedish Red Cross captain, Dr. Hans Arnoldsson, who had been put in charge of coordinating the logistics. The plan called for evacuating the women by foot to the nearby sub-camp of Malchow, from where a convoy of the Red Cross's white buses and ambulances would transfer the liberated prisoners to Denmark and eventually on to Sweden. The commandant could not ignore an order from the Reichsführer-SS, but the idea of releasing Jews was anathema to him. It was clear to both men that he had no intention of complying. It was left to Benoît to end the standoff. He reminded Suhren of the consequences of disobeying Himmler's expressed wishes. The SS commander finally acquiesced, authorizing the release of the Jewish women. In his 1947 memoir, *Aux Portes des Enfers*, Arnoldsson credits Benoît Musy with convincing Suhren to release the Jewish prisoners.[14]

The Red Cross fleet was hardly sufficient to move 8000 inmates,[15] and Göring eventually secured a freight train to transport an overflow of about 4000 of the women to Denmark. The operation took five days. There are conflicting accounts of how many of those rescued were Jewish. Göring would later claim 3000 Jews were freed from Ravensbrück alone. Norbert Masur gave the figure as 3500. While Arnoldsson was coordinating the operation, Göring and Benoît determined that there were an additional 2800 women, including 960 Jews, interned in labor camps around the Hamburg area.[16] These would be the last women added to the train convoys already under way.[17]

While the liberation of Ravensbrück was still in progress, Schellenberg summoned Count Bernadotte to a meeting at the Swedish consulate in Flensburg, purportedly to discuss the next step in the White Buses evacuation. Bernadotte was not prepared for his stunning overture. Hitler, the German intelligence chief revealed, would soon be dead. Himmler was now prepared to approach General Eisenhower to surrender. Would he be willing to arrange such an approach? Himmler was anxious to meet again with the count to work out the details, but Bernadotte stated that he believed there was no need for such a meeting. All that was required was a "letter of capitulation" from the German side.[18] Schellenberg pointed out this could prove problematic while Hitler was still alive. He suggested a meeting with Himmler at the Swedish consulate at Lübeck. The meeting was arranged for that evening at 10 p.m.

Just as the men sat down to talk, an air raid siren sounded, forcing them to seek refuge in the cellar. Here, by candlelight, Heinrich Himmler finally uttered the words that Schellenberg had been waiting to hear for two years. If a meeting could be arranged with General Eisenhower, he was willing to make a formal declaration: "I recognize that Germany has suffered defeat at the hands of the Western Allies. I am prepared to surrender unconditionally on the Western front and also to discuss the technical ways and means of arranging capitulation."[19] On one point, however, he still refused to yield. "To the Russians it is impossible for us Germans, and above all for me, to capitulate."[20] Bernadotte agreed to bring a letter to the Swedish foreign minister with the terms he was proposing, but only if Himmler formally included the surrender of Denmark and Norway to the Allies. Himmler agreed, with the proviso that the postwar occupation would not include Soviet troops. Shortly after midnight on April 24, Schellenberg left to accompany Himmler to his hotel before returning to escort Bernadotte to the Danish border.

It took mere hours for Himmler's offer of capitulation to reach the Western Allies. On April 25, only thirteen days after he was inaugurated, the new U.S. president, Harry S. Truman, placed a transatlantic call to his British counterpart, Winston Churchill, to discuss Himmler's offer. A declassified transcript reveals that neither leader was willing to sell out their erstwhile Soviet ally even though the war was all but won and Stalin was no longer indispensable to a military victory. This had been the purported reason that the Americans and British had declined to endorse previous ransom proposals:

CHURCHILL: [Himmler's refusal] to surrender on the Eastern Front looks like a last attempt to sow discord between the Western Allies and Russia. Obviously the Nazis would have to surrender to all the Allies simultaneously.

TRUMAN: That is right. That is exactly the way I feel. He has to surrender to all the Allies at once. . . .

CHURCHILL: We consider Himmler should be told that German folk, either as individuals or in units, should everywhere surrender themselves to the Allied troops or representatives on the spot. Until that happens, the attack of the Allies upon them on all sides and in all theaters where resistance continues will be prosecuted with the utmost vigor. . . . .[21]

The leaders agreed to cable Stalin immediately to inform him about Himmler's offer and reassure the Soviet chief that they would not accept anything less than an unconditional surrender to all three Allied powers simultaneously. These communications had been conducted in the strictest of secrecy, but it didn't take long for Himmler's offer to leak. On April 28, a correspondent for the British news agency Reuters reported that Heinrich Himmler had offered his unconditional surrender to the Western Allies. Only a few hours later, the BBC broke into its broadcast with the sensational news. For war-weary Britons, the report sparked premature celebrations. In Berlin, however, the news was not as well received. It was the job of one of Goebbels's aides to monitor Western broadcasts. Hearing the news, he immediately handed a summary of the report to Hitler's private secretary, Martin Bormann, in the Führerbunker where Hitler had retreated with his closest aides as the Reich crumbled around him. It was left up to Bormann to relay the news to the Führer.

Among those present in the bunker was Hanna Reitsch, a decorated Luftwaffe aviatrix who was fanatically devoted to Hitler and who had volunteered to fly leading Nazis out of Berlin ahead of the approaching Soviet forces if required. Captured after the war, Reitsch told American intelligence officers that she was present in the bunker when Hitler received the news about Himmler's negotiations. She described the Führer raging like a madman, face distorted as he shuffled up and down the corridor thrusting the report at everyone he met. "His color rose to a heated red and his face was almost unrecognizable," she recalled.[22]

Hermann Fegelein had been designated by Himmler as his liaison in the bunker, to relay information back and forth between Hitler and the Reichsführer-SS. Hitler immediately ordered Fegelein—who was also the brother-in-law of Hitler's mistress, Eva Braun—taken out to the Chancellery garden and shot as punishment for Himmler's betrayal. Next, he instructed the recently appointed Luftwaffe commander-in-chief Ritter von Greim to order Himmler's arrest. "A traitor must never succeed me as Führer," he reportedly screamed.[23] Hitler must have known that the arrest order was unenforceable, but it served as a powerful indictment. It was all the more significant because Hitler was at that moment planning his own suicide and Himmler—who he often referred to as *der treue Heinrich* (the faithful Heinrich)—would in all probability have been appointed his successor if not for the betrayal.[24]

The Führer made his position even clearer the next day when he sat down to write out his will. Along with this document, he composed a "political testament." The first section contains a lengthy treatise: "It is untrue that I, or anyone else in Germany, wanted war in Germany in 1939. It was desired and instigated solely by international finance conspirators of Jewish blood or working for Jewish interests," he wrote. After appointing Admiral Karl Dönitz as his successor, he turned his pen to the subject of Himmler: "Before my death, I expel from the party and all his offices the former Reichsführer-SS and Reich Interior Minister, Heinrich Himmler."[25]

In the same testament, the Führer had also chosen to expel another leading Nazi figure, Hermann Göring. Days earlier, the Luftwaffe chief—upon hearing that Hitler had retreated into his bunker to die—sent him a telegram delicately asking for permission to take over the Reich. If he failed to hear back, he would assume that the Führer had lost his "freedom of action" and would immediately assume the leadership. When Bormann received the telegram, he convinced the Führer that Göring's action amounted to a coup d'état. "Göring and Himmler, quite apart from their disloyalty to my person, have done immeasurable harm to the country and the whole nation by secret negotiations with the enemy, which they have conducted without my knowledge and against my wishes, and by illegally attempting to seize power in the State for themselves," Hitler declared.[26] Less than thirty-six hours later, he and his new wife, Eva Braun, swallowed cyanide tablets as Soviet forces closed in.

Hitler's death on April 30 appeared to have brought an end to the most monstrous crime in human history. His successor, Admiral Dönitz—though fiercely anti-Semitic and loyal to Hitler—was a military man who had played no part in the Final Solution. His first priority was to set the groundwork for a quick and orderly surrender. For the countless surviving inmates barely languishing in the camps, it appeared that liberation was now truly at hand. But as it turned out, Hitler's murderous claws were about to reach out from beyond the grave.

Among the most important concessions Himmler had agreed to during the spring of 1945 was a pledge he had made to Carl Burckhardt after Jean-Marie Musy had arranged a meeting with the vice-president of the ICRC in March. The Reichsführer had agreed to permit Red Cross officials to station themselves inside several major concentration camps, with the proviso that they remain for the duration of the war. Conditions were beginning to improve in many of the camps thanks to the welcome relief packages of food and medicine brought by the Red Cross monitors—known to the inmates as "angels from God."[27]

By the end of April, only two major concentration camps, Dachau and Mauthausen, remained unliberated by the Allies. In both camps, the population of inmates had swelled significantly in recent weeks due to the arrival of thousands of prisoners evacuated from other camps on forced marches. Built in 1933 to house political prisoners, Dachau had served as the Nazis' original concentration camp. Victor Maurer had been working for the Red Cross for less than a week when he was given his first assignment. He was dispatched from Geneva to accompany five carloads of food and medical supplies destined for a concentration camp outside Munich under the terms of an agreement brokered with the Nazis. His orders were to distribute the supplies to the prisoners and then stay in the camp for the duration of the war.[28] When the forty-five-year-old former hotel manager arrived on April 26 to "get the truth to the world about the dirty business going on there," he was not at first welcomed by the commandant. Two days later, on Saturday, April 28, he made another attempt. This time, he was allowed to enter and distribute the supplies. That night, Maurer was assigned to a bedroom in the camp barracks, room #203. When he emerged the following day, the commandant and most of his officers had fled, leaving the camp in the command of a lieutenant, Heinrich Wickert, and 130 guards.[29] The ICRC official spent the next twenty-four hours convincing Wickert and the guards that they would be held personally responsible for any atrocities committed against the prisoners once the Allies arrived. Unbeknownst to Maurer and his assistant, it was not the guards who posed the greatest threat.

As the Reich entered its death throes in mid-April, Ernst Kaltenbrunner seethed with anger while his superior, the Reichsführer-SS, continually defied Hitler's orders, seemingly intent on saving the last remnants of the parasitical Jewish race for reasons beyond the Nazi's comprehension. It was impossible to defy Himmler's directives, at least not directly. Instead, Kaltenbrunner conceived a fitting tribute to the Führer, who was holed up in Berlin watching his Reich disintegrate around him. Kaltenbrunner knew that Hitler had ordered the destruction of every last Jew before the liberation of the camps, and he was determined to carry out this directive. In mid-April, Kaltenbrunner summoned Berte Gerdes, the chief of staff of the Munich Gauleiter. Gerdes was instructed to come up with a plan "without delay" for the liquidation of Dachau as well as two auxiliary Jewish labor camps,

Landsberg and Mühldorf. All three camps were directly in the path of the advancing Allied armies and would soon be liberated. Under Operation Fire Cloud (*Wolke Brand*), the inmates of Dachau—with the exception of Aryan nationals of the Western powers—were to be "liquidated by poison." Gerdes was instructed to procure from the Gauleiter health chief the required quantity of poison, which would be placed in the inmates' food ahead of the arrival of the Allied liberators, killing sixty-seven thousand inmates.[30]

Victor Maurer had no knowledge of Kaltenbrunner's plan. But the Red Cross official knew that the remaining inmates at Dachau were in grave danger from crossfire if the German guards attempted to defend the camp from the oncoming American forces. For his part, Wickert had no desire to risk his life or those under his command, and so an agreement was reached between the two men. If the camp was surrendered peacefully, Maurer promised, the entire German contingent would be protected under the Geneva Convention, despite whatever atrocities had taken place there. Maurer knew that on the railroad siding leading to the camp were the rotting bodies of hundreds of prisoners who had arrived dead from a recent forced evacuation of Buchenwald, apparently killed by the strafing of Allied aircraft.

With the agreement in hand, Maurer picked up a broomstick, tied a white rag to one end, and called upon the German officer to accompany him out the camp gates. The two men walked up the road, where sporadic fighting was taking place between German and American soldiers. When they caught sight of an American motorized unit, Maurer waved his improvised white flag. Within moments, the Red Cross delegate and the German officer were surrounded by American army vehicles of the 42nd Infantry Division. Maurer approached the jeep of Brigadier General Henning Linden and said in broken English, "I am the representative of the International

Committee of the Red Cross. The camp at Dachau will be turned over to you according to an agreement I have reached with the officer in command of the remaining guards."[31] He outlined the agreement to Linden, who readily agreed to its terms. Minutes later, American soldiers drove through the gates and were greeted by thousands of inmates, ecstatic at their newfound freedom.[32] By an accident of timing, Kaltenbrunner's plan had been derailed.

Adolf Hitler committed suicide in his Berlin bunker the day after Dachau was liberated. The new German leader, Admiral Dönitz, knew that the remaining camps were on the verge of liberation by the Allies and, even if he knew of Hitler's liquidation decree, it was unlikely he would have considered carrying out such a monstrous order. Dönitz had no idea that Kaltenbrunner had already decided to carry on the late Führer's genocidal edict. Discouraged by the Dachau setback, the security chief took advantage of the leadership void caused by Hitler's death and set in motion the final phase of Operation Fire Cloud.

Mauthausen concentration camp was actually a series of three interconnected labor camps—Mauthausen, Gusen 1 and Gusen 2— that supplied slave labor to an underground Messerschmitt aircraft factory in the nearby Austrian town of Linz, where Hitler had grown up. On April 22, two ICRC officials had arrived at the gates of Mauthausen with truckloads of food supplies. They were not permitted to enter the camp at this time, but they were allowed to deliver supplies and take with them 817 French, Belgian and Dutch deportees under the terms of the Germans' recent agreement to allow the evacuation of the sick and elderly. The next day, an additional 183 French prisoners were released to ICRC official Charles Steffen.[33]

Louis Haefliger was a forty-one-year-old former bank employee from Zürich who had impressed his Red Cross superiors with his fierce determination on previous missions. Haefliger had been dispatched from Geneva headquarters to try again to station himself inside the camp, as per the agreement negotiated by Burckhardt.[34] On April 27, at the head of a column of nineteen white trucks bearing the Red Cross emblem, he encountered the camp commandant, thirty-nine-year-old Franz Ziereis, who informed him that his presence in the camp was "undesirable." This time, Haefliger held his ground and demanded that the SS commander stick by the terms of Himmler's agreement. "The terms stipulate that a delegate must be allowed to enter the camp, distribute the food parcels himself, and remain in the camp until it is finally liberated," the Red Cross official insisted.[35] Ziereis finally acquiesced after Haefliger threatened harsh retribution by the Allies following liberation.

Entering Mauthausen—a camp which he would later describe as the "Gates of Hell"[36]—Haefliger was shocked at the prisoners' condition. He immediately demanded that Ziereis allow them to bathe and be disinfected while their clothing was washed. He also discovered that the Red Cross packages brought in for the inmates a week earlier were being plundered by SS guards for their most valuable contents—condensed milk, chocolate, biscuits and butter.

Haefliger was assigned to bunk with an SS Obersturmführer named Reiner—like himself, a former bank employee—who came to admire how the Swiss delegate was able to bully the commandant. On May 2, Reiner confided to his flabbergasted Red Cross roommate a secret. Ziereis had installed a gas chamber at Mauthausen and had been "annihilating" hundreds of prisoners up until the arrival of the Red Cross. Although Haefliger could not have known about Himmler's orders months earlier to suspend the Final Solution, both the Allied governments and the ICRC had operated under the assumption that mass exterminations had long since been suspended. Now, Reiner confided an even more horrifying revelation. Ernst

Kaltenbrunner had ordered Ziereis to liquidate all the remaining inmates before the camp was liberated. "[Reiner] didn't hide the fact that if his confidence was betrayed, we'd both end up with a bullet in the back of our necks," Haefliger later recalled.[37]

According to Kaltenbrunner's plan—code-named "Feuerzeug" (lighter)—an air raid alarm would sound on May 5 or 6 when the Russians or Americans approached. The prisoners from Gusen 1 and 2—numbering some forty to sixty thousand—would then be assembled in the nearby underground aircraft factory, where twenty-four and a half tons of dynamite had already been placed in the walls and corridors.[38] Once the inmates were gathered, the explosives would be detonated, killing and burying the entire camp population. A Mauthausen clerk, Austrian-born Hans Marsalek, would later confirm this order. "I was to liquidate all prisoners on behalf of SS Obergruppenführer Dr. Kaltenbrunner; the prisoners were to be led into the tunnels of the factory Bergkristall and only one entrance was to be left open. Then this entrance was to be blown up by the use of explosives and the death of the prisoners was to be effected in this manner." Marsalek also claimed that the Mauthausen gassing plant, camouflaged as a bathroom, was built on the orders of the former garrison doctor, Dr. Krebsbach.[39] (Ziereis would later tell his Allied interrogators that the order to kill all the inmates came from Himmler and Kaltenbrunner and was to be carried out if "the front lines approached Mauthausen" but it is clear that Kaltenbrunner issued many orders in the name of Himmler and there is no direct evidence that the Reichsführer-SS ever issued or was aware of such an order.)

The next morning, Haefliger asked Reiner to summon the SS aircraft factory supervisor to Ziereis's office. When the supervisor arrived, Haefliger stormed into the commandant's office and demanded that Ziereis immediately countermand the order to blow up the factory. At first, the Nazi attempted to shrug off responsibility for the crime, claim-ing "It's not up to me to countermand orders from above."[40] Haefliger informed him that he would be tried and executed for war crimes if the order was carried out. The warning appeared to have the desired effect on the brutal commandant, who reluctantly issued a verbal order annulling the decree.[41] From that point on, Ziereis seemed to lose his will to resist. As Haefliger later recalled, "All of a sudden I realized that I was facing a different man, weak, trembling, old, discouraged."[42]

On May 3, while Haefliger was still trying to persuade Ziereis to peacefully surrender the camp, the German commandant broke down. Eventually, Ziereis announced that he was fleeing the camp with some of his troops to fight the Russians.[43] Before he left, he placed his house at the disposal of the Red Cross representative. Haefliger declined the offer. "I prefer to stay with the detainees rather than in this monster's comfortable villa," he wrote in his journal. "Ziereis leaves us, and Reiner and I walk back to the camp. There is great agitation in the camp; additional machine guns have been brought to the sentry posts. SS soldiers are constructing new machine gun nests. Everywhere the defenses are being strengthened. The camp is in ferment. And I inno-cently thought the camp would be handed over peacefully to the Russians or Americans. The situation is increasingly disquieting. The fate of 60,000 human beings hangs in the balance."[44]

On May 5, Haefliger proposed to his SS roommate that the two of them drive to the American combat zone and summon the army to liberate the camp before one of Ziereis's zealous protégés decided to carry out the Kaltenbrunner plan.[45] Reiner told him the guards didn't want to risk their lives defending the camp and were as impatient for the liberation as the inmates. He agreed to accompany the Red Cross delegate. Before they set out, Haefliger arranged for the appointed representative of the inmates to lower the swastika banner and replace it with a white flag when he saw the Americans arriving. The pair left the camp that afternoon in a car painted white to mark it as a Red Cross vehicle. Before he set off, Reiner made sure to remove the death's head insignia of the concentration cap SS from his camp.

A half hour outside Linz, they caught sight of a huge tank in the distance. Haefliger got out, picked up a branch and attached a white handkerchief to one end. Then he and Reiner started walking. Within minutes, they were surrounded by four Sherman tanks, each bearing the white star of the U.S. Army. The hatches opened and young soldiers armed with machine guns swarmed out. Haefliger's English was poor, but a GI who spoke German was summoned to interpret. They explained their mission and urged the Americans to quickly liberate the nearby camp. The commanding officer was skeptical, fearing heavy resistance by the remaining camp guards. This was not part of his orders. The division had not even been aware there was a concentration camp in the area.

Reiner gave his assurance that the guards would surrender peacefully. Then, seated at the side of an American officer in his white Opel—Reiner had already been arrested and taken into a tank—Haefliger led the advance guard of the American second division to the underground aircraft factory, where he pointed out the corridors still mined with dynamite and wired with aircraft bombs.[46] (A week after liberation, Colonel Edward Ardery, company commander of the U.S. Army's 56th Engineers Battalion, would be dispatched to the Gusen underground factory to disarm the munitions. "There were a lot of explosives in there," he later recalled. "I went in there to take them out so that it couldn't be blown up."[47]) The American GIs quickly continued at top speed on to Mauthausen. As they approached the camp, the chimney of the crematorium came into view, although the American soldiers had no idea what the strange structure represented.

When Haefliger's car turned the final curve, he and the officer saw the swastika lowered and replaced by the white flag of surrender.

The entry of the American soldiers was greeted with exuberant cheers. The inmates raced out of their barracks and disarmed the guards, many immediately exacting revenge by smashing rifle butts over the heads of their former tormentors and later lynching the most brutal.

As thousands of inmates celebrated their newfound freedom, none were aware that they likely owed their lives to an elderly Swiss fascist, a formidable ultra-Orthodox Jewish woman and a corpulent Finnish osteopath.

EPILOGUE

On the afternoon of May 21, 1945, three men in civilian clothing were stopped outside the Lower Saxony town of Bremervörde at a routine checkpoint manned by former Soviet POWs. They claimed to be recently discharged noncommissioned officers from a unit of the German Secret Field Police. One of the men—sporting an eye patch and civilian clothing—presented papers identifying him as Sergeant Heinrich Hitzinger. The men were detained for interrogation by the British occupation authorities. Two days later, Hitzinger was spotted behind a bush removing his eye patch and putting on the spectacles that made him instantly recognizable as the most wanted man in Germany. Confronted by the commandant, the purported sergeant finally dropped the facade: "I am Heinrich Himmler," he declared. After a thorough medical examination, the camp doctor ordered the notorious prisoner to open his mouth for inspection. Within seconds, Himmler bit down on the cyanide capsule he kept hidden in his teeth. Major Norman Whittaker, one of the British officers present at the scene, recorded the aftermath in his diary: "There were terrible groans and grunts coming from the swine," he wrote, noting that the doctor attempted in vain to resuscitate him. "It was a losing battle and this evil thing breathed its last at 23:14 hours."[1]

Himmler had apparently chosen suicide rather than attempt to defend the indefensible or dare to portray himself as a "humanitarian" with whom the West could enter into a productive alliance. His delusion on that score was shattered for good only a day before the German surrender, when the new Nazi leader, Admiral Dönitz, formally dismissed the Reichsführer-SS from all his posts on May 6. Up until that moment, Himmler still appears to have bought into the deception carefully cultivated by Kersten, Musy, the Sternbuchs and Saly Mayer—the idea that the Western Allies would be open to a compromise peace with the Nazis.[2] It was a charade that may well have conspired to rob Hitler of his ultimate goal—a *Judenrein* Europe.

Largely because of the chaos that prevailed during the last days of the Reich, along with the last-minute destruction of the Nazis' once meticulous records, there are no accurate figures for how many Jews survived the Holocaust or the camps. Estimates range from 300,000 to 500,000, including more than 200,000 Hungarian Jewish survivors, but not the nearly 10 percent of Polish Jewry who survived by escaping to the Soviet Union.[3] It is also difficult to estimate how many survived directly or indirectly as the result of the negotiations with Nazis during the final stages of the war. It is important to acknowledge the critical efforts of the WRB, the Joint, and the WJC as well as other rescuers throughout Europe. But it is hard to dispute the central role played by Jean-Marie Musy on behalf of the Sternbuch Rescue Committee, an effort that went far beyond the 1210 lives previously credited to him. His negotiations with Himmler and advocacy of Carl Burckhardt played a crucial role in allowing the presence of the Red Cross in concentration camps during the final weeks of the war; it likely prevented Kaltenbrunner's plan to dynamite and poison the surviving camp inmates. That was in addition to ICRC relief shipments that saved thousands more. The ICRC physician in charge also confirmed that Benoît Musy was responsible for ensuring the evacuation of thousands of Jews from Ravensbrück, negotiated by Kersten and Masur, and that he paved the way for Count Bernadotte's rescue operation. Benoît Musy was also instrumental in preventing a Buchenwald death march.

It may seem premature to claim that the deception engineered by the Sternbuchs, Mayer, Musy and others helped end the systematic exterminations of the Jews in the fall of 1944, but the evidence is certainly compelling.

In the decades since, there has been much debate within academia and the Jewish community about who deserves the credit for saving this remnant of European Jewry—or the blame for not doing more to rescue the nearly six million who perished, depending on one's perspective.[4] Nowhere has this debate been more fiercely argued than among the cast of characters who entered into negotiations with the Nazis during the final stages of the Holocaust.

Only weeks after VE day, Count Folke Bernadotte published an account in Sweden of his negotiations with Himmler and his own role in organizing the evacuation of the Scandinavians and Jews. In *The Curtain Falls*, Bernadotte casts himself in a heroic light while failing to even mention Felix Kersten's role in the rescue. Instead, he assigns sole credit to himself and to Walter Schellenberg. His memoir caused something of a sensation in Sweden, where he was widely lauded for his heroics. Largely on the strength of his newly acquired reputation, Bernadotte was appointed by the United Nations as a special mediator to resolve the violence that erupted following the UN Partition Plan for Palestine and subsequent May 1948 Israeli Declaration of Independence. Vilified for his role in negotiating the truce that followed, Bernadotte was assassinated by right-wing Israeli extremists in September 1948.

Five years later, Oxford University historian Hugh Trevor-Roper shredded Bernadotte's self-laudatory account in an *Atlantic Monthly* piece. "Of Count Bernadotte's activities in these negotiations, little need be said, for he was simply an agent, a 'transport officer,' no more," wrote Trevor-Roper, whose 1947 book, *The Last Days of Hitler*, had established him at the time as one of the leading historians of the Second World War.[5] Instead, he assigned most of the credit for the success of the negotiations to Felix Kersten, whom he deemed responsible for the liberation of the Scandinavian prisoners and several thousand Jews. The historian also takes at face value Kersten's claim that, according to Himmler, Bernadotte had at first refused to take any Jews. "He understands the necessity of our fight against world Jewry," the Reichsführer allegedly told his masseur. It's unclear whether it was Himmler or Kersten who fabricated this account, but there is little evidence to back up the claim. It wasn't the only questionable account in Trevor-Roper's piece.

He also repeated Kersten's sensational assertion that he had saved nearly three million "unreliable" Dutch citizens from deportation to the east in 1941 after he persuaded the Reichsführer against the move. "Himmler was at that time in a low state of health and particularly dependent on Kersten. Consequently, the move was postponed until after the war," writes Trevor-Roper, noting that these matters have been "well authenticated." When these stories were circulated, the Dutch government lauded Kersten as a national hero and even nominated him for the Nobel Peace Prize. Eventually, it became clear that the so-called authentication Trevor-Roper had relied on was documents forged by Kersten himself to bolster his claims.[6] Three decades later, the Oxford professor would again be duped by forgeries when he famously authenticated a series of sixty found volumes of Hitler's "lost journals" in April 1983. Weeks after he pronounced the "Hitler Diaries" genuine, forensic scientists revealed that they were in fact a crudely executed hoax perpetrated by the notorious German forger Konrad Kujau.

Still, Kersten's duplicity in the service of his own ego does not take away from his undeniable role in the release of the Ravensbrück inmates—attested to by Hillel Storch after the war—or his efforts to prevent the destruction of the concentration camps, which have also been independently corroborated. The World Jewish Congress credited him with saving at least sixty thousand Jews.[7]

Himmler's SS negotiator, Kurt Becher, would also later claim sole credit for preventing the evacuation of the concentration camps and for convincing Himmler to end the Final Solution in the fall of 1944, although these claims are highly dubious.

The unseemly debate over who deserved credit served to detract from the significance of the negotiations themselves and ignored the central role of a number of other key players, including the Musys and the Sternbuch rescue committee. For his part, Jean-Marie Musy remained mostly silent about his role in the negotiations. He and his son Benoît did provide testimony on behalf of Walter Schellenberg during the intelligence chief's Nuremberg war crimes trial in 1949 after he was indicted on four counts, including crimes against humanity. Their affidavits about his central role in the negotiations likely proved crucial in winning Schellenberg an acquittal on the most serious of these counts, and in his relatively light sentence of six years.[8] After the war, Benoît Musy would become a world-class motorcycle and race-car driver. He was killed in a crash in 1956, only four years after his father passed away in Fribourg at the age of seventy-six. Neither father nor son has been recognized as a Righteous Gentile Among Nations at Yad Vashem. Until their deaths, the Sternbuchs regularly praised both men as heroes who had "acted honourably on behalf of the Jewish people."[9]

For decades after the war, Saly Mayer's files were closed to most researchers—likely to hide from history his role in illegally ransoming Jews on at least two occasions. As a result, the accusations leveled by the Sternbuchs and others were allowed to go unchallenged until Yehuda Bauer and other historians eventually set the record straight.

As it turned out, Count Bernadotte was not the only central player in the negotiations who would be gunned down by Jewish extremists. On March 15, 1957, Rezső Kasztner was assassinated outside his Tel Aviv home by members of the same right-wing paramilitary group—the Stern Gang—that had gunned down the Swedish Red Cross vice-president a decade earlier. As details of his role in the negotiations had emerged after the war, Kasztner had been widely vilified for a number of alleged sins. Most notoriously, he had vouched for his chief SS negotiator, Kurt Becher, and helped Himmler's henchman escape prosecution for war crimes. Kasztner was also accused of failing to warn Hungarian Jewry of the Final Solution and of thus allowing hundreds of thousands to be deported to Auschwitz without resistance. At the same time, he had purportedly helped dozens of his own friends and family members to escape by securing them passage on the train. He was also accused of pocketing the so-called Becher deposit paid by the wealthiest passengers. In a sensational 1955 libel trial brought on his behalf by the Israeli government, these episodes received a full airing. Right-wing parties successfully used the trial as a high-profile forum to indict the ruling Mapai party for which Kasztner worked as a government spokesman. Although he was cleared of stealing the Becher deposit, the judge ruled that Kasztner had "sold his soul to the devil" in negotiating with Nazis. The verdict shook Israeli society to the core and led to the eventual fall of the cabinet and to Kasztner's assassination less than two years later. For five decades, Rezső Kasztner would be universally condemned for his role in the negotiations even though the Israeli Supreme Court reversed the initial judgment against him a year after his death. That attitude finally began to shift in 2007 when Yad Vashem declared Kasztner a "hero" who had been the "victim of a vicious smear campaign."[10] That same year, Hungarian-Canadian author Anna Porter published a riveting account titled *Kasztner's Train*, which helped rehabilitate his tarnished reputation.

The reassessment of Kasztner's actions coincided with a gradual willingness among historians to reconsider the controversial wartime negotiations between Jews and Nazis. When Edwin Black published *The Transfer Agreement* in 1984—about the Haavara pact—he recalled that even his own parents were deeply uncomfortable with the subject matter. By the time Yehuda Bauer's *Jews for Sale?* was released ten years later, the discussion of Jewish/Nazi negotiations was still controversial, but the initial backlash had abated.

Still, many chronicles of the Holocaust barely mention these negotiations, while others downplay their significance. Musy's mission is often accorded little more than a passing mention or even deemed a "failure" because *only* 1210 Jews were liberated. With some notable exceptions, the Sternbuchs' role is often overlooked completely.[11] It's possible that some historians are reluctant to focus too much attention on this chapter of history for fear of providing ammunition to Holocaust deniers and revisionist historians. Such individuals and groups could attempt to fixate on Himmler's actions in *saving* some Jews rather than on his role as the architect of history's worst genocide.

Even as the ransom negotiations have become part of the historical discourse, the extraordinary role of Orthodox Jews in Holocaust rescue efforts has been largely ignored or dismissed while most of the attention has focused on the successes or failures of the mainstream Jewish establishment.

In 1983, historian Lucy Dawidowicz published a powerful polemic in *Commentary* magazine under the headline "Indicting American Jews." In this essay, she takes issue with what she describes as the "ugly afterlife" of the Holocaust—the accusations that emerged after the war that American Jewish leaders stood idly by while the Jews of Europe were slaughtered. Inexplicably, she blames this phenomenon on the American left attempting to fan the flames of anti-Semitism. "Today the Left, heartland of anti-Zionism, bays loudly against the 'Jewish establishment' for having 'betrayed' the European Jews during the Holocaust," she writes. "It appropriates the cruel and ill-founded charges of collaboration which Hannah Arendt, in *Eichmann in Jerusalem*, leveled against the Jewish leadership in the Nazi-controlled ghettos in Eastern Europe, and applies them to the Jewish leadership of the United States."[12]

It is hard to deny the emergence of this phenomenon, but the fact is that most of the loudest voices leveling these accusations came from the right, not the left—often from those who themselves played a major role in these events. After the war, Rabbi Chaim Michael Weissmandl settled in New Jersey, where he spent much of the rest of his life bitterly accusing the so-called Zionist hierarchy—whom he described as "atheist degenerates known as Jewish statesmen"—of sabotaging ransom efforts in order to further the cause of Palestine. The former revisionist Zionist leader Peter Bergson also spent much of the postwar period attacking the Jewish establishment for failing to press the American government for rescue until it was too late.[13] He believed that much of European Jewry could have been saved had the world acted sooner and had the American Jewish leaders raised a greater outcry. In a 1978 interview, he was still calling on the leadership to admit that they had failed the victims of the Holocaust: "Whatever the motivations, it is important today—this is the one thing I don't understand—why thirty years later the Jewish leaders don't recant and say 'mea culpa'?"[14] In her own indictment, Dawidowicz doesn't entirely let the leadership off the hook. "As for American Jews, they too could certainly have done more, tried harder, shouted more loudly," she writes. "But I am not persuaded that in the end they would have accomplished much more than they did."[15]

Much of the criticism has been leveled against Stephen Wise, who was indisputably America's most influential Jewish leader during this period. The fact is that nobody did more to alert Americans to the evil of the Nazis than Wise during the months and years after Hitler came to power. The influential Reform rabbi galvanized tremendous grass-roots opposition, spearheaded a crippling economic boycott, and organized massive rallies attended by thousands, helping to turn much of America against Hitler long before the war began. The anti-Nazi movement he led was undeniably effective as it fought to creatively counter the poisonous elements fanning the flames of isolationism and anti-Semitism before Pearl Harbor. And yet once the news of the Final Solution began to circulate among the leadership in 1942, and words like *extermination* and *liquidation* became a part of the vocabulary, voices that were once forceful and passionate in their response to Hitler's crimes now appeared paralyzed and ineffective.

It is easy in retrospect to criticize what was undeniably a grossly inadequate response to the greatest crisis ever to confront the Jewish people. But after years spent reviewing hundreds of thousands of pages of correspondence, minutes of myriad meetings, archival files on three continents and trans-Atlantic cables from this cataclysmic period, I emerged with a much more nuanced picture. As I observed news of the Holocaust unfold in real time, it became apparent that the scale of the evolving tragedy was so vast and overwhelming as to be almost incomprehensible. A sense of impotence and utter powerlessness engulfed the leadership, which was soon swept aside by the assurances of the Roosevelt administration. The best way to save the Jews of Europe, they were told, was to defeat Hitler with the greatest military arsenal ever assembled. Indeed, in the battle against the Nazis, the Jews had finally found the American people and their government in common cause in a resolute determination to crush the Axis and restore freedom. Any attempt to undermine the war effort by criticizing the Roosevelt administration, they believed, would be seen as un-American and would almost certainly hinder, not help, the cause of the European Jews. Payment of ransom, most argued, would merely help prolong the German war effort, which was against the law and tantamount to treason.

Seen in this light, the response of the Jewish leadership at the time is almost understandable. However, it also makes all the more remarkable the extraordinary efforts of the Orthodox Jews, who answered to a different set of laws. While recriminations have swirled for decades around the actions of the mainstream Jewish leadership, little attention has been paid to the religious leaders who devoted themselves to rescue because the Torah commanded it. And while the establishment leaders had little to show for their efforts, the heroic accomplishments of the Vaad ha-Hatzalah, the Sternbuchs and others have for the most part been accorded little more than an historical footnote.

If the efforts of the Sternbuchs and the Musy mission played a crucial role in ending the mass exterminations, as newly uncovered evidence suggests, it stands without doubt as a monumental achievement. Why has this chapter of Holocaust history been so long ignored or downplayed? There is unquestionably a discernible bias that emerges linked perhaps to the status of ultra-Orthodox Jews as outsiders even within the Jewish community. As a secular Jew myself, I have witnessed this bias all my life and perhaps even held stereotypes of my own. For non-Jews, they are often perceived as completely alien, beholden to an extremist religious agenda.

A telling clue to these attitudes can be found in the transcript of an interview Roswell McClelland gave to Claude Lanzmann in 1978 while the French filmmaker was researching his epic nine-hour Holocaust documentary, *Shoah*. McClelland revealed that before taking up his post at the War Refugee Board in February 1944, an "old Jewish friend" warned him to be careful of Jews who will attempt to treat him like "the Wailing Wall"—people who will come to him "to tear their hair out and beat their poor heads against the wall" claiming that the world is coming to an end.[16] When he first encountered Isaac Sternbuch, the Swiss Orthodox Jew fit this description perfectly.

McClelland revealed that his first impression of Sternbuch was the "stereotype of a sort of medieval Rabbi out of a Polish ghetto." He admitted that he didn't know how to deal with somebody like Sternbuch, especially when he arrived at the WRB office saying, "We need a hundred million francs to save the Jews in Hungary, and if this is not forthcoming by next Tuesday morning, everybody will be dead. This was a little bit Sternbuch's approach . . . he gnashed his teeth and tore his hair out and the world was coming to an end." At this point in the interview, Lanzmann interjects. "Considering the things in retrospect, he was right," notes the French filmmaker. For nearly eighteen months, McClelland had battled the Sternbuchs at every turn, preferring to deal with Saly Mayer, whom he claimed had the "more rational" and "less emotional" approach to the problem. Three decades after those epic historical events, and with the benefit of hindsight, McClelland responded to Lanzmann, "He was, yes, I agree with you. He was right."[17]

Even David Wyman, who—along with his protégé, Rafael Medoff—has done more than any historian to publicize the rabbis' march of 1943, gives most of the credit for the creation of the War Refugee Board to Peter Bergson, who he appears to believe skillfully used the rabbis to further his goal of rescue. Wyman credits the WRB with saving more than 200,000 Jews while he largely downplays the role of the Orthodox leadership, even though the Vaad brought the rabbis together with Bergson and secretly financed rescue operations that the WRB shunned. Nonetheless, Wyman does chronicle the efforts of the Sternbuchs and acknowledges that their tractor bribe may have played a part in freeing the Bergen-Belsen Jews.

On the other side of the coin, the late David Kranzler published a number of books about the rescue efforts of various Orthodox figures, including Recha Sternbuch. Although his works provide valuable insight into the various players, they are noted for sometimes wildly exaggerating the accomplishments of the Orthodox while dismissing the efforts of other figures, and for repeating as gospel the long-discredited accusations against Saly Mayer. For years, Kranzler engaged in an historical feud with the first Wiesenthal Center director Efraim Zuroff, who in 2000 published a well-balanced and meticulously researched history of the Vaad ha-Hatzalah. Zuroff's apparent sin was correctly noting that throughout much of the war, the Vaad reserved its rescue efforts for saving Orthodox Jews.[18]

The uncomfortable reality is that, while much of the world abandoned the Jews and the American leadership dithered, a small disparate group came together to rescue the remnants of European Jewry. The rescuers included Zionists and anti-Zionists; Orthodox and secular Jews; pariahs such as Rezső Kasztner and Saly Mayer; and even some Nazis. The motives of some of these figures are still murky, as are their results. It would be far more satisfying to be able to paint a picture of a noble band of like-minded individuals as the heroes of the Holocaust. But history doesn't work that way.

In early January 1946, HIJEFS received an alarming telegram from Prague:

CONTINUAL POGROMS. OPPRESSION. FEAR. HORROR. IF NO IMMEDIATE HELP. WE HAVE RESPONSIBILITY FOR THE LIVES OF REMNANTS OF EASTERN JEWRY. ONE MILLION DOLLARS NECESSARY IMMEDIATELY.[19]

Sounding much like the frequent cables the committee had received from underground sources throughout the war, this appeal had in fact come from Recha Sternbuch, and the war had long since ended. The news of Germany's surrender on May 7, 1945, had done nothing to slow Recha's dedication to rescue. Within days, she had made her way to Germany, where she spent weeks coordinating relief parcels of kosher food to displaced-persons facilities set up on the sites of the former Nazi concentration camps. Few recipients of these parcels had any idea that the turbaned woman who delivered them might very well have played a key role in their survival.

Next, she traveled to France to investigate reports that hundreds of Jewish children had been placed with gentile families by parents before they were deported to the death camps. Here, Recha embarked on yet another mission. She founded a children's home and a yeshiva for Holocaust survivors in the French resort town of Aix-Les-Bains, which would become an important center for rescued children, as would a number of other such homes she established in the country. She also discovered that a significant number of Jewish orphans had been taken in by convents, where the children were now receiving a

Catholic education. She dedicated herself to removing these children to ensure that they were raised Jewish. Her preferred method involved negotiations with the diocese. Often, she would simply march in and bully the nuns into relinquishing their charges, announcing, "These children belong to the Jewish people." Hitler had left Europe with few enough Jews, she reasoned.

At the end of 1945, the Vaad designated Recha as their representative in Poland after reports reached the leadership that some Eastern Europeans had launched pogroms against Jewish survivors "to finish the job that Hitler started." Nazi Germany had fallen by the wayside, but Recha's mission of rescue continued on. For more than a quarter century after the war, she dedicated herself to the rebirth of European Jewry—determined to thwart Hitler's poisonous dream.

Recha Sternbuch died in Paris in 1971, two years after Isaac succumbed to cancer in Switzerland. Word of her incredible rescue efforts had spread, but in the Sternbuch household those things were never talked about. As Recha's children grew older, they frequently heard astonishing stories—sometimes three times in a week—from strangers describing how their mother had saved these people's lives. Whenever the children asked Recha to tell them about these feats of rescue, she demurred, as did Isaac. When grandchildren came along, they too clamored to hear the stories. But whenever she was asked to describe her role in saving thousands of Jews, Recha Sternbuch's response was always the same: "I didn't do enough."

APPENDIX

APPENDIX A

"Cease exterminations" cable

MESSAGE RECEIVED NOVEMBER 20, BERNE, SWITZERLAND

OUR DELEGATE BROUGHT FROM BERLIN THE PROPOSAL
TO DEPOSIT LARGER AMOUNT FOR A GRADUAL EVACUATION OF
JEWS FROM GERMANY. THE NEGOTIATIONS ARE CONTINUING.
FURTHER DETAILS FORTHCOMING. IN INTERIM SECURED
PROMISE TO CEASE EXTERMINATION IN CONCENTRATION CAMPS.
ON BASIS OF INTERVENTION BY NUNCIATURE IN BERNE THE
GERMAN GOVERNMENT CONFIRMED THIS PROMISE TO THE
VATICAN. ALSO WAS STATED THAT CAMPS IN UPPER SILESIA
WILL BE UNDER SUPERVISION OF INTERNATIONAL RED CROSS.
STERNBUCH

A cable discovered in the files of the Vaad ha-Hatzalah sent via the Polish diplomatic code from the Sternbuchs on November 20, 1944, reporting that Jean Marie Musy's negotiations with Himmler had resulted in a "promise to cease extermination in concentration camps." Five days later, Himmler issued an order prohibiting the "further killing of Jews."

APPENDIX B

Export permit

Saly Mayer of the JDC arranged for the Swiss government to issue this export permit for the illegal tractor bribe initiated by the Sternbuchs and other Orthodox rescuers. The Nazis had promised to "blow up the facilities at Auschwitz" if the delivery of the tractors was "begun seriously." Less than 72 hours after the tractor export permit was approved on November 22, 1944, the Auschwitz-Birkenau gas chambers and crematoria were destroyed by the Nazis.

APPENDIX C

"Good will of America" cable

```
STRICTLY CONFIDENTIAL * NOT FOR PUBLICATION

CABLE FROM BERN ARRIVED IN NEW YORK FEBRUARY 10th.

MUSY CAME BACK STOP THE RESULT OF HIS ACTION IS GOOD STOP HE PERSONALLY
BROUGHT THE TWO SONS OF RABBI KOTLERBERG STOP HE HAS ARRANGED THAT
EVERY WEEK COMMENCING FEBRUARY 9th A TRANSPORT OF AT LEAST 1200
PERSONS OR MORE ARRIVE.
WE MUST PAY FIVE MILLIONS SWISS FRANCS THAT MUST BE DEPOSITED IN
THE SWISS BANK TO THE CREDIT OF MUSY WHEN THESE TRANSPORTS ARRIVE STOP.
WHEN YOU RECEIVED OUR CABLE THAT THE FIRST CONVOY ARRIVED YOU MUST
PREPARE AND TRANSFER FOUR MILLION SWISS FRANCS.
WE HAVE CONVINCED THE GERMANS THAT THE GOOD WILL OF AMERICA IS MOST
DESIRABLE STOP

                                        STERNBUCH
```

A cable from the Sternbuchs to the Vaad ha-Hatzalah sent three days after former Swiss President Jean-Marie Musy had secured the release of 1210 Jews from Theresienstadt with the promise of regular evacuations to come. The deal was contingent on five million francs being deposited in Musy's name to be used for German Red Cross relief efforts after the war, but Himmler was more interested in "the good will of America" in order to secure a separate peace with the Western Allies.

PRIMARY SOURCES

AET – War crimes trial transcripts and interrogations of Adolf Eichmann, Jerusalem, 1961

TRIAL TESTIMONY

Dr. Ernest Abeles	Adolf Eichmann
Kurt Becher	Erich Von Dem Bach-Zelewski
Hansi Brand	Philip von Freudiger
Joel Brand	

AIAOJ – Agudath Israel of America Orthodox Jewish Archives, New York
AJCA – American Jewish Congress Archives, New York
AJHS – American Jewish Historical Society, New York and Boston
BA – Bundesarchiv, Berlin, Germany
CHARLES *Lindbergh Papers*
CLAUDE LANZMANN SHOAH COLLECTION – Steven Spielberg Film and Video Archive

INTERVIEWS AND OUTTAKES

Peter Bergson	Benjamin Murmelstein
Hansi Brand	Maurice Rossel
Hermann Landau	Andrew Steiner
Roswell McClelland	Rudolf Vrba

DDS – Diplomatic Documents of Switzerland

DGFP – *Documents on German Foreign Policy* (captured German diplomatic dispatches)

FDRL – Franklin Delano Roosevelt Presidential Library, Hyde Park, New York

Franklin Roosevelt Presidential Papers

Franklin Roosevelt Personal Papers

Henry Morgenthau Papers & Diaries

Stephen Early Papers

Eleanor Roosevelt Papers

Sumner Welles Papers

Harold Ickes Papers

FO – Records of the British Foreign Office, National Archives, Kew, U.K.

FRUS – Foreign Relations of the United States – Historical Documents

HFM – Henry Ford Museum and Archives, Dearborn, Michigan

HLA – Personal Archives of Sternbuch Rescue Committee Secretary Hermann Landau, Toronto, Ontario

HST – Harry S. Truman Library and Museum

ICE – Independent Commission of Experts, Switzerland – Second World War

Interim Reports – 1997–2000

Switzerland and Refugees in the Nazi Era

Switzerland, National Socialism and the Second World War

ICRC – Archives of the International Committee of the Red Cross, Geneva, Switzerland

IMT – Trial of the Major War Criminals Before the International Military Tribunal, Nuremberg

TRIAL PROCEEDINGS

Karl Dönitz

Hans Frank

Hermann Göring

Ernst Kaltenbrunner

Fritz Sauckel

Hjamar Schacht

Walter Schellenberg

Albert Speer

Joachim von Ribbentrop

AFFIDAVITS

Franz Göring

Hans Marsalek

Benoît Musy

Jean-Marie Musy

Dieter Wisliceny

INTERROGATIONS

Ernst Kaltenbrunner

Otto Ohlendorf

Walter Schellenberg

JDC – Archives of the American Joint Jewish Distribution Committee, New York

JRMC – Jacob Rader Marcus Center of the American Jewish Archives, Cincinnati, Ohio

JVL – Jewish Virtual Library

KFA – Julius Kühl family papers, Toronto, Canada

KHEC – Kleinman Holocaust Education Center, Brooklyn, New York

Isaac Sternbuch papers

Michael Tress Collection

LC – Library of Congress, Washington, D.C.

NAC – National Archives of Canada, Ottawa

NARA – National Archives and Research Administration, Washington, D.C., & College Park, Maryland

PRO – British Public Records Office, Kew, London, U.K.

RVR- Personal collection of Reek van Rijsinge, Amsterdam

SGA – Staatsarchiv, St. Gallen, Archives of St. Gallen Canton, St. Gallen, Switzerland

SM – Saly Mayer papers, JDC Archives, New York

STAAT – Bavarian State Library, Munich

SWC – Simon Wiesenthal Center

USHMM, Archive of the United States Holocaust Memorial Museum, Washington, D.C.

VH – Archives of the Vaad ha-Hatzalah, Yeshiva University, New York

WJC – World Jewish Congress Records, American Jewish Archives

WRB – Records of the War Refugee Board, Franklin Delano Roosevelt

Presidential Library, Hyde Park, New York
YU – Yale University Library
YVA – Yad Vashem—World Center for Holocaust Research, Jerusalem

AUTHOR INTERVIEWS

Hermann Landau, Toronto, Canada

Gerhart Riegner, Geneva, Switzerland

Edouard Musy, Fribourg, Switzerland

Arno Kersten, Sweden

Renée Landau, New York, NY

Stefan Keller, St. Gallen, Switzerland

Netty Segal (Recha & Isaac Sternbuch's daughter), New York, NY

Sarah Shapiro (Recha & Isaac's granddaughter), Jerusalem, Israel

Ruth Rottenberg Mandel, Jerusalem, Israel

Michael Kühl, Toronto, Canada

Janine Kühl Weinstock, Toronto, Canada

Moshe Landau, Cleveland, Ohio

Rabbi Moshe Kolodny, New York, NY

Bob Narev, Auckland, New Zealand

Sima Shachar, Beit Terazin, Jerusalem, Israel

Edwin Black, Washington, D.C.

Rafael Medoff, Washington, D.C.

Peter Munk, Toronto, Canada

Dr. Henri Lustiger Thaler, Brooklyn, NY

Dr. Igor Bartosik, Auschwitz-Birkenau Memorial and Museum, Poland

Hubert Berkhoug, NIOD, Amsterdam

HOLOCAUST SURVIVORS

Nathan Leipciger (Auschwitz)

Max Eisen (Auschwitz & Mauthausen)

George Brady (Auschwitz)

Johnny Freund (Auschwitz)

Sigmund Sobolewski (Auschwitz)

Edward Mosberg (Mauthausen)

NOTES

ONE: THE LIFEBOAT IS FULL

1   Jewish Virtual Library, "Belgium."
2   Antwerp World Diamond Center, "The 19th Century."
3   Kurlansky, *A Chosen Few*, p. 42.
4   Author interview with Renée Landau, October 23, 2015.
5   Author interview with Recha Sternbuch's daughter Netty Segal, October 22, 2015.
6   JVL, "Basle."
7   Joseph Friedenson and David Kranzler, *Heroine of Rescue*, Mesorah Publications: Brooklyn, 1984, p. 26.
8   Author interview with Recha Sternbuch's daughter Netty Segal, October, 22, 2015.
9   *Heroine*, p. 26.
10 Bezael Naor, *When God Becomes History*, p. 32.
11 November 2015 author interview with Ruth Rottenberg Mandel, the girl Recha and Isaac raised for almost ten years. Because Ruth's father was still alive, they did not consider it an adoption. When Ruth was fourteen, she returned to Belgium to live with her father.
12 Stefan Keller, *D'élit d'Humanité*, Éditions d'en Bas: Lausanne, 1994.
13 Six districts are classified as half-cantons.
14 Ibid.
15 "Switzerland, National Socialism and the Second World War," *Final*

Report of the Independent Commission of Experts Switzerland—Second World War (2002), p. 71.

16   Ibid.

17   Ibid.

18   Independent Commission of Experts Switzerland—Second World War, "Switzerland and Refugees in the Nazi Era" (1999) p. 47.

19   *Heroine,* p. 27.

20   ICE, p. 106.

21   Ibid., p. 107. An additional 252 refugees were granted this status between 1939 and 1945.

22   YVA, Shaul Ferrero, "Switzerland and the Refugees Fleeing Nazism: Documents on the German Jews Turned Back at the Basel Border in 1938–1939," *Yad Vashem Studies*, vol. XXVII, Jerusalem (1999) pp. 203–234.

23   ICE, p. 107.

24   *Unlikely Heroes*, 2003 documentary about Holocaust rescuers produced by Moriah Films, a division of the Simon Wiesenthal Center.

25   Ibid., p. 28.

26   YVA, Testimony of Carl Mogenroth about Emigration from Nazi Germany," File 0.3-8251.

27   "Witnesses to Kristallnacht," *Jewish Journal*, Nov. 6, 2014.

28   Shirer, p. 351.

29   ICE, p. 108.

30   "A Survey of Nazi and Pro-Nazi Groups in Switzerland: 1930–1945,"r. Alan Morris Schom, Simon Wiesenthal Center (June 1998), Ch. 17. In his report, Schom claims that Rothmund visited the Oranienburg concentration camp but that camp had been deactivated in 1936 and replaced with the Sachsenhausen facility, also located in Oranienburg. We can assume this is the camp that he refers to.

31   ICE, p. 109.

32   ICE, "Switzerland and Refugees," p. 76.

33   Mitya New, *Switzerland Unwrapped: Exposing the Myths*, I.B. Tauris: London and New York, 1997, p. 3.

TWO: THE SWISS SCHINDLER

1   *Heroine*, p. 30.

2   Keller, p. 176.

3   Measuring Worth website, "Exchange Rates between the US dollar and 41 currencies."

4   New, pp. 4–5.

5   Keller, p. 87.

6   *Unlikely Heroes*, op. cit.

7   ICE, "Switzerland and Refugees," p. 114.

8   *Heroine*, p. 36.

9   *Unlikely Heroes*, op. cit.

10 Author interview, October 23, 2015, with St. Gallen–based Swiss historian Stefan Keller, who wrote the definitive account, *Grüninger's Fall*, which has been the basis for a number of films and documentaries about the affair; YVA, "Paul Grueninger, Switzerland."

11 Meir Wagner and Moishe Meisels, *The Righteous of Switzerland: The Heroes of the Holocaust*, KTAV Publishing: Newark, 2001, p. 48.

12 Ibid.

13 Author interview with Recha Sternbuch's daughter Netty Segal, October 21, 2015.

14 Author interview with Ruth Rottenberg Mandel, November 2015.

15 Keller, p. 87.

16 Author interview with Recha Sternbuch's granddaughter Sarah Shapiro, November, 2015; *Heroine*, p. 42.

17 *Heroine*, pp. 35–36.

18 Ibid.

19 Wagner and Meisels, p. 36.

20 USHMM, *Holocaust Encyclopedia*, "Kristallnacht."

21 Ibid.

22 JVL, "Heydrich's Instructions for Kristallnacht," stenographic report on the Jewish Question at the Reich Air Ministry, Nov. 12, 1938.

23 YVA, File O.2/438.

THREE: BETRAYED

1   ICE, "Final Report," p. 109.

2   Schom, op. cit.

3   Keller, pp. 70–71.

4   Ibid.

5   Author interview with St. Gallen historian Stefan Keller, October 23, 2015.

6   Eyal Press, p. 36.

7   Wagner and Meisels, p. 38.

8   Ibid.

9   Ibid.

10 Ibid., p. 139.

11 Ibid., pp. 40–41; Keller, pp. 165–166.

12 Eyal Press, p. 17.

13 Mitya New, pp. 7–8.

14 Wagner and Meisels, p. 50.

15 Keller, p. 166.

16 Ibid.

17 Author interview with Stefan Keller, October 22, 2015.

18 *Heroine*, p. 34.

19 Hermann Landau, secretary of the Sternbuchs' rescue group HIJEFS would repeat this accusation to historian Stefan Keller in his book *Grüninger's Fall*. Landau did not live in Switzerland when Grüninger was active, so he was likely repeating what he had heard from the Sternbuchs, whose hostility against Mayer they both took to their graves.

20 Eyal Press, p. 17.

21 Author interview with Stefan Geller, October 2, 2015. Geller claims that Grüninger was a poor salesman and failed to make a go of the Basel store.

22 *Heroine*, p. 40.

23 Ibid.

24 Ibid., p. 40.

25 Ibid., p. 42.

26 Ibid., p. 43.

27 In *Heroine of Rescue*, Friedenson and Kranzler claim it was the prosecutor who made the contribution, but St. Gallen historian Stefan Keller insists it was in fact the judge. (Author interview with Keller, October 22, 2015.) Isaac Lewin of the Vaad later claimed it was "the Chairman of one of the Swiss political parties, Dr. Imhoff," who sent Recha flowers and a check for 100 Swiss francs.

FOUR: STRANGE BEDFELLOWS

1 John Toland, *Adolf Hitler: The Definitive Biography*, Knopf Doubleday: New York. The reference is contained in Hell's own notes from 1922, held at the Institut für Zeitgescheite, Munich, ZS 640, folio 6.

2 Adolf Hitler, *Mein Kampf*, Hutchinson: London, p. 620.

3 Ian Kershaw, *Hitler, the Germans and the Final Solution*, International Institute for Holocaust Research, Yad Vashem: Jerusalem, Ch. 4, p. 8.

4 Ibid.

5 USHMM, *Holocaust Encyclopedia*, "German Jewish Refugees— 1933–1939."

6 "Asks Laws to Admit Jews from Germany," *New York Times*, March 20, 1933, p. A1.

7 "Boycott advocated to curb Hitlerism," *New York Times*, March 21, 1933, p. 10.

8 JVL, "Nuremberg Trial Defendants: Julius Streicher."

9 Ibid.

10 "Nazi Reign a Blow to German Shipping," *New York Times*, July 27, 1933, p. A1.

11 Mike Wallace, "New York and the Nazis," p. 8.

12 Edwin Black, *The Transfer Agreement: The Dramatic Story of the Pact Between the Third Reich and Jewish Palestine*, Carroll & Graf: New York, 2001.

13 Black, p. 326.

14 Yehuda Bauer, *Jews for Sale: Nazi Jewish Negotiations, 1933–1945*, Yale University Press: New Haven and London, 1994, p. 6.

15 Solveig Eggerz, "Jewish Assimilation: Berlin as a Showcase," *Issues*, Summer 2000.

16 See my book, *The American Axis: Henry Ford, Charles Lindbergh and the Rise of the Third Reich* (St. Martin's Press: New York, 2003).

17 Ibid., *The American Axis*, pp. 1–2.

18 Marion A. Kaplan, *Between Dignity and Despair*, Ebsco Publishing: Ipswich, 1999.

19 Black, p. 123.

20 "Reich Migrants get Back 42% of Funds in Cash," *Jewish Telegraphic Agency*, May 25, 1936.

21 "Haavarah Winds up Reich-Palestine Transfer Operations; Handled $35,000,000 in 6 Years," *Jewish Telegraphic Agency*, Sept. 10, 1939. The figure cited is 105,000,000 German marks. Edwin Black cites the figure of 60,000 Jews who transferred to Palestine under the pact "in its various forms." In *Jews for Sale*, Yehuda Bauer writes that 20,000 German Jews emigrated to Palestine under the actual Haavara agreement, representing 37% of all German-Jewish immigrants to Palestine (Bauer, p. 10). This does not contradict Black's findings, but illustrates the complex machinery of Jewish emigration before the war and the vagaries of the pact itself, which is superbly outlined in Black's meticulously researched book.

22 Author interview with Edwin Black, February 22, 2016.

23 JVL, "Adolf Eichmann."

24 Jacob Boas, "A Nazi Travels to Palestine," *History Today*, vol. 30, no. 1, pp. 33–38.

25 Joseph Verbovszky, "Leopold von Mildenstein and the Jewish Question," master's thesis, Case Western University, May 2013.

26 Jacob Boas, "A Nazi Travels to Palestine," *History Today*, vol. 30, no. 1.

27 Jochen von Lang (ed.), *Eichmann Interrogated: Transcripts from the Archives of the Israeli Police*, Perseus Books Group: New York, 1999, p. 24.

28 Many of these German emigrants did not leave via the Haavara.

29 Verbovszky, p. 33.

30 "Eichmann Tells His Own Damning Story," *Life* magazine, Nov. 28, 1960. Four years before his capture by Mossad agents in Argentina in 1960,

Eichmann granted a series of tape-recorded interviews to a Dutch-born SS officer named Wilhelm Sassen who, like Eichmann, had fled to Argentina after the war to escape prosecution. After Eichmann's capture in 1960, Sassen sold the transcripts of the interviews to *Life* magazine which published the "confession" under Eichmann's byline in a two-part cover series headlined, "Eichmann Tells His Own Damning Story." In this feature, he gives the date of his trip to Palestine as 1935, but the details make it clear that he is referring to the aborted 1937 journey with Hagen.

31 AET, session 16, April 26, 1961.

32 Nicosia, *Zionism*, p. 135.

33 YV, N/11/465/E, "The 12 November meeting in the wake of Kristallnacht."

34 Ibid.

35 Ibid.

36 Richard Breitman and Allan J. Lichtman, *FDR and the Jews,* Belknap Press: Cambridge, 2003, p. 103.

37 "German Immigration Far Under the Quota," *New York Times,* June 26, 1938, p. A23.

38 FDRL, Morgenthau Diaries, March 18, 1938, p. 330.

39 Ibid.

40 "Little Prejudice Against a Woman, Jewish, Black or Catholic Presidential Candidate," *Gallup News Service,* June 10, 2003.

41 W.D. Rubinstein, *The Myth of Rescue: Why the Democracies Could Not Have Saved More Jews from the Holocaust*, Routledge: London and New York, 1997, p. 50.

42 "What FDR Said About the Jews in Private," *Los Angeles Times*, April 7, 2013.

43 Edwin Diamond, *Behind the Times: Inside the New York Times*, University of Chicago Press: Chicago, 1995, p. 67.

44 Breitman and Lichtman, p. 105.

45 FDRL, "Myron C. Taylor Papers," Intergovernmental Committee on Political Refugees Correspondence, 1938, President Roosevelt to Myron C. Taylor, April 26, 1938.

46 Jeffrey Gurock, *America, American Jews and the Holocaust,* Routledge: Florence, KY, 2013, p. 229.

47   Jeffrey Lesser, *Welcoming the Undesirables: Brazil and the Jewish Question*, University of California Press: Oakland, 1995, pp. 111–112.

48   "1938 Evian Conference Still Haunts Australia," *Christian Today*, Jan. 9, 2012.

49   Frank Bialystock's excellent 2000 book, *Delayed Impact: The Holocaust and the Canadian Jewish Community*, also provides valuable insight into Canada's attitudes.

50   Irving Abella and Harold Troper, "'The Line Must Be Drawn Somewhere': Canada and Jewish Refugees 1933–9," *Canadian Historical Review*, vol. 60, 1979, p. 184.

51   Ibid.

52   NAC, "Diaries of William Lyon Mackenzie King," March 29, 1938.

53   Ibid.

54   NAC, "Diaries of William Lyon Mackenzie King," Item 8114, Tuesday, June 29, 1937.

55   Ibid.

56   "The Traitor and the Jew: Anti-Semitism and the Delirium of Extremist Right Wing Nationalism in French Canada from 1929–1939," review by Donald A. Wright, *Canadian Woman Studies/Les cahiers de la femme*, vol. 14, no. 4, 1994, p. 122.

57   Abella and Troper, *NITM*, pp. 17–18.

58   Ibid., p. 30.

59   Minutes of Second Public Meeting, Evian Conference, July 7, 1938.

60   "Obama Admits Israel Has Good Reason for Scepticism over Iran Nuclear Deal," *The Guardian*, Nov. 24, 2013.

61   Ronnie S. Landau, *The Nazi Holocaust*, I.B. Tauris: London, 2006, p. 137.

FIVE: THE REICHSFÜHRER-SS

1   "German Army Attacks Poland," *New York Times*, Sept. 1, 1939, p. A1.

2   Author interview with Netty Segal, October 2015.

3   Wolfgang Gerlach, *And the Witnesses Were Silent*, University of Nebraska Press: Lincoln, 2000, p. 153.

4   YVA, TR-3/1209, Reichssicherheitshauptamt to SS Brigadeführer Thomas Brussels re: emigration of Jews, October 23, 1941.

5   Himmler, p. 42.

6   Richard Breitman, *The Architect of Genocide: Himmler and the Final Solution*, Pimlico: London, 2004.

7   Roger Manvell and Heinrich Fraenkel, *Heinrich Himmler: The Sinister Life of the Head of the SS and Gestapo*, Skyhorse: New York, 2007, note 6, p. 255.

8   Ibid., pp. 7–8.

9   Ibid., p. 9.

10 Ibid., p. 4.

11 Longerich, p. 34.

12 Ibid., p. 42.

13 Leon Poliakov, *The History of Anti-Semitism*, vol. 4, University of Pennsylvania Press: Philadelphia, 2003. p. 254.

14 Shirer, p. 38.

15 Ibid., p. 54.

16 Ibid., p. 65.

17 YVA, Photo archives, Album # FA142/29.

18 Manvell and Fraenkel, p. 13.

19 Longerich, p. 79.

20 Manvell and Fraenkel, p. 11.

21 Longerich, p. 79.

22 Detlief Muhlberger, *Hitler's Voice: Organization and Development of the Nazi Party*, Peter Lang: Bern, 2004, p. 182.

23 See my book *The American Axis,* pp. 49–52, for details of Ludecke's mission.

24 Manvell and Fraenkel, pp. 15–16.

SIX: EVACUATION TO THE EAST

1   Richard J. Evans, *The Third Reich in Power*, Penguin Press: London, 2005, p. 97.

2   Albert Speer, *Inside the Third Reich*, Macmillan: London, 1970, p. 45.

3   Longerich, p. 428.

4   USHMM, Center for Advanced Holocaust Studies; Wendy Lower, "The Holocaust and Colonialism in Ukraine"; Holocaust in the

Soviet Union Symposium Presentations, United States Holocaust Museum: Washington, D.C., 2005.

5   Browning, p. 255.

6   Ibid., p. 260.

7   IMT, Trial of the Major German War Criminals, "United States et al v. Hermann Wilhelm Göring et al., "Judgment of 1 October 1946."

8   Longerich, p. 622.

9   The title of Richard Breitman's 1991 study of Himmler's role in carrying out the Final Solution: *The Architect of Genocide: Himmler and the Final Solution*, Pimlico: London, 2004.

10 YVA, Armament in the Ukraine Inspector to Office of Wi Rü re: The Jewish Question, Yitzhak Arad, Yisrael Gutman, Abraham Margaliot (eds.), Documents on the Holocaust. Selected Sources on the Destruction of the Jews of Germany and Austria, Poland and the Soviet Union, Document no. 190, pp. 417– 419.

11 Breitman, p. 196.

12 AET, Defence witness, Testimony from Abroad, the Testimony of Erich Von Dem Bach-Zelewski, May 29, 1961; Bach-Zelewski claims that, according to his diary, the executions took place on August 17 but Christopher Browning writes that Himmler's appointment book for August 14 notes his "presence at an execution of partisans and Jews in the vicinity of Minsk." The Nazi claims that only 20 to 30 partisans and some Jews were shot, but other accounts put the number much higher.

13 Gerald Fleming, *Hitler and the Final Solution*, University of California Press: Berkeley, 1982, p. 50.

14 Browning, n. 21, p. 516. Browning cites the testimony of an unnamed SS man quoted in Ralf Ogorreck's 1996 German book *Die Einsatzgruppen und die "genesis der Endlosung,"* Berlin, 1996. He doesn't necessarily take the account as reliable. "The transition to shooting of Jews in Belorussia was neither so immediate nor so comprehensive as this testimony suggest," he writes, "but the testimony nevertheless supports the notion that the issue of shooting Jewish women and children was broached during the Himmler visit."

15 Browning, p. 107.

16 Breitman, p. 196.

17 Browning, p. 315.

18 Ibid., p. 188.

19 Rudolf Hoess, *Commandant of Auschwitz*, Phoenix Press: London, 2000, p. 183.

20 YVA, Documents on the Holocaust, Selected Sources on the Destruction of the Jews of Germany and Austria, Poland and the Soviet Union, Document 117, pp. 249–261.

21 AET, Eichmann Testimony, Jerusalem, session 107, July 24, 1961.

SEVEN: SAVING THE GUARDIANS OF THE TORAH

1 Author interview with Ruth Rottenberg Mandel, November 2015. Ruth's father would eventually marry Isaac's sister.

2 Ibid., p. 36, diary entry from January 4, 1941.

3 "Correspondent Describes Jewish Ghetto in Warsaw Dispatch," Jewish Telegraphic Agency, April 3, 1941. Some accounts claim the population as 400,000 but the *JTA* correspondent secured the figure of 510,000 from Waldemar Schoen, head of the resettlement division for the Generalgouvernement.

4 Charles G. Roland, *Courage Under Siege: Disease, Starvation and Death in the Warsaw Ghetto,* Oxford University Press: New York, 1992, p. 98.

5 Untitled Kühl memoir prepared for the immediate family by Julius Kühl's daughter, Janine Weinstock (in the author's possession).

6 Untitled Kühl bio, p. 7.

7 ICE, Final Report, p. 129.

8 Ibid., p. 110.

9 Alan Schom, "The Uninvited Guests: Swiss Forced-Labour Camps, 1939–44," Simon Wiesenthal Center: Los Angeles, 1998.

10 Ibid., p. 111.

11 Ibid., p. 112.

12 Author interview with Janine Weinstock, Kühl's daughter, October 2015; Untitled Kühl memoir, p. 7.

13 "Jews Mistreated in Swiss WWll Camps, Study Says," *Los Angeles Times*, Jan. 13, 1998.

14 Gutta Sternbuch, *Gutta: Memories of a Vanished World*, Feldheim: Nanuet, NY, p. 62.

15 Gutta Sternbuch, p. 76.

16 Interview with Gutta Eisenzweig Sternbuch, "Hotel Polski," Top Doc Films, 2010.

17 Ibid.

18 Measuringworth.com, "Exchange Rates Between the United States Dollar and 41 Currencies, 1940."

19 Efraim Zuroff, *The Response of Orthodox Jewry in the United States to the Holocaust*, Yeshiva University Press: New York, 2000, p. 24.

20 Zuroff, p. 91.

21 Zuroff, p. 163.

22 Friedenson and Kranzler, p. 47.

23 Author interview with Herman Landau, Toronto, Canada, August 2000.

24 Friedenson and Kranzler claim that the bar mitzvah took place at the Etz Chaim yeshivah, perhaps because Rabbi Botchko was the dean, but according to the Sternbuchs' daughter Netty Sternbuch Segal, the ceremony took place at the family home. Author interview with Netty Segal, October 2015.

25 Michael Robert Marrus and Robert O. Paxton, *Vichy France and the Jews*, Stanford University Press: Palo Alto, 1981, p. 3.

26 The Independent Commission of Experts studing Swiss wartime refugee policy puts the estimate at 3600, but University of Geneva historian Ruth Fivaz-Silbermann puts the figure at 2600. Table Ronde 26 Avril (2014), Université de Berne, Ruth Fivaz-Silbermann, Université de Genève.

27 Marrus and Paxton, p. 4.

28 USHMM, interview with Hermann Landau, 1979, Story RG-60.5007, 1979, Steven Spielberg Film and Video Archive, Claude Lanzmann Shoah Collection.

29 Author interview with Netty Segal, October 2015. Other details of the bar mitzvah ceremony come from the account of Friedenson and

Kranzler in *Heroine of Rescue* and Gutta Sternbuch in her 2005 memoir, *Memories of a Vanished World.*

30   Author interview with Netty Sternbuch Segal; Friedenson and Kranzler, p. 22.

EIGHT: THE STERNBUCH CABLE

1   Saul Friedlander, *The Years of Extermination*, HarperCollins: New York, 2007, p. 332.

2   USHMM, Christopher Browning, "Initiating the Final Solution: The Fateful Months of September–October 1941," Ina Levine Annual Lecture, March 13, 2003.

3   AET, District Court Sessions, Session 10, April 19, 1961.

4   USHMM, Timeline of Events, "Killing Operations Begin at Chelmno."

5   Friedlander, pp. 315–317.

6   USHMM, Holocaust Encyclopedia, "Sobibór: Chronology."

7   "Warsaw Ghetto is 'Hell on Earth,'" says eyewitness report, *Jewish Telegraphic Agency*, May 13, 1942.

8   "Allies Are Urged to Execute Nazis," *New York Times*, July 2, 1942, p. A6.

9   Max Frankel, "150th Anniversary: 1851–2001; Turning Away from the Holocaust," *New York Times*, Nov. 14, 2001.

10   Morse, p. 6.

11   Walter Laqueur and Richard Breitman, *Breaking the Silence,* Simon & Schuster: New York, 1986, pp. 100–102.

12   Laqueur and Breitman, p. 110.

13   Longerich, p. 573.

14   Ibid., p. 136.

15   Riegner, p. 41.

16   Arthur Morse, *While Six Million Died,* Overlook Press: Woodstock, 1967, pp. 7–9.

17   Author interview with Gerhart Riegner, October 2000; Riegner, p. 42.

18   Riegner would only confirm that Schulte was his source decades later.

19   In his 1967 book, *While Six Million Died,* Arthur Morse claims the Riegner cable was sent to Washington the same day, but in fact Elting

only prepared his memo on August 10 while the U.S. minister, Leland Harrison, transmitted it to Washington on August 11.

20 NA, RG 84, Box 7, 840.1 J, File 1942.

21 AJA, Box J12, Folder 22.

22 NA, 862.4016/2234, Harrison to Secretary of State, Aug. 11, 1942.

23 Wyman, p. 43.

24 Riegner, Gerhart. *Never Despair: Sixty Years in the Service of the Jewish People and the Cause of Human Rights*, Ivan R. Dee: New York, 2006 (ed.), p. 43.

25 Ibid., p. 44.

26 Stephen Wise, *The Challenging Years*, G.P. Putnam's Sons: New York, 1949, p. 275.

27 YVA, Shoah Resource Center, Announcement of the Evacuation of the Jews from the Warsaw Ghetto, July 22, 1942," Documents on the Holocaust, Selected Sources on the Destruction of the Jews of Germany and Austria, Poland and the Soviet Union, Document #128, 1981.

28 JVL, "Adam Czerniakow."

29 "The Mysterious Messenger," Jan. 1, 1984, Monty N. Penkower letter to *Commentary*.

30 Arthur Morse, *While Six Million Died: A Chronicle of American Apathy*, Random House: New York, 1968.

31 USHMM, interview with Hermann Landau, 1979, Story RG-60.5007, 1979, Steven Spielberg Film and Video Archive, Claude Lanzmann Shoah Collection.

32 Elias Sternbuch interview with Monty Noam Penkower, Dec. 1980.

33 Penkower, pp. 71–72; Morse, p. 16. Morse incorrectly interprets the word "Eisensweig" as "steelworkers" when in fact it was the last name of Elias's lady friend, Gutta, and was meant to tell him that she had escaped deportation.

34 AIA, Michael Tress Collection, Confidential Internal Reports, Moreinu Rosenheim's Diary During Wartime, Box A12.

35 AIA, Michael Tress Collection, Confidential Internal Reports, Moreinu Rosenheim's Diary During Wartime, Box A12, Cable Rosenheim to FDR, Sept. 3, 1942.

36 Monty Penkower, *The Jews Were Expendable: Free World Diplomacy and the Holocaust*, University of Illinois Press: Urbana and Chicago, 1983, p. 69.

37 Thomas Mann, *Listen Germany: Twenty-Five Radio Messages to the German People over BBC*, Knopf: New York, 1943, p. 76.

38 Anne Frank House 1942 Timeline, "The Deportations."

39 "Yad Vashem: Nazi Soap Stories 'Invention,'" *Haaretz*, Nov. 2, 2005.

40 Breitman, p. 6.

NINE: MARCH OF THE RABBIS

1 Joseph Goebbels, *The Goebbels Diaries: 1942–1943,"* Greenwood Press: Westport, CT., 1970, p. 241.

2 Friedenson and Kranzler, *Heroine*, p. 94.

3 The American Jewish Committee rep had another commitment but asked to be kept informed.

4 Ibid.

5 Nicholas John Cull, *Propaganda and Mass Persuasion: A Historical Encyclopedia, 1500 to Present*, ABC-CLIO: Santa Barbara, 2003, p. 25.

6 "The Mysterious Messenger," Jan. 1, 1984, Monty N. Penkower letter to *Commentary*. It was Penkower who found confirmation that the cables had been dispatched by Elias Sternbuch.

7 Wise, p. 276.

8 "Hitler Has Ordered Annhilation of All Jews by End of 1942, Washington Hears," *Jewish Telegraphic Agency*, November 25, 1942.

9 "Wise Gets Confirmations," *New York Times*, Nov. 25, 1942, p. 10.

10 Wyman, p. 52.

11 "American Jewry Will Mourn on Wednesday for Jews Murdered by Nazis in Europe," *Jewish Telegraphic Agency*," Nov. 30, 1942.

12 "Roosevelt Receives Jewish Delegation, Promises Aid to End Nazi Massacres of Jews," *Jewish Telegraphic Agency*, Dec. 9, 1942.

13 "11 Allies Condemn Nazi War on Jews," *New York Times*, Dec. 18, 1942, p. 1.

14 FDRL, WRB, Box 3, Bermuda Conference, Memorandum of Bermuda Conference on the Refugee Problem held April 19 to April 29, 1943. "Summary of Recommendations."

15 "Nazis Start Mass-Execution of Warsaw Jews on Passover; Victims Broadcast S.O.S., *Jewish Telegraphic Agency*, April 23, 1943.

16 YVA, Shoah Resource Center, The International School for Holocaust Studies, "Warsaw Ghetto Uprising."

17 Zuroff, p. 244.

18 Friedenson and Kranzler, p. 95.

19 AJCA, Minutes of Joint Emergency Committee on European Jewish Affairs, Mar. 15, 1943.

20 USHMM, *Holocaust Encyclopedia,* "Peter Bergson."

21 AJCA, Minutes of Joint Emergency Committee on European Jewish Affairs, Mar. 15, 1943, "Report on Discussions with the Jewish Army Committee."

22 "Save Doomed Jews, Huge Rally Pleads," *New York Times,* March 2, 1943, p. A1.

23 AJCA, Trager to Rosenblum, March 17, 1943.

24 Ibid., p. 240.

25 "Roosevelt Says U.S. Efforts to Save Jews of Europe Will Not Cease Until Nazis Crushed," *Jewish Telegraphic Agency,* July 26, 1943.

26 "Congressman Rogers Demands United Nations Agency to Save Jews in Europe," *Jewish Telegraphic Agency,* July 21, 1943.

27 "Oral History Interview with Josiah E. Dubois Jr.," Harry S. Truman Library and Museum, June 29, 1973; Wyman, p. 97.

28 The Jewish Chronicle Online, Anna Sheinman, "The Eden Declaration 70 years on," Dec. 13, 2012.

29 Breckinridge Long, Fred L. Israel, *The War Diary of Breckinridge Long: Selections from the Years 1939–44,* University of Nebraska Press: Lincoln, 1966, p. 307.

30 Breitman and Lichtman, *FDR and the Jews*, p. 218.

31 See Ch. 6 of my book *The American Axis* for details.

32 FDRL, Henry Morgenthau Jr. Presidential Diaries, May 20, 1940, p. 563.

33 Max Wallace, *The American Axis*, St. Martin's Press: New York, 2003, pp. 290–291.

34 Ibid.

35 Ibid.

36 Advertisement, *New York Times*, May 4, 1943, p. 17.

37 Account of Rabinowitz's grandson Jonathan Stern, "Testimony from Relatives of Those Who Marched," David S. Wyman Institute exhibit on the rabbis' march.

38 Wyman, p. 148.

39 It helped that one of the Orthodox activists, Irving Bunim, had long been a follower of Bergson's mentor, the Revisionist leader Ze'ev Jabotinsky. Bergson told Claude Lanzmann in 1978 that it was Rabbi Eliezer Silver, head the Union of Orthodox Rabbis and a leader of the Vaad who "issued the order" for the Rabbis to march and who marched at the head. Dr. Henri Lustiger Thaler, senior curator of the Amud Aish Memorial Museum, told me in September 2015 that the politically savvy Vaad/Agudath Israel leadership refrained from officially endorsing the rabbis' march for fear of alienating the Roosevelt administration. Instead, many members, including Silver, marched as individuals.

40 USHMM, interview with Peter Bergson and Samuel Merlin, New York, Nov. 15, 1978, Story RG-60.5020, Steven Spielberg Film and Video Archive, Claude Lanzmann Shoah Collection.

41 "Three Hundred Rabbis Submit Petition to Washington On Rescue of Jews From Europe," *Jewish Telegraphic Agency*, Oct. 7, 1943.

42 Zuroff, p. 258.

43 "Three Hundred Rabbis Submit Petition to Washington on Rescue of Jews from Europe," *Jewish Telegraphic Agency*, Oct. 7, 1943.

44 Encyclopedia of America's Response to the Holocaust, the David Wyman Institute for Holocaust Studies, "Rescue Resolution."

45 "580,000 Refugees Admitted to United States in Decade," *New York Times,* Dec. 11, 1943, p. A1.

46 "Jews Debarred," Celler declares, *New York Times,* Dec. 12, 1943, p. 8.

47 FDRL, Morgenthau Diaries, memorandum Paul to Morgenthau, Dec. 17, 1943; Hull to Morgenthau, Dec. 6, 1943; Morgenthau to Hull, Dec. 17, 1943.

48 FDRL, Morgenthau Diaries, Vol. 688, Jewish Refugees, Dec. 13–Dec. 31, 1943, Memorandum for the Files, Josiah E. Dubois Jr., Dec. 18, 1943.

49 FDRL, Morgenthau Diaries, Memo, Dubois to Morgenthau, "Report to the Secretary on the Acquiescence of This Government in the Murder of Jews," Jan. 13, 1944.

50 FDRL, Morgenthau Diaries, Vol. 694, Jan. 15, 1944, Minutes of Treasury Department meeting re: "Jewish Evacuation."

51 FDRL, Morgenthau Diaries, Vol. 694, Memo, January 15, 1944, "Personal Report to the President."

52 FDRL, Morgenthau Diaries, Vol. 694, Jan. 15, 1944, Minutes of Department of Treasury Department meeting re: "Jewish Evacuation."

53 FDRL, Ira Hirschman Papers, Box 2, Executive Order No. 9417, Establishing a War Refugee Board, Jan. 22, 1944.

TEN: THE RESCUE COMMITTEE

1   Author interview with Renée Landau, October, 2015.

2   Author interview with Renée Landau, May 2016.

3   Marrus and Paxton, p. 70.

4   Ibid., p. xvii.

5   "France Responsible for Sending Jews to Concentration Camps," *The Guardian,* Feb. 17, 2009.

6   Author interview with Renée Landau, October 2015.

7   KFA, "Julius Kühl family memoir," p. 36.

8   Ibid., p. 29.

9   Ibid.

10 Friedenson and Kranzler, p. 58.

11 KFA, "Julius Kühl family memoir," p. 31.

12 Ibid.

13 Gutta told a number of versions of this story in which she claimed that Recha had rescued the 12 Jews from "Germany" but the operation may very well have taken place in Vichy France or Austria.

14 Bauer, *JFS*, p. 63.

15 Ibid., p. 65.

16 IMT, "Testimony of Dieter Wisliceny," Jan. 3, 1946.

17 Ibid., p. 67.

18 IMT, "Testimony of Dieter Wisliceny," Jan. 3, 1946.

19 AET, testimony of Dr. Ernest Abeles, session 49, May 23, 1961.

20 Bauer, *JFS*, p. 69.

21 YVA, Shoah Resource Centre, "Slovakia."

22 Jewish Women's Archive, Encyclopedia, "Gisi Fleischmann," by Gila Fatran.

23 Bauer, *JFS*, p. 73.

24 Ibid., p. 74.

25 AET, testimony of Dr. Ernest Abeles, session 49, May 23, 1961.

26 USHMM, interview with Andrew Steiner, 1978–79, Story RG-60.501, Steven Spielberg Film and Video Archive," Claude Lanzmann Shoah Collection.

27 Steiner later told Claude Lanzmann that the fictitious man's name was "Joseph Rot."

28 USHMM, Steiner interview, op. cit.

29 Dr. Efraim Zuroff, "The Europa Plan," *Shalom: The European Jewish Times,* October, 2005.

30 Bauer, *JFS*, p. 75.

31 YVA, Exhibition, The Story of the Jewish Community in Bratislava; Bratislava During the Holocaust; "The Working Group," Video interview.

32 Bauer, *American Jewry and the Holocaust: The American Jewish Joint Distribution Committee, 1939–1945,* Wayne State University: Detroit, 1981, p. 368.

33 USHMM, interview with Andrew Steiner, 1978–79, Story RG-60.501, Steven Spielberg Film and Video Archive, Claude Lanzmann Shoah Collection.

34 Ibid., p. 370.

35 YVA, Exhibition, The Story of the Jewish Community in Bratislava; Bratislava During the Holocaust; "The Working Group," Video interview with Ondrej Steiner.

36 AET, testimony of Dr. Ernest Abeles, session 49, May 23, 1961.

37 Bauer, *AJH*, p. 370.

38 Ibid., p. 371.

39 Ibid., p. 372.

40 Bauer, *JFS*, p. 81.

41 Ibid., p. 81.

42 SM, roll 65, "Fleischmann to Mayer," July 28, 1943. I rely on Yehuda Bauer's translation from the original German.

43 Bauer, *AJH*, p. 375.

44 Bauer, *JFS*, p. 85.

45 AET, testimony of Dr. Ernest Abeles, session 49, May 23, 1961

46 Bauer, *JFS*, p. 85.

47 IMT, "Testimony of Dieter Wisliceny," Jan. 3, 1946.

48 AET, testimony of Dr. Ernest Abeles, session 49, May 23, 1961.

49 Ronald Florence, *Emissary of the Doomed: Bargaining for Lives in the Holocaust*, Penguin: London, 2010.

50 Bauer, *JFS*, p. 87.

51 Bauer, *JFS*, p. 78.

52 Bauer notes that at least $131,000 was transferred from the Jewish Agency in Istanbul to the Working Group during the spring of 1943.

ELEVEN: THE SPY CHIEF AND THE DEVIL'S DOCTOR

1 YVA, "About the Holocaust. Overview: How Vast the Crime?"

2 YVA, "From a Speech by Himmler Before Senior Officers in Poznan, October 4, 1943."

3 Karina Urbach, *Go-Betweens for Hitler*, Oxford University Press: Oxford, 2015, p. 299.

4 Breitman, *JCH*, pp. 418–419; Dulles, p. 419.

5 Gerald Reitlinger, *The SS: Alibi of a Nation*, Da Capo Press: Boston, 1989, p. 165. In a diary entry dated November 10, 1942, Felix Kersten would note that Himmler described Ciano as a "traitor" who the Führer would see "hanged" because he was seeking a separate peace with the Allies on behalf of Italy.

6 FRUS, *The Conferences at Washington, 1941–1942, and Casablanca, 1943* (1941–1943), p. 13.

7 Ibid., p. 9.

8 Waller, p. 9.

9   Kersten, *Memoirs*, p. 309.

10 Ibid., p. 11.

11 Kersten, *Memoirs*, introduction by Hugh Trevor-Roper, p. 10.

12 Ibid.

13 Shirer, p. 653.

14 Schellenberg, *The Labyrinth*, pp. 70–85.

15 IMT, Schellenberg testimony, Trial of Ernst Kaltenbrunner, January 4, 1946.

16 Ibid.

17 Ibid.

18 Walter Schellenberg, *Hitler's Secret Service*, Pyramid: New York, 1968, p. 153.

19 Kersten, *Memoirs*, p. 11.

20 Ibid., diary entry, Berlin, March 3, 1940.

21 Ibid.

22 Ibid., diary entry, November 10, 1942.

23 Ibid., p. 20.

24 Ibid., p. 21.

25 Ibid., pp. 25–26.

26 Ibid., pp. 217–218.

27 Walter Schellenberg, *The Labyrinth: Memoirs of Walter Schellenberg, Hitler's Chief of Counter-intelligence*, DaCapo Press: Boston, 2000, p. 306.

28 Ibid., p. 301.

29 NARA, RG 165, July 1945, "Report on the Case of Walter Schellenberg, British–US interrogation of Walter Schellenberg."

30 Schellenberg, *The Labyrinth*, pp. 308–309.

31 Waller, p. 69. Waller and others have described Langbehn as Himmler's lawyer but this doesn't appear to have been the case.

32 Allen Welsh Dulles, *Germany's Underground*, Da Capo Press: Boston, 1947, p. 148.

33 Ibid., p. 155.

34 Ibid., p. 159.

35 Ibid.

36 Kersten, *Memoirs*, diary entry, October 2, 1943.

37 Breitman, p. 441; CIA Library, "Reichsführer Himmler Pitches Washington: Dispatch from Wartime Sweden," John H. Waller.

38 Kersten, *Memoirs,* diary entry, October 3, 1943.

39 Ibid., diary entry, October 24, 1943.

40 Breitman, p. 418.

41 Reinhard Doerries and Gerhard L. Weinberg, *Hitler's Intelligence Chief: Walter Schellenberg,* Enigma Books: New York, 2013, p. 109.

42 Breitman, p. 441; CIA Library, "Reichsführer Himmler Pitches Washington: Dispatch from Wartime Sweden," John H. Waller.

43 Kersten, *Memoirs,* diary entry, Dec. 4, 1943. Like many of Kersten's diary entries, there is a discrepancy with the date given and Himmler's calendar. This conversation, if it occurred, is more likely to have taken place on December 9, the next time Himmler's appointment book records a meeting with Kersten.

44 Ibid.

45 Ibid.

46 Ibid.

47 FRUS, 740.0011 European War 1939/32649: Telegram, Herschel Johnson to Secretary of State, Jan. 10, 1944.

48 Breitman, p. 423.

49 Ibid.

50 Ibid.

51 Richard Smith, *OSS: The Secret History of America's First Central Intelligence Agency,* Rowman & Littlefield: Lanham, MD, 2005, pp. 197–98.

TWELVE: BLOOD FOR TRUCKS

1 USHMM, *Holocaust Encyclopedia,* "Hungary Before the German Occupation."

2 YVA, The International School for Holocaust Studies, "Historical Background: The Jews of Hungary During the Holocaust."

3 WRB, Box 66, Jews in Hungary (1), February–May 1944, "A Concise Survey of the Situation of Hungarian Jews, "Geneva, April 30, 1944.

4   Ibid.

5   Andrew Handler, *A Man for All Connections: Raoul Wallenberg and the Hungarian State,* Greenwood Publishing: Westport, CT, 1996, p. 33.

6   In *Jews for Sale?,* Yehuda Bauer names Freudiger, Weiss and Rezső Kasztner as the three, but when testifying at Eichmann's trial in 1961, Freudiger insisted he went with Kahan.

7   AET, Testimony of Hansi Brand, session 58, May 30, 1961. Some accounts claim the couple ran a glove factory, but Hansi describes their business as a "workshop" producing "knitted goods."

8   AET, Testimony of Joel Brand, session 56, May 29, 1961.

9   Bauer, *JFS*, p. 163.

10 Ibid.

11 WRB, Box 66, Jews in Hungary (1), February–May 1944, Harrison to State, April 24, 1944.

12 Brand initially recalled the date as April 16 but later remembered a meeting on his birthday, April 25.

13 AET, Testimony of Joel Brand, session 56, May 29, 1961.

14 At another point in his testimony, Brand quotes Eichmann as saying, "I am prepared to sell you a million Jews—goods for blood, blood for goods."

15 AET, Testimony of Joel Brand, session 56, May 29, 1961.

16 Ibid.

17 Ibid.

18 Ibid.

19 The pair initially escaped on April 7 but hid for three days before making their way past the outer perimeter on April 10, which is the date often cited. In his interview with Claude Lanzmann, Vrba gives the date of his escape as April 7. USHMM, interview with Rudolf Vrba, 1978–81, Story RG-60.5016, Steven Spielberg Film and Video Archive, Claude Lanzmann Shoah Collection.

20 "Rudolf Vrba, Escapees from Auschwitz who revealed the truth about the camp," *The Guardian*, April 13, 2006.

21 USHMM, interview with Rudolf Vrba, 1978–81, Story RG-60.5016, Steven Spielberg Film and Video Archive," Claude Lanzmann Shoah Collection.

22 AJC, War and Peace/Germany File, "Two eyewitness accounts of Auschwitz and Birkenau, German Extermination Camps—Auschwitz and Birkenau."

23 "Rudolf Vrba, Escapees from Auschwitz who revealed the truth about the camp," *The Guardian,* April 13, 2006.

24 Ibid.

25 Longerich, p. 694.

26 IMT, "Testimony of Dieter Wisliceny," Jan. 3, 1946.

27 This is also the figure cited in the official guide published by the Auschwitz-Birkenau Memorial Museum, titled *Auschwitz-Birkenau: The Past and the Present*. Höss claimed in his memoir that the figure of 2.5 million was supplied to him by Eichmann.

28 *Höss*, p. 215.

29 WRB—General Correspondence: German Extermination Camps [Part I: *Auschwitz Protocols*—press release and Vrba-Wetzler Report], "The extermination camps of Auschwitz and Birkenau in Upper Silesia," 1945.

30 AET, Testimony of Philip von Freudiger, Session 52, May 25, 1961.

31 USHMM, interview with Rudolf Vrba, 1978–81, Story RG-60.5016, Steven Spielberg Film and Video Archive, Claude Lanzmann Shoah Collection.

32 Vrba would later claim the meeting took place in June but the subsequent cables from Weissmandl and ensuing activities prove the date must have been in the vicinity of May 15.

33 USHMM, interview with Rudolf Vrba, 1978–81, Story RG-60.5016, Steven Spielberg Film and Video Archive, Claude Lanzmann Shoah Collection.

34 Ibid.

35 Ibid.

36 While McClelland's wife was a practicing Quaker, McClelland didn't consider himself an adherent of the religion, nor was he brought up as a member of the society, even though his mother was descended from Quakers.

37 WRB, Box 36, Representatives—Representatives and Special Attachés: Appointments (1) Hodel to Pehle, Feb. 10, 1944.

38 Zuroff, *Vaad*, p. 266.

39 Author interview with Renée Landau, October 2015.

40 Author interview with Hermann Landau, Toronto, August, 2000; USHMM, interview with Hermann Landau, 1979, Story RG-60.5007, Steven Spielberg Film and Video Archive, Claude Lanzmann Shoah Collection.

41 WRB, Box 70, Union of Orthodox Rabbis: Representation in Switzerland (I. Sternbuch) (1), January–June 1944, Cordell Hull to Harrison, Jan. 24, 1944.

42 Author interview with HIJEFS secretary Hermann Landau, Toronto, August 2000.

43 His confusion was likely caused by Isaac's position as the representative of the Union of Orthodox Rabbis.

44 USHMM, interview with Roswell McClelland, 1978–79(?), Story RG-60.5047, Steven Spielberg Film and Video Archive, Claude Lanzmann Shoah Collection.

45 Ibid.

46 VH, Box 36, Folder 132, Sternbuch & Donnenbaum to *Vaad*, July 13, 1944

47 USHMM, interview with Hermann Landau, 1979, Story RG-60.5007, Steven Spielberg Film and Video Archive, Claude Lanzmann Shoah Collection.

48 Ibid.

49 Ibid.

50 Ibid.

51 Author interview with Hermann Landau, Toronto, August, 2000; USHMM, interview with Hermann Landau, 1979, Story RG-60.5007, Steven Spielberg Film and Video Archive, Claude Lanzmann Shoah Collection.

52 WRB, Box 70, Memorandum, McClelland to DeJong, May 25, 1944, Union of Orthodox Rabbis: Representation in Switzerland (I. Sternbuch) (1), 1939.

53 WRB, Box 70, Union of Orthodox Rabbis: Representation in Switzerland (I. Sternbuch) (2), July–December 1944, Union of

Orthodox Rabbis: Representation in Switzerland (I. Sternbuch) (1), July–December 1944, Telegram, #3506, Harrison to State, June 2, 1944.

54 Bauer, *JFS,* p. 174.

55 AET, Testimony of Joel Brand, session 56, May 29, 1961.

56 Paul Lawrence Rose, "Joel Brand's 'Interim Agreement' and the course of Nazi-Jewish Negotiations 1944–45," *The Historical Journal,* vol. 34, no. 4 (Dec, 1991), p. 911.

57 Ibid., p. 912.

58 AET, Testimony of Joel Brand, session 56, May 29, 1961.

59 Bauer, *JFS*, p. 208.

60 AET, Kurt Becher statement, session 85, July 4, 1961.

61 Bauer, *JFS*, p. 198.

62 AET, Testimony of Hansi Brand, session 58, May 30, 1961.

63 Author interview with Peter Munk after Toronto screening of *Killing Kasztner, September, 2008*; Anna Porter, *Kasztner's Train*, Douglas & McIntyre: Vancouver, 2007, p. 233.

64 Ladislab Löb, *Rezső Kasztner: The Daring Rescue of Hungarian Jews: A Survivor's Account*, Random House: New York, 2011, p. 89.

65 Porter, p. 237.

66 AET, Testimony of Hansi Brand, session 58, May 30, 1961.

67 Ibid.

68 WRB, Box 79, Negotiations in Switzerland—Including German Proposals (3), McClelland to Secretary of State for WRB, #5197, Aug. 11, 1944.

THIRTEEN: AN UNLIKELY ALLY

1 "Inquiry Confirms Nazi Death Camps," *New York Times*, July 3, 1944, p. 3.

2 VH, Box 35, Folders 118-127, Memorandum to Pehle from Vaad, March ?, 1944.

3 WRB, Box 66, Jews in Hungary (2), February–May 1944.

4 Author interview with Renée Landau, October 2015.

5 FDR-63: Letter, John J. McCloy to John W. Pehle re: bombing of railway lines transporting Jews to death camps, July 4, 1944; Telegram, Harrison to Secretary of State, June 24, 1944 (transmitting McClelland cable of June 17).

6 USHMM, *Holocaust Encyclopedia,* "Why Auschwitz Was Not Bombed," McCloy to Kubowitski, Aug. 14, 1944.

7 USHMM, interview with Roswell McClelland, 1978–79(?), Story RG-60.5047, Steven Spielberg Film and Video Archive, Claude Lanzmann Shoah Collection.

8 Robert L. Beir, *Roosevelt and the Holocaust: How FDR Saved the Jews and Brought Hope to a Nation,* Skyhorse: New York, 2013.

9 "New Study Reveals FDR Opposition to Bombing Auschwitz," *New English Review,* Jan. 24, 2012.

10 The date is often incorrectly reported as June 18.

11 WRB, Box 40, Measures Directed Toward Halting Persecutions— Hungary, Vol. 1 (1), Morgenthau to Pehle, September 6, 1944.

12 Martin Gilbert, "Bombing Auschwitz: Fact and Myth," *The Times* (London), Jan. 27, 2005.

13 Ibid.

14 Eleonore Lappin, "Death Marches of Hungarian Jews through Austria in the Spring of 1945," *Yad Vashem Studies,* vol. 28, Jerusalem (2000) pp. 203–242.

15 DDS, Notice du Chef du Département politique, M. Pilet-Golaz, vol. 15, no. 20, Oct. 13, 1943.

16 YU, Irving Bunim Oral History Collection, interview of Irving Bunim by Rabbi Moshe Kolodny, Dec. 12, 1976.

17 Author interview with Agudath Israel archivist Moshe Kolodny, November 2016, who claimed he heard the story from historian Monty Penkower, who interviewed Morgenthau's Jewish secretary, Henrietta Klotz. She claimed she heard one of the men give instructions in Yiddish for Kalmanowitz to faint just before his collapse.

18 FDRL, Morgenthau Diaries, Book 718, April 6–7, 1944.

19 Ibid., Minutes of Treasury meeting, re: "Jewish evacuation," April 7, 1944, 11:30 a.m.

20 WRB, Box 70, Sternbuch to Union of Orthodox Rabbis, May 25, 1944, Union of Orthodox Rabbis: Representation in Switzerland (I. Sternbuch) (1), January–June 1944.

21 WRB, Box 24, Private Messages Sent—Vaad ha-Hatzalah (2), Vaad to Milefsky, Montevideo, May 1944.

22 Isaac Lewin and Ludwig Kryzanowski, "Attempts at Rescuing European Jews," *Polish Review*, part 2, vol. 24, no. 1 (1979), pp. 46–61.

23 WRB, Box 70, Sternbuch to McClelland, June 29, 1944, Sternbuch to Union of Orthodox Rabbis, May 25, 1944, Union of Orthodox Rabbis: Representation in Switzerland (I. Sternbuch) (1), January–June 1944.

24 WRB, Box 70, Union of Orthodox Rabbis: Representation in Switzerland (I. Sternbuch) (1), January–June 1945, "Confidential Biographocal Data, Jean-Marie Musy," prepared by American Legation, Bern, March 15, 1945.

25 Ibid.

26 Library of Congress, Exhibit, Revelations from the Russian Archives, "Anti-religious campaigns."

27 Daniel Sebastiani, *Jean-Marie Musy (1876–1952)*, doctoral thesis, Université de Fribourg, 2004, pp. 427–428.

28 Ibid., p. 904.

29 Ibid., p. 905.

30 Sebastiani, p. 905.

31 Ibid., p. 676.

32 Ibid., p. 684.

33 Ibid., p. 591.

34 Ibid.

35 Georges André Chevallaz, *The Challenge of Neutrality: Diplomacy and the Defense of Switzerland*, Lexington Books: Lanham, MD, 2001, p. 114.

36 Sebastiani, p. 813.

37 Ibid., p. 886.

38 USHMM, "France," *Holocaust Encyclopedia*.

39 Sebastiani, p. 887.

40 Ibid., p. 888.

41 VH, File #36, Folder 135, Testimony of Jean-Marie Musy, taken at Bern, Switzerland, Oct. 26, 1945, by Major Robert Haythorne, OUSCC.

42 Rose, *Archives of the Holocaust.* Interview with Dr. Reuben Hecht by Professor Monty Penkower, Haifa, January 6–7, 1982, p. 382.

43 VH, File #36, Folder 135, Testimony of Jean-Marie Musy, taken at Bern, Switzerland, Oct. 26, 1945, by Major Robert Haythorne, OUSCC.

44 Author interview, Hermann Landau, August 2000, Toronto, Ontario. Landau told me that by the end of his mission, no committee member believed that Musy was interested in the money, nor did he claim any compensation beyond his expenses.

45 Schellenberg, *The Labyrinth*, p. 378.

46 Musy would later claim he hadn't seen Himmler in four years, but records indicate that they met in January 1941, when Musy traveled to Berlin on behalf of Vichy France.

47 VH, File #36, Folder 135, Testimony of Jean-Marie Musy, taken at Bern, Switzerland, Oct. 26, 1945, by Major Robert Haythorne, OUSCC.

48 Ibid.

49 Paul Lawrence Rose, "Joel Brand's 'Interim Agreement' and the course of Nazi-Jewish Negotiations 1944–45," *The Historical Journal,* vol. 34, no. 4 (Dec. 1991), p. 921.

50 VH, File #36, Folder 135, Testimony of Jean-Marie Musy, taken at Bern, Switzerland, Oct. 26, 1945, by Major Robert Haythorne, OUSCC; HLA, "Rapport au Comité Suisse de l'Union of Orthodox Rabbis of the United States and Canada concernant l'action entreprise en vue de la libération des Israélites, détenue dans les camps de concentration allemande," Report by Jean-Marie Musy, Fribourg, 1945.

51 Ibid.

52 VH, File #36, Folder 135, Testimony of Jean-Marie Musy, taken at Bern, Switzerland, Oct. 26, 1945, by Major Robert Haythorne, OUSCC.

53 Ibid.

FOURTEEN: FALL OF THE KILLING MACHINE

1   USHMM, *Holocaust Encyclopedia*, "Auschwitz: Chronology." Some accounts claim the explosions happened on November 24, but the general consensus is that they took place on the 25th. Crematorium I, active from 1940 to 1943, had been converted into an SS air raid shelter a year earlier. A fifth building, known as Crematorium V, was left standing to be used for the cremation of any prisoners who died after November 1944.

2   USHMM, *The Holocaust Encyclopedia*, "Prisoner Revolt at Auschwitz-Birkenau."

3   YVA, Shoah Resource Center, "Horthy Offer."

4   WRB, Saly Mayer's Negotiations in Switzerland (1), Stettinius to Pehle, Aug. 17, 1944; YVA, Shoah Resource Centre, "Horthy Offer."

5   Yehuda Bauer, *Jews for Sale: Nazi Jewish Negotiations, 1933–1945*, Yale University Press: New Haven and London, 1994, p. 213.

6   Ibid., p. 217.

7   "Public Understanding of the Holocaust from WWII to Today," Roper Center of Public Opinion, Cornell University.

8   Ibid., p. 219.

9   WRB, McClelland to WRB, Aug. 11, 1944.

10 Ibid.

11 WRB, "American Jewish Joint Distribution Committee Licenses—Rescue Operations in Hungary and Balkans," McClelland to WRB (Harrison to State), July 5, 1944.

12 WRB, Box 77, Joel Brandt Proposal (1), Winant to Secretary of State, July 20, 1944.

13 WRB, Box 77, Joel Brandt Proposal (1), Telegram, Foreign Office to Spanish High Commission.

14 WRB, Box 78, Saly Mayer's Negotiations in Switzerland (2), Telegram, Hull to Harriman, American Embassy, Moscow, Oct. 20, 1944.

15 WRB, Box 24, Private Messages Sent—Vaad ha-Hatzalah (2), Sternbuch to Vaad, Oct. 20, 1944.

16 JDC, SM-65, Mayer to Fleischmann, Feb. 24, 1945.

17 The date is often incorrectly given as August 21, but McClelland reports on August 26 that he has just spoken to Mayer, who told him his meeting took place on Sunday, August 20.

18 Yehuda Bauer claims Mayer didn't want his "partners" to enter Switzerland, but the WRB records indicate that it was the Swiss who would not let the Nazis enter.

19 WRB, Box 79, Negotiations in Switzerland—Including German Proposals, Telegram, McClelland to WRB, Aug. 23, 1944.

20 WRB, Box 78, Saly Mayer's Negotiations in Switzerland (2), McClelleland to WRB, Aug. 26, 1944.

21 WRB, Box 78, Saly Mayer's Negotiations in Switzerland (2), McClelland to WRB, Sept. 16, 1944.

22 Eleonore Lappin, "Death Marches of Hungarian Jews through Austria in the Spring of 1945," *Yad Vashem Studies*, vol. 28, Jerusalem (2000) pp. 203–242.

23 AET, Testimony of Hansi Brand, session 58, May 30, 1961.

FIFTEEN: FORTY TRACTORS

1   Some still give the date as November 24 or 26.

2   Although the gas chambers were inexplicably left intact.

3   USHMM, "Liberation of Nazi Camps," *Holocaust Encyclopedia*.

4   YVA, Shoah Resource Center, "Aktion 1005."

5   Rozett and Spector, *Encyclopedia of the Holocaust*, p. 503.

6   Yehuda Bauer (reply), *Rescue Attempts during the Holocaust*, Proceedings of the Second Yad Vashem International Historical Conference, April 1974, Yad Vashem: Jerusalem, 1977, First session debate, p. 119.

7   IMT, affidavit 3762-PS, Colonel Kurt Becher, March 8, 1946.

8   Ibid.

9   IMT, Nazi Conspiracy and Aggression, affidavit of Dieter Wisliceny, Nov. 29, 1946, Nuremberg, Germany, UK-81.

10 IMT, Testimony of Ernst Kaltenbrunner, April 12, 1946, morning session.

11 IMT, Document 2605-PS, "Details of the Persecution and Massacre of Jews in Hungary 1941–1944," affidavit of Rudolf Kasztner sworn in

London to the United States Major Judge Advocate General chief counsel, Warren F. Farr, September 13, 1945.

12   Author interview with Sigmund Sobolewski, Oct. 15, 2016.

13   Author email interview with Dr. Igor Bartosik, October 20, 2016. Bartosik says he has never heard of the bodies buried in fields described by Sigmund Sobolewski.

14   Ibid.

15   Yehuda Bauer (reply), *Rescue Attempts during the Holocaust*, Yad Vashem: Jerusalem, 1977, First session debate, p. 119.

16   Author interview with Hermann Landau, August 2000.

17   WRB, Box 66, Jews in Hungary, July 1944, Folder 2, "McClelland Memo on whole tractor affair," July 21–22, 1944.

18   Ibid.

19   Ibid.

20   Ibid.

21   WRB, Box 79, Records formerly classified as "Secret," June 1944– August 1945, Negotiations in Switzerland Including German Proposals, Folder 1 McClelland to WRB, July 26, 1944.

22   Ibid.

23   Ibid.; WRB, Box 79, Records formerly classified as "Secret," June 1944–August 1945, Negotiations in Switzerland Including German Proposals, Telegram, Pehle to Leavitt, Aug. 9, 1944.

24   WRB, Box 79, Records formerly classified as "Secret," June 1944– August 1945, Negotiations in Switzerland Including German Proposals, Folder 1 McClelland to WRB, July 26, 1944.

25   SM-21, Telegram, Israel Rosenberg to Joseph C. Hyman, July 25, 1944.

26   WRB, Box 79, Records formerly classified as "Secret," June 1944– August 1945, Negotiations in Switzerland Including German Proposals, Telegram, WRB to McClelland (Leavitt to Saly Mayer), July 29, 1944.

27   Ibid.

28   SM-21 Memo, meeting with Vaad ha-Hatzalah, July 25, 1944.

29   WRB, Box 79, Records formerly classified as "Secret," June 1944– August 1945, Negotiations in Switzerland Including German Proposals, Telegram, McClelland to WRB, State, FEA, July 29, 1944.

30 WRB, Box 66, Jews in Hungary, July 1944, Folder 2, "McClelland Memo on whole tractor affair," July 21–22, 1944.

31 WRB, Box 79, Records formerly classified as "Secret," June 1944– August 1945, Negotiations in Switzerland Including German Proposals, Telegram, Stettinius to McClelland, Aug. 2, 1944. Stettinius is listed on the cable as "Acting Secretary of State."

32 KFHEC, Isaac Sternbuch papers (unclassified as of September, 2015), Sternbuch to McClelland, Aug. 24, 1944.

33 USHMM, interview with Hermann Landau, 1979, Story RG-60.5007, Steven Spielberg Film and Video Archive, Claude Lanzmann Shoah Collection.

34 VH, Box 36, Folder 132, Sternbuch to Vaad, Aug. 26, 1944.

35 Isaac Lewin and Ludwig Kryzanowski, "Attempts at Rescuing European Jews," *Polish Review*, part 2, vol. 24, no. 1 (1979), p. 58.

36 Paul Lawrence Rose disputes Yehuda Bauer's claim that the Saly Mayer talks prompted the release of the first contingent, noting that they had been brought to the border even before the talks took place, so Mayer can't claim credit for effecting the release. However, he overlooks a memo from Roswell McClelland on August 11 demanding the release of five hundred Jews as a goodwill gesture before Mayer would agree to meet with the SS (Gestapo) negotiators. This would suggest that Bauer's claim has some validity, although it still remains a possibility that the ten tractors were also a factor.

37 The only exceptions were those who had converted to Christianity before 1941 and a "special group" of three thousand that would be exempted under the protection of Horthy.

38 Bauer, *JFS*, pp. 214–215.

39 SM-21 Memo, meeting with Vaad ha-Hatzalah, July 25, 1944.

40 SM-JDC minutes, Report on Business Transacted, Aug. 30, 1944. In these minutes, Mayer reports on having met with Schwalb, Sternbuch, Donebaum and Freddiger. It's uncertain whether "Freddiger" refers to the Hungarian Orthodox leader Philip von Freudiger, who had initiated the tractor deal.

41 In *Jews for Sale*, Yehuda Bauer identifies Trümpy as connected to the German Messerschmitt company. In *The Man Who Stopped the Trains to Auschwitz*, Kranzler writes that he was the Swiss representative but gives his name as Curt Trümpy rather than Carl. JDC minutes, however, have Saly Mayer identifying him as Bührle's secretary, which allows him to go "to and fro." Oerlikon, like Messerschmitt, had significant German war contracts but, unlike Messerschmitt, Oerlikon was a Swiss company. In Monty Penkower's superbly documented book, *The Jews Were Expendable*, he identifies Trümpy as an "intermediary" between Bührle and Messerschmitt, which may account for Bauer's confusion.

42 "New Records Show the Swiss Sold Arms Worth Millions to Nazis," *New York Times*, May 29, 1997.

43 Bauer, *JFS*, p. 223.

44 Yehuda Bauer, "The Negotiations between Saly Mayer and the SS," *The End of the Holocaust,* ed. Michael Robert Marrus, Walter de Gruyter: Berlin, 1989, p. 175.

45 SM-21, SM-Joint, "Notes on the Latest Developments," October 31, 1944.

46 SM-21(2).

47 SM-21, Ausfuhrgesuch, #9876, Willy-Traktoren, Volksirtchalts Departement, Sektion für Ein und Ausfuhr, Bern, Nov. 16, 1944. The export permit was stamped by the Swiss authorities six days later, on November 22.

48 SM-21(2), Trümpy was in daily contact to determine the status of the order and almost certainly informed his Budapest SS contacts the same week that the tractors were ready to be delivered.

49 The reference to sheepskins stems from the fact that the Orthodox used the word *zellwoole* (wool) as a code word for sums of money. "Sheepskin" is presumably a poor English translation of the German.

50 WRB, Box 78, June 1944–August 1945, Saly Mayer's Negotiations in Switzerland (2), #5197, Bern to Secretary of State (McClelland to WRB), Washington, Aug. 11, 1944; SM-Roll 8, File 21, American Legation, Bern to Secretary of State (McClelland to WRB), Washington, Aug. 11, 1944.

51　WRB, Box 66, Jews in Hungary, July 1944, Folder 2, Kasztner and
Komoly to Schwalb, July 28, 1944. The letter is signed by Kasztner and
his Va'ada colleague Otto Komoly but Kasztner's name appears first
and he begins by using the first person "Ich" so we can presume it was
written by Kasztner.

52　The promise of 300 tractors had apparently originated with Rabbi
Weissmandl who relayed the fabricated story via Philip Freudiger in
order to prolong the stalled negotiations by suggesting that the tractors
represented the first installment of the goods the Germans had
demanded. Testifying at Eichmann's war crimes trial on May 25 1961,
seventeen years after the events in question, Philip Freudiger apparently
confused trucks with tractors when he was being questioned by the
deputy prosecutor, Gabriel Bach. According to Freudiger, Weissmandl
had told Wisliceny that "Mr. Freudiger had 250 trucks which they
could begin to deliver on account of the 10,000 [trucks]." Other
contemporary accounts, however, suggest that Weissmandl had in fact
revealed there were 300 tractors available in Switzerland, rather than 250
trucks. It is assumed that Freudiger's error accounted for this confusion,
although it is possible that Weissmandl also separately fabricated a story
about 250 trucks.

53　In the letter, Kasztner makes reference to Willy's boss ("*Willys chef*" in
the original German) which could only refer to Adolf Eichmann.

54　There is a strong possibility that Eichmann would have sent the Jews
to Austria even without a ransom being paid because Ernst
Kaltenbrunner had requested able-bodied Hungarian Jews to rebuild
Vienna which had recently suffered heavy Allied bombing.

55　Bauer, *JFS*, p. 223.

56　BA, NS 19/2776, Musy to Himmler, Nov. 18, 1944.

57　SM-21, Ausfuhrgesuch, #9876, Willy-Traktoren, Volksirtchalts
Departement, Sektion für Ein und Ausfuhr, Bern, Nov. 16, 1944.

58　VH, Box 36, Folder 132, Cable, Sternbuch to Vaad, Nov. 22, 1944.

59　Yehuda Bauer (reply), *Rescue Attempts during the Holocaust*, Yad Vashem:
Jerusalem, 1977, Proceedings of the Second Yad Vashem International
Historical Conference, April 1974, First session debate, p. 119.

SIXTEEN: DEAL WITH THE DEVIL

1 VH, Box 36, Folder 132, Sternbuch to Vaad, Oct. 31, 1944.

2 VH, Box 36, Folder 132, Sternbuch to Vaad, Nov. 21, 1944.

3 Rose, *Archives of the Holocaust,* pp. xii-xiii.

4 WRB, Box 70, Union of Orthodox Rabbis: Representation in Switzerland (I. Sternbuch) (1), July–December 1944, McClelland to WRB, Dec. 9, 1944.

5 USHMM, interview with Roswell McClelland, 1978–79(?), Story RG-60.5047, Steven Spielberg Film and Video Archive, Claude Lanzmann Shoah Collection.

6 Author interview with HIJEFS secretary Hermann Landau, who was present at all but the first meeting between the Sternbuchs and Musy.

7 Testimony of Reuben Hecht in Rezső Kasztner libel trial, Jerusalem District Court, June 4, 1954.

8 In *Jews for Sale?*, Yehuda Bauer incorrectly claims this second meeting took place on January 1 and another on the 15th, but Musy only met Himmler twice during their negotiations. There was no meeting on January 1.

9 Himmler wrote a note to himself about the meeting three days later with this question and suggested that he had posed the question to Musy, though we don't know exactly what was said at the meeting.

10 This was not true. The United States government did not charge an emigration tax. The U.S. had imposed an immigration tax of 50 cents per immigrant in 1882 to fund the salaries of immigration officials. This was gradually increased to $9 before the tax was eliminated entirely in 1921. Canada imposed a Chinese head tax of $50 in 1885 meant to discourage Chinese immigrants. This tax was gradually increased to $500 until 1923, when Canada passed the Chinese Immigration Act, which virtually abolished Chinese immigration for years until the act was repealed in 1947.

11 HLA, "Rapport au Comité Suisse de l'Union of Orthodox Rabbis of the United States and Canada concernant l'action entreprise en vue de la libération des Israélites, détenue dans les camps de concentration allemande," Report by Jean-Marie Musy, Fribourg, 1945.

12 NA, RG 242, Himmler aide-memoire, Jan. 18, 1945, T 175.

13 Ibid.

14 WRB, Box 70, Union of Orthodox Rabbis: Representation in Switzerland (I. Sternbuch) (1), January–June 1945; Vaad ha-Hatazalah Emergency Committee to Isaac Sternbuch, Feb. 19, 1945.

15 YU, Irving Bunim Oral History Collection, interview of Irving Bunim by Rabbi Moshe Kolodny, Dec. 12, 1976; Bunim, *Fire*, p. 138.

16 SM-22, Inter-office Memo, United Jewish Appeal, H. Peretz to Blitz and Bernstein, Dec. 22, 1944.

17 NARA, RG 165, July 1945, "Report on the Case of Walter Schellenberg, British-US interrogation of Walter Schellenberg."

18 WRB, Box 70, Union of Orthodox Rabbis: Representation in Switzerland (I. Sternbuch) (1), January–June 1945; McClelland to WRB, Feb. 6, 1945.

19 WRB, Box 70, Union of Orthodox Rabbis: Representation in Switzerland (I. Sternbuch) (1), January–June 1945; McClelland to WRB, Feb. 6, 1945.

20 Ibid.

21 WRB, Box 70, Union of Orthodox Rabbis: Representation in Switzerland (I. Sternbuch) (1), McClelland Memo, "Sternbuch-Musy-Himmler-Jewish Affair," Feb. 6, 1945.

22 Two members of the Danish Red Cross accompanied the ICRC delegate, Maurice Rossel.

23 USHMM, "Theresienstadt: The Red Cross Visit," *Holocaust Encyclopedia*.

24 JDC, "The Theresienstadt Ghetto," Report by Dr. M. Rossel, June 23, 1944.

25 IMT, Statement Under Oath by Franz Göring, Feb. 24, 1948.

26 AIA, Joan Fredericks Collection, interview with Walter Lode, 1969.

27 AIA, Joan Fredericks Collection, interview with Gertrude Narev.

28 Author interview with Bob Narev, February 11, 2016.

29 AIA, Joan Fredericks Collection, interview with Elisabeth (Bertha) Devries.

30 Ibid., interview with Greta Stanley.

31 WRB, Box 70, Union of Orthodox Rabbis: Representation in Switzerland (I. Sternbuch) (2), January–June 1945; Telegram # 1069, McClelland to State and WRB, Feb. 17, 1945.

32 "Rabbis Celebrate Freeing of Jewish Refugees," *New York Times,* Feb. 9, 1945; WRB, Box 79, Negotiations in Switzerland—Including German Proposals (3).

33 "Gestapo Agrees to Release Jews from Camps; 1200 reach Switzerland; more due today," *Jewish Telegraphic Agency,* Feb. 9, 1945.

34 VH, Box 36, Folder 132, Sternbuch to Vaad, Feb. 17, 1945.

35 Testimony of Reuben Hecht in Rezső Kastzner libel trial, Jerusalem District Court, June 4, 1954.

36 WRB, Box 78, German Proposals Through Sweden; "Summary," Union of Orthodox Rabbis to Sternbuch, April 3, 1945.

37 WRB, Box 70, Union of Orthodox Rabbis: Representation in Switzerland (I. Sternbuch) (2), January–June 1945; Memorandum, "Liberation of Édouard Herriot," Telegram #1175, Squire to State, Feb. 21, 1945.

38 WRB, Box 70, Union of Orthodox Rabbis: Representation in Switzerland (I. Sternbuch) (1), January–June 1945; Telegram # 913, MWA to State Department, Feb. 9, 1945.

39 VH, Box 36, Folder 132, Sternbuch to Vaad, Sent Feb. 12, received Feb. 17, 1945.

40 WRB, Box 70, Union of Orthodox Rabbis: Representation in Switzerland (I. Sternbuch) (1), January–June 1945; McClelland to WRB, Feb. 23, 1945.

41 YU, Irving Bunim Oral History Collection, interview of Irving Bunim by Rabbi Moshe Kolodny, Dec. 12, 1976; Bunim, *Fire,* p. 142.

42 WRB, Box 79, Negotiations in Switzerland—Including German Proposals (3) Minutes of Department of Treasury meeting, Feb. 27, 1945.

43 Ibid.

44 WRB, Box 79, Negotiations in Switzerland—Including German Proposals (5) Memorandum for the Secretary's Files, March 13, 1945.

45 YU, Irving Bunim Oral History Collection, Interview of Irving Bunim by Rabbi Moshe Kolodny, Dec. 12, 1976; Bunim, *Fire,* p. 148.

46 WRB, Box 79, Negotiations in Switzerland—Including German Proposals (4) Telegram # 907, State Department and WRB to Harrison and McClelland, March 2, 1945.

SEVENTEEN: WAITING IN VAIN

1 SM-22, "No Jews Have Been Liberated from Theresienstadt," *The Day,* February 26, 1945.

2 Felix Kersten, *The Memoirs of Doctor Felix Kersten*, Doubleday & Company: Garden City, NY, 1947, pp. 244–245.

3 IMT, interrogation of Schellenberg, Walter by Lt. Colonel S.W. Brookhart, Nov. 13, 1945

4 NARA, RG 165, July 1945, "Report on the Case of Walter Schellenberg, British–US interrogation of Walter Schellenberg"; Musy told McClelland that the Führer had been given transcripts from an underground Allied propaganda broadcast, *Atlantiksender,* but Schellenberg claimed in his memoirs that it was a decoded message emanating from Spain.

5 Interview with Dr. Reuben Hecht by Professor Monty Penkower, Haifa, January 6–7, 1982, *Archives of the Holocaust.*

6 Author interview, Renée Landau, October, 2015.

7 Schellenberg, *The Labyrinth,* p. 380.

8 Author interview with Hermann Landau, August 2000; HLA, "Rapport au Comité Suisse de l'Union of Orthodox Rabbis of the United States and Canada concernant l'action entreprise en vue de la libération des Israélites, détenue dans les camps de concentration allemande," Report by Jean-Marie Musy, Fribourg, 1945.

9 NARA, RG 165, July 1945, "Report on the Case of Walter Schellenberg, British–US interrogation of Walter Schellenberg."

10 JDC, Introduction to finding aid, Saly Mayer files.

11 SM-21, "S.M. Joint, Minutes, 14/02/45.

12 SM-21, "S.M. Joint, Minutes, 14/02/45, p. 3.

13 Ibid.

14 Rose, p. xviii.

15 SM-22, McClelland to Mayer, Feb. 28, 1945.

16 IMT, Testimony of Ernst Kaltenbrunner, April 12, 1946.

EIGHTEEN: DITHERING

1 BBC home service, April 19, 1945, Richard Dimbleby broadcasting.

2 Franklin Bialystok, *Delayed Impact: The Holocaust and the Canadian Jewish Community*, McGill-Queen's University Press: Montreal and Kingston, 2000, p. 25.

3 Ben Shephard, *After Daybreak: The Liberation of Bergen-Belsen, 1945*, Schocken: New York, 2005, p. 29.

4 Ibid., p. 30.

5 Ibid., p. 4.

6 ICRC, Daniel Palmieri, "The International Committee of the Red Cross in the First World War," Sept. 10, 2014.

7 ICE, "Switzerland and Refugees in the Nazi era," p. 96; Riegner, p. 48.

8 Riegner, pp. 48–49.

9 HLA, "Rapport au Comité Suisse de l'Union of Orthodox Rabbis of the United States and Canada concernant l'action entreprise en vue de la libération des Israélites, détenue dans les camps de concentration allemande," Report by Jean-Marie Musy, Fribourg, 1945.

10 Ibid.

11 WRB, Box 70, Union of Orthodox Rabbis: Representation in Switzerland (I. Sternbuch) (2), January–June 1945; Telegram # 731, Grew to McClelland, Feb. 17, 1945.

12 WRB, Box 70, Union of Orthodox Rabbis: Representation in Switzerland (I. Sternbuch) (1), McClelland Memo, "Sternbuch-Musy-Himmler-Jewish Affair," Feb. 6, 1945.

13 WRB, Box 68, ICRC: Relief (WRB) for Concentration Camps in Germany and German Occupied Areas (1), January–March 1945, Stettinius to McClelland, Jan. 17, 1945.

14 WRB, Box 68, ICRC: Relief (WRB) for Concentration Camps in Germany and German Occupied Areas (1), January–March 1945, McClelland to WRB and State, Jan. 22, 1945.

15 Ibid.

16 WRB, Box 68, ICRC: Relief (WRB) for Concentration Camps in Germany and German Occupied Areas (1), January–March 1945, Telegram #450, McClelland to WRB, Jan. 22, 1945.

17 Grew acted as secretary of state for much of 1945, while Stettinius attended international conferences.

18 WRB, Box 33, War Refugee Board, Vol. 3 (2) "Minutes of the Sixth Meeting of the War Refugee Board," February 20, 1945.

19 Ibid.

20 WRB, Box 68, ICRC: Relief (WRB) for Concentration Camps in Germany and German Occupied Areas (2), January–March 1945, McClelland to State and WRB, March 2, 1945.

21 Ibid.

22 WRB, Box 68, ICRC: Relief (WRB) for Concentration Camps in Germany and German Occupied Areas (2), January–March 1945, #438, O'Dwyer to McClelland, March 10, 1945.

23 WRB, Box 52, Programs with Respect to Relief and Rescue of Refugees— Evacuations to and Through Switzerland—Switzerland—New Program (3).

24 BBC, "15 April, On this Day, British Troops Liberate Bergen Belsen." British medical officer Brigadier Llewellyn Glyn-Hughes, reported that he had seen these "acts of cannibalism." Other reports claim that one in ten bodies had sections of their thighs removed.

25 WRB, Box 70, Union of Orthodox Rabbis: Representation in Switzerland (I. Sternbuch) (2), January–June 1945 Grew to McClelland (Vaad to Sternbuch), March 24, 1945.

26 WRB, Box 30, Situation in Germany and German-Controlled Territory (1) O'Dwyer to Goldman, March 12, 1945.

27 Kersten, "Contending with Plague Among the Prisoners," March 11, 1945, p. 176.

28 Schellenberg, *The Labyrinth*, p. 382.

29 WRB, Box 68, ICRC: Relief (WRB) for Concentration Camps in Germany and German Occupied Areas (1), January–March 1945; Draft wire, McClelland to State and WRB, Feb. 23, 1945.

30 WRB, Box 68, ICRC: Relief (WRB) for Concentration Camps in Germany and German Occupied Areas (1), January–March 1945; Telegram, McClelland to O'Dwyer and State Department, March 22, 1945.

31 WRB, Box 68, ICRC: Relief (WRB) for Concentration Camps in Germany and German Occupied Areas (1), January-March 1945; Draft wire, McClelland to State and WRB, Feb. 22, 1945.

32 WRB, Box 52, Programs with Respect to Relief and Rescue of
    Refugees—Evacuations to and Through Switzerland—Switzerland—
    New Program (3); Transcript of telephone conversation, Paris 4-1-1,
    between Mann, McClelland and O'Dwyer, March 29, 1945.

33 WRB, Box 52, Programs with Respect to Relief and Rescue of
    Refugees—Evacuations to and Through Switzerland—Switzerland—
    New Program (3); Memorandum for the Files, April 6, 1945.

34 The British liberators found evidence that eighteen thousand inmates
    had died during March alone. Several thousand more had succumbed
    in February, though the numbers are sketchy.

35 Irma Sonnenberg Menkel, "I Saw Anne Frank Die," *Newsweek,* July 21, 1997.

NINETEEN: AGREEMENT "IN THE NAME OF HUMANITY"

1   Kersten, *Memoirs*, p. 219.

2   USHMM, Mobile exhibit, "King Christian X of Denmark."

3   Count Folke Bernadotte, *The Curtain Falls: Last Days of the Reich*,
    Alfred A. Knopf: New York, 1945, p. 47.

4   Bauer, *JFS*, p. 245.

5   There are no precise figures on death march fatalities. The United States
    Holocaust Museum estimates that "possibly as many as 15,000 died."

6   USHMM, "Death March from Auschwitz," video testimony of Lily
    Appelbaum Malnik.

7   Shmuel Krakowski, "The Death Marches and Liberation," *The End of
    the Holocaust*, ed. Michael Robert Marrus, Walter de Gruyter: Berlin,
    1989, p. 489.

8   Kersten, *Memoirs,* diary entry, March 2, 1945, pp. 276–277.

9   Ibid., diary entry, March 5, 1945.

10 Ibid., diary entry, March 12, 1945.

11 Ibid.

12 FRUS, "Interest of the United States in the relief and rescue of Jews
    and security detainees in Germany and German-occupied territory,"
    Johnson to Secretary of State, 840.48 Refugees/3-2845, Telegram,
    March 28, 1941, pp. 1140–42.

13 Ibid.

TWENTY: AT DAGGERS DRAWN

1 Kersten, *Memoirs,* diary entry, March 17, 1945, p. 281.

2 FRUS, "Interest of the United States in the relief and rescue of Jews and security detainees in Germany and German-occupied territory," Johnson to Secretary of State, 840.48 Refugees/3-2845, Telegram, March 28, 1941, pp. 1140–42.

3 Ibid.

4 FRUS, 840.48 Refugees/4–345: Telegram, Stettinus to Johnson, April 7, 1945.

5 FO, 954, 23, Eden to Churchill, April 1, 1945.

6 Meier Sompolinsky, *Britain and the Holocaust: The Failure of Anglo-Jewish Leadership,* Sussex Academic Press: Sussex, 1999, p. 215; Steven Koblik, "No Truck with Himmler: The Politics of Rescue and the Swedish Red Cross Mission, March–May, 1945," *Scandia,* vol. 51, nos. 1–2, 1985, p. 185.

7 FO, 371, Mallet to Foreign Office, Feb. 25, 1945.

8 Masur claims that the WJC asked for volunteers for the mission and that he was finally chosen among "several members" who had volunteered.

9 Norbert Masur, "My Meeting with Heinrich Himmler, April 20/21, 1945; Report to the Swedish Section of the World Jewish Congress, Stockholm, Sweden, translated into English by Henry Karger, 1993.

10 Kersten, *Memoirs,* diary entry, April 21, 1945, p. 285.

11 Joseph Kessel, *The Magic Touch,* Rupert–Hart Davis: London, 1961, p. 237.

12 Masur, op. cit.

13 Ibid.

14 Kersten, *Memoirs,* diary entry, Oct. 28-29, 1941, pp. 115–116

15 Kessel, p. 239.

16 Masur, op. cit.

17 Kersten, *Memoirs,* diary entry April 21, 1945, p. 286.

18 Ibid.

19 Masur, op. cit.

20 Ibid.

21 Kersten, diary entry, April 21, 1945, *Kersten Memoirs,* p. 287

22 Ibid.

23 Masur, op. cit.

24 Kersten, diary entry, April 21, 1945, *Kersten Memoirs,* p. 288

25 Masur, op. cit.

26 Kersten, diary entry, April 21, 1945, *Kersten Memoirs,* p. 288

27 Masur, op. cit.

28 Ibid.

29 Ibid.

30 Kersten, *Memoirs,* pp. 272–273.

31 Ibid., p. 292.

TWENTY-ONE: RACE AGAINST TIME

1   Bernadotte, p. 66.

2   IMT, Testimony of Ernst Kaltenbrunner, April 12, 1946, morning session.

3   Schellenberg, *Labyrinth*, p. 386.

4   NARA, RG 165, July 1945, "Report on the Case of Walter Schellenberg, British–US interrogation of Walter Schellenberg."

5   HLA, Rapport au Comité Suisse de l'Union of Orthodox Rabbis of the United States and Canada concernant l'action entreprise en vue de la libération des Israélites, détenue dans les camps de concentration allemande," Report by Jean-Marie Musy, Fribourg, 1945.

6   Sune Persson, *Escape from the Third Reich*, Pen & Sword Books: S. Yorkshire, 2009, pp. 154–157.

7   WRB, Box 70, Union of Orthodox Rabbis: Representation in Switzerland (I. Sternbuch) (3), McClelland to State Department and O'Dwyer, April 9, 1945.

8   Ibid.

9   IMT, Statement Under Oath by Franz Göring, Feb. 24, 1948.

10 HLA, Rapport au Comité Suisse de l'Union of Orthodox Rabbis of the United States and Canada concernant l'action entreprise en vue de la libération des Israélites, détenue dans les camps de concentration allemande," Report by Jean-Marie Musy, Fribourg, 1945.

11 Alois Dörr trial transcript translated at helmbrechtswalk.com; Daniel Joseph Goldhagen, *Hitler's Willing Executioners: Ordinary Germans and the Holocaust*, Alfred A. Knopf: New York, 1996, p. 356.

12 Persson, p. 200.

13 Franz Göring, "Extract from My Diary concerning the liberation of persons from German Concentration camps," annex to "Schellenberg's report on his transactions with Count Bernadotte and events in the last weeks of the Reich."

14 Hans Arnoldsson, *Aux Portes des Enfers*, Éditions Je Sers: Paris, pp. 123–129.

15 Arnoldsson, who headed the operation, gave the figure rescued at 8000. Norbert Masur gave the figure as 7000, half of whom were Jewish.

16 Agneta Greayer and Sonja Sjostrand, "The White Buses: The Swedish Red Cross Rescue Action in Germany During the Second World War," The Swedish Red Cross: Stockholm, 2000.

17 When Soviet forces arrived on April 30, they found 3000 sick and elderly prisoners still in the Ravensbrück camp. USHMM, "Ravensbrück: Liberation and Post-war Trials," *Holocaust Encyclopedia*.

18 NARA, RG 165, July 1945, "Report on the Case of Walter Schellenberg, British–US interrogation of Walter Schellenberg."

19 Bernadotte, p. 112.

20 NARA, RG 165, July 1945, "Report on the Case of Walter Schellenberg, British–US interrogation of Walter Schellenberg."

21 FRUS, Diplomatic papers 1945, Volume III, European Advisory Commission, Austria, Germany, Document 536, "Transcript of trans-atlantic telephone conversation between President Truman and British Prime Minister Churchill."

22 "The Last Days of Hitler," *Life* magazine, Mar. 17, 1947, p. 119.

23 John Toland, *The Last 100 Days: The Tumultuous and Controversial Story of the Final Days of World War 2 in Europe*, Random House: New York, 2014.

24 Schellenberg told his Allied interrogators that Himmler believed he would be appointed as Hitler's successor as head of state "within the next day or two."

25 IMT, "Adolf Hitler's Final Political Testament," United States, Office of United States Chief of Counsel for Prosecution of Axis Criminality, *Nazi*

Conspiracy and Aggression, 8 vols. and 2 suppl. vols. (Government Printing Office, Washington, 1946–1948), VI, 259–263, Doc. No. 3569-PS.

26 Ibid.

27 ICRC, Address by Dr. Cornelio Sommaruga, president of the International Committee of the Red Cross, Geneva, to the Friends of the Magen David Adom in Great Britain Institute of Contemporary History and Wiener Library London, Chatham House, September 15, 1997.

28 ICRC, "Le CICR et les détenus des camps de concentration nation-aux-socialistes (1942–1945)," Sébastien Farré, *Revue Internationale de la Croix-Rouge*, vol. 94, 2012, p. 212.

29 IMT, PS-2728, affidavit of Victor Maurer, May 1, 1945, Report of the Atrocities Committed at the Dachau Concentration Camp Testimony – Exhibits 3–24, Vol. 2, War Crimes Investigation Team #6823.

30 IMT, Interrogation of Berte Gerdes, presented to Nuremberg tribunal, Jan. 2, 1946, morning session.

31 IMT, PS-2728, affidavit of Victor Maurer, May 1, 1945, Report of the Atrocities Committed at the Dachau Concentration Camp Testimony—Exhibits 3–24, Vol. 2, War Crimes Investigation Team #6823.

32 Having witnessed the bodies of prisoners in the open railway cars, the first American soldiers reportedly shot a number of SS guards on entering the camp.

33 Jean-Claude Favez, *The Red Cross and the Holocaust*, Cambridge University Press: Cambridge, 1999, p. 270.

34 WRB, Box 69, Miscellaneous Documents Concerning Other Concentration Camps in Germany, April–June 1945, Memorandum to Files, Roswell McClelland, June 6, 1945.

35 Drago Arsenijevic, *Voluntary Hostages of the SS*, Ferni Publishing: Geneva, 1979, p. 181.

36 ICRC, Address by Dr. Cornelio Sommaruga, president of the International Committee of the Red Cross, Geneva, to the Friends of the Magen David Adom in Great Britain Institute of Contemporary History and Wiener Library London, Chatham House, September 15, 1997.

37 "Report of Louis Haefliger," Christian Bernadac, *The 186 Steps*, Ferni: Publishing Geneva, 1978, p. 133.

38 Various accounts suggest that many civilians from nearby towns were also to be assembled and blown up to "prevent eyewitnesses."

39 IMT 3870-PS. Marsalek would claim that the order came from Himmler, but it is clear that Kaltenbrunner used Himmler's authority to issue many orders, especially in the final months of the war, when he was defying his superior's directives. During his interrogation after he was captured on May 23, Ziereis also verified the order: "Reichsminister Himmler and SS Obergruppenfuehrer (Lt. General) Kaltenbrunner ordered me to kill all inmates if the frontlines approached Mauthausen. I had orders from Berlin to blow up Mauthausen and Gusen including all the inmates. All inmates were to be brought into the Gusen mine and blown up." It is possible that Himmler did decide to issue an order to liquidate all the remaining prisoners after he realized that there would be no separate peace with the West, but there is no direct evidence to suggest this. In contrast, there is repeated testimony that Himmler had been attempting to counteract last-minute attempts to murder the remaining Jews. On October 27, 1945, SD inland intelligence chief Otto Ohlendorf was interrogated by the Nuremberg counsel, Colonel S.W. Brookhart. He revealed that it was Oswald Pohl who had ordered the liquidation of 60,000 Mauthausen inmates "in the face of an order from Himmler to the contrary."

40 Ibid.

41 ICRC, Rapport Haefliger, G 44/13–18, 24.05.1945,; "Le CICR et les détenus des camps de concentration nationaux-socialistes (1942–1945)," Sébasien Farré, *Revue Internationale de la Croix-Rouge,* vol. 94, 2012, p. 22; Kurt Becher would later claim that it was he who convinced Himmler to countermand Kaltenbrunner's plans.

42 Ibid., p. 335.

43 Ziereis was later captured by American forces after he was betrayed by his eighteen-year-old son.

44 Arsenijevic, p. 192.

45 Haefliger claimed the ICRC later forced him resign for this "breach of protocol," S. Farré, "The ICRC and the detainees in Nazi concentration camps (1942–1945)."

46 WRB, Box 69, Miscellaneous Documents Concerning Other Concentration Camps in Germany, April–June 1945, Memorandum to Files, Roswell McClelland, June 6, 1945.

47 Rudolf A. Hanschmied, Jan Ruth Mills & Siegi Witzany-Durda, *St. Georgen-Gusen-Mauthausen: Concentration Camp Mauthausen Reconsidered*, BOD: Madison, 2007, p. 221.

EPILOGUE

1 Stephen Tyas & Peter Witte, *Himmler's Diary 1945: A Calendar of Events Leading to Suicide*; "The Diary of Major Norman Whittaker, Lüneburg," Fonthill Media: Oxford and Charleston, SC, 2008.

2 Longerich, p. 733. Initially confronted by Dönitz about news of his "treachery" against Hitler, Himmler professed his innocence. He offered his services as "second in command" but the Grand Admiral refused, noting that his new government would be "non-political" in nature. Himmler returned repeatedly to Dönitz's headquarters in the days before his formal dismissal, apparently assuming he would still play a role.

3 YVA, "The Fate of Jews Across Europe;" USHMM, *Holocaust Encyclopedia,* "Hungary after the German Occupation."

4 According to Yad Vashem, "There is no precise figure for the number of Jews killed in the Holocaust. The figure commonly used is the six million quoted by Adolf Eichmann, a senior SS official. Most research confirms that the number of victims was between five and six million. Early calculations range from 5.1 million (Professor Raul Hilberg) to 5.95 million (Jacob Leschinsky). More recent research, by Professor Yisrael Gutman and Dr. Robert Rozett in the *Encyclopedia of the Holocaust*, estimates the Jewish losses at 5.59–5.86 million, and a study headed by Dr. Wolfgang Benz presents a range from 5.29 million to six million."

5   Hugh Trevor-Roper, "Kersten, Himmler and Count Bernadotte," *Atlantic Monthly*, February 1953.

6   Author interview with NIOD archivist Hubert Berkhoug, October 26, 2016. A Dutch government inquiry into Kersten's actions concluded that many of his claims were greatly exaggerated or fabricated entirely. The file is held at the Amsterdam-based NIOD (Institute for War, Holocaust and Genocide Studies).

7   "Dr. Kersten, Himmler's Therapist, Dead; Credited with Saving Jews," *Jewish Telegraphic Agency*, Apr. 22, 1960.

8   NA, RG 238, roll m897, 114.

9   Author interview with Netty Segal, October 2015.

10 "Holocaust museum seeks justice for 'misrepresented' Saviour of Jews," *Toronto Star*, July 24, 2007.

11 In *The Jews Were Expendable*, Monty Penkower includes a superbly researched chapter about the Sternbuchs' rescue activities. In *The Archives of the Holocaust*, Paul Lawrence Rose uses Reuben Hecht's archives to make the case that Musy's mission was instrumental in preventing the destruction of the remaining concentration camp inmates at the end of the war.

12 Lucy S. Dawidowicz, "Indicting American Jews," *Commentary*, June 1, 1983.

13 Bergson told Claude Lanzmann in 1978 that he "ceased being a Zionist" in 1943 because Zionism "failed" because "it did not clarify the national identity of those Jews who needed Palestine as those Jews who don't need it."

14 USHMM, interview with Peter Bergson and Samuel Merlin—New York, Nov. 15, 1978, Story RG-60.5020, Steven Spielberg Film and Video Archive, Claude Lanzmann Shoah Collection.

15 Lucy S. Dawidowicz, "Indicting American Jews," *Commentary*, June 1, 1983.

16 USHMM, interview with Roswell McClelland, 1978–79(?), Story RG-60.5047, Steven Spielberg Film and Video Archive., Claude Lanzmann Shoah Collection.

17 Ibid.

18 In 2006, Zuroff refused to appear at an event honoring wartime rescuers because Kranzler had also been invited. "Kranzler accused me of purposely falsifying research in order to increase sales of my own book on this topic," Zuroff explained at the time. "I therefore cannot endorse any initiative that acknowledges or rewards him." Kranzler defended his scholarship: "I challenge anybody to evaluate my own work, which is based on primary evidence and many original manuscripts."

19 KFHEC, Unclassified Isaac Sternbuch folder, Recha Sternbuch to HIJEFS, undated telegram, 1946.

BIBLIOGRAPHY

BOOKS

Abella, Irving and Harold Troper. *None Is Too Many: Canada and the Jews of Europe, 1933–1948,* Lester and Orpen Dennys: Toronto, 1983.

Arendt, Hannah (ed.). *Eichmann in Jerusalem: A Report on the Banality of Evil,* Penguin Classics: London, 2006.

Arsenijevic, Drago. *Voluntary Hostages of the SS*, Ferni Publishing: Geneva, 1979.

Bauer, Yehuda. *American Jewry and the Holocaust, The American Jewish Joint Distribution Committee, 1939–1945*, Wayne State University Press: Detroit, 1981.

Bauer, Yehuda. *Jews for Sale? Nazi Jewish Negotiations, 1933–1945,* Yale University Press: New Haven and London, 1994.

Bernadac, Christian. *The 186 Steps,* Ferni Publishing: Geneva, 1978.

Bernadotte, Folke. *The Curtain Falls: Last Days of the Reich*, Alfred A. Knopf: New York, 1945.

Bialystok, Franklin. *Delayed Impact: The Holocaust and the Canadian Jewish Community*, McGill-Queen's University Press: Montreal and Kingston, 2000.

Black, Edwin. *The Transfer Agreement: The Dramatic Story of the Pact Between the Third Reich and Jewish Palestine*, Carroll & Graf: New York, 2001.

Black, Edwin. *The War Against the Weak: Eugenics and America's Campaign to Create a Master Race*, Four Walls Eight Windows: New York, 2003.

Breitman, Richard, and Allan J. Lichtman. *FDR and the Jews,* Belknap Press: Cambridge, 2003.

Browning, Christopher. *Collected Memories: Holocaust History and Postwar Testimony*, University of Wisconsin Press: Madison, 2002.

Browning, Christopher. *The Origins of the Final Solution: The Evolution of Nazi Jewish Policy, September 1939–March 1942*, University of Nebraska Press: Lincoln & Yad Vashem Jerusalem, 2004.

Bunim, Amos. *A Fire in His Soul: Irving M. Bunim, 1901–1980, the Man and his Impact on American Orthodox Jewry*, Feldheim: Nanuet, NY, 1989.

Caestecker, Frank, and Bob Moore. *Refugees from Nazi Germany and the Liberal European States,* Oxford: Berghahn Books, 2010.

Chevallaz, Georges. *The Challenge of Neutrality: Diplomacy and the Defense of Switzerland*, Lexington Books: Lanham, MD, 2001.

Dawidowicz, Lucy. *A Holocaust Reader,* Behrman House: New York, 1976.

Dean, Martin. *Collaboration in the Holocaust: Crimes of the Local Police in Belorussia and the Ukraine, 1941–1944*, St. Martin's Press: New York, 2000.

Doerries, Reinhard, and Gerhard L. Weinberg. *Hitler's Intelligence Chief: Walter Schellenberg*, Enigma Books: New York, 2013.

Dulles, Allen Welsh. *Germany's Underground*, Da Capo Press: Boston, 1947.

Favez, Jean-Claude. *The Red Cross and the Holocaust*, Cambridge University Press: Cambridge, 1999.

Flanagan, Ben, and Donald Bloxham (eds.). *Remembering Belsen: Eyewitnesses Record the Liberation,* Mitchell Vallentine & Co.: Elstree, 2005.

Fleming, Gerald (ed.). *Hitler and the Final Solution*, University of California Press: Berkeley and Los Angeles, 1982.

Florence, Ronald. *Emissary of the Doomed,* Penguin: London, 2010.

Friedenson, Joseph, and David Kranzler. *Heroine of Rescue,* Mesorah Publications: Brooklyn, 1984.

Gilbert, Martin. *Auschwitz and the Allies,* Holt, Rinehart and Winston: New York, 1981.

Grobman, Alex. *Battling for Souls: The Vaad Hatzala Rescue Committee in Post-Holocaust Europe*, Ktav: Jersey City, 2004.

Grundmann, Siegfried. *The Einstein Dossiers: Science and Politics—Einstein's Berlin Period*, Springer Science and Business Media: Berlin, 2006.

Gutman, Yisrael, and Michael Berenbaum. *Anatomy of the Auschwitz Death Camp,* University of Indiana Press: Bloomington, 1998.

Gutman, Yisrael, and Efraim Zuroff (ed.). *Rescue Attempts During the Holocaust: Proceedings of the Second Yad Vashem International Historical Conference—April 1974,* Yad Vashem: Jerusalem, 1977.

Handler, Andrew. *A Man for All Connections: Raoul Wallenberg and the Hungarian State,* Greenwood Publishing: Westport, CT, 1996.

Hanschmied, Rudolf A, Jan Ruth Mills and Siegi Witzany-Durda. *St. Georgen-Gusen-Mauthausen: Concentration Camp Mauthausen Reconsidered,* BOD: Madison, WI, 2007.

Hilberg, Raul (ed.). *The Destruction of the European Jews,* Holmes & Meier: Teaneck, NJ, 1985.

Hitler, Adolf, *Mein Kampf,* Hutchinson & Co.: London, 1940.

Hoess, Rudolf (ed.). *Commandant of Auschwitz,* Phoenix Publishing: London, 1995.

Kaplan, Marion A. *Between Dignity and Despair,* Ebsco Publishing: Ipswich, 1999.

Kersten, Felix (ed.). *The Kersten Memoirs: 1940–1945,* Ishi Press International: New York and Tokyo, 2011.

Kersten, Felix. *The Memoirs of Doctor Felix Kersten,* Doubleday: Garden City, 1947.

Kessel, Joseph. *The Magic Touch,* Rupert–Hart Davis: London, 1961.

Kirsch, Jonathan. *The Short, Strange Life of Herschel Gryszpan,* W.W. Norton & Company: New York, 2013.

Kranzler, David. *The Man Who Stopped the Train to Auschwitz: George Mantello, El Salvador and Switzerland's Finest Hour,* Syracuse University Press: Syracuse, 2000.

Kranzler, David. *Thy Brother's Blood: The Orthodox Jewish Response During the Holocaust,* Mesorah: Brooklyn, 1987.

Laqueur, Walter and Richard Breitman, *Breaking the Silence: The Germans Who Exposed the Final Solution,* Simon & Schuster: New York, 1987.

Lipstadt, Deborah. *Beyond Belief: The American Press and the Coming of the Holocaust, 1933–1945,* the Free Press: New York, 1986.

Longerich, Peter (ed.). *Heinrich Himmler*, Oxford University Press: Oxford and New York, 2012.

Manvell, Roger, and Heinrich Fraenkel. *Heinrich Himmler: The Sinister Life of The Head of the SS and Gestapo*, Skyhorse: New York, 2007.

Marrus, Michael R. *The Holocaust in History*, Key Porter Books: Toronto, 2000.

Marrus, Michael Robert (ed.). *The End of the Holocaust*, Walter de Gruyter: Berlin, 1989.

Marrus, Michael Robert (ed.). *The Nazi Holocaust, part 8: Bystanders to the Holocaust*, vol. 1, Walter de Gruyter: Berlin, 1989

Marrus, Michael Robert, and Robert O. Paxton. *Vichy France and the Jews*, Stanford University Press: Palo Alto, 1981.

Marton, Kati. *A Death in Jerusalem*, Pantheon: New York, 1994.

Medoff, Rafael. *Blowing the Whistle on Genocide: Josiah E. DuBois and the Struggle for a U.S. Response to the Holocaust*, Purdue University Press: West Lafayette, 2008.

Morse, Arthur. *While Six Million Died: A Chronicle of American Apathy*, Random House: New York, 1968.

Muller, Filip. *Eyewitness Auschwitz: Three Years in the Gas Chambers*, Ivan R. Dee: New York, 1999.

Neufeld, Michael J., and Michael Berenbaum (ed.), *The Bombing of Auschwitz: Should the Allies Have Attempted It?* University Press of Kansas: Lawrence, in association with the U.S. Holocaust Museum, 2003.

New, Mitya. *Switzerland Unwrapped: Exposing the Myths*, I.B. Tauris: London and New York, 1997.

Penkower, Monty Noam. *The Jews Were Expendable: Free World Diplomacy and the Holocaust*, University of Illinois Press, Urbana and Chicago, 1983.

Perry, Michael, William W. Quinn and the Seventh U.S. Army Staff. *Dachau Liberated: The Official Report*, Inkling: San Francisco, 2000.

Persson, Sune. *Escape from the Third Reich*, Pen & Sword Books: S. Yorkshire, 2009.

Porter, Anna. *Kasztner's Train*, Douglas & McIntyre: Vancouver, 2007.

Randolph L. Braham. *The Politics of Genocide: The Holocaust in Hungary*, Wayne State University Press: Detroit, 2000.

Redles, David. *Hitler's Millennial Reich: Apocalyptic Belief and the Search for Salvation,* NYU Press: New York, 2008.

Rees, Laurence. *Auschwitz: A New History*, Public Affairs: New York, 2005.

Riegner, Gerhart (ed.). *Never Despair: Sixty Years in the Service of the Jewish People and the Cause of Human Rights*, Ivan R. Dee: New York, 2006.

Rose, Paul Lawrence (ed.) with Herbert Druks. *Archives of the Holocaust: An International Collection of Selected Documents,* Vol. 12, "Hecht Archive. University of Haifa," Garland: New York and London, 1990.

Rozett, Robert, and Shmuel Spector (ed.). *Encyclopedia of the Holocaust,* Lambda: Brooklyn, 2000.

Rubinstein, William. *The Myth of Rescue: Why the Democracies Could Not Have Saved More Jews from the Nazis*, Routledge: New York, 1997.

Schellenberg, Walter. *Hitler's Secret Service,* Pyramid: New York, 1968.

Schellenberg, Walter. *The Labyrinth: Memoirs of Walter Schellenberg, Hitler's Chief of Counter-intelligence*, Da Capo Press: Boston, 2000.

Shephard, Ben. *After Daybreak: The Liberation of Bergen-Belsen, 1945,* Schocken: New York, 2005.

Shirer, William. *The Rise and Fall of the Third Reich*, Simon & Schuster: New York, 1960.

Smith, Richard. *OSS: The Secret History of America's First Central Intelligence Agency*, Rowman & Littlefield: Lanham, MD, 2005.

Sompolinksy, Meier. *Britain and the Holocaust: The Failure of Anglo-Jewish Leadership*, Sussex Academic Press: Sussex, 1999.

Speer, Albert. *Inside the Third Reich,* Macmillan: London, 1970.

Tanenbaum, Roy. *Prisoner 88: The Man in Stripes,* University of Calgary Press: Calgary, 1998.

Toland, John. *Adolf Hitler: The Definitive Biography*, Knopf Doubleday: New York, 2014.

Tyas, Stephen, and Peter Witte. *Himmler's Diary 1945: A Calendar of Events Leading to Suicide*; "The Diary of Major Norman Whittaker, Lüneburg," Fonthill Media: Oxford & Charleston, 2008.

Urbach, Karina. *Go-Betweens for Hitler,* Oxford University Press: Oxford, 2015.

Urofsky, Melvin I. *The Voice That Spoke for Justice: The Life and Times of Stephen Wise,* SUNY Press: Albany, 1982.

Vincent, Isabel. *Hitler's Silent Partners: Swiss Banks, Nazi Gold and the Pursuit of Justice,* Alfred A. Knopf Canada: Toronto, 1997.

Von Lang, Jochen (ed.). *Eichmann Interrogated: Transcripts from the Archives of the Israeli Police,* Perseus Books Group: New York, 1999.

Wagner, Meir, and Moishe Meisels. *The Righteous of Switzerland: The Heroes of the Holocaust,* KTAV Publishing: Newark, 2001.

Waller, John H. *The Devil's Doctor,* John Wiley & Sons: New York, 2002.

Wyman, David (ed.). *The Abandonment of the Jews: America and the Holocaust: 1941–1945,* Pantheon: New York, 1985.

Zuroff, Efraim. *The Response of Orthodox Jewry in the United States to the Holocaust,* Yeshiva University Press: New York, 2000.

ARTICLES

Boas, Jacob. "A Nazi Travels to Palestine," *History Today,* vol. 30, issue 1.

Dawidowicz, Lucy. "Indicting American Jews," *Commentary,* June 1, 1983.

"Eichmann Tells His Own Damning Story," *Life* magazine, Nov. 28, 1960.

Ferrero, Shaul. "Switzerland and the Refugees Fleeing Nazism: Documents on the German Jews Turned Back at the Basel Border in 1938–1939," *Yad Vashem Studies,* vol. XXVII, Jerusalem, 1999.

Koblik, Steven. "No Truck with Himmler: The Politics of Rescue and the Swedish Red Cross Mission," March–May, 1945, *Scandia,* Vol. 51, nos. 1–2 (1985).

Lappin, Eleonore. "Death Marches of Hungarian Jews through Austria in the Spring of 1945," *Yad Vashem Studies,* vol. 28, Jerusalem (2000).

REPORTS

Schom, Alan Morris. "A Survey of Nazi and Pro-Nazi Groups in Switzerland: 1930–1945," Simon Wiesenthal Center, June 1998.

"Switzerland, National Socialism and the Second World War," *Final Report of the Independent Commission of Experts Switzerland—Second World War* (2002).

World Jewish Congress. "The Sinister Face of Neutrality: The Role of Swiss Financial Institutions in the Plunder of European Jewry," 1996.

ACADEMIC PAPERS

Erwin, Norman. "Confronting Hitler's Legacy: Canadian Jews and Early Holocaust Discourse, 1933–1936," Ph.D. thesis, Department of History, University of Waterloo, 2014.

Sebastiani, Daniel. "Jean-Marie Musy (1876–1952), un ancien conseiller fédéral entre rénovation nationale et régimes autoritaires," thèse de doctorat, Université de Fribourg, 2004.

JOURNALS

Abella, Irving, and Harold Troper. "'The Line Must Be Drawn Somewhere': Canada and Jewish Refugees 1933–9," *Canadian Historical Review,* vol. 60, pp. 178-209, 1979.

Bourgeois, Daniel. "Une lettre de Heydrich a Ribbentrop sur Vichy," *Revue d'histoire moderne et contemporaine (1954–),* vol. 18, no. 2 (Apr.– Jun. 1971), pp. 296–307.

Breitman, Richard. "A Deal with the Nazi Dictatorship?: Himmler's Alleged Peace Emissaries in Autumn 1943," *Journal of Contemporary History,* vol. 30, no. 3 (Jul. 1995), pp. 411-430.

Ceruti, Mario, Jean-Claude Favex and Michèle Fleury-Seemüller. *Documents diplomatiques suisses, 1848–1945. Vol. XI: 1.1.1934–31.12.1936,* Review by: Jonathan Steinberg, *The English Historical Review,* vol. 108, no. 428 (Jul. 1993), p. 769.

Dieckhoff, Alain. "Une action de sauvetage des juifs européens en 1944–1945: l'affaire Musy," Erlanger, Simon. "Real, Imaginary and Symbolic Roles of Jews in Swiss Society," *Jewish Political Studies Review,* vol. 22, nos.1–2 (Spring 2010), pp. 59-73.

Journal of Contemporary History, vol. 29, no. 1 (Jan. 1994), pp. 39–51.

Koblik, Steven. "Sweden's Attempts to Aid Jews, 1939–1945," *Scandinavian Studies,* Vol. 56, No. 2 (Spring 1984), pp. 89-113

Lewin, Isaac, and Ludwik Krzyzanowski. "Attempts at Rescuing European Jews with the Help of Polish Diplomatic Missions During World War II," *The Polish Review,* vol. 22, no. 4 (1977), pp. 3–23.

Lewin, Isaac, and Ludwik Krzyzanowski ,"Attempts at Rescuing European

Jews with the Help of Polish Diplomatic Missions During World War II: Part II," *The Polish Review*, vol. 24, no. 1 (1979), pp. 46–61.

Lewin, Isaac, and Ludwik Krzyzanowski. "Attempts at Rescuing European Jews with the Help of Polish Diplomatic Missions During World War II," Part IV, *The Polish Review*, vol. 29, no. 4 (1984), pp. 71–86.

Palmer, Raymond. "Felix Kersten and Count Bernadotte: A Question of Rescue," *Journal of Contemporary History*, vol. 29, no. 1 (Jan. 1994), pp. 39-51.

Penkower, Monty Noam. "The World Jewish Congress Confronts the International Red Cross during the Holocaust," *Jewish Social Studies*, vol. 41, no. 3/4 (Summer–Autumn 1979), pp. 229–256.

Revue d'histoire moderne et contemporaine (1954–), vol. 36, no. 2 (Apr.–Jun. 1989), pp. 287–303.

Rose, Paul Lawrence. "Joel Brand's 'Interim Agreement' and the Course of Nazi–Jewish Negotiations 1944–45," *The Historical Journal*, vol. 34, no. 4 (Dec. 1991), pp. 909-929.

Ulman, Jane. "Witnesses to Kristallnacht," *Jewish Journal*.

ACKNOWLEDGMENTS

If Recha and Isaac Sternbuch had had their way, this story likely would never have been told. That's why I am eternally grateful for the cooperation and assistance of their family, who have generously assisted me in my quest. Thanks to the Sternbuchs' daughter, Netty Segal; their granddaughters Sarah Shapiro and Devora Wolpin; their niece Ruth Rottenberg Mandel; and their cousins Hermann and Renée Landau. Thanks also to the family members of the other key players for their assistance: Jean-Marie Musy's grandson Edouard Musy; Felix Kersten's son Arno Kersten and Julius Kühl's daughter Janine Weinstock and his grandson Michael Kühl.

This book would also never have been possible without the valuable assistance of many people whom I gratefully acknowledge. First, my agents at Westwood, John Pearce and Chris Casuccio, for sticking with it and believing in this project. I am also indebted to my editor, Diane Turbide, at Penguin Random House Canada, for shepherding the manuscript and supporting me all the way through a grueling process while I navigated the minefield of Holocaust-era research to assemble the pieces of this important story.

When wading through tens of thousands of wartime documents from archives throughout the world, one of the greatest challenges is always ensuring accurate translation. I owe a huge debt to John Noyes, professor of German at the University of Toronto, for helping me assemble a team of capable German translators. Thanks to Folkard Fritz for helping decipher Rezső Kasztner's spotty German, Klaudia Meier, Simone van Tongeren (Dutch and German), Katharina Heinz, Sonja Mertz, Robert Muff and Joseph El-Cassabgui. For French translation, I relied on Margaret van Nooten, who went above and beyond the call of duty. And thanks also to Lev Jaeger for both Hebrew translation and valuable input about the manuscript in progress. Thanks as well to my international team of researchers: Greg Murphy (Washington, D.C.); Dina Leytes; Carolyn Gammon (Berlin); Simone van Tongeren (Amsterdam); Devhra Bennett Jones (Cleveland).

Many thanks to the countless unsung archivists and librarians who generously assisted in my research over the past sixteen years, especially John Taylor at the U.S. National Archives in Maryland; Shulamith Berger at Yeshiva University in New York; Misha Mitsel at the archives of the American Jewish Joint Distribution Committee in New York; the late Gerhart Riegner at the World Jewish Congress in Geneva; Tami Kinberg and Sima Shachar at the Beit Theresienstadt Museum in Israel; the staff of the United States Holocaust Memorial Museum in Washington, D.C., and the Franklin Delano Roosevelt Presidential Library and Museum at Hyde Park, New York; Boni Joi Koelliker at the American Jewish Historical Society Archives; Rabbi Moshe Kolodny at the Agudath Israel Orthodox Jewish Archives; Emmanuelle Moscovitz at Yad Vashem; the USC Shoah Foundation Institute for Visual History and Education; Stefan Keller at the Paul Grüninger Foundation in St. Gallen, Switzerland; Rafael Medoff at the David Wyman Institute for Holocaust Studies; and Hubert Berkhoug at the Netherlands Institute for War Documentation in Amsterdam, along with Reek van Rijsinge for sharing his extraordinary collection of Felix Kersten's personal papers.

I want to also thank Dovid Reidel at the Kleinman Family Holocaust Education Center in Brooklyn for allowing me to access the center's Sternbuch family archives and other important materials related to Orthodox Jews and the Holocaust even before the center's new Amud Aish Memorial Museum was formally opened and before much of the archival material could be classified.

I am indebted to the groundbreaking scholarship around this aspect of the Holocaust contributed by historians such as Monty Noam Penkower, Yehuda Bauer, Paul Lawrence Rose, and the invaluable Holocaust historiography compiled by Michael Robert Marrus.

It is never easy for Holocaust survivors to share their stories and relive the nightmare. I would like to acknowledge the generous cooperation of Nathan Leipciger, Max Eisen, George Brady, Johnny Freund, Sigmund Sobolewski and Edward Mosberg.

I am grateful for the loving support of my partner, Morag; my son, Dashiell; and my family: Mel Wallace, Jeremy Wallace, Robin Pachter, Hope Wallace, Hannah, Henry, and Emma Wallace.

Thanks also to Geoffrey York, Irene Piek, Sheldon Goldberg, the United Jewish People's Order, the Sarah and Chaim Neuberger Holocaust Education Centre, David Nanasi, Ian Halperin, Noah Lukeman, the Anne and Max Bailey Centre for Holocaust Studies, Ester Reiter, Diana Ballon, Helen Armstrong, Reeve Lindbergh, Shlomit Segal, Evan Beloff, Jacquie Charlton, Marnie Wohl, Jeremiah Bennett, Barbara Davidson, Mango, Sarah Latha-Elliott, Joe Jacobs, Edwin Black, Steve Simon, Tanja Rohweder, Robert Weiner, David Swift, Dick and Seema Marcus, Willa Marcus, Todd Shapiro, Mark Hiller, Lynette Boulet and Carla Ursini; plus Justin Stoller, Victoria Ryk, Tara Tovell, and others at Penguin Random House Canada.

INDEX